CAMBRIDGE COMMONWEALTH SERIES

General Editor: Professor E. T. Stokes

Politics and Christianity in Malawi 1875–1940

CAMBRIDGE COMMONWEALTH SERIES

Toward 'Uhuru' in Tanzania: G. Andrew Maguire

Developing the Third World: the experience of the nineteen-sixties: Ronald Robinson (ed.)

Mackinnon and East Africa 1878–1895: A Study in the 'New Imperialism': John S. Galbraith

The Durham Report and British Policy: A Critical Essay: Ged Martin

The Making of Modern Belize: Politics, Society and British Colonialism in Central America: C. H. Grant

These monographs are published by the Syndics of the Cambridge University Press in association with the Managers of the Cambridge University Smuts Memorial Fund for the Advancement of Commonwealth Studies.

Politics and Christianity in Malawi 1875-1940

The impact of the Livingstonia Mission in the Northern Province

JOHN McCRACKEN
Senior Lecturer in History, University of Stirling

CAMBRIDGE UNIVERSITY PRESS
CAMBRIDGE
LONDON · NEW YORK · MELBOURNE

Published by the Syndics of the Cambridge University Press
The Pitt Building, Trumpington Street, Cambridge CB2 1RP
Bentley House, 200 Euston Road, London NW1 2DB
32 East 57th Street, New York, NY 10022, USA
296 Beaconsfield Parade, Middle Park, Melbourne 3206, Australia

First published 1977

Printed in Great Britain by
Western Printing Services Ltd, Bristol

Library of Congress Cataloguing in Publication Data

McCracken, John, 1938–
Politics and Christianity in Malawi, 1875–1940.

(Cambridge Commonwealth series)
Bibliography: p.
1. Missions – Malawi, 2. Christianity – Malawi.
3. Malawi – Politics and government. I. Title.
BV3625.N8M32 968.9′7 76-27905

ISBN 0 521 21444 0

Contents

	List of maps	vi
	Preface	vii
	Abbreviations	xii
	Note on terminology	xiii
1	Malawi in the nineteenth century	1
2	David Livingstone and the origins of Livingstonia	17
3	Commerce and Christianity: the Yao experience	34
4	Missionary penetration and African responses 1878–91	57
	Kaningina and Bandawe: the pioneer settlements	57
	Livingstonia and the Blantyre atrocities	65
	Mission prospecting	71
	Bandawe: the origins of a Christian revolution	73
	Crisis in Ngoniland	85
	North and south of the lake: the Maseko Ngoni and the Ngonde	100
5	Popular Christianity and the making of a new elite, 1891–1914	110
6	The Overtoun Institution	132
7	Church and State, 1891–1914	157
	The Scottish missions and the colonial occupation	157
	Presbyterian attitudes	175
8	The origins of independency	184
9	Church and school, 1914–40	221
	The impact of war	221
	The educational debate	232
	The Christian community	243
10	The politics of privilege	256
	Native associations	257
	Independent churches	273
	Local politics	285
	Conclusion	292
	Bibliography	295
	Index	311

Maps

1	Malawi: peoples and places	xiv
2	The Livingstonia mission: sphere of influence	xv
3	Northern Ngoniland and Tongaland	74
4	Malawi in south central Africa	154
5	Provincial and district boundaries of Malawi c. 1910	185

Preface

The Livingstonia Mission of the Free Church of Scotland has long been recognised as one of the most important of the Christian missions introduced into Central Africa in the late nineteenth century. Founded at Cape Maclear in October 1875 just over 100 years ago, the mission established important diplomatic and educational contacts with a variety of people in northern Malawi in the fifteen years prior to the colonial occupation and later was instrumental in bringing many of them into the Presbyterian Church. The educational network it created, centred on the Overtoun Institution, became perhaps the most effective, certainly the most admired, in Central Africa and provided the early training for many of Malawi's inter-war leaders.

Yet for all its apparent success, Livingstonia fostered tensions which it was unable to control or eradicate. The early eruption of Christian independency in the Northern Province, pioneered by the Watch Tower movement, demonstrated that Livingstonia was unable to cope successfully with all the moral dilemmas – some of its own making – which faced early Christians in the north. Moreover, the active involvement of many of its members in various forms of political activity resulted as much from their disillusionment with the mission as from attitudes which it had fostered. Livingstonia may have been the seedbed of the Nyasaland African Congress, as Malawi's President, Dr H. K. Banda has suggested, but the connections were complex and sometimes indirect.

This book is a revised and extended version, containing considerable new material, of a PhD thesis presented at Cambridge in 1967. In it I have attempted to relate the story of the mission to certain political and economic developments taking place within Malawi from the late nineteenth century. Two controversial features are the major importance I attach to the attitudes and policies of the missionaries and the emphasis I place on the political dimension of African Christianity in the making of modern Malawi. It is my contention that without an understanding of the particular character of Livingstonia and the extent to which it differed from other missions in Central Africa, the nature of its impact would be dangerously obscured. Similarly, without an understanding of the cultural influence of the mission and of the frustrations and divisions which it generated, politics in the Northern Province could all too easily be reduced to so many 'proto-nationalist' or 'nationalist' gestures.

At the same time, I have attempted to throw light on three issues of general interest to historians. First, in discussing David Livingstone's ideas and their relationship to economic change, I have tried to isolate with some degree of precision the nature of the economic impact of a single mission. The 'Commerce and Christianity' strategy which Livingstonia's early sponsors espoused was ineffective in restructuring economic systems prior to the establishment of colonial rule, but latterly it played a significant part in the satellisation of Malawi as a labour reserve for southern Africa. To that extent the book touches on the study of underdevelopment in Africa. Secondly, in studying the relationship between Livingstonia and the various peoples with which it came into contact from the mid 1870s I have attempted to contribute to the wider debate concerning African responses to mission penetration. I argue that a religious crisis relating to the expansion of the slave and ivory trade made possible the extension of Christianity in certain areas, but that conversion on a wide scale only took place after local elites for a variety of reasons had associated themselves with the mission, and when African intermediaries existed in sufficient numbers to evangelise successfully. Finally, in considering the consequences of mission involvement, I have explored the issue of social differentiation. Access to mission schools and membership of the Presbyterian Church provided certain Malawians with the opportunity to acquire jobs and influence that they would not otherwise have possessed. Lack of similar opportunities led to resentment among less privileged groups and thus to the creation of alternative movements. Christianity was at once a response to the enlargement of economic scale and a deeply divisive force.

This book does not set out to be a definitive history of the Livingstonia Mission or of the Livingstonia Presbytery of the Church of Central African Presbyterian. The role of the Presbyterian Church in Zambia is considered only as it relates to events in Malawi; the dramatic story of Livingstonia's part in the campaign against the Federation of Rhodesia and Nyasaland lies beyond the period covered here. Nevertheless, I hope it will be read by individuals interested in the African Church and in a remarkable Scottish venture as well as by those whose principal concern is with the modern history of Malawi. In some respects the story of Livingstonia is a tale of promise unfulfilled – of an organisation which for a short period seemed capable of transforming the lives of many thousands of central Africans, but which, as time went by, undertook a decreasingly ambitious and effective role. But that would be too critical a judgement. In a variety of ways influences emanating from Livingstonia's early years are still of significance today.

The book is principally based on the extensive records of the Livingstonia Mission, the Foreign Missions Committee of the Free Church of Scotland and the Church of Central Africa Presbyterian. The bulk of these records are now located in two major centres: the National Library of Scotland and the Malawi National Archives. Those in the National Library are particularly valuable for the first twenty-five years of the mission's history up to about 1900; those in the Malawi National Archives, deposited on loan from the CCAP, are of greatest value from about 1900 up to the mid 1920s. It is noticeable that the standards of record-keeping sharply declined after the departure of Robert Laws from Livingstonia in 1927.

In addition, I have made use of the papers of Dr James Stewart, deposited in the National Archives of Rhodesia, the papers of Robert Laws, A. G. Macalpine and Frederick Morrison (an African Lakes Company employee) deposited in the Edinburgh University Library, a further collection of papers concerning Robert Laws held by the Department of Religious Studies, Aberdeen University, and a collection of letters written to Laws, held by Professor Shepperson, Edinburgh. These manuscript sources have been supplemented by the printed Reports of the Livingstonia Mission, by the two periodicals produced by the mission, *Aurora* and *The Livingstonia News*, and by various periodicals published in Scotland, notably *The Free Church of Scotland Monthly Record*.

Four other sources have been of particular value. For the Malawi regions in the late nineteenth and early twentieth century and for certain information on the Watch Tower movement I have made considerable use of the following series in the Public Record Office, London: FO 84, FO 2 and CO 525. Much of my information on the Seventh Day Baptists in the Northern Province is drawn from photocopies held by the University Library, Malawi, of Charles Domingo's correspondence with Joseph Booth and others. For African political activities in the twentieth century much of my information is drawn from District and Provincial records, which survive from the beginning of the twentieth century, and from central Secretariat papers dating from 1918 in the Malawi National Archives. Finally, for information on education between the wars I have made use of the relevant files in Edinburgh House, London.

Unlike most modern Central African historians, the student of Livingstonia and of the Northern Province of Malawi can build on foundations laid by a generation of gifted amateurs, some of whom were active participants in the events they describe. It need hardly be said that the perspectives of the earliest historians of Livingstonia, James W. Jack and W. P. Livingstone, are substantially different from my own. Nevertheless their works are based on an extensive study of Free Church records most of which have been accurately used. I have also benefited from a number of studies by missionaries, in particular those written by W. A. Elmslie, Mrs A. R. Fraser, Donald Fraser and T. C. Young. It is easy to demonstrate that there are weaknesses and inaccuracies in their accounts which modern scholarship is now beginning to rectify. Nevertheless without the contribution to scholarly research made by churchmen and missionaries the task of the historian of Malawi today would be infinitely more difficult than it is.

Acknowledgements

I wish to thank the British Council for aid in financing my first visit to Central Africa in 1964. Later research visits to Malawi and Zambia in 1966, 1970 and 1972 were assisted by the University College of Dar es Salaam, the University of Stirling and the Carnegie Trust for Scotland.

My interest in African history was awoken by Ronald Robinson who also suggested the topic of the thesis out of which the book has grown and provided me with initial supervision. Eric Stokes was unfailingly persistent, patient and encouraging as supervisor and later as editor. George Shepperson placed his extensive collection of primary material at my disposal and subjected the thesis to a number of scholarly criticisms. Jaap van Velsen gave me access to his unrivalled collection of research notes on native associations and on northern Malawi and illuminated my understanding of Central African affairs. From Roderick Macdonald, Bridglal Pachai, Andrew Ross and Roger Tangri I received additional useful information as well as unstinted hospitality.

There can have been few more stimulating environments for the aspirant

African historian than that provided by the University College of Dar es Salaam in the late 1960s. For better or worse, the historical perspectives that underpin this book were largely moulded in that period. For the insights they provided I am indebted to more of my former colleagues than I can name, but particularly Terence Ranger, John Iliffe, John Lonsdale and Andrew Roberts. Any misconceptions that remain are my own.

Among teachers, churchmen and others who came to my aid while conducting research were the Rev. Neil Bernard, the Rev. Chiswakhata Mkandawire, the Rev. Mr and Mrs Hamish Hepburn, the Rev. Mr and Mrs Tom Colvin, the Rev. Charles Chinula, Mr A. E. Muwamba, the Rev. Z. P. Ziba, Mr Hanock Ngoma and Mr Donald Moxon. My particular thanks is due to Miss Betty Neech who typed the various drafts of the book with exemplary patience and efficiency.

For access to written material I must thank the General Secretaries of the Livingstonia and Blantyre synods of the Church of Central African Presbyterian and the custodians of the Malawi National Archives, the National Archives Lusaka, Zambia, the National Archives, Salisbury, Rhodesia, the Public Record Office, London, the British Museum, Rhodes House, Oxford, the National Library of Scotland, the University Library, Malawi, Cambridge University Library, Edinburgh University Library, the Department of Religious Studies, Aberdeen, Edinburgh House, London and the Foreign and Commonwealth Office Library, London.

Certain passages in chapters 2, 3 and 4 originally appeared in articles I wrote for *The Early History of Malawi* (1972) and *Livingstone: Man of Africa Memorial Essays* (1973) both edited by Bridglal Pachai. I am grateful to the Longman Group Ltd for allowing me to reproduce them.

This book is dedicated to the memory of Jane McCracken, my first wife. Having typed most of the first draft of the thesis, she accompanied me to Malawi in 1966 and assisted in the collection of material. She died following a road accident in which we were involved while returning to Dar es Salaam. That it appears in print at all is a tribute to my wife, Juliet. Without her constant encouragement and assistance I doubt whether it would ever have been completed.

Abbreviations

ALC	African Lakes Company
AMEC	African Methodist Episcopal Church
ANC	African National Church
BCAG	*British Central Africa Gazette*
BSAC	British South Africa Company
CCAP	Church of Central Africa Presbyterian
CMS	Church Missionary Society
CS	Chief Secretary
CSHFMR	*Church of Scotland Home and Foreign Missionary Record*
CO	Colonial Office
DC	District Commissioner
DRC	Dutch Reformed Church
EUL	Edinburgh University Library
FCSMR	*Free Church of Scotland Monthly Record*
FCS	Free Church of Scotland
FCOL	Foreign and Commonwealth Office Library
FMC	Foreign Missions Committee
FO	Foreign Office
ICU	Industrial and Commercial Workers Union
IRM	*International Review of Missions*
JAH	*Journal of African History*
KAR	Kings African Rifles
LMS	London Missionary Society
LWBCA	*Life and Work in British Central Africa*
LWBMS	*Life and Work Blantyre Mission Supplement*
MNA	Malawi National Archives
MoNA	Mombera's Native Association
NLS	National Library of Scotland
NNNA	North Nyasa Native Association
PC	Provincial Commissioner
S of S	Secretary of State
UFCFMR	United Free Church of Scotland Foreign Mission Report
UMCA	Universities Mission to Central Africa
WNNA	West Nyasa Native Association

Terminology

Proper names in Malawi have been spelt in many different ways over the last hundred years. I normally follow recent usage except where a new name (e.g. Nsanje for Port Herald) might confuse the reader or where I quote direct from a contemporary source. The term 'Malawi' is used for the geographical region covered by the modern nation state and 'Nyasaland' for the British protectorate. 'Zambia' likewise is used for the geographical area and 'Northern Rhodesia' for the colony. 'Tanganyika' describes throughout the mainland region of what up to 1918 was German East Africa and from 1964 has been Tanzania. 'The Northern Province' in Malawi has taken different forms at different times. I use it consistently to describe the region of Livingstonia's influence running roughly from Karonga to Kasungu. The terms 'Malawian' and 'Nyasa' are both used in describing that country's inhabitants.

Following popular practice in Malawi I write of the 'Free Church of Scotland', though in 1900 it amalgamated with the United Presbyterian Church to become the United Free Church and in 1929 reunited with the Church of Scotland. Note also: 'Livingstonia' is the name both of the Free Church of Scotland mission and of the central station, the Overtoun Institution, founded at Khondowe in 1894; Mankhambira's fortified village, Chinteche, should not be confused with the government post, Chinteche Boma, established a few miles to the south about 1902.

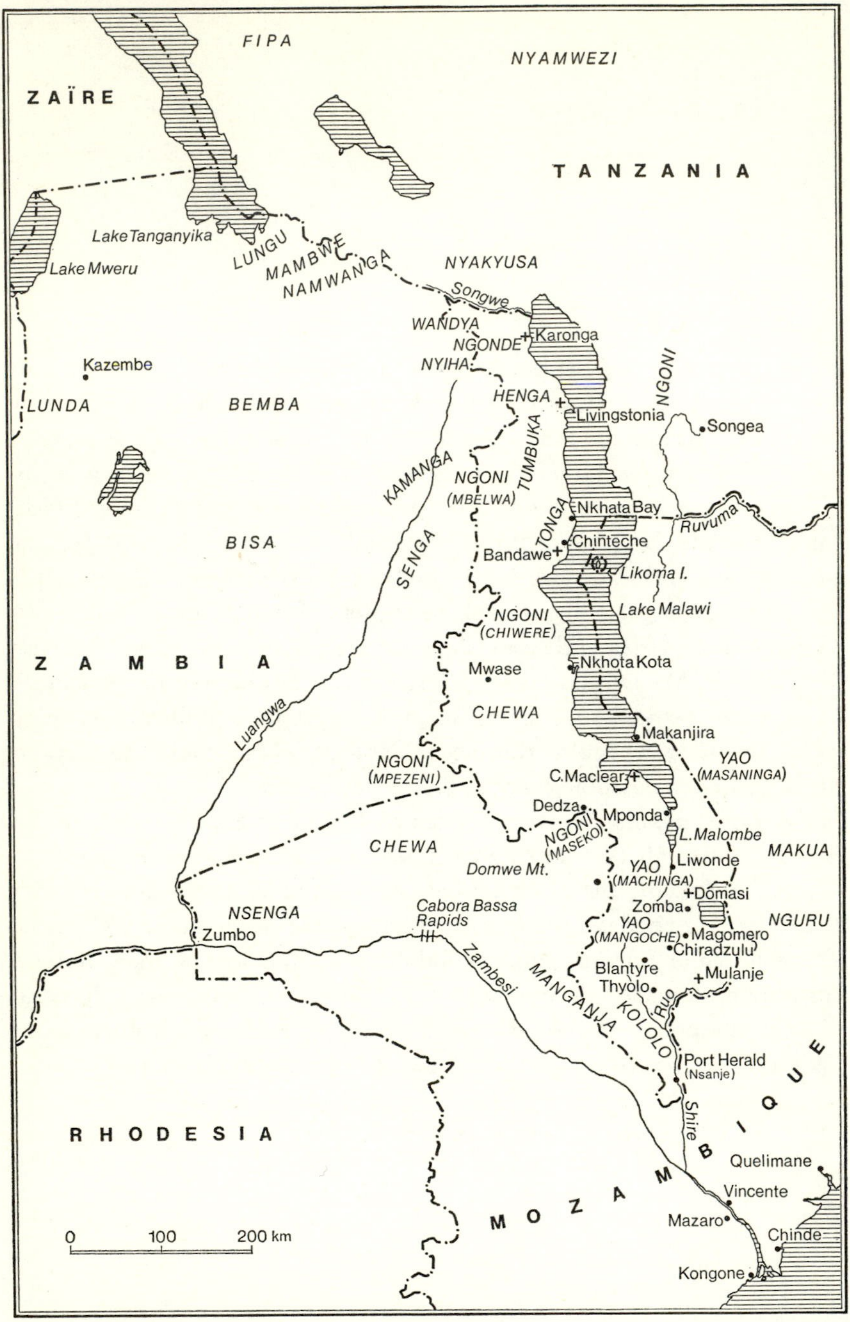

Map 1. Malawi: peoples and places
Names in brackets represent more modern names

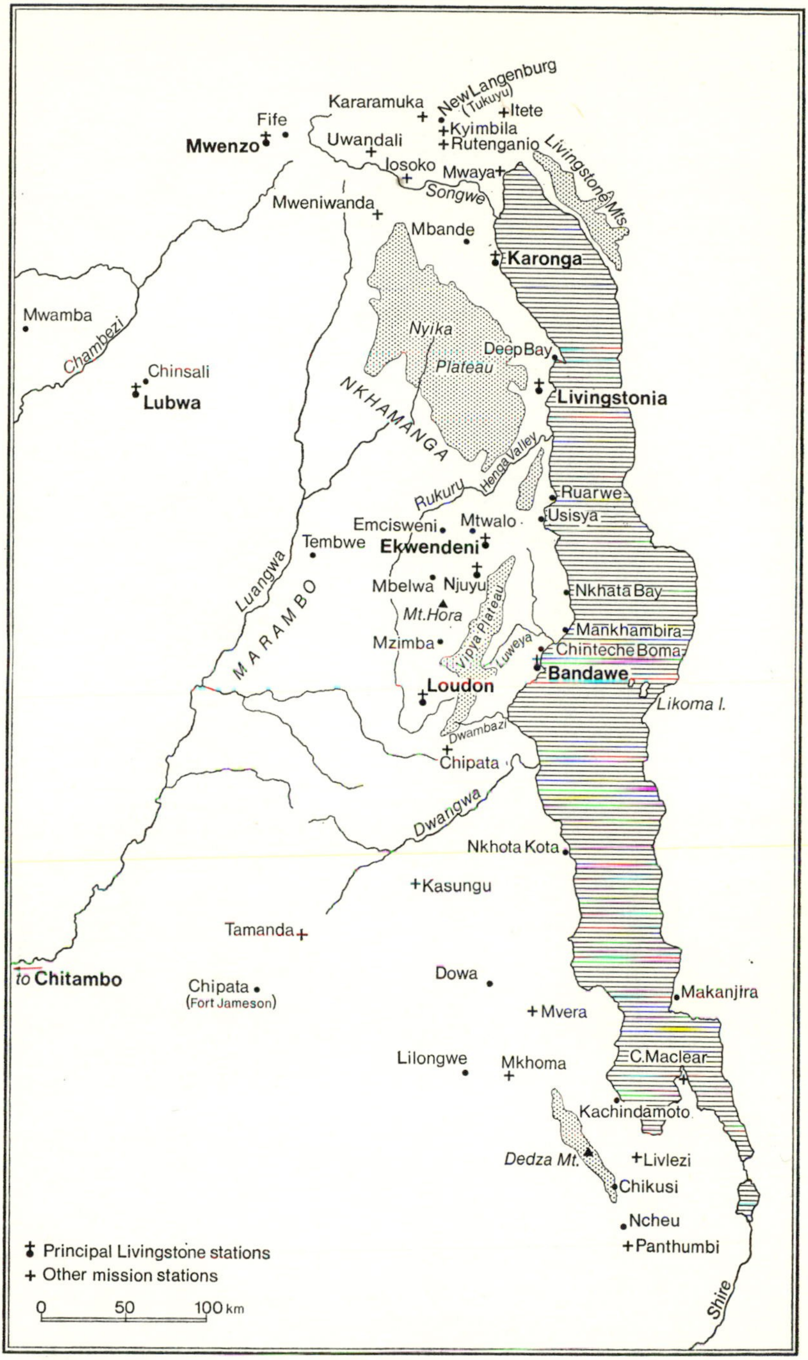

Map 2. The Livingstonia mission: sphere of influence

I

Malawi in the nineteenth century

Malawi is a long, narrow country, the length of Britain, but only half its area. Its boundaries are artificial ones, the creation of statesmen in the conference rooms of Europe. Yet to some extent, they give shape to a certain rough geographical and even historical unity, for the whole area is part of the southern extension of the Rift valley, which transverses the country from Lake Malawi in the north to the Shire valley in the south, with high plateaux rising on either side.

Although the main, precolonial trade routes ran at right angles to this trough, cutting across or round the lake to link the lands of Kazembe and Katanga in the interior, with the east coast ports of Kilwa, Zanzibar, Quelimane and Mozambique, the principal migrations into the country have followed the lines of its dominant physical feature. Down the valley on the west side of the lake from the fourteenth century, came members of the Phiri clan (also known as Maravi), the founders, by the sixteenth century, of an extensive, centralised, state system. Further to the west, on the Luangwa–Lake Malawi watershed, the Ngoni under Zwangendaba moved northwards in the early 1840s. Twenty years later, missionaries and explorers used the water system of the valley, linking the Indian Ocean via the Zambesi and Shire rivers with the lake, to establish the first permanent European settlements in this part of the Central African interior. Indeed, the water system became one of the great formative factors of Malawi's colonial history, for while it proved sufficiently effective as a means of communication to permit the founding of the early missionary settlements, its deficiencies, increased each year by the gradual silting up of the Shire river from the mid 1870s, placed a major obstacle in the path of large-scale white settlement, and thus contributed to the continuance of strong missionary influence in default of any other.

Equally illusory has been the promise offered by the area's natural resources. With its relatively high rainfall for Central Africa – ninety-five per cent of the country receives an average of over thirty inches of rain a year, the minimum amount required for successful dry land farming – its reasonably fertile soil and numerous outcrops of iron ore and other minerals, Malawi, from the earliest years of white penetration, has been the object of economic interest and hope. But, over the years, its mineral resources have been found to be unworkable and much of its soil has been declared unsuited to cash-crop production on a large scale. Economic development has always been round the next corner. Moreover, economic resources are unevenly distributed. Large variations in rainfall and soil exist within short distances but, by and large, the most reliable supplies of rain as well as the most fertile soils are found in the southern and central districts, a fact reflected in the greater density of population in these areas. It is not only the absence of a railway or the policies of Malawi's colonial rulers that made the 'dead North' so economically unproductive.[1]

By the 1870s, when the first, permanent, European settlers arrived in the country, a political situation of considerable complexity had been created through the clash of intruding peoples. Most inhabitants of Malawi in the first half of the nineteenth century were agriculturalists living in dispersed village settlements. Those living in central Malawi and south of the lake in the Shire valley and highlands shared a common language, Chichewa – spoken with considerable regional variations – and a common culture and clan organisation. Under a Phiri ruler, Karonga, the first centralised state in the region had been founded south west of the lake in the sixteenth century, but this had collapsed in the seventeenth century to be replaced by two major kingdoms: that of Undi, which stretched west from central Malawi over extensive portions of eastern Zambia and north western Mozambique; and that of Lundu in the south east, including the Shire highlands and lower Shire valley. Lacking effective centralising institutions, these states suffered from the failure of their rulers to maintain a monopoly over the collection of ivory tribute and by the increasing success of Yao and Bisa traders, from at least 1720, in squeezing the Maravi out of the major trade routes to the coast. Sub-chiefs like Mankokhwe established their virtual independence by the end of the eighteenth century, and the states also suffered from the activities of the Portuguese and their Chikunda retainers, who raided for slaves and ivory throughout the Zambesi valley. By 1880, the Lundu kingdom was restricted to the lower Shire valley and the king was a powerless cipher. As for Undi, his authority had already begun to deteriorate by 1831, when the Portuguese explorer, Gamitto, travelled through his territory,

[1] J. G. Pike and G. T. Rimmington, *Malawi, a Geographical Study*, London, 1965, 70, 90, 135–42; Swanzie Agnew, 'Environment and history: the Malawian setting' in Bridglal Pachai (ed.), *The Early History of Malawi*, London, 1972

and the decline accelerated during the next three decades. Village groupings re-emerged as the most important political units, but sufficient cultural distinctions remained for the inhabitants of Lundu's kingdom to be identified as Manganja, as opposed to the members of Undi's state and the tributary kingdoms attached to it, who became commonly known as Chewa.[2]

A somewhat different pattern was followed among the Maravi's northern neighbours: the Tumbuka and related peoples to the west of the lake, the Tonga on the lake shore itself and the Ngonde in the plain to the north west. Despite their sense of tribal identity, the Tonga and Tumbuka are 'mixed peoples, with mixed cultures having mixed histories'.[3] The Tonga are an amalgamation of at least four different groups, some of Chewa origin, some from the north, while the Tumbuka likewise have been influenced both by the matrilineal Chewa in the south and by patrilineal peoples from western Tanzania. Both originally lacked large-scale, centralised authorities, though among the Tumbuka, certain chieftaincies, notably that of Luhanga, controlled more than a single clan. In about 1780, however, a group of Balowoka (possibly Yao) traders, attracted by untapped supplies of ivory, entered Nkhamanga and established a loose confederation over the elephant-rich country running from the modern border of Zambia to the lake. The power of this Chikulamayembe dynasty derived from its control of ivory rather than from bureaucratic or military strength. By the 1820s it was beginning to decline as new, rival traders were attracted to the area.[4]

Godfrey Wilson has suggested that the Ngonde were also affected by ivory traders who reached them from the east side of the lake, but in a recent thesis Owen Kalinga has demonstrated that no such trading contacts existed prior to the late nineteenth century. The Ngonde were related not to the other groups in Malawi, but to those patrilineal peoples of western Tanzania who possessed in common a distinctive form of

[2] J. M. Schoffeleers, 'Livingstone and the Mang'anja Chiefs' in Bridglal Pachai (ed.), *Livingstone: Man of Africa, Memorial Essays 1873–1973*, Longman, 1973, 113–15; H. W. Langworthy, 'Chewa or Malawi political organisation in the precolonial era' in Pachai, *Early History*, 118–20

[3] H. Leroy Vail, 'Religion, Language and the Tribal Myth: the Tumbuka and Cewa of Malawi', Paper presented at a conference on the history of Central African religion, Lusaka, 1972

[4] J. van Velsen, 'Notes on the History of the Lakeside Tonga of Nyasaland', *African Studies*, XVIII, 3, 1959, 108–13; H. L. Vail, 'Suggestions towards a reinterpreted Tumbuka history' in Pachai, *Early History*, 150–60; T. Cullen Young, *Notes on the History of the Tumbuka–Kamanga Peoples in the Northern Province of Nyasaland*, London, 1932, 31–47, 82–4

centralised monarchy, the so-called Ntemi chieftainship. Originally the Kyungu or Ntemi had been a sacred religious figure, living like the Lwembe of the culturally similar Nyakyusa north-east of the Songwe river, in strict religious seclusion. But for reasons possibly connected with the favourable environment of the Karonga plain and the large settled population attracted to it, the Kyungus from the last third of the eighteenth century entered more actively into secular politics and succeeded in limiting the powers of their counsellors. They also gradually extended the boundaries of the Ngonde state and established reasonably effective control over outlying villages.[5]

Despite the political effects of the ivory trade, its role in the economies of most of the peoples of Malawi around 1800 was comparatively slight. Cattle were herded in areas free from tsetse fly, iron ore was mined in regions where it was plentiful and crops were cultivated with a skill which was to impress later European observers. 'The Manganja are an industrious race; and in addition to working in iron, cotton, and basket-making, they cultivate the soil extensively', David Livingstone wrote, following his initial visit to the Shire highlands.

> Large crops of the mapira or Egyptian dura (*Holcus sorghum*), are raised, with millet, beans, and ground-nuts; also patches of yams, rice, pumpkins, cucumbers, cassava, sweet potatoes, tobacco, and hemp, or bang (*Cannabis sativa*). Maize is grown all the year round. Cotton is cultivated at almost every village . . . Iron ore is dug out of the hills and its manufacture is the staple trade of the southern highlands. Each village has its smelting-house, its charcoal-burners, and blacksmiths.

Livingstone believed that local trade was extensive, a conclusion confirmed by modern research. 'A great deal of native trade is carried on between the villages, by means of barter in tobacco, salt, dried fish, skins, and iron.'[6]

Upon this pattern of predominantly agricultural activity two new features were imposed in the nineteenth century. The first was the extension and enlargement of long-distance trade to the coast. Up to the 1820s, the Arabs and Swahili on the east coast of Africa had been content to provide markets for caravans from the interior which were controlled by African peoples such as the Bisa, the Nyamwezi and the Yao. From this

[5] Godfrey Wilson, *The Constitution of the Ngonde*, Rhodes–Livingstone Papers No. 3, 1969; O. J. Kalinga, 'The Ngonde of Northern Malawi c. 1600–1895', PhD thesis, London, 1974, 115–55

[6] David Livingstone, *Narrative of an Expedition to the Zambesi and its Tributaries*, London, 1865, 110–14

period, however, the demand for slaves, stimulated by the growth of plantations on the French islands of the Indian Ocean and on Zanzibar and Pemba, and for ivory, as a result of the vogue in Europe for luxury articles made of that material, led to the first full-scale Swahili penetration inland. The actual numbers involved were small, but the Swahili had the advantage over their African competitors of access to capital lent by Indian financiers in Zanzibar and to the most modern firearms available in Central Africa, with which they equipped mercenary allies. They were not at first generally concerned with extending their territorial powers, though in the 1840s a trader from Zanzibar, Salim bin Abdallah, settled at Nkota Kota on the west shore of Lake Malawi, where he established a successful commercial staging post and agricultural settlement.[7] Instead, they concentrated in the Malawi regions on dominating the northern trade routes to Nkota Kota and Deep Bay and left the south to the Yao with whom individual Swahili had frequent commercial dealings. Their expansion however was not without political consequences. Apart from Nkota Kota, where Salim bin Abdallah and his successors emerged as powerful local rulers from about 1863, Swahili traders played an active role in the Tumbuka area controlled by the Chikulamayembe. 'Smashing the Balowokas' trade monopoly, these traders dealt with local village leaders who did not hesitate to sell slaves to the traders for cloth, beads, and other such merchandise.' By trading with the Swahili, local Tumbuka leaders augmented their economic position at the expense of the Chikulamayembe dynasty and rendered it virtually impotent. By the mid-nineteenth century, the Chikulamayembe empire was politically divided and economically in decline.[8]

In contrast to the Balowoka, the Yao benefited from trading contacts with the Swahili, which went back at least to the seventeenth century. These people scattered from their homeland in northern Mozambique in the 1850s partly, it would appear, as a result of internal dissensions, partly because of defeat at the hands of the Makua. Four separate groups moved into the southern part of Malawi, where they came into contact with the Manganja, with whom they lived for a time in comparative harmony. Disputes arose, according to Livingstone, because of the inability of the

[7] George Shepperson, 'The Jumbe of Kota Kota and some aspects of the history of Islam in British Central Africa' in I. M. Lewis (ed.), *Islam in Tropical Africa*, London, 1966, 196. See also Major Forbes to Commissioner Johnston, 17 July 1894, FO 2/67

[8] Vail, 'Tumbuka history', 160–1. See also Marcia Wright and Peter Lary, 'Swahili settlements in Northern Zambia and Malawi', *African Historical Studies*, IV, 3, 1971

Manganja to provide food supplies to meet the demands of the considerable body of traders. 'When the provisions became scarce, the guests began to steal from the fields, quarrels arose in consequence', and violent warfare broke out.[9] Unlike the Manganja, the Yao appear to have had no tradition of centralised political organisation, but through their involvement in the east coast trade prominent military and commercial leaders had emerged who owed their power to the acquisition of slaves and the distribution of cloth. Possession of firearms may also have contributed to their military superiority, though the few flintlocks they held in the 1860s are likely to have been of more importance in prestige terms than as effective military instruments.[10] At all events, the Yao were generally successful in the fighting and within a few years reduced the Manganja to the status of subjects or else drove them down to the Shire valley. Culturally and in some respects, politically, the Yao resembled the Maravi peoples. Like them they were matrilineal and matrilocal and deeply involved in subsistence agriculture. Their contacts with the east coast, however, as pioneers of the Arab trading frontier, introduced a new factor into political relations south of the lake. By the 1870s, coastal influence was apparent among the Yao in the type of houses built, the clothing worn and the fact that at least one chief, Makanjira, on the south eastern shore, had been converted to Islam. The major Yao settlements near the lake, Mponda's and Makanjira's, were substantial townships containing up to 8000 inhabitants. Dhows were built at Makanjira's, as at Nkota Kota, to carry caravans across the lake. Coastal produce – notably coconuts – were cultivated 'with the object,' so Abdallah wrote 'of making the Lake-shore resemble the Coast'.[11]

Moreover, the chieftaincies formed were based on the prowess of their leaders in the closely allied occupations of trade and war, and in their hold over supplies of ammunition and guns. As Mitchell has explained:

> Enterprising individuals were . . . able to achieve some personal fame by entering the slave trade. The wealth they acquired from this – beads, calico, gunpowder and guns – was in itself valueless in a society where few commodities were available for exchange. But on the other hand, it could be used to purchase or to capture slaves to

[9] Livingstone, *Narrative*, 171

[10] E. A. Alpers, 'The Yao in Malawi: the importance of local research' in Pachai, *Early History*, 171–3

[11] Robert Laws, *Women's Work at Livingstonia*, Paisley, 1886, 4; Diary of Frederick Morrison, entry for 8 March 1885; Yohanna B. Abdallah, *The Yaos*, Zomba, 1919, 43–4. See also Edward A. Alpers, 'Trade, State and Society among the Yao in the nineteenth century,' *JAH*, x, 3, 1969

> enlarge a man's own retinue. A successful trader therefore tended to be also a successful soldier and slave owner. The more slaves he owned and the larger his stock of ammunition, the more dependents he could secure. A man of some military ability could build up his power fairly rapidly and could, when he had done so, set out with his force as a chief on a military excursion into foreign parts.[12]

It was through their trading links with the coast that these men won supporters; any attempt to destroy that trade would be to hit at the basis of their power.

The second major intrusion into the Malawi regions came originally from the south. In the 1820s, the rise of the Zulu in Natal was accompanied by the splitting away of a number of groups of desperate marauders. One of these was the band of refugees under the sub-chief Zwangendaba, who became known as Ngoni. After stopping for some years near Delagoa Bay, the Ngoni moved northwards through Mashonaland, raiding as they went and incorporating the captives into their state. In 1835 they crossed the Zambesi near Zumbo, halted for four years in Nsenga country and then continued their northward advance up the Malawi–Luangwa watershed as far as Ufipa on the east side of Lake Tanganyika, where Zwangendaba died about 1845. A succession dispute followed, which resulted in the splitting away of several groups in different directions. One group made its way northwards up the east coast of Lake Tanganyika to Unyamwezi; the remainder stayed together until after the death of the regent Mgayi. Then two comparatively small secessions took place: the first was that of Zulu Gama, a non-royal ruler who took his followers eastwards to Songea; the second was headed by Chiwere Ndhlovu to the hills south west of Lake Malawi where he settled among the Chewa. Meanwhile, the dispute between Zwangendaba's sons was settled only after Mpezeni had taken his followers south, first into Bemba country and then, about 1871, into the area near Chipata in modern Zambia. Mperembe, another brother, also spent some time west of the Luangwa river, before being defeated by a coalition of Bemba chiefs about 1870, after which he rejoined the Ngoni of Mbelwa. Meanwhile, Mtwalo, a third claimant, had placed himself under the rule of Mbelwa, a fourth, about 1857. Advancing up the Henga valley and into the rolling highlands beyond, this group reduced most of the Tumbuka to subjection and destroyed the last vestiges of the Chikulamayembe state. Much earlier, the Maseko Ngoni had come north independent of Zwangendaba and had settled in the area of Domwe mountain to the

[12] J. C. Mitchell, 'An Outline of the social structure of Malemia area', *Nyasaland Journal* IV, 2, 1951, 21–2

south of Dedza. They had then crossed the Shire river under their leader Mputa and moved up the east side of the lake, making contact with Zulu Gama's Ngoni. Following Mputa's death, the Maseko retraced their steps to Domwe mountain and settled there permanently in the late 1860s.[13]

Thus by the 1870s four Ngoni kingdoms, as well as several smaller splinter groups, were established in the Malawi regions. Mbelwa dominated the northern hills, Chiwere the area inland from Domira Bay, Mpezeni the eastern Zambian plateau, and the southern Ngoni the Dedza highlands.

Despite succession disputes, which constantly threatened the unity of the various kingdoms in the second half of the nineteenth century, the Ngoni's Zulu-type tactics and weapons, and their formidable military organisation were sufficient to enable them to mount attacks against other societies which could rarely be resisted. Unlike the Yao, the Ngoni lacked all but the most minor contacts with the east coast trade, their main economic activities being those of pastoralists and cattle keepers. Frequent raids were made upon their neighbours, partly to obtain supplies of cattle and grain, and partly to take captives, not for the slave trade, but for incorporation into their state, particularly as the dependants of the chief and his senior lieutenants. Indeed the whole political structure depended on raiding, and thus upon the maintenance of an efficient army. In a society lacking almost entirely the conventional forms of wealth, power lay in the number of men a man might control. But whereas among the Yao this could be achieved indirectly through success in trade, the Ngoni relied almost entirely on the direct method of capture in war. Moreover, it was through raiding and the organisation of the state for war that recent captives were themselves assimilated and provided with the opportunities for advancing their own positions. Like the Zulu, the Ngoni had a system of age regiments, into which boys of approximately fifteen were incorporated every few years. Through the songs and dances they learned, as well as through the discipline of military training, the captives were culturally assimilated, to a greater or lesser extent, into Ngoni society. In the regiments, successful warriors, whatever their backgrounds, could compete for positions of military leadership. Ng'onomo, the senior general in the northern Ngoni paramountcy by the 1870s, was the son of a captive from near Delagoa Bay. Chiwere Ndhlovu, eventually the leader

[13] This account is taken substantially from J. A. Barnes, *Politics in a Changing Society*, Oxford, 1954, 7–23. Additional information appears in J. D. Omer-Cooper *The Zulu Aftermath*, London, 1966 and Bridglal Pachai, *Malawi: the History of a Nation*, London, 1973, 22–37

of an independent Ngoni group, was an Nsenga by birth and himself a former captive.

Europeans entering the Malawi regions in the 1860s and 1870s described that area as 'one of the dark places of the earth, full of abominations and cruelty'.[14] The Shire highlands, with its dense population and comparatively limited supplies of ivory was agreed to be one of the major sources for the slave trade, though any estimate as to the actual numbers involved must be treated with considerable caution. According to Consul Rigby, 19 000 slaves, most of them from the Malawi region, were passing through the customs house at Zanzibar in the early 1860s and considerable numbers were also exported from Kilwa in this period and from the Portuguese ports as well. Slaves were captured in raids made for this purpose, but as Livingstone noted, Manganja headmen also sold unwanted people from their villages – criminals, those convicted of witchcraft and friendless orphans who lacked for influence. There is evidence to suggest that, as the demands for slaves intensified, rulers altered legal procedures to make it easier for them to sell their subjects.[15]

Recent studies have tended to modify this point by stressing the positive consequences of long distance trade and of the Ngoni invasion. It is certainly true that destruction was not universal. Despite the repeated forecasts of extensive depopulation in the Malawi regions, the imminent annihilation of the Manganja in the 1860s and of the Tonga in the 1880s, the observed fact is that Malawi, of all parts of Central Africa, is the one with the highest density of population and has been so since the earliest records were kept.[16] By extending the area of central control, Ngoni raids brought justice to a divided people through the sword, so Ngoni historians have suggested.[17] Some groups of Senga in northern Malawi deliberately settled under Ngoni rule in order to avoid their raids; another group of Tumbuka at Ruarwe paid a regular tribute and thus avoided attack.[18]

[14] J. W. Jack, *Daybreak in Livingstonia*, Edinburgh, 1901, 18

[15] David Livingstone to Dr Candlish, 12 March 1862 NLS 7793; Livingstone, *Narrative*, 125–6; E. A. Alpers, *The East African Slave Trade*, Nairobi, 1967, 19–20

[16] See Lord Hailey, *An African Survey*, London, 1938, 108. According to the highly suspect figures which Hailey used, the density per square mile of population in Nyasaland in 1935–6 was 42.6 compared to 4.7 Northern Rhodesia, 8.6 in Southern Rhodesia, 13.8 in Mozambique and 14.3 in Tanganyika

[17] Margaret Read, *The Ngoni of Nyasaland*, London, 1956, 88–9; Y. M. Chibambo, *The Ngoni of Nyasaland*, London n.d. (1942), 60

[18] Steele to Smith, 15 August 1894, NLS 7873; Morrison Diary, 22 September 1885

Nevertheless, it would be wrong to underestimate the dramatic impact of the new intruders. The Ngoni disrupted long-distance trading patterns. By 1865, their raids had put an end to the lucrative trade in ivory and copper between Kazembe and Lake Malawi, though in later years, Yao and Swahili traders still moved inland from Mponda's into the Luangwa valley in search of ivory and struck up the lake to Nkota Kota and from there occasionally to Katanga.[19] At the same time, the northern trade route between the Mweru–Ulungu area and Karonga and Deep Bay increased in importance, in part due to the African Lakes Company, which opened a depot at Karonga in 1884.

Moreover the increasing demand for ivory had profound effects on the major export economies. As caravans required provisioning, settlements like Makanjira's, Mponda's and Nkota Kota were drawn into the commercial production of food crops long before the arrival of the British. Visiting Makanjira's in 1876, a Scottish missionary commented: 'We passed through large fields of Indian corn, mapira, cassavas, ground-nuts and rice, the soil being a sort of black sand.'[20] Rice, maize, onions, vegetable marrows, pawpaws, and mangoes were all grown for sale at Nkota Kota in the mid 1880s. Traders came from far and wide to buy salt at Mponda's, the major mart near the lake for this most valuable commodity.[21]

What was happening was less the expansion of the local economy as its restructuring to meet demands emanating from the coast and from Europe. If we accept that even in the comparatively well populated Malawi regions, labour rather than land was the scarce commodity, the sale of slaves and the incorporation of captives into Ngoni regiments cannot have been other than harmful to local systems of agricultural production. With the retreat of cultivators into heavily stockaded villages and into mountain or lakeside sanctuaries far from fertile land, agricultural productivity in many regions is likely to have declined. It is of course possible that the unusually severe famine of 1862, like the collapse of cotton growing in the Shire highlands at the same time, attested to by several observers, was a consequence of a temporary phenomenon – the Yao invasion – and had no long term repercussions.[22] More likely, how-

19 Andrew D. Roberts, 'Pre-colonial Trade in Zambia', *African Social Research*, 10, 1970, 730; Morrison Diary entries for 3, 8, 16, 25 June, 14 July, 3 August 1885

20 Livingstonia Mission Journal, entry for 17 February 1876

21 Edwards to Johnston, 17 July 1894, FO 2/67; Morrison Diary entries for 18 September, 17 November, 8 December 1885; 2 March 1883

22 See Reginald Foskett, (ed.), *The Zambesi Journal and Letters of Dr John Kirk*, Edinburgh, 1965, Vol. II, 507; Livingstone, *Narrative*, 464–5

ever, these events were related to wider changes within the Malawi economy, resulting in the increased prosperity of a minority and the increased suffering of the rest. As Austen has pointed out, 'The commodities entering the main trade circuits – whether overseas exports such as ivory and slaves or internally consumed goods like salt, iron, copper and fish did not directly draw upon the major productive sector of most of the indigenous economy', which remained predominantly one of subsistence agriculture.[23] The success of the Bisa earlier in the nineteenth century suggests that ivory trading in particular did not automatically require the control of substantial military resources. Nevertheless, from the scattered evidence provided by the early Livingstonia missionaries, it is clear that by the 1870s few small long-distance traders remained, the most successful entrepreneurs being rulers like Mponda, able to mobilise large bands of elephant hunters and of porters to carry ivory to the coast. However, state domination by itself was no guarantee of commercial success. An influx of traders could as easily result in the collapse of a centralised polity as it could in the enlargement of the ruler's power.

In this situation few generalisations are available to explain the success or failure of particular societies. One centralised power, that of Mwase Kasungu, gained strength and prestige from successfully combating the Ngoni; another, that of the Chikulamayembe, admittedly already weakened by the influence of Swahili traders, collapsed at the first blow. One group with a certain tradition of centralised authority, the Manganja near the lake, were brought within the confines of an intruding state; another group without any tradition of centralisation at all, the Tonga, found unity of a sort in resistance. The nature of the impact, rather than the political structure of the societies concerned, appears to have played the determining role.

Yet one broad distinction can be drawn. In the southern districts, the Yao and the Maseko Ngoni between them, with some help from Mpezeni's Ngoni to the west, came to dominate the Maravi round the lake and in the Shire and Dedza highlands by the 1870s, though not without considerable fighting, witnessed by the first UMCA party ten years earlier. Only in the Shire valley did the Manganja succeed in averting the invasion, and there strong and determined military leaders such as the *prazo* owner, Paul Marianno Vas dos Anjos, the adventurer Chibisa and a handful of Kololo refugees introduced by Livingstone were able to

[23] Ralph A. Austen, 'Patterns of Development in Nineteenth-Century East Africa', *African Historical Studies*, IV, 3, 1971

carve chieftaincies for themselves out of the pervailing conditions of uncertainty.[24]

In the north, however, the reluctance of Swahili merchants to burden themselves with territorial responsibilities, meant that, despite the expansion of the northern Ngoni, at least three pockets of agriculturalists remained independent. The Ngonde, though fiercely attacked by the Ngoni at the time of Zwangendaba's march north, were left virtually unmolested by Mbelwa and the Bemba on the far side of the Luangwa valley. Not until 1887, when the first attempts were made by Arab traders, headed by Mlozi, to establish their suzerainty, did they come under considerable pressure once more. Further south, Mwase Kasungu, the only Chewa leader to maintain substantial political power, was able to utilise his control over the trade route running inland from Nkota Kota to obtain a substantial supply of firearms, which he used to defeat an Ngoni impi sent against him in the 1860s. Subsequently he was able to make an alliance with Mbelwa, who in return for the military aid he supplied, agreed to leave him unscathed. Finally, the Tonga, though hard pressed by Mbelwa's Ngoni from the 1850s, still retained their independence. Considerable numbers of Tonga, particularly women and children, were captured by the Ngoni and incorporated into the segment within the kingdom controlled by the headman, Mayayi Chiputula Nhlane. They managed to preserve their cultural identity, however, partly because of their close proximity to Tongaland. In the mid 1870s, they revolted and fled down to their brethren at the lake shore, who were now settled in four or five fairly large stockaded villages. In the south, missionaries from the 1870s were to deal almost exclusively with new intruding political leaders; in the north they were to make significant contacts with the old cultivators.

Three further points can be made. British pioneers often assumed that they were entering a largely closed society with little concept of the wider world. In fact, through the influence of the Swahili, the Yao, the Portuguese and the Bisa, Malawi at the time of their arrival was already intimately connected by trade with a great sweep of country extending from the coast as far as Katanga. The influence of the Sultan of Zanzibar was of no great weight in the region, but it is not without significance that the Jumbe of Nkota Kota, himself an official representative of Seyid Burgash, regularly corresponded with the Sultan right up to the 1890s. For this reason, the British and the policies which they might be expected to follow were not unknown. Apart from a handful of freed slaves and

24 M. D. D. Newitt, '*Portuguese Settlement on the Zambesi*', London, 1973, 255–81; Schoffeleers, 'Livingstone and the Manganja Chiefs', 116–28

mission dependants, who had established links with early European expeditions in the 1860s, several of Malawi's inhabitants had been in direct contact with the British at the coast by the time that the Scottish missions were established. One such was an English-speaking Arab, met by the Livingstonia Mission party on their pioneer visit to Lake Malawi in 1875, who had been to Zanzibar and 'seemed unable to connect the English flag with anything else than the suppression of the slave trade'.[25] Another, also an English-speaking Arab, the master of one of the Jumbe's dhows, had served for a time on a British man-of-war.[26] The view that missionaries were universally regarded in incomprehension as exotic creatures bringing 'a new magic which promised greater wealth or power' is singularly far from the mark.[27]

Also misleading is the belief that the various 'tribal' groups described reflected distinct political entities. It is convenient to write of a 'Yao invasion' of the Shire highlands, but only in the knowledge that Yao territorial chieftaincies were as likely to clash with each other as they were with rival Ngoni or Manganja polities. To some degree at least, tribal labels indicate economic not ethnic identity. Thus Makanjira, the most powerful of the Yao chiefs on the lake, was in fact of Chewa origin, as was Chabisa a leading ally of the Ngoni, Mpezeni. The senior councillors of the Swahili Jumbe of Nkota Kota were respectively a Bemba and a Yao. The Yao chief Mponda frequently allied himself with the Ngoni, Chikusi, against his trading rival, Makanjira. And Makanjira returned the compliment by supporting Chifisi, the claimant to Chikusi's throne. Economic interest rather than 'tribal' sentiment was the basis of political action.

Although it is not easy to determine whether the economic crisis of the mid nineteenth century resulted in a general religious crisis, recent research has demonstrated that various religious institutions in Malawi were undergoing considerable pressures at the time that the missionaries arrived. Following Vail, we may assert that most people in the Malawi regions shared three basic religious beliefs: the first in the existence of witches, who were held to be responsible for otherwise unexplained misfortune, and who could be detected by doctors who frequently made use of the *mwavi* poison ordeal; the second in the spirits of the dead, who functioned as intermediaries between the living and the world beyond; and the third in a High God, worshipped through a number of large and

[25] Livingstonia Mission Journal entry for 14 October 1875, NLS 7908

[26] ibid. entry for 22 November 1875

[27] See M. L. Chanock, 'Development and change in the history of Malawi' in Pachai, *Early History*, 437

influential territorial cults.[28] It is tempting to argue that various developments in the nineteenth century – the eruption of the Ngoni and their attempts to assimilate Chewa and Tumbuka captives into their kingdoms, the perversion of legal systems by rulers anxious to sell their subjects, and the creation of stockaded villages, into which large numbers of disparate people were thrust – all had the effect of exacerbating witchcraft tensions, thus increasing the use of the *mwavi* ordeal.[29] 'Increase of tension' is in danger of becoming a portmanteau explanation of religious change in Africa, somewhat akin to the 'rise of the middle classes' as an explanation of political change in Europe. But while it is important to recognise that the *mwavi* ordeal was frequently used by the Chewa in the 1830s, before the Ngoni invasions and the expansion of long-distance trade, there is no gainsaying that waves of witchcraft accusations took place in several regions at the end of the nineteenth century. *Mwavi* was adopted by the Ngoni and widely employed in both the northern and southern kingdoms during the 1870s and 1880s, and it was also much used by the Tonga and at Mponda's court in the 1890s.[30]

It is also possible that, as more people were caught up in long-distance trade, the idea of a personal active God became more attractive than it had been previously. Horton has argued that, in small-scale societies, 'lesser spirits underpin the events and processes in the microcosm of the local community'. But as social relations widen through involvement in commerce, in migrant labour, or perhaps even in nomadic pastoralism, the emphasis on lesser spirits (relevant only to a specific locality) fades and the supreme God appears of greater importance.[31] Taken too far, this theory can be dangerously self-fulfilling. As a belief in a High God normally coexisted with a belief in lesser spirits, it is often extremely difficult to determine whether one was becoming more powerful than the

[28] Vail, 'Religion, Language and the Tribal Myth'. Vail relates these beliefs to the southern Tumbuka alone. In generalising more widely I am presenting a deliberately over-simplified sketch of the variegated pattern of beliefs existing among different peoples.

[29] For a similar argument see Terence Ranger, 'Introduction' in T. O. Ranger and John Weller (ed.), *Themes in the Christian History of Central Africa*, London, 1975, 6–8

[30] A. C. P. Gamitto, *King Kazembe*, Lisbon, 1960, vol. 1, 73–4, 104–6; W. A. Elmslie, *Among the Wild Ngoni*, Edinburgh, 1901, 62–6; Ian Linden, *Catholics, Peasants and Chewa Resistance in Nyasaland, 1889–1939*, London, 1974, 24

[31] Robin Horton, 'African Conversion', *Africa*, XLI, 2, 1971; Horton, 'Conversion: Impact versus Innovation', Paper presented at a meeting of the African Studies Association of the United Kingdom, Liverpool, 1974

other. Practically all Central African peoples, from at least the beginning of the nineteenth century, were involved to some degree in a variety of economic relations beyond the village level, so it is not difficult to demonstrate that those who had developed a strong sense of a High God had also witnessed an extension of economic scale. The difficult questions to answer are why long-distance traders like the Yao, involved in contacts with the east coast from at least the seventeenth century, should be converted to Islam in large numbers only from the 1890s, or how far an involvement with an African High God facilitated or hindered conversions to Christianity or Islam. Nevertheless, the central thrust of Horton's argument appears to be valid. Converts to Christianity or Islam were frequently made, in the late nineteenth century, from among peoples like the Yao or the lakeside Tonga who were in the process of becoming fully integrated into the world economy. Other converts were members of certain specialised groups – caravan porters, elephant hunters and, naturally, mission dependants – who had been removed from their place of origin and hence developed a cultural identity associated with their particular employment.[32] African religious institutions in certain places were capable of responding to the extension of economic scale with no less success than Christianity. Schoffeleers has shown how the M'bona cult, associated with the Manganja, revived after the main cult centre had been destroyed by incoming marauders in the 1860s and became a factor of importance in the Shire valley during the twentieth century. But it is not without significance that, in several parts of Malawi, territorial cults appear to have suffered permanently from the destruction of their centres and the scattering of officials during the Ngoni invasions. The main centre of the Chisumphi cult, associated with the northern Chewa, was ransacked by a band of Chikunda in the early 1860s and later destroyed by the Ngoni. The Tumbuka chieftaincy with which the Chikang'ombe shrine was associated was also destroyed by the Ngoni during the middle of the century. Religious cults were better equipped than political institutions to survive such blows. Nevertheless, particularly in northern Malawi, they did not completely recover.[33]

Pondering on the weak impact of Christianity on Africa up to the late

[32] See Allan Isaacman, 'The Origin, Formation and Early History of the Chikunda of South Central Africa', *JAH* XIII, 3, 1972

[33] J. M. Schoffeleers, 'The Chisumphi and M'boni cults in Malawi: a comparative history', Paper presented to a conference on the history of Central African religion, Lusaka, 1972; Schoffeleers, 'The Interaction of the M'bona cult and Christianity, 1859–1963', in Ranger and Weller, *Christian History*; Vail, 'Religion, Language and the Tribal Myth'

nineteenth century, Robert Laws reached the conclusion 'that God could not trust Christendom with the knowledge of it until the Christian conscience was awake . . . to the iniquity of slavery'.[34] An alternative approach would be to turn Laws's solution on its head. Most Central Africans, most of the time, found satisfactory answers to the moral problems which confronted them in the extraordinary variety of religious institutions which they possessed. If from the late nineteenth century, Christianity offered some people more satisfactory solutions, the restructuring of local economies and the emergence of new social groups may well have influenced their decision. In that sense, as Horton writes, Christianity can be seen as a catalyst – a stimulator and accelerator of changes which were already in the air.[35]

[34] Robert Laws, 'Address at the opening of the synod of the C.C.A.P.', Blantyre, 13 October 1926, Liv. Corr. Box 3

[35] Horton, 'African Conversion', 104

2

David Livingstone and the origins of Livingstonia

At 6.30 a.m. on 12 October 1875, a small steamer pushed its way out of the Shire river into the open waters of Lake Malawi and thus brought to a climax a process set under way over sixteen years earlier by David Livingstone. Early in his career in Africa, Livingstone had reached the conclusion that while, individually, Africans were no better and no worse than Europeans, collectively, their defective social and economic institutions condemned them to a low place on the scale of human existence. The answer, he believed, lay not so much in individual conversions as in the general improvement which would result from the opening of the African continent to free trade and its incorporation in a world economy dominated by Britain. 'Sending the Gospel to the heathen must . . . include much more than is implied in the usual picture of a missionary, namely a man going about with a Bible under his arm', he wrote in a passage markedly at odds with modern theories of structural underdevelopment.[1]

> The promotion of commerce ought to be specially attended to as this, more speedily than anything else, demolishes the sense of isolation which heathenism engenders, and makes the tribes feel them mutually dependent on, and mutually beneficial to each other. . . My observations on this subject make me extremely desirous to promote the preparation of the raw materials of European manufacturers in Africa for by that means we may . . . introduce the negro family into the body corporate of nations, no one member of which can suffer without the others suffering with it.

The creation of a cash-crop economy, dominated by European traders would have the additional advantage, he argued, of uprooting the slave trade; for if Europeans were prepared to buy the ivory, cotton and other products of Africa in return for their own goods, it would no longer be

[1] David Livingstone, *Missionary Travels and Researches in South Africa*, London, 1857, 28

necessary for Africans to sell their own people to get the guns, powder and cloth which they desired.

The first essential was to reduce transport costs from the interior to a level where bulk commodities like cotton and sugar could be profitably sold on the British market. Livingstone rejected the overland route from the south on the grounds that the presence of tsetse fly in the Zambesi valley made impossible the use of oxen and that commercial transactions would be impeded by the protectionist Boers. Fever and physical obstacles in Angola made the west coast route no more inviting. Head porterage as employed by the Mambari was an effective means of transporting goods of high value and comparatively low bulk, like ivory, but it was too cumbersome and expensive to be used for items of 'legitimate' trade. For a time, the east coast route via the Zambesi looked more promising. Livingstone shared with many of his contemporaries a belief in the transforming effect of steam power, but he recognised that the enormous amounts of capital required to build railways in Africa were unlikely to be raised outside the boundaries of a European colony. Steamships, however, were a realistic alternative. That great waterway, the Zambesi, could be exploited in the same way as the St Lawrence in North America by steamers which would push past the decaying Portuguese settlements in the low-lying coastal regions and open up markets and sources of raw material in the healthy Bataka plateau beyond. But the discovery, made in November 1858, that the Cabora Bassa rapids presented an insuperable barrier to navigation brought the Zambesi project to a halt, and forced Livingstone to look north to the Shire river, a tributary of the Zambesi. In April 1859 he and John Kirk, the young Scottish doctor and botanist to the Zambesi expedition, left the cataracts some hundred miles up the Shire, and travelled through the highlands to the north-east, an area which they both regarded as suitable for white settlement. Four months later, they returned to this region with a larger party and on 17 September reached Lake Malawi. Livingstone, having noted the large amount of commercial activity taking place around the south end, concluded that if British merchants were to purchase cotton and ivory there, they might 'cut off the slave trade of a large district at its source'.[2] In September 1861, he came back again with a small sailing boat, which was dragged past the cataracts half way up the Shire, the only obstacle to navigation from the coast to the lake. He sailed two thirds of the way up the western shore, as far as Nkata Bay, before returning convinced that here was the second region where a small colony could be established.

[2] Livingstone to the Earl of Malmesbury, 15 October 1859, printed in Wallis, *Zambezi Expedition*, vol. II, 332

To Livingstone the Malawi regions provided three essential ingredients for the successful introduction of commercial settlements. In the first place, the waterway via the Zambesi and Shire to Lake Malawi provided a means of communication which, despite the cataracts, the shallowness of the river, mudbanks and the stormy conditions often found on the lake, was infinitely superior to anything he had come upon before. The threat that the Portuguese might levy prohibitive tariffs at the Zambesi mouth was a drawback sufficiently severe to lead Livingstone into two explorations of the Ruvuma, a river, as he noted, 'exterior to Portuguese claims'.[3] But by the end of 1862 it was clear that for those who believed that the best means of linking the interior with the coast was by steamer, the Shire–Lake Malawi route was the only one to aim for.

Secondly, the population, in comparison to that of most of Central Africa, was dense. Livingstone described it in 1861 as 'prodigious – no part of Africa I have seen so teems with people as the shores of Lake Nyasa'.[4] He admitted that this might be a temporary phenomenon, explained in part by the fact that the fishing season was in full swing at the time of his visit, and that a number of refugees had fled from their homelands to the lake. More cogent reasons, perhaps, were the favourable natural resources of that region and, again by Central African standards, the comparatively bounteous rainfall.

Finally, from a superficial view, the Manganja of the Shire valley and highlands already appeared to have laid the foundations for a successful cash-crop economy. Yao intruders had not yet undermined their independence at the time of Livingstone's first visits and they still maintained the agricultural skills which had excited Gamitto among the Chewa in 1831, growing those crops of tobacco, sugar-cane and above all cotton which Livingstone was most anxious to develop.[5] Summarising the results of his expedition of 1859, he reported that cotton was cultivated at almost every village and that one of the varieties to be found was 'of excellent quality, and considered in Manchester to be nearly equal to the best Orleans'.[6]

> We have opened a cotton and sugar producing country of unknown extent [he told Lord Malmesbury in 1859] which, while it really seems to afford reasonable prospects of great commercial benefits to our own country, it presents facilities for commanding a large section of the slave market on the East coast and offers a fairer hope of its

[3] George Shepperson (ed.), *David Livingstone and the Rovuma*, Edinburgh, 1965, 16

[4] Livingstone to Tweedie, 2 November 1861, NLS 7792

[5] Gamitto, vol. 1, 117

[6] Livingstone, *Narrative*, 111

extirpation by lawful commerce than our previous knowledge of the country led us to anticipate.[7]

Having discovered a suitable area, Livingstone was now faced with the problem of inducing a missionary or commercial group to settle there. An active opponent of missionaries who attempted to convert Africans to Christianity without trying to alter the environment in which they lived, he cared little whether the establishments were of mission stations as such or of communities of commercially-minded and God-fearing laymen. His own expeditionary party was originally regarded as the nucleus for a colony to be established on the upper reaches of the Zambesi, where it would demonstrate the advantages of self-help and act as a middleman between the English merchant and the African producer of raw materials. Later in 1859 he turned his attention to the creation of a colony of 'good Christian Scotch families' with their ministers and elders in the Shire highlands, and was prepared to spend £2000 to £3000 for this purpose.[8] He regarded very favourably the scheme of a party of Scottish artisans under an English leader to set up an independent settlement on the lake. 'They are probably hardy, frugal and industrious', he told Lord Russell, 'and seem just the men we need brought to hand without our seeking.'[9]

In the event, the first response to his appeal came from a body that was only marginally interested in the expansion of the export economy. This was the Universities Mission to Central Africa, whose foundation was immediately inspired by Livingstone's speeches at Oxford and Cambridge in 1857, but perhaps owed more to the growing desire shown by High Anglicans of a Tractarian disposition in the late 1850s to enter actively into mission work both at home and abroad. Although the mission, after its establishment at Magomero in 1861, tried to base itself on Livingstone's model of an agricultural and Christian settlement, aiming 'to encourage the advancement of science and the useful arts', it was uneasy and uncomfortable in this role. Four of the first seven members of the staff were priests with little or no experience of the simplest carpentry or agricultural skills. Its successes were to be those of the spirit, its failures largely those of practical competence.[10]

Thus, it was not until the arrival in Central Africa of James Stewart

[7] J. P. R. Wallis, *The Zambesi Expedition of David Livingstone 1858–1863*, London, 1956, II, 332

[8] George Seaver, *David Livingstone: his life and letters*, London, Lutterworth, 1957, 342; W. G. Blaikie, *The Personal Life of David Livingstone*, London, 1880, 261

[9] Livingstone to Russell, 29 December 1862, FO 84/1177

[10] The best account remains Owen Chadwick, *Mackenzie's Grave*, London, 1959.

that Livingstone was confronted by someone who responded fully to the implications of his challenge. Stewart in 1859 was a twenty-seven-year-old student at New College, the Free Church of Scotland theological hall in Edinburgh. In his youth, on his father's farm, he had developed the ambition 'to lead an expedition to some unexplored region'. From the late 1850s the wave of exploration in East Africa – Burton and Speke's exploits as well as those of Livingstone – had turned his attention in that direction.[11] An amateur scientist, the author of two botanical text-books, he shared with Livingstone his faith in the beneficial effects that would result from the increased production of raw materials in the new continents for the use of industrialists in the west, and in particular was fascinated by the latter's descriptions of the cotton-growing potentialities of the Zambesi region. Livingstone urged the cultivation of cotton in Africa not only for the benefits it would bring to Africans themselves, but because a healthy market there would enable manufacturers to bypass the slave-owning American states from which most of Britain's raw cotton came. From the early 1850s the apparent political and economic instability of the American cotton states was forcing opinion in Britain towards Livingstone's conclusion. India had been tried as a source of supply but results at first had been unsatisfactory, while an attempt to get production expanding in West Africa had met with little success.[12] By 1860 the issue had become sufficiently urgent to make Stewart feel that one of his major concerns must be to safeguard the prosperity of Lancashire by seeking out alternative supplies in the regions to which Livingstone had pointed.[13]

At first Stewart looked for help to the Foreign Missions Committee of his church; but though Dr Tweedie, the convenor, declared himself ready to assist in communicating with Livingstone on the subject of a new industrial mission in Central Africa, he was not prepared to authorise Stewart to go there. It was only sixteen years since the Disruption of the Church of Scotland in 1843, when some third of the ministers of the church, including all the foreign missionaries, had walked out in protest against what they regarded as the intolerable interference of the civil jurisdiction of the state in spiritual matters. Remarkable progress had been made since then in providing new salaries and churches, as well as in keeping up old projects. Foreign missions actually received more than

[11] James Wells, *Stewart of Lovedale*, London, 1908, 5–7; James Stewart, *Livingstonia its Origin*, Edinburgh, 1894, 3–4

[12] R. J. Gavin, 'Palmerston's Policy towards East and West Africa, 1830–1865', Cambridge PhD, 1959–60, 169–70, 231

[13] Wells, 23

twice as much in 1848–9 from the Free Church than they had done in 1842 from the undivided Church of Scotland. But the main task was clearly to consolidate the old rather than to take on new responsibilities.[14]

Stewart accordingly took a step that was later to be of importance for Livingstonia. He turned away from the church and in the winter of 1860–1 began seeking financial support from businessmen, academics and local politicians in Glasgow, Manchester and Liverpool. The result was distinctly gratifying. Despite his inexperience, Stewart displayed a flair, which he was to demonstrate repeatedly in later years, for tapping the consciences of the rich and extracting money for his projects. Through his efforts, a committee of eighteen men was formed, headed by the Lord Provost of Edinburgh and including in Drs Candlish and Tweedie, two of the most influential members of the Free Church, along with representatives from all three industrial cities. A statement about the proposed mission was drawn up in the following terms:[15]

> The principle on which the mission is proposed to be founded is that of making it as speedily as possible self-supporting. And this is to be attempted by introducing other labourers than ordained ministers and teachers. There seems to be a felt necessity that a direct and open effort should be made to follow up the labours of missionaries by industrial and civilising appliances.

Even more indicative of the economically revolutionary character planned for it was a note made by James Stewart in his diary:[16]

> If the mission comes to be established one of the most important things – in fact the most valuable of all things would be to take a steam-engine of two four or six horse power at once with abundance of belts and mills to fit. There should be at least a saw mill, a steel flour mill; a coffee mill; and planing machines of the forms at work in that factory at Leith Walk Edin.

Modernisation would come to Malawi in the shape of the fan-belt and the steam engine.

The subsequent failure of Stewart's scheme has been described in detail elsewhere.[17] By the time he arrived in the Shire highlands on a tour of reconnaissance the situation had changed entirely from what it had been

[14] J. R. Fleming, *A History of the Church in Scotland, 1843–1874*, Edinburgh, 1927, 19–25, 63–66; E. G. K. Hewart, *Vision and Achievement, 1796–1956*, London, 1960, 38–9, 60

[15] Stewart, *Livingstonia*, 10

[16] Stewart, Journal entry for 12 July 1861, Stewart Papers ST1/2/1, Salisbury

[17] The best modern account of Stewart and his involvement with Malawi is: Sheila Brock, 'James Stewart and David Livingstone' in Bridglal Pachai (ed.), *Livingstone: Man of Africa*, London, 1973

on Livingstone's first visit. Fierce fighting had broken out between the Mangoche Yao migrating southwards to the Shire highlands and the Manganja whom they found in possession. As the Manganja were subdued or driven down to the valley, slave-trading by Arab and semi-Portuguese agents increased and petty military overlords rose to overshadow established rulers. The cultivation of cotton and other crops, which Livingstone noted on his early explorations, was brought to a standstill and the situation was made worse by prolonged drought.

Furthermore, the Universities Mission had itself suffered a number of crushing setbacks. Military involvement on the side of the Manganja against the Yao had not only made its position in the Shire highlands untenable, but had aroused strong criticism in England. Fever took its toll among the most able of the staff; communications with the coast, in the absence of a mission steamer, were found to be almost impossible to maintain; agricultural development, in the absence of anyone qualified to introduce it, never got off the ground.

For Stewart, whose melancholy and entirely platonic shipboard romance with Mrs Livingstone cast a shadow over his entire relationship with her husband, doubts as to the practicability of the explorer's scheme had occurred weeks before his arrival off the mouth of the Zambesi.[18] His first visit to the Shire highlands in 1861 confirmed his worst suspicions. Almost no cotton could be found and such slow and primitive methods of spinning were in use that it was clear that no commercial benefit could be gained from them. Turning his full resentment against Livingstone he therefore cast the latter's *Missionary Travels* into the Zambesi – 'so perish all that is false in myself and others' – and departed back to Britain.[19] There, in November 1863, he presented his committee with a report that catalogued the obstacles overlooked in Livingstone's earlier dispatches. The Zambesi–Shire route, he noted, was shallower and more difficult to navigate than any earlier account had suggested. Portuguese hostility could result in the levying of prohibitive duties. The climate of the river valley was unfavourable to the health of white men.[20]

> I cannot help feeling and stating that if the information sent home by the Livingstone Expedition during the first two years of its

[18] Stewart, Journal entries for July–November 1861, 2 and 8 January 1862, Stewart Papers ST1/2/1. Almost all account of this most interesting period in Stewart's life is omitted from the published edition of his journals: J. P. R. Wallis (ed.), *The Zambesi Journal of James Stewart, 1862–1863*, London, 1952

[19] Wallis, *Zambezi Journal*, 190

[20] James Stewart, 'Report on the Practicability of the establishment of a Mission on the river Zambezi', November 1863, Stewart Papers, ST1/1/1

existence had been as clear and definite as has been the experience of those who since that time have gone to that country, much labour and perhaps human suffering might have been spared.

His committee could only accept the implications of the advice and promptly disbanded itself. In the same year, it was decided to evacuate the Universities Mission to Zanzibar, a decision preceded a few months by that of the British government to withdraw Livingstone's Expedition.

The failure of the Zambesi Expedition marks a turning point in official British government attitudes to East Central Africa. Up to the 1860s Livingstone's views were closely allied with those of at least one important school of Government opinion. With Palmerston and his followers, Livingstone had based his opinions on a belief in the essential identity of character in all races. He was convinced that Africans and Asians could easily be made Christians, customers and valuable producers of raw materials, if only their defective and unprogressive institutions – of which the worst was the slave trade – were destroyed or reformed.[21]

It followed that as long as Palmerston was in office, Livingstone's schemes received government support. An initial Exchequer grant of £5000 was made for the Zambesi Expedition, the salaries of the staff were paid, a steamer suitable for inland navigation was ordered and on Livingstone himself was conferred the somewhat nebulous authority attached to the title of 'Her Majesty's Consul in the District of Quilimane on the Eastern Coast of Africa'. At the same period, the government in its search for a suitable entry into the interior gave active support to the East Africa expedition of Burton and Speke in 1856 and to the Niger Expedition of 1857. Livingstone in the late 1850s was not so much the independent explorer as the agent of a continent-wide campaign inspired from Whitehall.[22]

But from the early 1860s the official view was changing fast. The 1857 Rising and the Taiping Rebellion provided evidence from India and from China that the reaction to European expansion might be more complex than had been originally imagined. The comparative failure of all three African expeditions caused officials to question the basis of their policy, a belief in the rapid improvability of non-Europeans.[23] At the Foreign Office, Russell proved far less sympathetic to plans of expansion than his

[21] For a lively description of these attitudes see Ronald Robinson and John Gallagher with Alice Denny, *Africa and the Victorians*, London, 1961, 1–26

[22] Gavin, 214; Reginald Coupland, *Kirk on the Zambesi*, 75–6

[23] For mounting criticism in Britain against the Zambesi Expedition see Shepperson, *David Livingstone and the Rovuma*, 34–8. For a wider perspective see Gavin, 263–6; Robinson and Gallagher, 5–6

predecessor, Clarendon, had been. Kirk, who visited him following the withdrawal of the Zambesi Expedition, 'was quite prepared for Earl Russell's cold manner, and don't expect anything to be done if he can help it'.[24] Two months later, in October 1864, Waller found the same atmosphere prevailing. 'The Dr is in bad odour at the Foreign Office entre nous,' he told James Stewart, 'and they hate the name of the Expedition.'[25] Palmerston's death, a year later, only solidified the breach between official opinion and that of the Livingstone school. Apart from the aid grudgingly given to the great explorer on his final expedition, the government henceforth refrained from providing financial assistance or administrative support to private missionary or exploring parties. Appeals for help for Livingstonia in the 1870s and 1880s were to be brushed aside. The mission was to spend its formative years isolated from the British government and hence forced into undertaking responsibilities for which it had not entirely bargained.

Shorn of official support, Livingstone during the next decade continued to emphasise the importance and practicality of introducing small colonies into the interior. Publicly, and in private correspondence, he deplored the withdrawal of the Universities Mission, called for the establishment of a British steamer on the lake and wrote enthusiastically of the contribution to be made by Scottish agents. Stewart's visit to the Malawi region had taken place at an inopportune moment, he acknowledged in his published account of the Zambesi Expedition: 'Though, had this Scotch perseverence and energy been introduced, it is highly probable that they would have reacted, most beneficially, on the zeal of our English bretheren, and desertion would never have been heard of.'[26]

It is unlikely, however, that such chauvinist sentiments would have had much effect in altering the naturally wary approach of missionary societies to the interior after the failures of the 1860s, had they not been accompanied by developments of a more tangible nature. Historians have tended to give Livingstone almost the monopoly of credit for the sudden expansion of missions to Central Africa in the 1870s and 1880s. And undoubtedly the exploits of his last expedition – the false report of his murder, the meeting with Stanley and, finally, the picturesque death at Ilala – all contributed to a massive resurgence of interest in his work. In October 1869, three years before his meeting with Stanley, to which Jeal ascribes the beginning of the Livingstone myth, Horace Waller was able to inform the explorer 'that the interest in this country about you is as

[24] Wallis, *Zambesi Expedition*, Li

[25] Horace Waller to Stewart, 18 October 1864, Stewart Papers, ST/1/1/1

[26] Livingstone, *Narrative*, 414

intense as I ever could wish it to be . . . The Geographical Society might in short be called the Livingstone Society for the last two years. Sir Roderick's vehement denial, Young's most successful clear-up of Moosa's lie have all tended so to surround you with a halo of romance such as you can't imagine.'[27]

Yet even when these events are taken into account one may still question whether they had more effect in outweighing Stewart's earlier objections than did the increased economic involvement of Europeans in East Africa from the 1870s. The decisive step was probably the opening of the Suez Canal in 1869 and the consequent improvement of communications up the East Coast through the creation in 1872 of a monthly mail service between Aden and Durban via Zanzibar run by the British India Steam Navigation Company, a Scottish firm owned by William Mackinnon.[28]

For ten years the Free Church, with other societies, had ignored Livingstone's appeals. But with the establishment of a monthly line of steamers up the coast the Foreign Missions Committee under the leadership of Dr Alexander Duff, formerly a notable missionary in India, turned its attention in that direction.[29] In January 1874 Duff met Sir Bartle Frere at a dinner following a lecture the latter had given in Edinburgh. Frere had recently returned from a visit to Zanzibar and the East Coast which had impressed him as a suitable field for missionary labour.[30] He suggested that the Free Church should take up work among the Somalis, a people he had admired in Aden as labourers and out-of-door servants. Duff got Murray Mitchell, the secretary of the Committee, to write to Dr John Wilson, the head of the Free Church College, Bombay, asking his opinion of the proposed mission, and requesting that he 'send some natives of India without delay to see and report upon the field'.[31] Wilson approved heartily of the proposal and promised, according to Murray Mitchell, to send not Indians but 'two if not three Natives of

27 Waller to Livingstone, 25 October 1869, Waller Papers; Tim Jeal, *Livingstone*, 337–53

28 Reginald Coupland, *The Exploitation of East Africa, 1856–90*, London, 1939

29 Alexander Duff, *The Proposed Mission to Lake Nyassa*, Edinburgh, 1875, 8

30 Henry Bartle Edward Frere (1815–84) had a distinguished career as a civil servant in India, which culminated in his appointment in 1862 as Govenor of Bombay. He became a confidant of Livingstone and in 1872 was sent to Zanzibar to negotiate an anti-slavery treaty with the Sultan. His views on mission work are contained in the study he wrote following his visit to Zanzibar and the east coast: Sir Bartle Frere, *Eastern Africa as a Field for Missionary Labour*, London, 1874

31 J. Murray Mitchell to Dr J. Wilson, 8 January 1874, NLS 7770

East Africa – connected apparently with a Galla tribe – whom he considers well fitted to go out and act as pioneers'.[32]

This was the situation when early in 1874 James Stewart, now the head of the Lovedale Institution, South Africa, returned to Scotland to raise money for the daughter college of Blythswood. In April he attended Livingstone's funeral in Westminster Abbey. A month later he drew up a memorandum on 'Livingstonia, Central Africa', the gist of which was presented to the General Assembly of the Free Church in a speech delivered on 19 May. 'Somali land', Stewart commented, 'is in every way unsuitable' for a Free Church mission. 'It can never be a place of entrance in to the continent, or of exit from it. Its productions must be comparatively limited and its soil is not remarkably fertile.' The southern end of Lake Malawi, on the other hand, could be reached from the coast by water with only a single interruption. With Lovedale as 'the base of operations' for the new mission, its success would not be in doubt.[33] Such a station 'placed on a carefully selected and commanding spot in Central Africa [would] grow into a town, and afterwards into a city and become a great centre of commerce, civilisation and Christianity'.[34]

Stewart's proposal came at a timely juncture for the Free Church authorities. Their own plan for Somaliland had failed to create much interest in Scotland, and even its architects were quickly won over.[35] Bartle Frere was reported to be much taken with the new scheme, though he did not want the Somali country to be entirely given up, while Wilson wrote from Bombay giving the information – new apparently to Murray Mitchell, and he thought to Duff as well – that Livingstone himself had suggested the borders of Lake Malawi as the locale for a Free Church Mission.[36] Not only was the Free Church's decision to found a mission in East Africa unconnected with Livingstone's appeals, its authorities were ignorant of the area he had selected for evangelisation. Only the fortuitous appearance of Stewart and his suggestion of a title and location for the new mission connected Livingstone with its foundation at all.

It may seem ironic that a man who has been described as 'the busiest among his detractors in the field and afterwards at home' should have

[32] Murray Mitchell to Sir Bartle Frere, 20 March 1874, ibid.

[33] James Stewart, 'Memorandum on "Livingstone" Central Africa', May 1874, Stewart Papers ST1/1/1

[34] Stewart in his speech to the General Assembly on the Free Church of Scotland, May 1875, quoted in J. W. Jack, *Daybreak in Livingstonia*, Edinburgh, 1901, 26

[35] Minutes of the acting FMC of the Free Church of Scotland, entry for 21 July 1874, Church of Scotland Offices, Edinburgh

[36] Murray Mitchell to Dr Wilson, 30 July 1874, NLS 7770

been the architect of a scheme to commemorate Livingstone in this way.[37] The cynic could no doubt say that Stewart was less concerned with creating a suitable memorial than with getting support for his own pet scheme for the development of a new inland mission as a satellite for Lovedale. But this would only be a partial truth. Stewart's views had moderated since the fiasco of his first visit to the Zambesi region. In the intervening decade he had begun to correspond once more with Livingstone on reasonably friendly terms, and remained favourable to his belief in missionary operations that were 'very much more extended than what is usually embraced in the phrase "*a mission station*"'.[38] He looked eagerly to the dramatic economic transformation of Africa, believing at one stage that, if Livingstone could prove that there was continuous water communication between Lake Tanganyika and the Nile, then 'you have the American Lakes over again and may have a Chicago yet at X' [on the south-west corner of Lake Tanganyika].[39]

The geographical hopes were to be proved vain, but the desire to create a purified Chicago in Central Africa remained a fundamental part of Stewart's plans, both in his decisive rejection of Somaliland because of its alleged economic deficiencies, and in his advocacy of the Malawi regions because of the promise that area appeared to offer for the development of an export economy. Livingstone's ideas may not have weighed with the authorities of the Free Church in their decision to found an East African mission; but for those who were to finance and administer Livingstonia, their influence was of considerable importance.

Evidence of this influence appeared from the first in Livingstonia's administrative structure. Though he recognised the need to secure the approval of the Foreign Missions Committee for his scheme, Stewart looked for financial support to men of the same type as those who had helped him on his earlier expedition. Aided by his brother-in-law, John Stephen, the son of a wealthy shipbuilder, he organised a private meeting in the Queen's Hall, Glasgow, on 3 November 1874, which was to prove of importance to the mission. The Glasgow businessmen present demonstrated their acceptance of his assessment of the economic potential of the Lake Malawi area by unanimously agreeing to 'the desirableness and practicability of the enterprise and of planting an industrial and educational settlement at the region indicated'.[40] A special committee was

[37] Seaver, *David Livingstone*, 434

[38] Stewart to Livingstone, 4 October 1864, Stewart Papers ST1/1/1

[39] Sketch-map, n.d., ibid.

[40] Minutes of a meeting in the Queen's Hall, Glasgow, 3 November 1874, NLS 7913

appointed to raise funds on an interdenominational basis, and branches were soon formed in Edinburgh, Aberdeen and Dundee. Within a few days, sums of £1000 apiece had been promised by James White of Overtoun, the owner of a vast chemical manufacturing works at Rutherglen, by James Stevenson, the founder of a rival firm of chemical manufacturers, and by James Young, a close friend of Livingstone, founder of the shale oil industry and owner of the enormous 'Young's Paraffin Light and Mineral Oil Company'. Other large donations were received from Alexander Stephen, chairman of the shipbuilding firm at Linthouse and Stewart's father-in-law, from George Martin, who ran a successful export business with branches in Batavia, Singapore and Manila, from William Mackinnon, the founder of the British India Steam Navigation Company, and from his nephew Peter, a fellow director.

By itself such information is not particularly striking. Few missions to Central Africa in the nineteenth century could not boast some connection with the wider commercial world; most, in taking on new responsibilities, sought a parallel rise in income through the personal generosity of wealthy individuals like Robert Arthington or in special appeals such as the Church of Scotland was to set in motion over Blantyre.[41] But whereas these were normally short-term affairs, replaced soon after the new mission had been established by some system of associations through which quite small sums could be drawn from large numbers of people, Livingstonia continued to rely on the same, small, predominantly Glaswegian group of Free Church industrialists, without support from official Free Church funds, right on into the first decade of the twentieth century.[42] It was not until 1914 that Livingstonia finally came under the financial auspices of the Free Church Foreign Missions Committee. Between 1886 and 1890, for example, twenty-nine contributions, at least thirteen of them from Glasgow, produced £8106 14s 6d out of £15933 15s 6d raised. By 1890, White's son, John Campbell White, the donor of an estimated total of £50 000 to the mission, was giving £600 a year on salaries alone, as well as contributing heavily towards the cost of new buildings.[43] New large-scale subscribers appeared in the 1880s, among them William Henderson, Chairman of the Aberdeen Line of Steamers, George Barbour, who

[41] Arthington, 'the miser from Leeds', helped found Baptist and LMS mission settlements in Central Africa and frequently offered aid, though on unacceptable terms, to Livingstonia. A. M. Chirgwin, *Arthington's Millions*, London, n.d., 44–5

[42] Andrew C. Ross, 'Scottish missionary concern 1874–1914: a golden era?', *The Scottish Historical Review*, vol. LI, 151, April 1972

[43] George Smith, *The Lake Regions of Central Africa*, Edinburgh, 1891

managed various companies from Edinburgh and Sir John Cowan, the owner of paper mills at Penicuick; but generally it was the earliest supporters who remained most loyal, and when they died they were often not replaced.

It was not by chance that Livingstonia received the special attention of philanthropic industrialists in Scotland. Most of the men who supported her, critical perhaps of the system of patronage within the Church of Scotland that left the power of appointing ministers in the hands of a group of land-owning gentry, now less wealthy than themselves, had joned the Free Church at the time of the Disruption and were primarily responsible for keeping it solvent during the next thirty years. Lavish in their support of philanthropic schemes in Scotland, they still tended to be chary of giving aid to the destitute poor, whose plight might be assumed to be a consequence of their own folly, and looked instead towards less culpable, and more exotic, objects of charity further afield. The needs of '"Darkest England" with its sunken tenth of 3 000 000, many of whom had themselves to blame for being of that number', could not compare, believed John Campbell White, with those of '"Darkest Africa" with its 180 millions, who through no fault of their own, were sunk in vice and misery'.[44] It is perhaps significant that Campbell White, despite his acts of charity, did nothing to rectify the appalling conditions of work in his own factory at Rutherglen until Keir Hardie publicly exposed them in 1899.[45]

To this general attraction of the African continent as a scene of philanthropic endeavour was added the particular allurements of Livingstonia: first the fact that it was designed to commemorate the great missionary explorer, supreme publicist of the spiritual values inherent in Victorian industry; and second that it was deliberately sited near Lake Malawi on the expectation that that region, with its excellent waterway to the coast, would become a centre of economic activity. Industrialists of Campbell White's stamp were not directly concerned with the hypothetical profits they might make from the exploitation of Central Africa. Only William Mackinnon among Livingstonia's early supporters had financial interests that might have benefited from such work, and Mackinnon, though obsessed by grandiose schemes for African development, lost interest in the Lake Malawi region from 1879.[46] But they were

44 Quoted in ibid. See also Fleming, 38–42, 63–5

45 Donald Carswell, *Brother Scots*, London, 1927, 207–8; W. H. Marwick, *Economic Development in Victorian Scotland*, London, 1936, 158–9

46 John S. Galbraith, *Mackinnon and East Africa 1878–1895: a Study in the 'New Imperialism'*, Cambridge, 1972, 29–70

all firm believers in economic progress. They shared the opinion of an anonymous correspondent to the *Church of Scotland Missionary Record* when he wrote:[47]

> The complaint that missions are a burden or a waste ought for ever to cease; for just the opposite of this is true. They are profitable in every way; they are a grand outlying business investment – in the way of protecting commerce, of promoting manufactures and of stimulating trade. They bring up savage men to a higher appreciation of themselves, to realise their wants and needs, and thus awaken in them healthful tastes. So this grand missionary movement is being felt in our markets that supply the new and increasing wants of the world. In this way profits are reaped and business is benefited.

Money given to Livingstonia thus could be conceived of as an investment, but a long-term one in which the investors themselves might not share the profits. New markets would be created through it, new producers of raw material would appear and the commercial world as a whole would benefit. And Africa would be a part of that world; Africans would benefit morally and commercially with the rest.

A natural corollary to the concentration of financial support among a few individuals was the concentration of administrative power in the same hands. Among most Protestant missions, the CMS excepted, control of policy remained embedded in an ecclesiastical hierarchy. Livingstonia, by contrast, was administered separately by its financial supporters. Early arrangements for it were made personally by James Stewart, with some support from Alexander Duff, John Stephen, James Stevenson and other industrialists. It was not till 1877, however, after Stewart had returned to Africa, that official recognition was given to their position, through the creation of a joint sub-committee to deal with Livingstonia's affairs, consisting of representatives of the Foreign Missions Committee of the Free Church and the Glasgow Livingstonia Committee – a body initially set up to collect subscriptions.[48] This body, which held its first meeting on 6 November 1877, was nominally subordinate to the Foreign Missions Committee of the Free Church, which nominated nine of its fifteen original members and had the power of vetoing its proposals. In fact several of its nominations, including Stevenson and John Stephen, were businessmen and members of the Glasgow Committee. Nine of the first fifteen were laymen, a proportion that was maintained in later years when the size of the Committee increased. By 1891, half of the Com-

[47] *Church of Scotland Home and Foreign Missionary Record*, October 1876, 188

[48] Livingstonia Sub-Committee minute book, 1–2, NLS 7912

mittee were appointed from Glasgow, where it held its meetings, and twenty-four out of thirty-two were laymen. In its early days the sub-committee was intended to 'be of great service by ripening questions for decision by the General Committee'.[49] But Murray Mitchell, secretary of the Foreign Missions Committee in 1878, admitted that 'hardly ever will its recommendation be set aside'.[50] In practice the Foreign Missions Committee became the rubber stamp for the smaller body, not once vetoing its proposals and interfering hardly at all in its affairs. 'I find the Foreign Mission Committee of the Free Church really don't do much themselves about Livingstonia,' wrote Maclagen, secretary of the equivalent committee of the Church of Scotland in 1879. 'There is a special Livingstonia Committee consisting chiefly of Glasgow people who practically manage everything reporting to the F.M. Committee what they do.'[51]

Not all members of the committee attended regularly, and much was left to the secretary of the Foreign Missions Committee, an ex-officio member of the sub-committee, who dealt with all official communications with Livingstonia and acted as the link between the two committees and between them and the head of the mission. As long as Murray Mitchell, a retired Indian missionary, was secretary, the post was of only limited importance. But in 1879, he was replaced by Dr George Smith, editor of *The Edinburgh Daily Review*, and Smith regularly attended meetings of the sub-committee and frequently contributed to discussions.[52] Yet even Smith was a lightweight when compared with the first three convenors: James Stevenson, convenor until May 1880, James White and John Campbell White, who succeeded his father in May 1884. The influence of the businessmen was weakened by their lack of knowledge of conditions in Africa, by the length of time it took for correspondence to reach the lake from Scotland – up to five months in the 1880s – and by the distractions that a busy life imposed on many members of the committee. Yet, as holders of the purse strings, they were always able to apply the ultimate sanction. No plan requiring substantial expenditure could be put into operation without their prior agreement. No European agent could be appointed to the mission who did not pass their scrutiny.

The composition of Livingstonia's expeditionary party demonstrates the expectations of those responsible for its selection. As commitments at

[49] Murray Mitchell to Stewart, 2 January 1878, NLS 7770

[50] ibid., 13 February 1878

[51] Maclagan to Herdman, 20 June 1879, NLS 7544

[52] Smith, like Kipling, began his career as a newspaperman in India. He was the author of several weighty studies of Indian missionaries and statesmen.

Lovedale prevented Stewart from going, its leadership was vested in the hands of E. D. Young, a warrant officer in the Royal Navy, who had been seconded to the Zambesi Expedition in 1852 and led the Livingstone search expedition to Lake Malawi in 1867. Only one ordained missionary was appointed, the young United Presbyterian Robert Laws, along with five artisans: a sailor, an engineer, a gardener, a blacksmith and a carpenter. Later reinforcements maintained non-clerical dominance, though from the 1880s new skills began to be demanded: the first teacher was appointed in 1882, the first nurse in 1897. Out of thirty-one European appointments made in the first ten years, sixteen went to 'artisans' – seamen, ships' engineers, gardeners, carpenters, joiners and weavers – and six to others in primarily technical occupations – captain of the mission steamer and civil engineer. Only thirteen agents went out from Scotland as ordained missionaries before 1900; thirty-one went as artisans.

The character of the artisans is a key to the nature of the mission. As dourly devout and as restlessly ambitious as Livingstone, they saw in Central Africa a gateway to personal achievement. To Stewart and his business friends their role was clear. After establishing a settlement they would attract Africans to live there, teach them technical skills and provide demonstrations of European industry. For the artisans themselves, however, their appointment was to be a prelude to greater advancement. Of the five who sailed from London on 21 May 1875, two were later to become doctors, one a clergyman and one a respected trader. For the first time the theory of the 'industrial mission' was to be put to the test by men well qualified to do so.

3
Commerce and Christianity: the Yao experience

The seven years following the arrival of the pioneer Livingstonia party in Africa was a period of experiment during which the disadvantages of the Christian colony strategy were made increasingly clear. Bearing in mind advice given by Livingstone to the convenor of the Foreign Missions Committee nearly fourteen years earlier, the missionaries brought with them a small prefabricated steamer so constructed that it could be taken to pieces at the foot of the Murchison cataracts and rebuilt when the journey round the rapids had been completed. On 23 July 1875 they arrived aboard a German schooner off the Kongone mouth of the Zambesi and quickly set to work recruiting gangs of local Africans for the arduous task of bolting together the steel plates of their vessel. On 3 August the *Ilala* was launched and a week later the journey upstream began. A temporary setback came with the capsizing of an accompanying sailing boat, the death of two of its crew and the loss of most of the missionaries' personal possessions. But by 6 September the foot of the rapids had been reached and contacts with Makololo chiefs had been successfully established.

The close alliance forged by Livingstone with the Makololo refugees he had introduced from Barotseland played an important part in the missionaries' plans. When Stewart first travelled up the Shire in 1862, they were still living together in one village as Livingstone had left them.[1] During the next thirteen years they spread out through the lower Shire valley, establishing their dominance over the local Manganja through the use of firearms and the sale of ivory and creating a loose political federation, headed by Ramakukan but with Chipatula, Masea, Malilima and others virtually independent beneath him.[2] Aliens in a hostile land and lacking the Yao's coastal contacts, the Kololo, as Laws pointed out, were

[1] Wallis, *Zambesi Journal of James Stewart*, 90

[2] W. H. J. Rangeley, 'The Makololo of Dr. Livingstone', *Nyasaland Journal*, XII, 1, 1959, 84–91; Stewart to his wife, 9 August 1876, Stewart Papers ST1/1/1

'placed between two markets' and hence 'would welcome any communication with the English'.[3] When visited by the missionaries in early September, they responded by bringing firewood and provisions for sale, and by sending their villagers to work. Within a month, up to 1000 porters had been recruited, the steamer had been dismantled (with the exception of the boiler) into fifty-pound loads, the sixty-mile trek past the rapids had been accomplished and the steamer had been rebuilt and relaunched. On 11 October, the *Ilala* sailed through Lake Malombe and anchored opposite the Yao chief, Mponda's village at the river crossing south of the larger lake. The next day, having received from Mponda permission to settle where he wanted at Cape Maclear, Young called for the Old Hundredth to be sung as the first steamer to enter Lake Malawi moved onto its waters.[4] Just under a week later, on 17 October, after a first, short tour of reconnaissance, the landing at Cape Maclear was finally effected. 'Livingstonia is begun', wrote Laws, 'though at present a piece of canvas stretched between two trees is all that stands for the future city of that name.'[5]

To understand the response to mission penetration in East Central Africa in the late nineteenth century, it is necessary to recognise two important factors distinguishing the economic and political conditions prevailing in that region from those existing on the west side of the continent. In West Africa, the centralised societies of the interior were almost entirely Islamic in character or at least had Muslim teachers able to meet the demands for a literate bureaucracy: Christian missions were simply not required. In the eastern interior, on the other hand, even among such centralised states as Buganda, into which the Arabs had penetrated in the 1840s, Muslim influence was still limited in the 1870s and the demand for foreign technicians and instructors, capable of giving assistance in the agonising process of state modernisation, remained strong.

By contrast, while trading cities of West Africa, connected to the Atlantic seaboard tended to welcome missionaries during the period of their transference from a slaving to a more sophisticated economy, in East Africa the existing trading interests rejected the missionaries outright. Chiefs in Old Calabar or Lagos might well respond to the educational blandishments of the CMS or the United Presbyterians; their continued economic prosperity depended on the development of a literate

[3] R. Laws to A. Duff (?) 21 February 1876, NLS 7876

[4] Livingstonia Mission Journal entries for 11 and 12 October 1875, NLS 7908

[5] R. Laws to 'a friend at home', 19 October 1875, printed in *East Central Africa Livingstonia* in *The Livingstonia Mission 1875–1900*

professional elite, capable of competing and collaborating with the Europeans on equal terms.[6] It was fruitless, however, for Thomas Clegg, fresh from his success in persuading African agents to cut out European middlemen at Abeokuta, to implore Livingstone on his Zambesi expedition 'to get chiefs or wealthy traders if there are such to consign their produce direct to Manchester'.[7] African entrepreneurs of the type Clegg envisaged were thin on the ground in East Africa, and those traders who might have filled this role had their contacts fixed with the Indian Ocean economy, dominated by Arabs and Swahili, rather than with the British.

Furthermore, the communications systems used by Europeans to reach the Malawi regions militated against peaceful contact with the resident traders. On the Kenyan and Tanganyikan mainland, European pioneers, most of them explorers and government agents who were prepared to cooperate with Swahili traders to some extent, followed their trade routes into the interior and made allies of those chiefs the Swahili had befriended. Further south, however, Livingstone's failure to discover a link between the Ruvuma and Lake Nyasa ensured that the prevailing line of European advance should run counter to the existing paths of trade rather than along them. As the pioneers on this route were mainly missionaries noted for their hatred of the slave trade and were convinced, with James Stewart, that Arabs and Swahili were as 'full of all deceit and lying and contempt and hatred of Christianity as the very Devil himself', it was not surprising that opportunities for collaboration were notably limited.[8] While missionaries in West Africa sought to reform or extend existing patterns of trade, missionaries near Lake Malawi aimed rather to replace or destroy them.

For Livingstonia, these conditions provided the background to much of her work in Malawi up to the 1880s. One possible course of action her agents might have taken was to place themselves under the protection of the ruler of a strong centralised state and attempt to reform from within. In fact the northern Ngoni, the best substitutes the Malawi regions offered for the more complex polities of Buganda and Barotseland, were much admired for their military virtues by the missionaries Stewart and Laws, who were well aware of the strategic value to be gained from influencing a people so militarily dominant. As among other missions, however, the theoretical value of working from within a centralised polity was out-

[6] J. F. A. Ajayi, *Christian Missions in Nigeria, 1841–1891: the Making of a New Elite*, London, 1965, 53–6, 133–5

[7] T. Clegg to Livingstone, 29 August 1860, Stewart Papers ST1/1/1. For Clegg's attempts to train African traders see Ajayi, 84–6, 210–14

[8] Stewart Journal entry for 2 September 1861, Stewart Papers ST1/2/1

weighed in practice by the attractions of independence and the necessity of providing a port for the mission steamer by the lake shore. It was this, more than any desire on principle to settle among weak societies, that led the pioneer party to Cape Maclear, a hilly promontary at the south end of the lake which E. D. Young had visited and admired on his 1867 expedition. One drawback to the site, as Laws observed, was its distance from the nearest villages; another, noted by Stewart on the very day of his arrival, was its confined situation, shut in by rocky hills and lacking agricultural land.[9] For a time indeed Stewart believed that 'there would be no difficulty in making this place an excellent small town and certainly a good mission station'.[10] But as the months went by his opinion grew steadily less favourable. The plain fact was, he told his wife in July 1877, Young had placed the mission on the edge of a barren, tsetse-infested plain, unfriendly to animal life. To Captain Elton he was even more critical. 'As a harbour – excellent', he replied to one of the consul's questions; 'as a mission station – nearly useless'.[11]

The years spent by the missionaries at Cape Maclear were essentially a period of adjustment in personnel and policies alike to the realities of the African situation. In common with all pioneer missions, much time was spent in combating the physical challenges of the new environment. In the first year, a row of houses was built facing the lake, and a wooden fort was constructed against possible invaders; the ground was drained, gardens cultivated and a start made at building a timber slipway for the *Ilala*. E. D. Young, however, though an experienced sailor, had few of the talents that make for effective missionary leadership. To James Stewart, who replaced him at the head of a party of reinforcements, including four African evangelists from Lovedale, in October 1876, his work had about it 'a commonness and absence of all comfort inside and out that is to me very unsatisfactory'.[12] But Stewart was no more successful than Young in creating a harmonious community. Aged over forty when he arrived at Cape Maclear, he believed himself to be too old to respond to the challenge of his own creation. Impatient to get back to Lovedale, he was consumed by 'a slow burning anger . . . that I should be kept toiling away at rough work which suited me 20 years ago but does not suit me at all now'.[13]

9 Livingstonia Mission Journal entry for 17 October 1875; Stewart to his wife, 21 October 1876, Stewart Papers ST1/1/1

10 Stewart to his wife, 24 October 1876, ibid.

11 Stewart to his wife, 22 July 1877; Stewart, 'Reply to Questions proposed by Capt. Elton', 22 August 1877, ibid.

12 Stewart to his wife, 22 November 1876, ibid.

13 Stewart to his wife, 1 June 1877, ibid.

Under the strain imposed upon him by malaria he became so despotic and irritable that at least one observer thought he was going out of his mind.[14] It was only after his departure in December 1877 and the elevation of Robert Laws to the headship that Livingstonia got fully under way as an effective community.

Aged only twenty-four at the time of his arrival in Africa Laws, the son of an Aberdonian cabinet-maker, was originally regarded as a temporary member of the expeditionary party, but stayed on for fifty-two years in the service of the mission and became a legend in Malawi during his lifetime.

Austere, taciturn, with little gift for public speaking, he had an appetite for work that is almost unbelievable. A fully qualified doctor, he looked after the health of the mission party in the pioneer years and gave simple medical assistance to hundreds of out-patients, mostly with the aid of Epsom Salts and rhubarb pills.[15] He kept meteorological observations, collected linguistic material, maintained a voluminous official correspondence and taught the first pupils who came to the station from May 1876. Under his influence the Scottish agents read the Greek New Testament together and conducted Sunday services in neighbouring Yao and Manganja villages at which they demonstrated through picture-book and magic lantern displays the spherical form of the earth, its revolutions round the sun, the cause of day and night, God's purposes with man.[16] Hardly a major exploratory or diplomatic mission was undertaken in the first decade without Laws, and hardly a decision of any substance was not referred to him. Up to the appointment of Donald Fraser and James Henderson in the mid 1890s he had no intellectual peer among the missionaries and even after their arrival, his ideas, though regarded as narrow and old fashioned by the new generation of agents, were arguably more far-sighted than any that replaced them.

Under Laws, the first coherent attempt was made to put Livingstonia's enclave policy into action. The alternative to working within a powerful state was to set up an artificial settlement which could act as the nucleus for the introduction of 'legitimate' commerce in opposition to the slave trade. From the earliest days, the Scots made exploratory and evangelistic visits to villages on the Cape Maclear peninsula and to the more important settlements further north on the lake. These visits, however, were regarded

[14] This was the pioneer trader, H. B. Cotterill who communicated his fears to Horace Waller. See Waller to Secretary, Free Church FMC, 28 May 1877 NLS 7872

[15] Medical Report for 1876 and 1877. Livingstonia Mission Journal.

[16] Livingstonia Mission Journal entries for 14 November 1875, 16 and 30 January 1876.

as being of less importance than the building up of the central station as a populous and thriving township. On purely practical grounds there was good sense in attracting Africans to reside there, thus creating a labour force which could assist in the formidable tasks of constructing houses and growing crops. At a deeper level Livingstonia was seen as an 'institution' where Africans could be educated in an environment free from the pressures of their own social background, and inspired by the example of European industry. With Alexander Riddel most missionaries believed:

> that the separation of the people from their tribal chief is, humanly, the only conceivable way in which they can be laid open to the reception of Christianity. For as long as they owe allegiance to the hereditary Chief of their tribe, they must use the tribal tatoo mark and be subject to his will in all public ordeals, involving their nominal belief in witchcraft and a host of inferior spirits or demigods which cannot coexist with a belief in the Divine revelation.[17]

Most of the difficulties confronting Livingstonia at Cape Maclear stemmed from the political and economic environment in which the mission found itself situated. By the mid 1870s the migration of the Masaninga and Machinga Yao into the Malawi regions had resulted in the creation of a number of territorial chieftaincies near the south end of the lake, those most frequently visited by the missionaries being Makanjira's, established on the eastern shore about 1872, and Mponda's on the river-crossing to the south. Of diverse origin these chieftaincies were led by rulers, among whom Mponda was a typical example, who owed their power less to conventional hereditary rights than to their success as traders and raiders.[18] Monopolising the ownership of guns and ammunition in their states, they actively involved themselves in the east coast trade in ivory, copper and slaves, and turned their central villages into entrepots where caravans from the west could be provisioned and where Arab middlemen could operate in profitable security.

At a superficial level these men were not averse to the establishment of alliances with the mission. Products of a competitive and unstable environment, they envied Livingstonia's material wealth and looked to exploit her wider technological connections. Mponda, for example, though a drunken braggard in the eyes of the censorious Scots, was also a much-

17 Riddel to Dr Macrae, 8 January 1880, NLS 7872

18 According to Rangeley, Mponda, the son of the chief in a matrilineal society, used his power as a war leader to seize control of the chieftainship, following the death of his father about 1866, W. H. J. Rangeley, 'The Amacinga Ayai', *Nyasaland Journal*, XVI, 51–3

travelled trader with a keen eye for economic gain. In 1866 he had impressed Livingstone as being 'immensely interested in everything European'.[19] Ten years later he informed Young that he wished to accompany him to England 'that he might learn to make guns, gunpowder and cloth, the three all-important things to an African chief'.[20] He gave the Scots permission to settle in his territory and for several years used them sporadically as medical advisers, sending a villager to the station to be operated upon for a cyst, and requesting medicine for his wives 'that they might have more children'.[21] Laws could 'present no glowing report of a series of brilliant operations', but he treated the chief and his dependants for minor ailments with such success that in 1885 when Mponda was dying it was to Laws that he turned for medical aid.[22] As specialists in this field, even more, as itinerant technicians repairing the occasional firearm, mending musical boxes and giving arsenic to deal with marauding leopards, the missionaries were widely accepted, and treated, if not with favour, at least without active hostility.

But this acceptance was limited to the most peripheral of activities. Despite his request, made in 1876, that the missionaries should drive the Ngoni out of the country, Mponda was sufficiently secure politically in the 1870s to have little need for such military assistance as the Scots could provide.[23] In that decade, the chieftaincy was largely free from the succession disputes which erupted after his death, and the Maseko Ngoni, though undoubtedly a danger, were kept in check by a combination of superior firearms and careful diplomacy. By 1885 Mponda was paying Chikusi, the Maseko paramount, an annual tribute in cloth and salt for which he received the assurance that 'the Agoni would not be permitted to make raids on his territory' along with the promise of their help in any war in which he might be involved with the Songea Ngoni or his rival Makanjira.[24] Such a treaty was by no means an infallible safeguard, but it is significant that during the 1870s, the Ngoni did leave Mponda largely unmolested, while continuing to raid into the Shire highlands, the home of the less powerful Mangoche Yao. Driven from the south end of the lake by their Machinga cousins, this group had fewer opportunities for accumulating Enfield rifles and thus were readier to seek the protection

[19] Livingstone, *Last Journals*, 106–7

[20] Livingstonia Mission Journal entry for 14 April 1876

[21] ibid. entries for 20 January, 1–2 March 1876

[22] Medical Report for 1876 and 1877 ibid., Diary of Frederick Morrison, entries for 23 February, 5 May 1885, EUL

[23] Livingstonia Mission Journal entry for 1 March 1876

[24] Morrison Diary entry for 5 May 1885; Consul Hawes to FO, 7 July 1886, FO 84/1751

offered by the Blantyre Mission of the Church of Scotland, established in the Shire highlands in 1876. On his initial tour of reconnaissance, Henry Henderson, the pioneer Blantyre agent, noted that 'the Ajawa (Yao) . . . are being much harassed by the Ma Viti (Ngoni)' and found Chief Kapeni near Blantyre 'most anxious for the English to settle with him. He and indeed all the people I have conversed with have quite the idea that the "English" will bring peace and safety with them.'[25] Mponda, in contrast, though he treated Young and Laws with courtesy, did not repeat his request for military support, and remained deeply suspicious of the missionaries' intentions.

The major factor preventing the tactical alliance from being transformed into a more lasting relationship was the incompatible aims of the parties involved. To Mponda the maintenance of political power was connected more fundamentally than the missionaries imagined with the continuation of coastal trade. It was not just that the authority of Yao chiefs stemmed from the profits to be made from trips to the Zanzibar coast and Quelimane. More important, Yao economies had clearly been restructured by the 1870s in response to the demands of the export market. Slave wives, of whom Mponda possessed some seventy or eighty, played a crucial role in the enlargement of a Yao chief's lineage, for whereas the freeborn sons of a chief were primarily subjected to the authority of their maternal uncles, the sons of slaves remained at their father's village and swelled the ranks of his dependants.[26] Domestic slaves as well as unpaid members of the subordinate Manganja population were employed on ivory hunting expeditions and on caravans to the coast. Other slaves worked on the land with freeborn Yao and grew the surplus food crops with which caravans were provisioned. Without the coastal trade, Makanjira's dhows would have lacked for passengers. In the absence of Arab caravans the salt sold by Mponda's dependants would have been less in demand.[27] Ivory expeditions created the markets for rice and maize which were grown at both chiefs' villages. Arab traders supplied the flintlocks and, by the 1880s, the Enfield rifles upon which the military strength of the Yao was increasingly based. To abandon trade with the east coast, as the missionaries demanded, would have been to weaken the sinews of the

[25] Henderson to Macrae, 8 July 1876, quoted in CSHFMR, November 1876, 199–200

[26] Edward A. Alpers, 'Trade, State and Society among the Yao in the Nineteenth Century', *JAH*, x, 1969, 411–13

[27] The sale of salt from neighbouring salt-pans was an important feature of trade at Mponda's. See Livingstone, *Last Journals*, 106; Morrison Diary, entries for 23 January, 2 March 1883

local economy and to undermine the authority which the chiefs had painstakingly acquired.

It is hardly surprising, therefore, that little attention was paid to the mixture of moral exhortation and threat which Young poured on the major lakeside rulers, from the *Ilala* in the first few months of the mission settlement. Instructed by their home committee that 'active interference by force initiated on your side is in no case and on no account whatever to be resorted to', the missionaries resorted to bluff in searching a dhow near the south end of the lake, or in warning the Jumbe of Nkota Kota to mend his ways.[28] By 1882, the bluff had been called outright. Slave traders prepared caravans at Nkota Kota without any attempt at concealment. Dhow captains circled the *Ilala* to show off their wares and shouted abuse at the steamer's crew.[29]

In this situation much depended on the efficacy of Livingstone's scheme to restructure local economies through the introduction of legitimate trade. A short-lived venture, made in 1876 by an idealistic young schoolmaster, H. B. Cotterill, demonstrated some of the problems to be faced. Financed by James Stevenson, William Mackinnon and James Young, all leading supporters of Livingstonia, Cotterill hoped to use the steel sailing boat gifted to him by the boys of Harrow, to buy ivory on the lake and sell it direct to Europe. But in the absence of adequate transport facilities to the coast, his costs were high and his profits non-existent. Within three months of his arrival at Cape Maclear, Stewart had dismissed Cotterill's project as 'almost certain to be a failure', and instead was asking that a mission trading store should be opened, partly to save the mission the substantial costs of buying imported goods from independent traders and partly as a means of selling to the Yao the calico, axes and needles which the Arabs would otherwise provide.[30]

In Scotland, however, the home authorities were not convinced that it was wise for the mission to take a direct part in commerce. Permission to open a trading store of the type that Stewart had visualised was refused, though the first convenor of the committee, James Stevenson, expressed his wish to 'openly countenance and in many ways co-operate with

[28] 'Instructions to Lake Nyasa Party given by the Foreign Missions Committee of the Free Church', *Eastern Central Africa*, Livingstonia Mission Journal entries for 14 October, 10 December 1875

[29] Morrison Diary, entry for 7 December 1882

[30] Stewart to Cowan, 24 November 1876; to Duff, 4 December 1876, NLS 7876. Advised by Laws 'that I was not fitted for the rough life', Cotterill returned to Europe in 1877 and settled as a tutor in Dresden. See Cotterill to Laws, 22 January 1880, Shepperson Collection

Christian men engaged in honourable commerce'.[31] For Stevenson, missions like Livingstonia were only one among several instruments of change working for the absorption of East Central Africa into the world economy. He believed that their role of creating a prosperous elite of agricultural producers would come to nothing if transport costs were not considerably reduced and commercial firms founded to exploit the new conditions. All three tasks were interrelated.

From the mid 1870s, Stevenson combined his interest in Livingstonia with schemes for improving communications into the heartland of Central Africa. With Livingstone he believed that its commercial prospects would be best served by using the waterway from the mouth of the Zambesi to Lake Malawi and beyond.[32] But he was also fearful of the damage the Portuguese government could inflict through prohibitive tariffs and hence looked to an alternative overland route north of the Portuguese possessions. In 1876 he joined William Mackinnon in his project to build a waggon road from Dar es Salaam inland.[33] But when, a year later, the Portuguese government reduced transit dues on the Zambesi to a nominal three per cent, he succeeded in persuading the Livingstonia sub-committee to agree to supply a steamer for the lower Shire, and also to contribute towards the cost of a road past the Murchison cataracts.[34]

For Stevenson, however, these measures were secondary to his central plan of introducing commerce through the creation of a trading company. His initial scheme for a 'Commercial Adventure in Central Africa', to be conducted on business principles and separate from the mission, was laid before the Free Church Committee in October 1876.[35]

But it was not until after the Portuguese government had reduced transit dues that the first practical steps towards forming a company were taken. Stewart had wished for no more Europeans to be sent out, asserting that 'what we want is more calico to employ more labour'.[36] To James White he confessed his suspicion of over-ambitious plans:

> I wish to say that while it would be of great benefit to have a *small store* here I hope none of my friends or the friends of the mission in Glasgow will have anything to do with *big trading*

[31] Smith to Duff, 15 March 1876, *NLS* 7770

[32] Stevenson to Smith, 19 November and 10 December 1894, NLS 7873

[33] H. W. Macmillan, 'The Origins and Development of the African Lakes Company 1878–1908', Edinburgh University PhD 1970, 84–91

[34] Livingstonia sub-committee minutes entry for 7 August 1877, NLS 7912

[35] Memo by James Stevenson to FMC of the Free Church of Scotland, 17 October 1876, NLS 7872

[36] James Stewart, 'Report on Livingstonia', 3 March 1877, Stewart Papers STI/I/I

> *schemes* for Lake Nyassa at present . . . Trade must grow little by little and a large expenditure at first means certainly a big loss.[37]

But the committee was not to be warned. Under Stevenson's promptings it recommended, late in 1877, the creation of a new commercial body, independent of the mission but closely related to it. Two brothers, John and Fred Moir, were appointed as managers and Stevenson prepared the prospectus. In July 1878 'The Livingstonia Central Africa Company' was officially incorporated. Its three directors, Stevenson himself, John Stephen and James Young junior, were all members of the Glasgow sub-committee as were a majority of its original twelve shareholders.[38] Hardly a subscriber to the company, up to 1886, was not also a subscriber to Livingstonia.[39] The *Ilala* was transferred to the Company's use for three years and from 1880 it was agreed 'that all artisans already employed or that may be employed by the Mission or the Trading Company should be engaged on the footing that if required they should transfer their services from the one to the other of these bodies'.[40]

It is hardly surprising that the African Lakes Company, as the new body was known from 1881, had little success in seducing the Yao from their allegiance to the east coast trade. With a working capital of £6000 in the early 1880s, the company attempted at one and the same time to control the whole European carrying trade of Central Africa from the Zambesi to Lake Tanganyika, to trade over the same area and to develop cash-crop production in the Shire highlands – and all this with a staff which as late as 1886 numbered only twenty Europeans. The result is vividly shown in a letter from Fred Moir to his father in March 1880:

> As regards procuring ivory, we have been under supplied with men. Every man we had (till within the last six months of last year) has been employed *almost solely* working on repairing the steamer or recruiting at Blantyre. Every pound of ivory sent home on account of the Company has been bought or shot by your two sons and besides this we had the whole of the details of keeping notes of goods when & where shipped and delivered which took up a great deal of valuable time which might have been more profitably spent purchasing produce.[41]

Despite the extravagant claims made earlier for the Zambesi–Shire

37 Stewart to White, 28 February 1877, enclosed in McClure to R. Young, 18 May 1877, NLS 7877

38 Prospectus of the Livingstonia Central Africa Company, 1879, NLS 8021

39 Macmillan, 'African Lakes Company', 104

40 Livingstonia sub-committee minutes entries for 18 March 1878 and 9 March 1880, NLS 7912

41 F. Moir to Dr Moir, 12 March 1880, Moir Papers

waterway, it was soon evident that Livingstone's route offered few advantages for aspirant cash-crop producers. Because of the low level of water in the river and the numerous sand banks, both the *Ilala* and the *Lady Nyassa* – put into service by the Moirs in September 1878 – were small, shallow craft whose carrying capacity was so limited that they could only be profitably employed in transporting goods of fairly high value. The use of porters between the river and the Shire highlands further increased transport costs with the result that by 1881 the Moirs had tacitly abandoned their plans for assisting in the development of peasant production and instead were concentrating on the export of ivory. The results have been studied by Hugh Macmillan.[42] Hindered as much by its ineffective transport system as by the ban on the sale of guns and gunpowder, the two managers found it almost impossible to break the Yao and Arab monopoly. The prices they offered were frequently rejected by Yao traders who could make greater profits by selling their ivory at the coastal ports. In consequence, up to 1883, the company was forced to rely upon white hunters – some of them sportsmen on safari from Britain – to shoot most of the ivory it exported. In the next three years, extensive purchases were made from Arab entrepreneurs at Karonga, but the trade in slaves was not thereby affected and Yao economic patterns continued as before. Frequent caravans still passed through Mponda's in the early 1880s and the number of Arab visitors to the entrepot appears to have increased. Some forty coast men were noted in the town in March 1883, apparently companions of the chief who had returned with him from Zanzibar after a six-month trading expedition during which he had obtained 'a goodly number of Enfield rifles . . . a number of boxes full of cloth, also a round sum of money'.[43] A Lakes Company employee observed 'hundreds of Arabs on shore' at Mponda's in June 1885, and 'sixty-nine slaves tied together with chains' at the village in the following August.[44] Mponda's successor was 'entirely in the hands of the coast men who surround him', Consul Hawes noted in June 1886, 'and every care is taken on their part to prevent the trade slipping out of their hands'.[45]

The reasons why there was no transition from the slave trade to legitimate commerce in the Malawi regions have often been misunderstood. No doubt the inefficiency of the Moir brothers, their limited resources and Christian scruples contributed to their ineffectuality. But these were not the major factors. The central reason why slaves continued to be sold in

[42] Macmillan, 'African Lakes Company', 211–17
[43] Morrison Diary entry for 2 March 1883
[44] ibid. entries for 8 June and 3 August 1885
[45] Hawes to FO, 3 June 1886, FO 84/1751

Central Africa was that slave labour was a fundamental feature of most Central African societies. Duff Macdonald, the Blantyre missionary, noted in the 1880s that while Yao chiefs frequently sold slaves on the export market, they also used them effectively 'farming, building, making baskets, sewing garments and such masculine pursuits'.[46] Where land was plentiful and labour in short supply wage labour was expensive, as the company discovered to its cost. By the 1890s it had begun to demand that the colonial government use forms of coercion in recruiting the porters and labourers whom it wished to employ. It is true that domestic slavery is not incompatible with the export of agricultural produce, but as transport costs remained high, the sale of agricultural surpluses was largely confined to the local Malawi market. In this situation the company survived financially by adapting to the existing economy. By opening a market for ivory on the lake, it provided an outlet for the larger traders which they found increasingly useful in the 1880s as political conditions in the East African interior worsened.[47] But a market of this type, far from reducing slavery, had the effect of contributing to its expansion. Ivory expeditions, as the Livingstonia missionaries commented, were frequently the occasion for the impressment of slaves or at least of servile Manganja villagers. The sale of ivory on the lake made it easier to transport slaves to the coast. And as small ivory traders virtually never sold their wares to the company, it was the powerful slave-owning rulers, the Arabs of Karonga, the Jumbe of Nkota Kota, Makanjira and occasionally Mponda who benefited from its presence.[48]

The failure to create a viable new economic structure on the lake was accompanied by a growth in tension between Livingstonia and the neighbouring Yao chieftaincy. Founded as a colonial enclave, the mission drew its pioneer settlers and thus its early intermediaries from those on the periphery of the tribal system: ambitious but disappointed village headmen and individuals with special skills, who sought to exploit them under European protection; the rejects and the dispossessed. Some sixty or seventy strong in February 1877, their numbers rose to 347 in August 1878 and to 590 in 1880.[49]

[46] Macdonald, *Africana*, 147. My analysis here is influenced by A. G. Hopkins, *An Economic History of West Africa*, London, 1973, 23–7

[47] In addition to the marketing facilities it provided, the company from the mid 1880s operated a skeleton postal service between Nkota Kota, Mponda's and Zanzibar. Morrison Diary entries for 1 October and 21 February 1886

[48] Cape Maclear Journal, entry for 6 May 1879, NLS 7909

[49] Cape Maclear Journal, August 1877; Diary of John Gunn, entry for 16 December 1878, printed in an Aberdeen newspaper, NLS 7906; W. P. Livingstone, *Laws of Livingstonia*, London, n.d. (1921), 194–5

These settlers can be described under three main headings. An important group were the incomers to Malawi, several of them freed slaves returning to their homeland, and some residents on the Mozambique coast. In Young's pioneer party were four liberated Africans – Lorenzo Johnston, Thomas Boquito, Samuel Sambani and Frederick Zarakuti – the first three Yao, the fourth Manganja. These men had been members of the group of slaves rescued by Bishop Mackenzie and Livingstone in the Shire highlands in July 1861. Sheltered at Magomero, where Sambani and Zarakuti had become special favourites of Lovell Procter, they had been brought down to Cape Town on the collapse of the mission and had lived there for some ten years.[50] Four other Africans were recruited at the Kongone mouth of the Zambesi and a further group of porters were engaged at Mazero to assist in transferring the mission's goods up river. Several of this group left the mission after they had accomplished the tasks for which they had been appointed, but several more stayed on, including Boquito, who accompanied Henderson on his pioneer expedition to the Shire highlands in 1876 and Sambani, Young's interpreter, already an experienced traveller.[51] From 1876, they were joined by a handful of members of the polyglot African community living near the Zambesi mouth, brought up to the lake by missionaries and other visitors as personal servants and interpreters. Two former slaves from Quelimane were brought to the station by James Stewart in 1876 and Consul Elton brought a third in 1877.[52] Another arrival was Joseph Bismark, the son of an African planter from Quelimane. Bismark already knew some French and Portuguese when he took employment in 1876 with W. B. Thelwall, an artist representing the *Illustrated London News* who travelled up to the lake with the second Livingstonia party. After Thelwall's death in a shooting accident in 1878, Bismark worked as an interpreter and teacher with the Blantyre Mission before becoming one of the first successful African capitalist farmers in Malawi and an elder of the Presbyterian church.[53] His career paralleled that of Charles Domingo, the son of a cook employed by the Lakes Company at Quelimane, who was brought to Malawi in 1881 by the Lovedale evangelist William Koyi

[50] Livingstonia Mission Journal 1875 prefatory note, NLS 7908; N. R. Bennett and M. Ylvisaker (ed.), *The Central African Journal of Lovell J. Procter 1860–1864*, Boston, 1971, 191, 316, 347, 449

[51] Livingstonia Mission Journal, entries for 19 November 1875, 21 February 1876; CSHFMR, 1 November 1896, 199–200

[52] Stewart to his wife, 10 October 1876, Stewart Papers, ST1/1/1; Diary of John Gunn, entry for 17 February 1879, 7906

[53] 'A Brief History of Joseph Bismark' by Himself, *Occasional Papers of the Department of Antiquities*, Zomba, 1969, no. 7, 49–54

and who later played a part of considerable importance in the religious life of the Northern Province.[54] A number of Swahili agents were also employed on an experimental basis in 1879. But though the artisan John Gunn described them as 'fine, frank, useful fellows', who 'make good overseers', they ceased to work at the mission after a couple of years. Boquito and Sambani also returned to the Cape Colony when their period of engagement was completed and there they were joined by Zarakuti, whose dramatically licentious behaviour led to his expulsion from the mission. All three returned to Malawi about 1881 and were employed as agents by the African Lakes Company some fifteen miles from Blantyre.[55]

Unjustly ignored in official histories of the mission, the contribution made by members of this group in the pioneer years was undoubtedly of considerable importance. At a time when the Scots were isolated from their neighbours by the barriers of language and custom, it was Boquito, Sambani, Bismark and the others who supervised work gangs at the station, kept open communications with the coast, interpreted for missionaries on their travels and explained to potentates like Mponda the purpose of the mission and the reasons for its presence.

By the end of 1876, two further groups of settlers had begun to arrive at Cape Maclear. The first consisted of Makololo princes with their Manganja servants, sent to the station on the instruction of their fathers to receive a Western education. Anxious to cement their relationship with the mission, the Kololo rulers in 1875 promised Young to send some of their numerous children to the mission. A year later, Ramakukan and Moloko each consigned a son to Stewart on his way up the river and these were joined during the next few months by the sons of several other headmen. These young men brought with them as companions and personal servants a number of Manganja subordinates, so that by August 1877, out of forty-five Makololo, so-called, resident at Cape Maclear, not more than nine were the sons of headmen.[56]

At first the experiment worked happily, with about half the group receiving simple lessons from the South African evangelists Shadrach Ngunana and William Koyi and the rest performing manual tasks under the supervision of the Scottish artisans. To the Makololo, however, Scottish discipline was intolerably confining. In October 1877, the eldest

[54] W. P. Livingstone, *Laws*, 194–5, See also pp. 210–218 below

[55] Diary of John Gunn entries for 14 September 1877, 23 April 1879, NLS 7906; John Moir to his sister, 15 January 1881, Moir Papers

[56] Stewart, 25 March 1877, quoted in *Daily Review*, 31 May 1877; Black, 31 October 1876, quoted in *FCSMR*, March 1877, 61; Cape Maclear Journal census August 1877, NLS 7909

son of Ramakukan, Kampata, walked out of the station following an argument, taking nine of the younger boys with him. Persuaded to return, he was punished by being refused work and thus was deprived of the opportunity to buy cloth.[57] A few weeks later he left the mission permanently and in January 1878 was back in the lower Shire valley with most of his compatriots. In May they were joined by the sons of Masea, the last chief to request the return of his children.[58] The Makololo's hopes that the mission would send a teacher to live among them had been disappointed and they were further annoyed, one artisan believed, 'because we do not supply them with guns and powder at their pleasure'.[59] They therefore decided to send their sons to the much closer school at Blantyre, but left the Manganja serfs to continue their education at Livingstonia. Among these were several who committed themselves entirely to the mission, notably Albert Namalembe, the first convert, baptised in March 1881, and John Brown Mvula, the second convert, baptised the following year.[60]

Meanwhile refugees – many of them dissident villagers exchanging the authority of one chief for another – were providing the third and most substantial source of settlers. The process was begun by Chimlolo, a Yao dependent of the UMCA at Magomero and Chibisa's in the early 1860s who had won a certain influence among the English as a reliable leader of porters.[61] In February 1876, he began work at Livingstonia and by January of the next year he had settled five members of his household around him.[62] Over the next few months, Chimlolo's example was followed by three neighbouring headmen, Mpasa, Makandanji and Kapangasina, the latter a Manganja vassal of Mponda's, who was changing his political allegiance. These men came at the head of extended families with up to twenty-two members, including wives and children; built villages under mission protection instead of living at the station itself as the Makololo did and incorporated in them a motley collection of followers most of whom gave as their reason for seeking refuge their fear

57 Cape Maclear Journal entries for 6–10 October 1877

58 Laws, to Stewart, 30 January, 28 March and 20 May 1878, Stewart Papers ST1/1/1

59 *Glasgow Herald*, 8 February 1877; Diary of John Gunn, 25 July 1878, NLS 7906

60 Laws to Stewart, 30 January 1878, Stewart Papers, ST1/1/1; *FCSMR*, September 1881, 220; November 1882, 326

61 *Journal of Lovell Procter*, 373, 382, 406; Henry Rowley, *The Story of the Universities Mission to Central Africa*, London 1866, 304, 439, 449

62 Livingstonia Mission Journal entries for 14, 19 and 27 February 1876; Cape Maclear Journal, August 1877, Appendix

of being enslaved. A few came from as far away as Nkota Kota in the north and the lower Shire valley in the south but most were local Manganja escaping from Yao hegemony. It was their language rather than that of the Yao that the missionaries used at Cape Maclear. By 1895, when the first census of the South Nyasa district was taken, the three villages at Old Livingstonia were all considered to be Manganja-occupied.[63]

The initial success of the Scottish mission in attracting refugees to its settlement throws into sharp relief the difficulties in precolonial days facing all expeditionary parties which undertook temporal responsibilities independent of any external political authority. One such problem concerned the control of missionaries over dependants at their station. At Cape Maclear, the early settlers were given food supplies until they could grow their own crops and in return were expected to adhere to a variety of regulations. They were forced to live in certain villages, to build only square huts, not round ones, and to send their children to school. They were advised to attend meetings on Sundays and to work for the mission, and were warned against beer drinking and polygamy although the latter was not absolutely forbidden. When acts of violence or theft took place, the missionaries responded by fining the offender so many yards of calico or by placing culprits in the stocks, constructed in July 1877. Later a prison was built in which one Golingo was confined for twenty-four days in September 1878 for deserting an expedition to which he had been recruited as a porter.[64] More serious offences were dealt with by expelling the offender from the station, though Laws was opposed to this method, which he believed to be no punishment for some individuals and a very grave one indeed for others who fell into the hands of the slaver. Offenders were also sometimes flogged, a punishment of which Laws, with some reservations, approved.[65] Attempts were made from time to time to give an air of legality to the proceedings, by convening councils of local settlers to give judgement or by asking neighbouring headmen to do so. But these tribunals tended to have little real power and were employed only on the initiative of the Europeans.

A second problem concerned Livingstonia's relations with her Yao neighbours. As the number of dissident villagers rose, to perhaps 550 by mid 1880, their defiance of the authority of local rulers began to provoke

[63] *BCAG*, September 1895, 1

[64] Cape Maclear Journal entries for 2 July, 19 and 31 December 1877, 6, 21 September, 1 October 1878

[65] ibid. entry for 19 June 1878; Laws to Stewart 20 May 1878, Stewart Papers STI/1/1; Laws to Smith 18 March 1880, quoted in Livingstonia sub-committee minutes, entry for 2 June 1880, NLS 7912

angry reactions. The early settlers, Chimlolo, Kapangasina and Mpasa appear to have established villages at Livingstonia less because of their fear of being enslaved than because they were ambitious to extend their political power. Later they acted as intermediaries between the new refugees and the mission and increased the numbers of their followers by incorporating them into their villages, a practice in which they were helped by the mission policy of refusing to repatriate refugees to their masters unless some crime could be proved against them. In an area where control of manpower rather than control of land was the key to power and wealth, the results were catastrophic. Several headmen in the vicinity of the lake lost followers to the mission, the greatest sufferers being two vassals of Mponda, Chualo and Sogoli whose villages were situated on the eastern shore of the southern promontory some distance from the station. In March 1876, a handful of Sogoli's villagers came to work for a few days at the station. Ten months later, in January 1877, the first defectors followed and were allowed to remain, despite the fact that Sogoli sent his brother to ask for their return. Several more absconded during the next few months, including one of the headman's own wives.[66] When Sogoli visited the station on 24 August 1878 his village had virtually disintegrated. 'Three years ago', he told the missionaries,

> the English came into the country with a steamer. They called on Mponda asking him to stay in his country and saying that they wished to live at peace with all men. Mponda gave them ground to settle on, and he never since stirred up strife or war. What had he done? Nothing! His people were leaving him and finding shelter with the English. A large number of his own (Sogoli's) people had run to the English (here he recited the names of those who had left him) so that his village was now completely shattered. He had sent after these people but each one was allowed to plead his own cause and the result was that none of them were restored to him.[67]

The reactions of both sides were predictable. The missionaries told Sogoli that they would always shelter oppressed persons against whom no charges had been made; Sogoli responded in the only way open to him. Even before his dramatic appeal he had made attempts to kidnap dependants on whom verbal persuasion had failed to work. But this caused intervention. On 1 June 1878 one of the Scottish artisans, Crooks, led an armed posse to Sogoli's village to retrieve a boy snatched from one of the mission villages. A brawl followed and the party was forced to

66 Livingstonia Mission Journal entry for 19 March 1876; Cape Maclear Journal entries for 29 January, 11, 15–16, 21 February, 9 October 1877

67 ibid. entry for 24 August 1878

spend the following night watching for possible attackers.[68] Other kidnapping incidents were followed by the seizure of those Yao thought to be responsible, their imprisonment and in one case the flogging of a ringleader. African agents of the mission were struck and insulted in neighbouring villages; neighbouring headmen shunned the station for fear of instant arrest.[69]

Problems of this type were aggravated by the fact that during the early years the ordained missionaries were often absent from the central station. Diplomatic and pioneering expeditions were frequently made and in addition, in December 1876, at the urgent request of Henry Henderson, the missionaries took over responsibility for Blantyre, then according to Stewart 'at a standstill and in danger of utter collapse'.[70] Stewart himself, his cousin (a civil engineer) and Laws all spent periods there attempting to get the place in working order, before the arrival of the Church of Scotland's first ordained missionary, Duff Macdonald, in 1878. The result was that artisans were frequently left for extended periods in positions of authority. During 1878, a typical year, they were in charge at Cape Maclear for over 200 days. This is of importance in explaining some of the discrepancies that emerged between theory and practice in the working of the mission. At a time when malaria and blackwater fever killed off nearly one in four of the mission staff, only men of considerable initiative and ambition would consider going out to Central Africa.[71]

Of the first five Livingstonia artisans, two, Johnston and Riddel, went later to Aberdeen University and became respectively a doctor and a clergyman; a third, McFadyen, also became a doctor and a fourth, Simpson, after years in the service of the Lakes Company, set up as an independent trader and then as a prosperous planter.

But this ambition was more commonly given rein in the wielding of power over Africans. Two members of the staff, Crooks in 1879 and McCurrie later at Bandawe had to be dismissed for respectively striking and shooting at men in their employment.[72] As events at Bandawe were to show, almost every time an artisan was left in charge of a station the mission entered more aggressively into local politics, and the number and severity of punishments inflicted at the station increased.

68 ibid. entries for 1–5 June 1878

69 ibid. entries for 23 September 1878; 2, 20 November, 12–17 April 1879

70 Stewart to Duff, 20 December 1876, NLS 7876

71 Out of eighty-one members of staff appointed to Livingstonia between 1875 and 1900, all young and fit on appointment, eighteen died on service in Malawi and eleven were invalided back to Scotland

72 Cape Maclear Journal entries for 4 March and 3 May 1879; Bandawe Station Journal entry for 16 September 1887, NLS 7911

By 1881 the political situation that confronted the Scots at Cape Maclear was in some respects less favourable than it had been at the time of their arrival six years earlier. Neighbouring headmen still continued to request the aid of the mission in dealing with such natural hazards as man-eating leopards and marauding elephants; one local chief, Kasanga, had attempted to place his village under mission protection when he went on a trading venture to Bisa country.[73] But, by and large, Livingstonia's relationship with her neighbours had become alarmingly isolated. Furthermore the increase in numbers had brought the difficulties that Stewart had foreseen. Shortage of fertile land meant that several prospective settlers had to be turned away as there was no means of feeding them. As the settlement expanded the problem of sanitation grew acute and the fever rate increased. Laws had initially opposed Stewart's proposal to move the site, but by 1880 his resistance was stilled. In October 1881, six years almost to the day since the arrival of the missionaries, the *Ilala* sailed north to Bandawe, half way up the west coast of the lake, taking with her the last Europeans from the station.[74]

The history of Cape Maclear from the 1880s reveals all too clearly the failure of Livingstonia to make a significant impact on the lakeside Yao. Although most of the scholars and servants attached to the mission moved up to Bandawe, the village settlements remained. These Laws placed under the headship of Chimlolo, whom he made responsible for civil jurisdiction, with the aid of a tribunal of councillors. An advanced scholar, Andrew Mwana Njobvu was put in charge of Sunday services and of the school at the settlement, while another, Harry Zamatgona, was given the care of the store and ordered to buy salt to be bartered for provisions at the other stations.[75] A year later, an evangelist, Charles Konde, supported by the Bandawe congregation at the rate of three shillings per month was sent to replace Njobvu and he in turn was replaced in 1884 by the mission's first convert, Albert Namalembe, who remained there until his death in 1908.[76]

The immediate effect of the missionaries' departure was to weaken their influence on the promontory. Numbers attending school dropped from an average of forty to about eight or nine in June 1882. Three months later the day school had ceased to function and Sunday services

[73] Cape Maclear Journal entries for 4 March and 3 May 1879

[74] Laws, 28 October 1881, quoted in *FCSMR*, March 1882, 83

[75] *FCSMR*, December 1883, 357

[76] W. Scott to R. Laws, 30 October 1884, Shepperson Collection; *Livingstonia News*, August 1908, 40

were attended only by women.[77] In the absence of Europeans at the station, Chimlolo and Mpasa behaved increasingly as independent village headmen. Chimlolo sold women and children from his village into slavery; Mpasa received settlers fleeing from Makanjira without asking permission of the mission. Both men employed the *mwavi* poison ordeal in disputes with Livingstonia's African agents.[78] Chimlolo actively assisted the Lakes Company during a crisis on the lower Shire in 1884. Subsequently, however, he was banished to Karonga on account of his dictatorial treatment of the Cape Maclear settlers and was allowed to return only in 1892.[79] As for Mpasa, he provoked the anger of Mponda II by refusing to give food to the chief in January 1887, with the result that Mponda's men began 'committing thefts in the neighbourhood and giving great annoyance to the people in the mission village'. It was only with the reassertion of Mponda's sovereignty in the area that the outbreak of war was avoided.[80]

The arrival of Namalambe and, to a lesser extent, the foundation in 1887 of a new station at Livlezi, near enough for the Europeans to make regular visits, restored temporary vitality to the settlement. Consul Hawes in June 1886 declared himself to be 'much pleased with the intelligence and ability shown by some of the boys' in the village school which Namalambe was running.[81] By 1894 three schools were in operation there with a combined membership of 224 and nearly 400 people were regularly attending Sabbath services.[82]

But once again, early promise went unfulfilled. In contrast with the small group at Cape Maclear who identified themselves with the Lakes Company and with Livingstonia, most of the Yao became increasingly wary as the European presence began to loom large. The expansion of Islam provides a striking contrast to the failure of the commerce and Christianity strategy. Evidence of coastal influence among the Yao was much apparent in the mid 1870s in the 'several good square houses' seen by both Young and Stewart on their first visits to Mponda's in the carved

[77] Harkness to Laws, 21 June 1882, 11 September 1882, Shepperson Collection

[78] Morrison Diary, entries for 25 April, 13 May 1883, 24 March, 16 September 1885

[79] Harkness to Laws, 12 January 1885, Shepperson Collection; Sharpe to H. H. Johnston, 17 December 1892, enclosed in Johnston to Rosebery, 2 January 1893, FO 2/54

[80] Morrison Diary entries for 14 and 18 January 1887; Hawes to Laws, 3 April 1887, Shepperson Collection

[81] Hawes to FO, 3 June 1886, FO 84/1751

[82] Dewar to Smith, 12 January 1895, NLS 7878

doorposts and lintels at his village and in the kanzu-clad Swahili living there. But with the exception of Makanjira's, where Consul Elton noted in 1877 'a mwalimu established here, who teaches reading and the Koran', Islam had not been adopted, even as a court religion, and it still seemed possible that Christianity might fill the spiritual gap within their widening social horizons which the Yao were experiencing as members of an international trading community.[83]

Ten years later, the battle had clearly been lost. In 1885, Makanjira's head village, with its population of between 3000 and 4000 was a replica of a coastal community. According to one observer, the inhabitants 'all, or nearly all, speak the Zanzibar language. The houses also are nearly all after the same style . . . All the people we saw were very well clad in good blue or Zanzibar cloths.' Coastal produce, mangoes, pawpaws and coconuts, were grown near the town and Muslim education continued to flourish: 'There is a large schoolhouse where a mwalimu teaches the children Swahili and instructs them in the Koran.'[84] Mponda was buried according to Muslim rites in 1885, by which time several of his young men were said to be believers.[85] Six years later his town had a dozen Koranic schools, run by their own *waalimu*. They appear to have acted as the 'scribes or clerks' of the chief and conducted an extensive correspondence with traders like the Jumbe of Nkota Kota.[86] As the movement spread out from the court it took on a popular flavour. By 1895, Namalambe was reporting from Cape Maclear 'that *Islam* is spreading among the younger men, especially those who are much at Mponda's'. Christianity was at a standstill.[87] Fifteen years later, a missionary reported that the triumph was complete: 'Among the Yao on the lake shore it is becoming the natural thing to be a Mohammedan – they look on it as

[83] E. D. Young, *Nyassa: a Journal of Adventures*, London, 2nd edition, 1877, 61; Stewart to Duff, 26 October 1876, quoted in *The Daily Review*, 16 February 1877; J. F. Elton, *Travels and Researches among the Lakes and Mountains of Eastern Africa* (ed. by H. B. Cotterill), London 1879, 228–9. See also Edward A. Alpers, 'Towards a History of the Expansion of Islam in East Africa: the Matrilineal Peoples of the Southern Interior', in T. O. Ranger and I. N. Kimambo (eds.), *The Historical Study of African Religion*, London, 1972

[84] Morrison Diary entry for 8 March 1885; Consul Goodrich to FO, 19 March 1885, FO 84/1702

[85] Hawes to FO, 3 June 1886, FO 84/1751

[86] Ian Linden, *Catholics, Peasants and Chewa Resistance in Nyasaland, 1889–1939*, London, 1974, 26; Morrison Diary entry for 21 February, 1886; Alpers, 'Expansion of Islam', 185–6

[87] Livingstonia Mission Report, January–July 1895, 1

their natural religion. The Yao who does not accept it will soon find himself a stranger among his own people.'[88]

Missionary educational advances had also been rejected. By 1928, out of a total population of over 55 000 in Liwonde District, less than a thousand were attending an officially recognised school, and the standard, the local Resident reported, 'is so poor that it is worse than useless and most disheartening to any who aspire to enlightenment'.[89] Even the government schools established the same year in that area (the first in Malawi) failed to overcome the suspicion attached to any institution thought to be connected with Christianity, and by 1934 they had been abandoned altogether.[90] The Yao near the lake, though not those further south in the Shire highlands, were divorced, to a significant extent from educational opportunities.

[88] Report of the Third Nyasaland Missionary Conference, 1910, 39

[89] Resident Liwonde to Director of Education, Zomba, 7 June 1928, MNA s1/1067/28

[90] See file entitled 'Educational Facilities for Mohammedans', MNA, s1/1067/28

4
Missionary penetration and African responses 1878-91

Kaningina and Bandawe: The pioneer settlements

The move from Cape Maclear to Bandawe marked a new stage in the history of the Livingstonia Mission. Not only did it take Livingstonia for the first time into what was to become the main centre of its work in Malawi, the Northern Province, it also brought it into intimate touch with a political situation quite alien to that at the south end of the lake, and one in which missionary influence was to be positively welcomed. Moreover, it marked an important change in mission policy, a change from what may be called the 'residential mission' concept in which the principal aim was to attract Africans to a central station where they could be brought up away from the 'temptations' of their own society, to one in which the mission acted primarily on the village level with only a small, though admittedly important, residential element.[1]

The first suggestion that Livingstonia might found a new station on the lake came in October 1876 from James Stevenson who was seeking missionary support on the trade route north for his 'commercial adventure'.[2] Dr Stewart took up the matter and in 1877, during a tour of the lake, landed at the Tonga village of Mankhambira and walked a hundred miles south to Nkota Kota. As a result of this journey observation posts, each manned by a single European supported by a small staff of Africans, were set up in November 1878 at Bandawe, on the lake shore, and at Kaningina in the foothills inland.[3] They both survived until October 1879, when the Kaningina post was closed, apparently because Laws was afraid of the difficulties which might arise on account of its exposed position in the no-man's land between the Ngoni in the hills and the Tonga. Although Bandawe was now the obvious site for a new settlement,

[1] See Oliver, '*Missionary Factor*', 60

[2] Memo. by James Stevenson, 17 October 1876, NLS 7872

[3] Stewart, 'Summary of Instructions and Hints for 1878'; Bandwe Station Journal entry for 28 November 1878, NLS 7910

it was regarded with little enthusiasm either by the missionaries or by the committee at home. Laws feared that in the absence of any central local authority the mission would risk being involved in inter-village disputes; while Simpson, an artisan who had spent several months at the post, described it together with Kaningina and Cape Maclear as being 'all on the lake and all more or less unhealthy owing to the near vicinity of swamps and marshes'.[4]

Not until October 1880 was Laws given permission to move the whole party to Bandawe, and even then it was made clear that the new station was not to replace Cape Maclear as the main settlement of the mission, but was only to be used as a temporary outstation till a better site was found. Advice was given against spending more on the cost of the buildings than was absolutely essential, and Laws was told that he 'should as soon as possible complete your search of the Livingstone Mountains for a settlement at least as good as Blantyre's'.[5]

This reluctance to settle at Bandawe did not arise only from the unhealthiness of the low-lying site and its manifest inadequacy as a harbour, 'open to every wind that blows' and with 'no protection from the waves'.[6] A further factor was the embarrassing enthusiasm with which many lakeside Tonga villagers living in the vicinity of the new settlement responded to the mission's presence. Yao rulers, by their refusal to become closely involved with the mission, had rendered its influence powerless. Tonga headmen, through their eagerness to associate themselves with the missionaries, almost drove the Scots away.

The Tonga had many reasons for allying themselves with Livingstonia. At a simple level, political circumstances in the 1870s predisposed them to look for reliable allies. Raided by the northern Ngoni from the 1850s, they had retained a tenuous independence by retiring into a number of large, fortified villages, the most important ones being those of Mankhambira and Kangoma at Chinteche and of Marenga, Chikuru and Chimbono at Bandawe. Considerable numbers of Tonga, many of them women and children, had been captured by the Ngoni, but in the mid 1870s they rebelled and many fled down from the hills to the lake shore and took refuge with their brethren.

The opinion of early historians that only the fortuitous appearance of the missionaries saved the Tonga from destruction has been challenged by van Velsen who suggests that Ngoni power was declining at this

[4] Livingstonia sub-committee minutes entry for 2 June and 21 September 1880, NLS 7912

[5] Smith to Laws, 7 April 1881, NLS 7908

[6] Morrison Diary entry for 7 December 1882

time.[7] The subject is a complicated one which will be considered in more detail later but here it must be emphasised that in the 1870s the position of the Tonga was by no means beyond redemption. At Marenga's stockade in 1877, Stewart noted that 'provisions did not seem scarce, pombe [African beer] evidently was abundant; and though besieged the inhabitants were evidently holding their own'.[8] Chinteche, too, situated on a sandy spit between the Luweya river and the lake, and surrounded by a double, in places, triple stockade, was no easy place to assault. When Laws visited Mankhambira in 1877 in his much enlarged town, containing 'a vast number of temporary huts (*msassas*), occupied by people driven in from the surrounding villages by war with the Maviti', the chief boasted that though he had been twice attacked by the Ngoni, he had managed to drive them off each time.[9] One witness commented:

> Monkhombira [sic] recently repulsed Chipatula's forces with considerable slaughter, and he has the trees in the vicinity of his village decorated with scalps. It may be accounted for, however, by the fact that Monkambira has largely recruited from the Angoni[;] hundreds of Chipatula's subjects, because of his excessive cruelty having fled from him and associated themselves with Monkhambira.[10]

Nevertheless, though the Tonga were not without hope, their plight was still sufficiently desperate to make them welcome the mission as a diplomatic ally and as a source of military strength. Its assistance, Laws believed, was cherished not simply on account of its technical powers, but because of the metaphysical qualities it was supposed to possess. Mankhambira, in 1877, urgently requested Stewart to give him '*monkwala*, or medicine, to destroy his enemies, the Maviti', and Laws noted, in an ominous pointer to the future, that nothing would persuade him that they had not got any.[11]

Two further factors are important in explaining the involvement of the mission in local politics. Firstly, in the absence of any central territorial authority, the mission was frequently appealed to as a comparatively independent third party in disputes between village headmen. The growth of stockaded villages may well have increased internal political rivalry,

[7] Van Velsen, 'The Missionary Factor among the Lakeside Tonga of Nyasaland', *Human Problems* xxvi, December 1959, 5

[8] Dr James Stewart, 'The Second Circumnavigation of Lake Nyasa', *Proceedings of the Royal Geographical Society*, 1879, 67

[9] ibid. 66; *FCSMR*, April 1878, 86

[10] Diary of John Gunn, entry for 9 November 1878, NLS 7906

[11] Stewart, 'Second Circumnavigation', 66; *FCSMR*, April 1878, 86

for each village remained an autonomous political unit in which the authority of the stockade chief was frequently challenged by the heads of smaller villages who had taken refuge for protection. The result was that Tonga headmen sought alliances not just in order to ward off Ngoni attacks, but perhaps more frequently to assist them against other Tonga rivals.

Secondly, there is evidence to suggest that political pressures in the previous twenty years had created something of an economic void among the Tonga which the mission was able to fill. The move into stockaded villages which began before Livingstone's visit in 1861, undoubtedly increased the ability of the Tonga to resist Ngoni attacks but also reduced the effectiveness of agricultural producers, who had previously employed a system of dispersed settlement, living close to the land they cultivated. Little evidence exists on the introduction of cassava into Tongaland, but for at least one observer in the early 1880s its emergence as the Tonga staple crop was a direct consequence of Ngoni raids for food. 'One great enticement to make war on the Atonga is the state of their gardens', Frederick Morrison noted in 1882.

> The Angoni are men who believe more in love and war than in work . . . so that if they are hungry they meet their wants from an Atonga garden. This causes the Atonga to grow a food which the Angoni do not like called 'Chakow'. . . A few of them grow a little maize but it is considered a risk.[12]

Grain crops which required to be harvested and stored were easy targets for a military invader. Cassava, though less nutritious, could be left in the ground till required for consumption and thus was more difficult to steal.

As cassava is extremely high-yielding, by no means all refugees who poured into the fortified villages were required to cultivate the crop. But at the same time, coastal trade which so deeply influenced the Yao made only limited demands on man-power resources in Tongaland. Elephants, Mankhambira stated in 1875, were little hunted by the Tonga, though by that date a black (probably Yao) trader was buying ivory from him and some Tonga were hunting elephants with heavy spears rather than with the guns and poisoned arrows in greater use elsewhere.[13] Mankhambira denied that Arabs purchased slaves from him, though this statement was contradicted in 1885 by Consul Goodrich, who described Chinteche as 'a well known centre of the slave trade' and Mankhambira, by then

[12] Morrison Diary, entry for 10 December 1882

[13] Livingstonia Mission Journal entry for 4 December 1875, NLS 7908
Morrison Diary entry for 17 May 1883

dead, 'as a noted slave-dealer in Livingstone's time'.[14] Several parties of Arabs, loaded with ivory, passed Kaningina on their way from Ngoniland to Nkata Bay in 1879, and another party was noted at Zoani's village not far from Bandawe.[15] Some Tonga also practised the hazardous occupation of trading direct with the Ngoni. In 1884 the chiefs Fuka, Chikuru and Zoani were all reported to 'have gone in for a wholesale trade in slaves' in that direction.[16]

But these ventures were individual ones, affecting some Tonga chiefs more than others and not being central to their control of political authority. Despite the proximity of Nkota Kota, traders rarely made long expeditions across the lake in the 1880s and coastal influences were not apparent in Tonga clothing, houses or agricultural products. Thus the mission, in putting forward its economic demands, did not confront Tonga rulers with a challenge they felt unable to meet. More fundamentally, in seeking to employ workers on a wage basis, the mission was making contact with a people whose local subsistence economy had already been severely disrupted but who were not yet fully integrated into the economy of the coast. For many Africans, involvement in the new colonial economy was the end product of a brutal and painful process in which Europeans used their superior strength to destroy African competition. For the Tonga, however, the process was markedly different. Despite the variety of local products – not just cassava, but fish, cotton, sugar-cane, sesame, ground nuts and tobacco – their economy was so limited in the 1880s that many were prepared to enter wage employment, at least for a restricted period.

The immediate effect of this situation was to bring about a crisis in Livingstonia's relations with her neighbours which was not to be fully resolved till after the establishment of colonial rule. Following the foundation of the two outstations late in 1878, Kaningina rapidly developed as a focus both for those discontented Tonga who normally resided in Ngoni country and for those other Tonga who, having fled from the Ngoni and settled under Mankhambira, complained that they were being treated as slaves by him, and asked permission to settle with the English.[17] On January 1879, little more than six weeks after the founding of the station, 314 villagers attended the Sunday service. By September it was reported

[14] Goodrich to FO 19 February 1885, FO 84/1702

[15] Kaningina Station Journal entries for 6–7 February, 28 August 1879; Bandawe Station Journal entry for 27 August 1879, NLS 7910

[16] ibid. entry for 6 November 1879; J. A. Smith to Laws, 25 January 1884, Shepperson Collection.

[17] Kaningina Station Journal entries for 15 May, 24 June 1879

in Scotland that upwards of 2000 people had come under missionary rule at Kaningina, though many of these appear to have been temporary visitors, who used the presence of the mission as a protective shield against the Ngoni while they gathered their upland crops. Once the cassava had been collected and eaten, attendances at church fell away, and most people returned to their villages.[18]

At Bandawe in the heart of Tongaland, progress was less spectacular but more sustained. Having received permission from the chief Marenga to settle in his district, Stewart, in December 1878, recruited forty labourers who were set to work bringing in wood and grass for his house.[19] Other villagers were employed as personal servants, as herdsmen for the mission's small herd of livestock, and as agricultural workers clearing the land for its crops, but no large-scale settlement at the station appears to have taken place, congregations being drawn largely from the neighbouring villages of Marenga and Chimbono. By April 1879 some 250 people were regularly attending the evangelical meetings; while the school was said to be attended by between 70 and 100 pupils.[20]

These stations, although nominally under mission control, were staffed exclusively by laymen, not noted for their tact and forbearance. Bandawe was at first in the charge of James Stewart, the civil engineer, who brought to his work at the station the experience of a career in the Indian Civil Service, working on the Sirhind Canal in the Punjab; while Kaningina was organised by Alexander Riddel, an agriculturalist from the pioneer party. When Stewart left on 19 January 1879, artisans took charge of both stations; Allan Simpson who was to become a trader in the Shire valley spending nearly a year at Bandawe and Miller, later an employee of the ALC, replacing Riddel at Kaningina.

Freed from even the slender bonds of control imposed on them at Cape Maclear, these men initiated policies which involved both the imposition of a savage code of discipline on workers at the station and deliberate involvement in Tonga affairs. It may be argued that Simpson, in introducing flogging as a disciplinary measure at Bandawe, was simply resorting to the punishment of his schooldays in Kirkcaldy where the tawse had been in frequent use. On 12 January 1880 he flogged thirty-one herdsmen working for the mission and commented in schoolmasterly tones, 'it has had a better effect than all the moral lectures that could have been coined for them'.[21]

18 ibid. 19 January 1879; *FCSMR*, August 1879, 193; September 1879, 223; January 1880, 14

19 Bandawe Station Journal entries for 28, 30 November 1878

20 *FCSMR*, August 1879, 193

21 Bandawe Station Journal entry for 12 January 1880

But Scottish precedent could hardly explain the frequent excursions made by the missionaries outside their settlement. Although the station at Bandawe was held on sufferance from Marenga, Stewart ignored his sovereignty in attempting to impress on the Tonga the necessity of their conforming to an arbitrary code of conduct. On 30 December 1878, he warned Marenga of the need to keep peace in the country.[22] Thereafter he and his successors intervened repeatedly to quell riots and prevent kidnapping and slave trading, sometimes resorting to force when verbal persuasion went unheeded.

Early in January 1879 Stewart sent the first miniature police-patrol into action to rescue a woman and child from a village near the station and to give the offenders a flogging.[23] Simpson, when he heard reports of kidnapping in neighbouring villages, 'sent messengers to their chiefs to stop the work else I would come down and flog them'.[24] In June he put his threat to effect by seizing two men involved in a bout of fighting and sentencing them 'to 14 lashes each and a fine of 8 fowls'.[25] Later, in August, after a young man 'much attached to the mission', but not resident there, had been stolen during the night and sold to a party of Arabs at Zoani's village, Simpson sent off an armed patrol in pursuit. They arrived in time to rescue the young man, but not to capture the Arabs, one of whom was shot in the leg as he tried to escape. Zoani himself was heavily fined after Simpson had threatened to burn down his village.[26]

In many of these incidents the missionaries were actively encouraged by individual Tonga. In the absence of any final court of appeal, such as Mponda provided near Cape Maclear, disputes between headmen tended to be taken to a third party, frequently the mission. Miller received his first request for arbitration in March 1879, and by April was adjudicating on a full-scale *mlandu* involving the chiefs Marenga and Kangoma.[27] Simpson frequently heard cases; he noted on 11 September 1879, 'brought daily from a distance in some cases of 10 miles'.[28] His judgements on what were technically civil matters were often ludicrously idiosyncratic, involving, as they sometimes did, the punishment by fines or flogging of both parties for offences neither believed to have taken place.[29] But they

[22] ibid. entry for 30 December 1878
[23] ibid. entry for 10 January 1879
[24] ibid. entry for 17 June 1879
[25] ibid. entry for 29 June 1879
[26] ibid. entry for 27 August 1879
[27] ibid. entries for 8 March, 4–5 April 1879
[28] ibid. entry for 11 September 1879
[29] See entry for 24 May 1879

had compensations for certain Tonga, principally Marenga and Chimbono, the headmen living near the station, who appear to have brought up cases largely as a means of involving the mission on their side in local disputes. In September 1879, reports of slaving at Mankhambira's reached Bandawe only to be contradicted the next day. Chimbono himself, Simpson learnt, had been deliberately putting the reports out 'in order to try and get our help to settle some old quarrel between him and the chief he blamed for slaving'.[30] It is reasonable to assume that for each case the missionaries found to be fraudulent, there were others where they were successfully duped.

These exploits could not continue indefinitely unchecked by the Livingstonia authorities. On 15 October 1879 Laws arrived at Bandawe on his first visit of inspection. The next day he noted in the station's journal:

> I think there has been shewn too markedly a tendency to decide native disputes. When any dispute is brought by the parties to the station for decision it is right to advise on the matter if possible; but in matters entirely inter-native, the executive should be left to themselves not undertaken by the mission.[31]

However, the mission's involvement in politics could not be so easily stopped. Four days after Laws's visit a fight took place between two headmen, Gulungula and Malanda near Bandawe, resulting in the death of four men and the wounding of eleven others. Simpson reluctantly took no action in the matter at first, but three days later he entered fully into the dispute by calling the various parties to a conference.[32] In the next four months he arbitrated frequently in cases and dealt out punishments with a heavy hand – ordering at least one flogging of a man beyond the auspices of the station.[33]

Laws too was dissatified with the position. He realised that behind the behaviour of his staff lay a larger problem involving the practicability of residential mission policy in the prevailing conditions of unrest. To the sub-committee in Scotland he put the question:

> Is the Livingstonia Mission to be regarded as a Mission, like the early ones to the South Sea Islands, trusting to God for protection, though outwardly at the mercy of the natives when they think fit to rob or murder its members or is the Livingstonia Mission to be

30 ibid. entries for 21 and 22 September 1879

31 ibid. entry for 16 October 1879

32 ibid. entry for 20–1 October 1879

33 ibid. entries for 11 November, 1 and 3 December 1879, 12 and 21 January 1880

> regarded as a Christian Colony, having its foreign relationships and internal administration?

He refused to admit that one method was more Christian than the other, but acknowledged that the exercise of civil powers had brought problems:

> The exercise of Magesterial Functions by the head of the Mission I think rather hinders than furthers his work as a minister of the Gospel. In the eyes of the natives he is apt to be looked upon more in the character of a chief than as a teacher and friend to whom they can come for instruction and guidance.[34]

Livingstonia and the Blantyre atrocities

These reflections coincided with and in part resulted from the widespread publicity given to the Blantyre atrocities. When Dr Stewart arrived at the station in December 1876 he found work there at a standstill, the place completely disorganised and the missionaries, with the single exception of the young gardener, John Buchanan, discontented and demoralised. Under Stewart and his cousin who replaced him in May 1877, a colony was slowly created consisting, as at Cape Maclear, of an elite of coastmen and foreigners, Makololo scholars and a large number of refugees who settled in villages under mission protection round the station.[35]

Under the civil engineer the first steps were taken in imposing discipline and in attempting to counter the rash of thefts occurring in the vicinity of the settlement. But what smacked of the vigour of the Punjab degenerated after Stewart's departure and the arrival in July 1878 of Duff Macdonald, Blantyre's first ordained Church of Scotland missionary, into culpable mismanagement and gratuitous cruelty. Macdonald, a gentle scholar whose anthropological studies are still of the greatest value, permitted the laymen at the station to initiate policy in temporal matters and carry it into effect. In two months February–March 1879, an alleged murderer was executed with 'melancholy clumsiness', one man was repeatedly flogged for a crime which, it transpired later, he had not committed, while a second, convicted of having thrown away a box of tea he was employed to convey to Blantyre, was flogged with such appalling severity that he died later on the same day.[36]

[34] Laws to Smith, 3 February 1880, quoted in Livingstonia sub-committee minutes, entry for 2 June 1880, NLS 7912

[35] Stewart to Duff, 26 December 1876, NLS 7876; Duff Macdonald, *Africana*, vol. II, 22–5

[36] This account is largely based on Hanna, *Nyasaland and North-Eastern Rhodesia*, 26–34. See also Andrew Chirnside, *The Blantyre Missionaries – Discreditable Disclosures*, London, 1880.

In Britain the response to these punishments was tremendous. First news of the execution reached the Church of Scotland Foreign Mission officials in April 1879, and a meeting was almost immediately convened at which Dr Macrae, convenor of the Blantyre sub-committee, upheld the missionaries' actions on the grounds, as he was later to tell the General Assembly of his Church, that assumption of civil jurisdiction was essential in the type of Christian colony that Livingstone had visualised and of which Blantyre was meant to be a model.[37]

But this opinion was a minority one. From Sir Arthur Gordon, Governor of Fiji, Dr George Smith learnt the disturbing news that 'As to the legal position of the civil rulers of your settlement, I am afraid I can only say that it does not exist.' If the missionaries were charged under the Foreign Jurisdiction Acts they 'would probably be convicted of illegal assault'.[38] On 23 March the Established Church Committee told Macdonald that his position 'must be understood as excluding the power and jurisdiction known as civil government'. Offences committed at Blantyre were to be dealt with by 'the civil authority of the natives', and deportation used in serious cases.[39]

Up to now the events at Blantyre had only been made known to a small circle of churchmen in Britain. Early in the spring of 1880, however, a pamphlet setting out the main facts was published by Andrew Chirnside, a traveller who had spent some months in the Malawi regions.[40] It received wide publicity in the British press and aroused the concern of the Aborigines Protection Society and of the Foreign Office. The Church Committee, fearful lest its failure to act would bring about the intervention of the British government, appointed Dr Rankin of Muthill, a keen supporter of mission work with a personal involvement in Blantyre, to go out on a Commission of Inquiry along with a lawyer, Alexander Pringle of Yair. Their reports were presented to a special commission of the General Assembly held on 2 March 1881, where the decision was taken to withdraw Macdonald and the two artisans principally involved.[41] More important, the whole policy implicit in industrial missions was put in question.

[37] Speech to the General Assembly quoted in *Edinburgh Courant*, 3 March 1881

[38] Quoted in Livingstonia sub-committee minutes entry for 3 September 1879, NLS 7912

[39] Committee to Duff Macdonald, 23 March 1880, printed in Church of Scotland Assembly Papers 1880, 156–7

[40] Chirnside, *The Blantyre Missionaries*

[41] A full report of the proceedings is given in the *Edinburgh Courant*, 3 March 1881

Pringle suggested that neither social nor economic reform was required to any large extent:

> I see that the natives in that particular part of Africa stand in no special need of anything but Christianity and education. They already stand well as compared with the world at large in regard to habits of cleanliness, and to most other habits excepting some which might be amended through the direct influence of Christianity.

As for agricultural reform, the missionary could teach Africans nothing: 'they know enough, and more than he does, about gardening in the tropics'.

He added, 'I would have the missionaries selected on account of their qualifications as teachers and not as artisans'.[42]

The significance to Livingstonia of these events were deep and obvious. When news of the execution at Blantyre reached Scotland in 1879 the first reaction of the Church of Scotland's committee had been to call a joint conference with the Livingstonia sub-committee, the situation of the two missions being considered so similar. Riddel and Johnston, the Free Church artisans, assisted at this inquiry and told the Blantyre Committee that the execution was 'the best thing that could be done in the circumstances', and that a similar policy was followed at Livingstonia. Riddel, in addition, published a reply to Chirnside's pamphlet, so inept as to do his cause more harm than good.[43]

In November, 1879, however, a letter arrived from Dr Stewart, now back at Lovedale, which shattered this temporary unity. Stewart declared his fixed opposition 'against either Mission taking into their hands the power of life and death', and stated that he was 'utterly and without qualification of any kind opposed to flogging or the use of the lash or of any such punishments at a Mission Station'. 'During fourteen years,' he wrote, 'I have never once found it necessary to raise my hand to a native in that fashion.' Livingstonia, he suggested, should stop using the road south through Blantyre to avoid getting involved in any of that mission's quarrels.[44]

Stewart's comments were made after the storm had broken and he had been informed of the illegality of the missionaries' actions, and it may be

[42] Alexander Pringle, 'The continuation of the Blantyre Mission', Church of Scotland Assembly Papers, 1881, 194–5

[43] Riddel to Smith, 8 January 1880, NLS 7887; to Laws, 8 March 1880, Shepperson Collection; Alexander Riddel, *A Reply to 'The Blantyre Missionaries: Discreditable Disclosures'*, Edinburgh, 1880

[44] Quoted in Livingstonia sub-committee minutes entry for 13 November 1879, NLS 7912

questioned whether he had always been so completely opposed to civil action. Riddel and the Blantyre sub-committee had no hesitation about casting doubts upon his sincerity: 'Knowing as we do Dr Stewart's theory and practice on this and other matters, we could hardly believe our ears when we heard a direct contradictory [sic] to all his conduct while with us at Livingstonia and Blantyre.'[45] Even his cousin, the engineer, believed that Stewart 'had acted very inconsistently in opposing the exercise of magisterial powers after all that he said and did'.[46]

The Livingstonia sub-committee, however, accepted Stewart's statement completely. Orders were given in December 1879 for the road on the right bank of the Shire only to be used and Riddel was warned against having any further dealings with the Established Church.[47]

In the resultant brawl all the old antagonisms between the Church of Scotland and the Free Church surfaced. Both Rankin and Pringle in their reports blamed James Stewart, CE, for having introduced corporal punishment into their settlement and suggested that the policy later followed, closely resembled 'the well-known practice at Livingstonia'.[48] Rankin carried the controversy to the pulpit and the correspondence columns of *The Scotsman* with a vehemence that embarrassed even his own supporters. In reply the Free Church issued a statement denying the charges made by Rankin and Pringle and placing responsibility for events at Blantyre squarely back on Established Church shoulders. 'I regret to say,' wrote Dr Smith to Laws at the height of the controversy, 'that the Established Church Committee has ungenerously and by misrepresentation tried to shield themselves by reflecting on our staff without whom their Mission would not have been in existence.'[49] The wounds inflicted in these months took over a decade to heal.

Meanwhile, the Livingstonia sub-committee was working to legalise its own mission's civil position, before it too was exposed to the torch of publicity. The initial scheme was to petition the British government for a consul; but this was opposed by Sir Arthur Gordon, who pointed out

45 Riddel to Smith, 8 January 1880, NLS 7872

46 Stewart to Laws, 10 February 1–81, Shepperson Collection. For a detailed discussion of this incident generally favourable to Dr Stewart see Sheila M. Brock, 'James Stewart and Lovedale: A Reappraisal of Missionary Attitudes and African Response in the Eastern Cape, South Africa, 1870–1905', PhD. Edinburgh, 1974, appendix.

47 Livingstonia sub-committee minutes entry for 10 December 1879; Riddel to Laws, 8 March 1880, Shepperson Collection

48 'Report of the Committee for the Propagation of the Gospel in Foreign Parts – the Blantyre Mission Case', 13, 17, 51–2. Copy in NLS 7904.

49 Smith to Laws, 3 June 1880, NLS 7771

that a consul could exercise jurisdiction only over British subjects, and that 'if he were a man not friendly to the Mission (and the Foreign Office would likely name such a man) he would have infinite opportunities of doing mischief'.[50]

Alternative proposals were also rejected and finally the sub-committee, faced by the likelihood that many refugees would put themselves under the control of the mission when it was moved to Bandawe, declared in February 1880 that 'they did not regard their Mission as the nucleus of a state' and that 'they thought that it would be inexpedient for the Mission to undertake generally the civil administration of its territory'. Offences should normally be dealt with by deportation, but members of the mission would be allowed to exercise their discretion in special cases. Laws hoped to continue to give sanctuary to fugitive slaves but was opposed by Consul O'Neill, acting on instructions from the Foreign Office, who informed the heads at Blantyre that missionaries had no legal right to receive freed slaves and with this decision the sub-committee concurred.[51]

By 1881, therefore, both missions had received similar instructions to abjure from temporal action and discard much of their colonial apparatus. At Blantyre, however, the mission remained on its old site and continued to be responsible for the group of villages around it. Under its brilliant new head, David Clement Scott, formal education, hitherto neglected, was emphasised at the expense of agricultural work. Scott, however, a disciple of Macrae, whose 'far reaching view and broad estimate of Mission Work' he particularly admired, made little attempt to change the basic residential nature of the mission, either at Blantyre or at the new stations of Domasi and Mlanje, founded in 1884 and 1890 respectively.[52] Only a small network of village schools were set up around these stations and Christian and educational influence existed largely within the charmed circle of the mission.

Powers of jurisdiction, shorn of the excesses of the earlier period, were also retained. Scott deeply admired many aspects of African culture, and was particularly impressed by the *mlandu*, 'a meeting for discussion of some claim or right . . . the most characteristic word of African politics, itself a charter of limited government and appeal to right and sufficient

[50] Livingstonia sub-committee minutes, entries for 3 September and 6 June the latter with enclosure Gordon to Smith, 16 June 1879, NLS 7912; Maclagan to Herdman, 20 June 1879, NLS 7544

[51] ibid. entries for 6 February, 4–5 April 1880

[52] *LWBCA*, April 1897. The memorial to Macrae is one of the most prominent in Blantyre Church today

reason'.[53] The mission seems to have almost completely succeeded in avoiding conventional punishments, using conciliation rather than retribution wherever possible. Even in April 1888 *mlandu*, according to the mission's own magazine 'have been very numerous and exceed recording'. Blantyre was still the 'colony', the 'nucleus of a state' it had been in earlier days.[54]

For Livingstonia, however, the change in policy was dramatic and genuine. It coincided with the move of the central station from one region to another, and was reinforced by the fact that the new station, Bandawe, was widely regarded as only a temporary settlement upon which little expenditure should be lavished. Above all, it was welcomed and actively supported by the resident missionaries, rather than being opposed and thwarted by them, as at Blantyre. With the decision of the sub-committee not to re-employ Riddel and to send James Stewart CE to the north-west of the lake on road-building work, the 'interventionalist' school was shorn of two of its leading members and Laws's position as prime shaper of policy was strengthened. A strong believer in the tradition of Livingstone in the economic role of the mission, Laws had also from the mid 1870s sought to extend its influence over a wide area through African evangelists and had worried at the too-close identification of Christianity with all aspects of Western civilisation. As early as February 1876 he had dreamed of putting catechists and African teachers 'at the villages along the lake coast and river banks to the extent of from 700 to 800 miles within reach of our steamer', and later gave special instructions to evangelists making the journey from Cape Maclear to the neighbouring village of Mpongo that they should use canoes on occasion rather than the station rowing-boat, to prevent the spread of the Gospel being associated entirely with European technology.[55]

When he arrived at Bandawe in 1881, therefore, Laws was quick to inform the settlers who had already made their home at the station 'that here it was not intended that Civil Jurisdiction should be exercised by the English Missionaries and that they must decide where they would like to settle'. Those villagers who would not remain behind at Cape Maclear were forced to put themselves under the protection of one of the Tonga chiefs. For the rest it was repeated 'that it was only those at school or apprentices, or those in the steamer who would live with us'.[56]

[53] D. C. Scott, *A Cyclopaedic Dictionary of the Manganja Language spoken in British Central Africa*, Edinburgh, 1892

[54] *LWBCA*, April 1888

[55] Laws to Duff (?), 21 February 1876, NLS 7876; *F.C. of S. Monthly Record*, June 1881, 146; W. P. Livingstone, *Laws*, 179

[56] Bandawe Journal entry for 18 April 1881, NLS 7911

Mission prospecting

The establishment of the pioneer settlements in Tongaland was followed over the next decade by the founding of Free Church stations in three new areas west of Lake Malawi. The first and in many ways the most important was the station opened at Njuyu, near Hoho village in the northern Ngoni paramountcy. Worried by the false information the Ngoni were receiving concerning his contacts with the Tonga, Laws in September 1878 visited the home of the headman Mayayi Chiputula Nhlane, who he believed, erroneously, to be the Ngoni paramount chief. As Chiputula had recently died and his son had not been installed, few firm contacts were established. But early in December at the time of the founding of the Kaningina observation post William Koyi made direct contact with Mbelwa, the real paramount. On 20 December he returned again with Alexander Riddel and held a long discussion with the chief, his thirty-eight councillors and ninety-four village headmen.[57] Later in January 1879, Laws made his own first visit at the urgent request of Mbelwa, and the chief subsequently requested the missionaries to build a kraal close to his senior village. A broken collar-bone suffered by Miller when he fell from his *machilla* on the way up to the highlands prevented one visit, while James Stewart CE countermanded another on the grounds that it might compromise the mission with the Tonga.[58] Further delay resulted from the failure of the mission to recruit suitable agents. Laws noted in August 1877 that the Xhosa, William Koyi, could communicate easily with the Ngoni he met at Mankhambira's, and in all later expeditions to the Ngoni capital Koyi attended as an invaluable intermediary and interpreter.[59] Laws therefore attempted to recruit further Zulu or Sotho-speaking Lovedale graduates for work at the pioneer station, but Dr Stewart declined to send any more of his students until Cape Maclear had been evacuated, and the Rev. Pambani Mzimba, the first ordained African minister connected with the Free Church in South Africa, was forced to withdraw when his Presbytery refused to let him go.[60] It was not until May 1882 that Laws arranged at a ceremonial meeting with Mbelwa, for

[57] *FCSMR*, March 1879, 66–7, Kaningina Station Journal entries for December 1878, NLS 7910

[58] Miller to J. Stewart, CE, 8 June 1879, Shepperson Collection; J. Stewart CE to Main 9 July 1879 in Livingstonia sub-committee minutes 14 October 1879

[59] *FCSMR*, April 1878, 86

[60] G. Smith to Laws, 18 July 1881, NLS 7770; Brock 'James Stewart and Lovedale', 350. Mzimba's eventful career makes it interesting to speculate what his influence would have been in Malawi. In 1898 he broke with the Scots and founded the African Presbyterian Church.

a missionary to be resident at Njuyu. James Sutherland, an agriculturalist from Wick, joined the pioneer Koyi in July; they were reinforced in February 1885 by Dr W. A. Elmslie, only six months before Sutherland's death.

Meanwhile, yet another new station had been opened at Mweniwanda's village to the north-west of the lake. Its real founder was James Stevenson, who as far back as 1877 had seen the Nyasa–Tanganyika plateau as the terminus of trade for the great lakes, and a favourable spot for the distribution of goods over a wide area. In 1879, as part of his master-scheme for improving communications from the Shire to Lake Victoria, Stevenson recommended that the Livingstonia sub-committee should join with the London Missionary Society, now at work on Lake Tanganyika, to finance the building of a road between the two lakes. The committee, however, were understandably reluctant to support a venture which could be of no conceivable direct benefit to their own mission. Stevenson, therefore, was forced to take up the matter on his own initiative. After discussions with James Stewart CE, he told the Livingstonia sub-committee in February 1881 that he was prepared to put up £4000 for the road as long as certain conditions were met to ensure its use as a busy trade-route. Firstly, he asked that Livingstonia should establish a station near the south end of the road and the LMS one near the north end – no doubt to ensure a supply of trained porters and clerks for trading stations near the road. Second, he demanded that the African Lakes Company should extend its operations to Lake Tanganyika and that the LMS should abandon the route they had hitherto used to the coast overland to Zanzibar, and instead agree to bring up all goods via the Shire and Lake Nyasa.[61] The LMS jibbed at this last proposal, though its officials agreed to send out any steamers they might have built for them in the next two years by the water route, and for a time the whole scheme was in jeopardy. But the Livingstonia sub-committee, its faith in economic development as yet undimmed, promptly accepted its share of the bargain, and Stevenson decided to stand firm.[62] In May 1881 Stewart left Britain accompanied by two Scottish artisans to begin work on the road and to construct the first buildings of the new station at Chirenje near Mweniwanda's village, fifty miles inland from the lake, which he had chosen on a preliminary survey for strategic reasons. His death in August 1883 took place before the first missionary, the Rev. J. H. Bain, arrived to take charge of the

[61] Stevenson to Directors, Livingstonia Mission enclosed in Livingstonia sub-committee minutes, 15 February 1881; *FCSMR*, June 1881, 144

[62] Livingstonia sub-committee minutes entries for 15 February, 4, 26 April 1881; Smith to Laws, 7 April 1881, NLS 7771; Hanna, *Beginnings*, 45–6

station, and it was not until June 1884 that Bain was able to get properly down to work.

In accepting Stevenson's proposal, the Livingstonia committee unwittingly shifted the whole axis of the mission to the north. Up to this time it had seemed likely that the next station to be founded would be one extending inland from Cape Maclear to southern Ngoniland. Laws visited the Maseko Ngoni chief, Chikusi, in August 1878, before he made any contacts with the northern branch, and Stewart specially advised a year earlier that 'some effort should be made to conciliate the Maviti chiefs at the south end of the lake'.[63] With the switch of attention north, interest languished, and it was not until late in 1885 that Albert Namalambe persuaded Chikusi's councillors to allow Dr David Kerr Cross to found a station in their country.[64] The pull of the north end, however, was now exerting its influence. Bain's uncertain health made it necessary for him to have a companion, and Cross in 1886 was deputed to this task. Not till November 1887 was the new station founded, and then it was not begun in Ngoniland proper, as Laws had advised, but in the Livlezi valley beneath the Dedza highlands, an area inhabited largely by Chewa.

Bandawe: the origins of a Christian revolution

With the proliferation of Free Church stations over a stretch of country extending four hundred miles down the lake, the societies of northern Malawi were faced during the 1880s and 1890s with the necessity of reaching some relationship, however tenuous, with the new intruder. What that relationship was, whether it involved the rejection of missionary influence, or the acceptance of some part, or of what part, was determined by a whole host of variables including the nature of the individual society and its religious institutions, the circumstances of local politics and the strength and character of the missionary appeal. With local factors of such importance, the end results might appear fortuitous, yet their significance cannot be doubted. If we accept that the different reactions of African societies to the advent of European colonialism was itself a factor influencing the nature of the colonial settlement, then it is important to recognise that those reactions in their turn were profoundly affected by the character and extent of missionary contact in the years before the colonial invasion. More significant, the varied response of different societies, and groups within societies in the pioneer period to the oppor-

[63] Stewart, Summary of Instructions and Hints for Livingstonia, 1878, 2–3, *FCSMR*, March 1879, 66

[64] Letter from Albert Namalambe 13 February 1886 printed in *FCSMR*, August 1886, 240

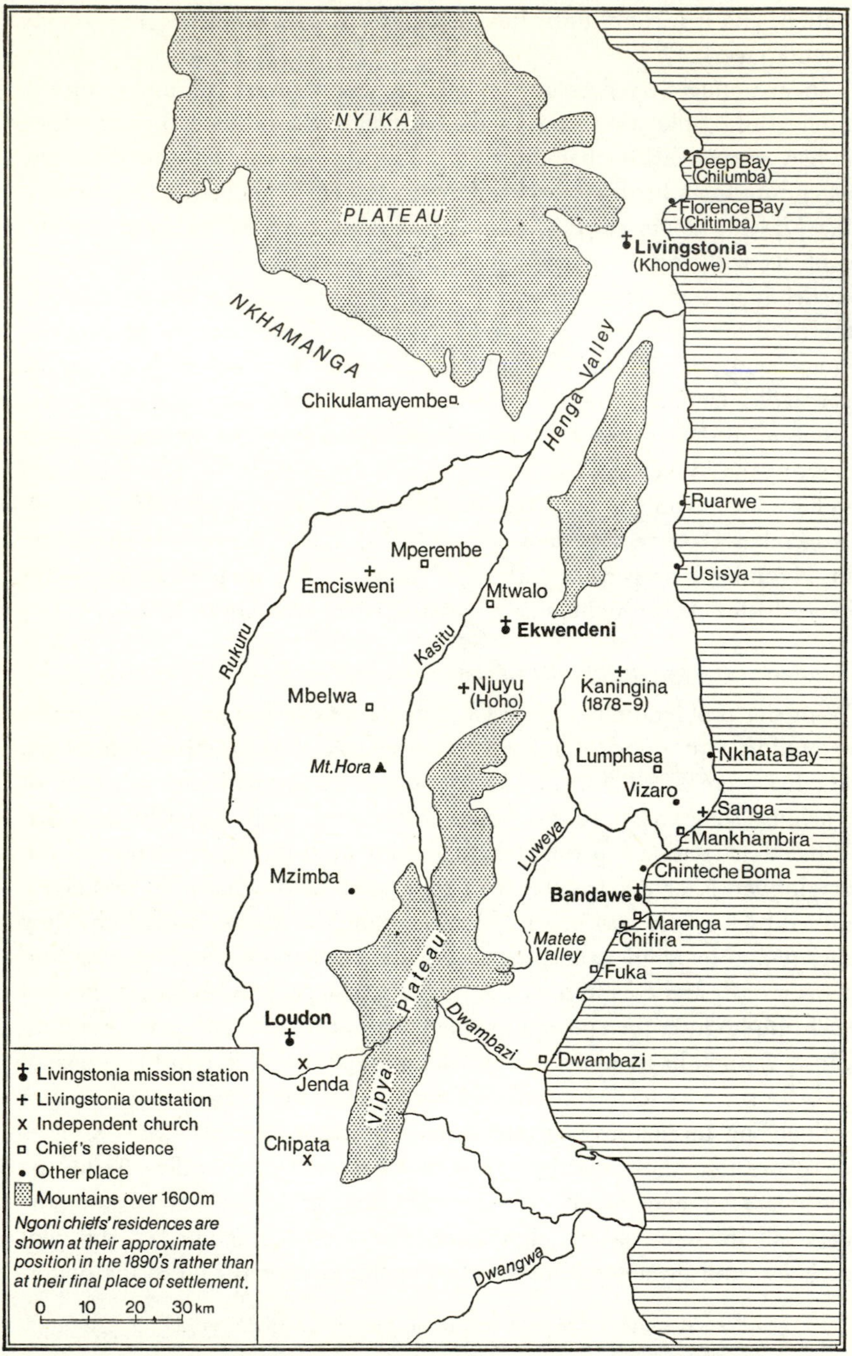

Map 3. Northern Ngoniland and Tongaland
Names in brackets represent more modern names

tunities provided by the missionaries fundamentally influenced the political and educational patterns that later emerged. In that sense, some of the foundations for the African history of colonial Malawi were laid in the fate of missionary endeavour in the immediately preceding period.

The most dramatic example is that of the lakeside Tonga, a people numbering not more than 60 000 as late as the 1950s, militarily weak and politically divided, whose positive response to the Livingstonia Mission enabled them to become the leading African beneficiaries of the colonial regime, and to some extent the leading political participants within it. Defined in the terms that C. C. Wrigley has used for Buganda, it is clear that no Christian revolution took place in Malawi; there was no transfer of power within an existing society from a traditional ruler to a new body of dynamic converts.[65] Defined in a broader sense, however, it may be argued that such a revolution occurred. Spearheaded by the activities of the first generation of Christian converts, a profound change in the relations of the lakeside Tonga with the wider world took place in the thirty years before 1914. It is to the nature of these changes and the process by which they were brought about that I now will turn.

There is a sense in which the background to the Christian revolution lay in the political relations existing between the Tonga and Livingstonia by the 1880s. From the foundation of the central Bandawe station in 1881 the missionaries resolutely followed their new instructions by refusing sanctuary to escaped slaves and refugees, turning away squatters from mission land and rejecting pleas aimed at involving them in inter-village disputes. Aberrations did occur, usually during Laws's absence from the station, when caution was thrown to the winds and orders were disregarded. In April 1886, for example, Bain, irritated beyond endurance by a series of robberies at the station, led out an armed expedition against a well-known thief from a neighbouring village and burned down his hut after threatening to burn the whole village if it was not pointed out to him.[66] Later in 1892 wholesale intervention took place during the short-lived reign of Dr David Fotheringham who in seeking to emulate the feats of his well-known brother, the manager of the African Lakes Company, gave refuge and help to all who came seeking it. In obedience to his instructions a whole village community was brought under armed guard from Chinteche to Bandawe for protection, the station was fortified with walls built between the main buildings so that attacks could be resisted and an ammunition depot was established, manned by mission

[65] C. C. Wrigley, 'The Christian Revolution in Buganda', *Comparative Studies in Society and History*, II (1959)

[66] Bandawe Station Journal entry for 8 April 1886

dependants whom Fotheringham had taught to shoot.[67] In general, however, the mission went to great lengths to avoid such involvement, and was only dragged unwillingly into local politics as a result of efforts by Tonga headmen to win its support against the Ngoni, or against one or other of their Tonga rivals.

The escape of Tonga refugees from Ngoniland in 1875 and the devastating defeat of the regiment sent in pursuit marked the beginning of a troubled period in Ngoni history during which few raids on Tongaland took place. A year later, in 1876, Henga subjects led by the warlord Kanyoli also rose in revolt and, over the next few years, the Ngoni were fully occupied in a series of bitter battles out of which the Henga emerged, bloodied but still independent.[68] During this period, Tumbuka refugees as well as Tonga congregated at Chinteche and several groups of Ngoni subjects made their way quietly to the lake shore and settled with Tonga relatives.[69]

In 1881, however, the Ngoni experienced a temporary resurgence of power. Many of their earlier difficulties appear to have arisen from the rapid accumulation of captives, and their subsequent failure to assimilate them fully within their society. Hence the two revolts, though they diminished the number of Ngoni subjects, did leave the state a more coherent body. When a group of Tumbuka subjects attempted to break away in 1880 they were decisively defeated at Mount Hora.[70] Raids into Tongaland followed and from February 1882 some Tonga used the mission as an intermediary through whom they paid the Ngoni a tribute in cattle, probably bought elsewhere.[71] By 1884, the Tumbuka subjects who had fled with the Tonga and even some Tonga themselves had begun to leave the stockaded villages and return to their former overlords. 'Marenga came in today telling us that a great many of his people had left and gone back to the Angoni', a missionary noted in April 1884. 'A good many of the Atonga have been doing this of late.'[72] Ngoni raids took place in the Matete valley and near Chinteche, with the result that a large number of refugees settled around Marenga's in November 1884. Demands for protection grew more insistent, especially after the visit to

67 Fotheringham to Laws, 4 April 1892; G. Aitken to Laws, 19 January 1892; Elmslie to Laws, 27 June 1892, NLS 7896

68 Saulos Nyirenda, 'History of the Tumbuka–Henga People', trans. and ed. by T. C. Young, *Bantu Studies*, 1930; Young, *Notes*, 118–26

69 *FCSMR*, April 1878, 86; Bandawe Station Journal entries for 14 and 22 January 1879, 13 January 1880, NLS 7910

70 T. C. Young, *Notes*, 118; Chibambo, *My Ngoni*, 4–15

71 Diary of Dr Laws, entry for 15 February 1882, Laws's Papers, EUL

72 Bandawe Station Journal Entry for 24 April 1884

Bandawe of Consul Goodrich in February 1855, who mediated in various diplomatic issues. 'The war spirit of the Angoni is evidently roused,' reported Dr William Scott in April 1885, commenting on a raid on a village near Chinteche, 'for they are making attacks on all sides.'[73]

This was the situation when, on 25 August, a representative of the African Lakes Company offered the Tonga treaties of protection as a first step, so it was hoped, in the granting of civil powers to the company by the British government. With the exception of Kangoma from Chinteche, all chiefs willingly signed. Henceforth, they declared, 'they were the children of the white man . . . no longer "Atonga" but "Amandalo"' ('*Mandala*' being the name by which the company was universally known). It was in vain for the missionaries to protest 'that they were not our people. We are not chiefs but teachers and would not fight unless to protect our lives.'[74] If the Tonga found difficulty in distinguishing between one group of white men and another, to distinguish between Livingstonia and the Lakes Company was virtually impossible. So closely tied together were the two bodies that the company borrowed the *Ilala* from the mission for four years before buying her outright in 1882 and employed several artisans who had formerly worked for the mission. Company employees like Frederick Morrison assisted in religious services on occasions at Bandawe and Cape Maclear throughout the 1880s and Morrison continued to describe the *Ilala* as 'the mission steamer' as late as 1886.[75] Moreover, the missionaries, though privately sceptical of the treaties, publicly presented an attitude of support. Though they protested their detachment from the company, they were quick to chide Kangoma for having 'cast off the white man and refused to sign the treaties' and warned him that, because of his behaviour, 'he need look for no help from us'.[76]

It was natural, therefore, for the Tonga to look to the mission to uphold the company's treaties in face of increasing Ngoni pressure. The polite requests for protection of 1884 were transformed into insistent demands in the following year. On 12 October 1885, some five headmen, led by Fuka, Chikuru and Chimbono, visited the station: 'They say that they were the children of the white man and were about to be killed by the Angoni. In virtue of the "Kalata" we must help them when attacked by

[73] ibid. entry for 11 May 1885

[74] ibid. entries for 22, 25 and 28 August, 12 October 1885

[75] Morrison Diary entries for 14 December 1884, 18 October 1885, 13 February 1886

[76] Bandawe Station Journal entry for 4 November 1885; J. A. Smith to Laws, 14 December 1885, Shepperson Collection

their enemies.'[77] Families settled on the beach in temporary shelters in order to be close to the mission station. Chimbono forbade his followers to bring wood to the mission steamer when the missionaries denied him assistance.[78] The conditions were being created in which, in September 1887, Laws flatly refused to allow Tonga women and children to take refuge in the mission stockade in the face of a major Ngoni attack, hourly threatened, and Chimbono responded by preventing Laws from sending his own wife and child to safety and from loading stores onto the *Ilala*.[79]

The crisis from August to October 1887 when an assault by the whole Ngoni army appeared imminent seemed significant to Laws and his colleagues in retrospect principally for their eventual success in averting armed conflict through negotiations with Mbelwa. More important to the Tonga, however, was the provision in the agreement that the mission would ignore attacks on Chinteche if Bandawe was left unmolested.[80] Here was proof not only of the value of the missionaries as political allies, but also of the selective nature of that value: the fact that benefits to be gained from contacts with Livingstonia were limited to selected villages even within a single society. Just as more attention was given to the security of villages close to Bandawe than to the security of those further away, so villages near Bandawe could acquire calico and other goods through meeting the economic demands of the mission while Chinteche and other outlying regions still had to rely almost exclusively on Arab traders for their external economic contacts. It was not surprising that Consul Goodrich in 1885 noted a distinction between the attitudes of headmen at Bandawe who were friendly to the white men and those at Chinteche where 'the attitude of the people was decidedly hostile'. Mankhambira was 'both frightened and annoyed at my having paid him three visits in the last few months'; his people on one of the consul's visits refused to sell him provisions.[81]

What is important here is less the hostility aroused by the mission – too valuable a potential ally to be totally antagonised – than the friction generated between those Tonga chiefs, notably Marenga, who gained from its proximity, and those who did not. Fighting broke out in July

77 Bandawe Station Journal entry for 12 October 1885

78 Morrison Diary entry for 21–2 October 1885

79 Bandawe Station Journal entries for 13 September and 25 September to 4 October 1887; Mrs Laws to her parents, 11 October 1887, Laws's Papers, EUL

80 Laws to Smith, 8 November 1887 quoted in *Scottish Leader*, 27 January 1888, NLS 7906

81 Goodrich to FO, 24 April 1885, 1 June 1885, FO 84/1702

1881 between Marenga, Katonga and Chimbono, all headmen living near Bandawe, and Mankhambira, who, it was claimed, was trying to establish his paramountcy over all the Tonga.[82]

Later disputes followed along similar lines with attempts being made to involve the mission in the struggle between Mankhambira and Kangoma for supremacy at Chinteche, and between the three headmen, Marenga, Chimbono and Chikuru, near Bandawe. In February 1885 matters reached a head in a full-scale battle between Marenga on the one side representing those forces which had gained from the mission's presence and Chikuru, Chimbono and Mankhambira on the other. Marenga told the missionaries of the friendship he had always had with the white man:

> For this he asserted that all the other Atonga chiefs hated him and were ready at any moment to fight against him. He wished us to help him against Tshikuru reminding us of the treaties he had signed and of our promises to help him. This being denied him he at once pled for powder; and again he had to be denied. He left us in anger saying he had all along been the friend of the white man and now in his hour of need we had cast him off.[83]

The immediate consequence was that missionaries acting with impeccable neutrality, gave medical aid to both sides, and managed to patch up a provisional peace. In the long run, however, their influence was weighted inevitably towards Marenga and his allies – as much for geographical reasons as for any other.

The transformation of this tactical alliance into a more fundamental relationship can be explained in the following way. The political advantages gained by some Tonga headmen from associating with the mission were powerfully reinforced by the emphasis on individual achievement inherent in Tonga society. As van Velsen has demonstrated, cohesion was achieved among the Tonga not through a common allegiance to some central authority, but rather through 'widely dispersed ties interlinking a variety of groups and individuals'. Most freeborn Tonga had two sets of kinship ties, patrilineal and matrilineal, the latter being the more important, and were thus able to choose from a wide range of alternatives as to where they should settle and with whom they should establish political or economic contacts. Where each freeborn Tonga male was a potential chief, liable to hive off to found his own village, or at least to leave one village in order to place himself under a more enterprising headman, it

[82] Bandawe Station Journal entries for 9–10 July 1881
[83] ibid. entry for 23 February 1886

was necessary for headmen to utilise all existing advantages to establish their personal leadership.[84]

One such potential advantage was the education offered by the missionaries. In contrast to the southern Malawi situation where the first proper school at Cape Maclear was regularly attended in 1879, three years after its foundation, by only some thirty to forty mission dependants, Tongaland rapidly became the scene of extraordinary educational enthusiasm. A small school was started at the Bandawe observation post, from which nine pupils were sent in September 1879 to continue their education at Cape Maclear.[85] On the founding of the central station this school was restarted, and by January 1884 was attended by over a hundred pupils, including more than a dozen boarders, several from villages in the Matete valley and from Kuwira. Marenga asked that a school should be established at his village as early as August 1879, but this request was not followed up till 1883 owing to the missionaries' insistence that he must build the school himself without payment. Fuka, a headman some four miles from Bandawe, followed his example, though his school was burnt down by the Ngoni before it was completed, while Mankhambira from Chinteche also asked for a teacher.[86]

In the pioneer years the attractions of education for the Tonga may well have lain primarily in the opportunities it gave them to strengthen the alliance with the mission. Mankhambira specifically asked for a European teacher to reside with him, and rejected the African offered instead.[87] With the decline of Ngoni pressure after 1887, rivalry between headmen increased and brisk competition took place for the limited numbers of teachers available. New schools were opened in 1888 at Marenga's, Chikuru's and Fuka's and a year later three further schools were started at Chinteche, at Dwambazi and in the Matete district. By 1890 the average attendance in the whole district was 2279, an exceptional figure that declined as the novelty of the schools wore off. Nevertheless, in 1894, eighteen schools were open with 1000 pupils regularly attending.[88]

Among most of the leading societies welcoming education in East

[84] J. van Velsen, 'The Establishment of the Administration in Tongaland; *Historians in Tropical Africa*, Salisbury, Southern Rhodesia, 1962, 2; van Velsen, *The Politics of Kinship*, Manchester, 1964

[85] Bandawe Station Journal entries for 26 December 1878, 16 September 1879; Livingstonia Mission Report, 1880, 2

[86] Bandawe Station Journal entries for 24 August 1879, 25 June, 31 July, 13 October, 10 December 1883

[87] ibid. entries for 12 September 1885, 23 February 1886

[88] *FCSMR*, June 1890, 175; Livingstonia Mission Report, 1894, 3

Central Africa at this early period a prime motive appears to have been the desire to strengthen and modernise the existing political structure. The Lozi, we are told, as late as 1906 'regarded education as a means of providing the Lozi state with qualified secretaries, clerks, interpreters and artisans'.[89] For the Tonga, however, the lack of any sophisticated bureaucracy whose internal functions could be improved by missionary teaching ensured that education should be regarded essentially as an outward-looking force, providing the techniques for grappling with the newly-intrusive Western world.

Here Livingstonia's economic influence was complimentary to the work of her schools. Although her agents at Cape Maclear had been principally concerned with intervening in the ivory trade many of them believed that more fundamental results would come from the encouragement of cash-crop peasant production. Both there and at Bandawe small quantities of cotton, tobacco, india-rubber and sugar-cane were bought up, in the hope of stimulating their growth, and a firm policy of purchasing food supplies from beyond the station was introduced, so that the mission could provide the nucleus of a market.[90]

In practice, the comparative absence of local customers and the high transport costs to the coast ensured that the mission's efforts would be unavailing. The purchase of food supplies, estimated by Laws in 1878 to include three tons of grain a week, led, he believed, to the extension of cultivation near Cape Maclear by Yao and Manganja producers.[91] But even here, the effects were limited. The mission used the steamer to collect supplies from a wide area and thus put little pressure on local agricultural communities. Large, regular supplies of provisions were purchased at entrepots – particularly at Mankanjira's – where surplus food crops were already being grown by the 1870s to meet the demand of trading parties travelling to and from the coast.[92] Indeed, without the supplies of maize, sorghum and rice, produced at Makanjira's in response to the slave trade, Livingstonia would have been hard put to survive. Instruction given to pupils and apprentices at Bandawe in such various skills as carpentry, brickmaking, sewing, storekeeping and, from 1889, printing, was not of

[89] Terence Ranger, 'African Attempts to control Education in East and Central Africa 1900–1913', *Past and Present*, 21, 1965, 59–60, 63

[90] Stewart 'Summary of Instructions and Hints', 2

[91] *FCSMR*, July 1878, 165

[92] A typical day's purchase at Mankanjira's taken from the Cape Maclear Journal, entry for 1 March 1877 was: Green maize, 1870 lbs; dried maize 700 lbs; mapira (sorghum) 700 lbs; rice 104 lbs; nuts 40 lbs; pumpkins 80; fowls 75

the type that could be transmitted with benefit beyond the mission. Most Africans employed – more than fifty at a time at Cape Maclear and up to a hundred at Bandawe – were dragooned into labour squads to carry out such work as hoeing and weeding in the mission gardens using methods no more efficient than those they employed at home.

But if the mission failed in its attempt to introduce agricultural and technical innovations, it did play a crucial role in creating the migrant labour system that was to become the central feature of Malawi's colonial economy. Teachers in village schools and workers building mission houses and cultivating its land were paid regular wages, partly in cloth and beads, but also in British money which was introduced by Laws in 1879 and could be exchanged for articles at the local store.[93] More calico was expended on the purchase of food supplies from neighbouring villages to feed the boarders at Bandawe school. All this contributed to the growing demand among the Tonga for European goods – a demand which could not be satisfied by the returns to be achieved from intensified agricultural production or the low wages the mission provided: one shilling per month for teachers in 1883, and three and a half yards of cloth per week for ordinary workers. The solution lay in seeking work elsewhere; and here the Tonga were helped by their fortunate proximity to the lake, and the readiness of Livingstonia to collaborate with the Lakes Company in shipping workers down to the Southern Province, on contracts lasting for six months or a year. Head porters and, from the early 1890s, agricultural labourers were much in demand by the African Lakes Company, which also employed an increasing number of African clerks and storemen. Believing that even porterage was a beneficial educational experience, Laws organised a labour bureau, issuing written contracts and guaranteeing the return of workers when their time was expired.[94] The first Tonga were sent south in 1885 and returned as deck passengers on the *Ilala* in November of that year. On 16 March 1886, a further party of thirty-three Tonga went off by steamer to Mandala and, in November, twenty-five more were recruited as porters for periods varying between six months and a year.[95] Later in May 1888 another 200 were recruited as mercenaries for the company's army, fighting Arab traders at the north end of the lake, and were taken overland to Karonga by Alfred Sharpe, and they in turn were followed in August by a second detachment, recruited from

93 Livingstonia Mission Report, 1880, 2

94 See Laws, 'Native Education in Nyasaland', Boston, 1929. Liv. Corr. Box 3; *Aurora*, April 1900; Macmillan 'African Lakes Company', 191

95 Morrison Diary, 12 November 1886, 16 March 1886; Bandawe Station Journal entries for 16 March, 29 November 1886, NLS 7911

Marenga.[96] In 1894 Laws estimated that 1400 Tonga migrants were working in the company's employment, while 4000 more were under settlers in the Shire highlands. As he noted: 'The whole of these have not come under the influence of Christian teaching in the Bandawe neighbourhood . . . but the way for their filling up the gap in the demand for labour has been opened up by the work and influence of the mission among the tribe.'[97]

For much of this work, the possession of a missionary education can have been of little value. The mercenaries, for example, received their main rewards from looting Arabs with the help of firearms supplied by the young Captain Lugard.[98] But some jobs did exist, not just as teachers, where an ability to speak a few words of English, and to read and write was of real commercial value. Many of the Tonga employed by the ALC were said to be 'captains of the boats and canoes and in positions of more or less trust and usefulness' and others in the service of the administration constituted 'the bulk of . . . irregular police at all the European stations between Nyasa and Tanganyika'.[99] It was inevitable perhaps that many Europeans should be aware only of the Tonga's dependence upon them: 'They are a pure importation of the white man,' wrote Dr Wordsworth Poole in 1896, '[who] work well when beaten and kept in hand.'[100] But the dependence was by no means a one-way affair. At a time when most of their neighbours were still struggling to reach some *modus vivendi* with the new intruders, the Tonga were consolidating their position as 'the Krumen of this Protectorate', the intermediaries upon whom much of the colonial system was ultimately based.[101] In the late 1870s, it had been Yao entrepreneurs involved in the east coast trade who were the leading African representatives of the international economy in Malawi. In the late 1890s, it was Tonga migrant clerks and foremen employed within the settler economy of southern Africa who had taken on this role. The transition involved a certain loss of African economic independence. But, as the pioneers in the migrant labour system, mission-educated Tonga retained far more options than were open to most migrants from elsewhere.

96 *FCSMR*, October 1888, 307. Lugard to Buchanan, 10 September 1888; to Laws, 31 August (approx!) (1888), Shepperson Collection

97 Laws to Dr Smith, 10 September 1894, NLS 7878

98 Lugard to Laws, 31 August (approx!)

99 *Report on First Three Years Administration . . . of . . . British Central Africa*, 1894, 24; Laws to Dr Smith, 10 September 1894. NLS 7878

100 Wordsworth Poole to his mother, 19 February 1896, MNA PO1/1

101 Sharpe to Sir C. Hill, 14 January 1897, FO 2/127. Sharpe's reference is to the Kru people of the Windward coast many of whom worked in European ships and trading stations from the eighteenth century

These developments, political, educational and economic, represent the extension of missionary influence at a popular level unparalleled outside Buganda in East or Central Africa at this period. Yet the mission remained isolated in certain respects. Despite their readiness to accept education and employment from the British, the Tonga were reluctant to take the final step of religious conversion. Early baptisms at Bandawe took place exclusively among dependants brought up from Cape Maclear such as John Brown Mvula, Charles Konde, Andrew Mwana Njobvu and John Kurukuru. The first Tonga converts were not made till 1889, eleven years after the founding of the observation post, and these, like other early converts were mostly teachers and scholars of whom it was said: 'Some had been at school with us at Cape Maclear, others joined us as occasional scholars soon after work was begun at Bandawe.'[102] In 1890 the total number of communicants in the whole mission including Cape Maclear and Ngoniland, was only fifty-three.[103]

Tonga religious institutions were less of an impenetrable barrier to Christian influence than the village-based Nyau cult of the Chewa and Manganja, but they provided the Tonga with satisfactory answers to many of the social and spiritual problems which confronted them. According to A. G. Macalpine, the missionary with the greatest experience of Tongaland, the Tonga believed in a high god, Chiuta, creator and sustainer of life, but concerned themselves more frequently with the spirits of the dead, who had power over the future of the living, and sometimes possessed mediums or 'soothsayers' (*mchimi*), men of influence whatever their rank.[104]

In comparison with the *mchimi*, the missionaries, none of whom learnt Chitonga before 1894, must have appeared disturbingly alien.[105] It is true that African agents held village services regularly throughout the 1880s. Hymns were sung at these services to Scottish tunes, the favourite being 'Scots Wha Hae' and simple biblical addresses were delivered, most of them dealing with redemption and sin.[106] Yet as most of the pioneer agents were Manganja and Yao, their links with the villagers were often slender. Cut off from Tonga society, they lacked for men like Mankham-

[102] *FCSMR*, August 1889; April 1890, 106

[103] Livingstonia Mission Report, 1886–90, 5.

[104] A. G. Macalpine, 'Tonga Religious Beliefs and Customs', *Journal of the African Society*, v, 1905–6; vi, 1906–7. For the Nyau cult see Matthew Schoffeleers and I. Linden, 'The Resistance of the Nyau Societies to the Roman Catholic Missions in Colonial Malawi' in Ranger and Kimambo, *Historical Study of African Religion*.

[105] A. G. Macalpine, 'Account of experiences with the Livingstonia Mission'

[106] Morrison Diary entry for 14 December 1884

bira the special political attractions possessed by the Europeans. At the same time, they tended to follow the artisans in gratuitously interfering in local affairs. At the observation post Fred Zarakuti's action in seizing two women and a child from Arab slavers and taking their calico and a gun might have been ascribed to an excess of zeal had he not promptly turned the women to use as the nucleus for a personal harem – an action he defended on the grounds that it did not contravene the law as he had seen it at Cape Town.[107] During the 1880s several incidents occurred in which Livingstonia pupils or agents seized supposed wrong-doers and otherwise acted violently towards neighbours, and were themselves attacked by aggrieved Tonga in return. In August 1885, for instance, a party of schoolboys who had seized a man from Chikuru's village for ill-treating a woman, and were bringing him bound to the station, were attacked by an armed band of villagers who fired at them and stole their loads.[108] Later in January 1887 Chimbono brought what Laws believed to be an entirely baseless accusation of adultery against one of the agents Pagani which resulted in the headman placing a boycott on the sale of all food to the station when satisfaction was not granted to him. The case was not settled till the chiefs around Marenga's had intervened and Laws had threatened to depart from Bandawe.[109]

Crisis in Ngoniland

In contrast to the Tonga, the northern Ngoni appeared unlikely candidates for conversion. Elsewhere individual missionaries and traders like Robert Moffat among the Matabele and Carl Wiese with Mpezeni's Ngoni succeeded in striking up personal friendships with rulers of new states created by marauding refugees from South Africa, but their formidable military systems, as Moffat recognised, were too vigorous to be pushed aside by the challenge of Christianity, while their need to raid or control subject peoples threw such hazards in the path of colonial plans for labour recruitment and economic exploitation that armed conflict with Europeans very often resulted.[110]

To this general pattern northern Ngoniland provides an exception. Superficially Mbelwa's Ngoni differed little from their kinsmen to the

107 Bandawe Station Journal entries for 14 May, 29 August, 2 September 1879, NLS 7910

108 Bandawe Journal entry for 5 August 1885, NLS 7911

109 ibid. entries for 11–14 January, 21 March 1887

110 Moffat's views are strikingly expressed in J. P. R. Wallis (ed.), *Matabele Journals of Robert and Emily Moffat*, 1945, 256–7. For a general survey of Ngoni responses see J. K. Rennie, 'The Ngoni States and European Intrusion' in Stokes and Brown, *The Zambesian Past*, 302–31

south. They dominated at the height of their influence an area said to be 30 000 square miles in dimension, populated by Tonga, Tumbuka, Henga, Ngonde, Chewa, Bisa and others. Whereas 'in all the other districts the missionaries were hailed', so Elmslie claimed, 'as the friends and protectors of the people [the Ngoni] needed not our protection as they were masters of the country for many miles around'.[111]

On a deeper level, however, the northern Ngoni were subjected to pressures which made them particularly receptive to missionary advances. In the first place, the balance of power in their favour, on which depended the continued vitality of the state, was beginning to tilt against them by the 1880s. Ngoni military successes were based on their powers of cohesion and the use of the short stabbing spear and oxhide shield. These had been sufficient to win them numerous striking victories during their northwards march, but they were less effective when pitted against agricultural peoples who had withdrawn into prepared stockaded villages, particularly if such peoples possessed the new improved firearms with increased velocity which were beginning to become available in East Central Africa by the last two decades of the nineteenth century.

The significance of these organisational and technical innovations first became apparent in the 1860s when the Chewa chief Mwase Kasungu defeated a Ngoni impi with the aid of guns sold to him by traders from Nkota Kota.[112] Over a decade later Mankhambira's successful defence of the Chinteche stockade against several attacks gave warning that Tonga villages were now less vulnerable than they had previously been. The sharp reverse suffered by an impi in 1882 at Nkota Kota where the Jumbe had accumulated up to two thousand firearms, was further evidence that Swahili trading settlements were also too formidable to be raided with impunity.[113]

The Ngoni, it is true, still won victories from time to time in open warfare. Frequent raids were made on Tonga cultivating their upland gardens during the 1880s, and a successful attack on the Bemba took place in 1887.[114] Nevertheless, a serious loss of confidence appears to have afflicted some leaders during the decade. Elmslie wrote in 1886 that the tentative move to the Mzimba district was a sign of relative decline in Ngoni power:

[111] Elmslie, *Wild Ngoni*, 78

[112] Cullen Young, *History of the Tumbuka–Kamanga*, 130

[113] *FCSMR*, April 1878, 86. Bandawe Journal entry for 28 October 1885; Diary of Dr Laws entry for 20 November 1882, Laws's Papers, EUL

[114] Elmslie to Laws, 7 November 1887, NLS 7890. For a detailed discussion of Bemba–Ngoni relations see Andrew D. Roberts, *A History of the Bemba*, London, 1973, esp. 363–76

> The end of the Angoni Kingdom as a marauding tribe is not far distant. Hemmed in on every side they must give in soon and the fact that they are looking for an uncultivated country as a new settlement means a great deal in the history of a tribe which has never broken up ground for itself but swallowed up the gardens of other tribes.[115]

Even Ng'onomo, the military commander, was pessimistic about his army's abilities when confronted by new forms of organisation. According to Elmslie, he told Mbelwa that it was only through the aid of the Senga with their guns that the Bemba had been defeated. Without their support he refused to attack Chinteche in 1887.[116]

While these external pressures may have played a part in persuading Ngoni leaders of the need to adopt alternate functions to those integral to a raiding economy, certain internal divisions were probably of greater importance in explaining the nature of Ngoni response to the arrival of the missionaries.

First among these divisions was the tension created by those subject peoples who still felt themselves at odds from their captives. In most Ngoni societies, recent captives were efficiently assimilated by being distributed all over the country under Ngoni leaders in such a way that they were unable to retain their old loyalties, and turned instead to the new. In northern Ngoniland, however, many of the captives taken from neighbouring tribes were permitted to remain together in groups under their own local chiefs and to follow their own laws and customs. This distinction which contributed to three breakaways of people of a common stock – Tonga, Henga and Tumbuka – in the 1870s, remained an issue of importance on into the 1880s. In 1885, for example, Elmslie reported numerous rumours of a forthcoming rising by Tumbuka which, though it came to nothing, caused 'a good deal of trouble in Agoniland'.[117]

A further source of tension was provided by captives such as the Nsenga and the Thonga of Mozambique taken before or shortly after the crossing of the Zambesi. Because chieftaincies in the northern kingdom were reserved almost exclusively for members of the royal clan, the Jere, this group had little opportunity of rising to the highest political office. On the other hand, the most able among them were highly prized as councillors by the chief of each segment, and they were also in demand as diviners, and *sing'anga* (medicine doctors), an occupation practised by

115 Elmslie to Laws, 22 November 1886, Shepperson Collection

116 Elmslie to Laws, 10 December 1887, NLS 7890, 13 May 1888, NLS 7891

117 Chibambo, *My Ngoni*, 39–41; Elmslie to Laws, 29 January 1885, Shepperson Collection

few of the original refugees from Shaka.[118] Because it was believed to be unfitting for the chief, the symbol of common unity within the segment or state, to interfere too frequently in domestic disputes, real power tended to slip towards the lieutenants. Consul Goodrich, who visited Mbelwa in April 1885, noted that 'The affairs of the country are managed by a council of indunas who merely notify to Mombera their decisions so that the chief himself has but little power.'[119]

By the mid 1880s customs were being introduced by councillors, notably the secret sale of slaves to Arab traders, of which the true Ngoni were said to disapprove. The position of the most senior chiefs, even of the paramount, was being put in question. According to George Williams, the last of the Lovedale graduates to be employed by the Livingstonia Mission, 'The fact is that Mombera would really make friends with the mission, for the councillors are using all their power to undermine his influence in fact if it was in their power they would wrest the kingdom out of his hands.'[120] Elmslie saw matters in a similar, though possibly exaggerated, light. The councillors, he reported in February 1886:

> are freed slaves and hate us because they cannot get their ends attained in the downthrow of the Angoni since we and only we maintain the Jeri dynasty. Mombera is powerless . . . The Jeris give evidence of the great moral truths of the Bible. They made slaves till now not 200 remain of the Angoni and all the power is in the hands of these freed slaves.[121]

Finally, tension existed between the paramount and his peers, the heads of the major segments within the state. As Barnes has shown, the snowball state system had a built-in tendency towards fission which did not necessarily presage its collapse or decay. In ideal circumstances, each son of a segment holder created his own segment when he came of age, drawn both from recent captives and from individuals from the older segments. Expansion thus continued at a great rate till the moment was reached when the paramount chief with the very slender central powers available to him would be unable to control the now unwieldy kingdom. One or more segments would therefore break away to found their own state, and the process would continue as before.[122] But if fission was a natural ingredient of the Ngoni state system, this did not prevent conflict between

118 Margaret Read, *The Ngoni of Nyasaland*, 49–50, 137

119 Goodrich to FO 24 April 1885, FO 84/1702

120 G. Williams to Laws, December 1884, Shepperson Collection

121 Elmslie to Cross, 8 February 1886, Shepperson Collection. For a similar situation among Mpezeni's Ngoni see Barnes, *Politics*, 46

122 ibid., 57–61

the paramount and his subordinate chiefs being almost endemic, particularly among the northern Ngoni where rivalry at the top took place within a single clan. Mbelwa not only had the example of the ominous break-up of the kingdom following his father's death constantly before him, he must also have been acutely aware that at least one chief, Mtwalo, had rights as good as his own to the paramountcy, while another, Mperembe, had actually broken away from the kingdom for a while before returning. As Mbelwa's own personal segment was smaller than those of some of the other chiefs, he had little reserve power at his disposal with which to maintain unity. Elmslie in 1885 spoke of enmity between Mbelwa and Mtwalo and the fear that 'The tribe may divide as Mtwaro is trying to set up as chief.' Mbelwa, he thought, 'seems going wrong as chief and irritating his people by disturbing them. He goes about alone now and he has recently taken cattle he had at kraals of Angoni and given them to the Atimbuka to keep.'[123] Even the followers of Chiputula Nhlane, members of a comparatively insignificant segment, found it possible to plan a breakaway to Mzimba when Mbelwa issued a judgement against them.[124]

It was against this background that Mbelwa faced Livingstonia during the 1880s. Clearly he regarded its agents as men of some importance, not only because of their wealth and technical skills, but also because of certain supernatural powers they were supposed to possess. To the Ngoni who made extensive use of medicines to strengthen their army in battle and deprive the enemy of courage, Mankhambira's claim 'that the English had given him plants which would strengthen him for War' must have appeared as convincing as his second threat 'that the steamer was away for an English army and there was another coming by land to drive the Angoni out of the country'.[125] It was hardly surprising that Mtwalo in October 1879 asked Miller 'that I should wash his body with medicine to protect him from his enemies who wished to kill him' – particularly as the missionaries, with doubtful propriety, had dangled before the Ngoni the claim that acceptance of Christianity permitted the believer to enter upon the fruits of Western power.[126] 'I showed them a Bible,' wrote Riddel of his first visit to Mbelwa,

> and told them it was it that made our nation rich and powerful . . .
> I then gave a sample of the Commandments and some of the leading

[123] Elmslie to Dr Smith, 29 May 1885 quoted in *FCSMR*, October 1885; Elmslie to Laws, 23 December 1885, Shepperson Collection

[124] G. Williams to Laws, 27 January 1887, NLS 7890

[125] Kaningina Station Journal entry for 20 December 1878, NLS 7910

[126] ibid. entry for 1 October 1879

> virtues it inculcated. I said if they received it, it would make them wise and happy and teach them how to become wealthy by fair means and not by robbery.[127]

Ngoni visitors to Bandawe in December 1880 were entertained by a magic-lantern display consisting of 'some pictures of battles, big guns, a regiment on the march . . . numerous forts on the Mediterranean'. They were also shown 'a photo of the Zulu king now caught' (Cetshwayo), an ominous indication of the fate awaiting those who opposed British military might.[128]

Mbelwa was thus in no position to ignore the mission as a political force, even though the military nature of the Ngoni kingdom offered him few opportunities for utilising it in the type of constructive role visualised for CMS agents by Mutesa of Buganda. Instead he followed a policy in which two principles appeared of primary importance: the first the desire to isolate the mission from any potential rival, Tonga, Tumbuka–Ngoni[129] or Ngoni; the second, the wish to prevent it antagonising others by making its material assets widely available.

In the earliest phase it was the first principle that dominated. Miller in 1878 and Laws a year later were both warmly welcomed by Mbelwa and strenuous efforts were made to attract them away from Bandawe up to the paramount's district. Councillors told Miller of their delight in having the missionaries with them: 'We welcome the Msungu to our country and look upon them as a wife come to be married to Mombelwa and we will all rejoice at the union.' Numerous goats and cattle were promised to them if they should decide to settle and the missionaries' residence with the Tonga was much deplored. 'Why do you not come up and live with us?' the councillors asked Laws, 'can you milk fish that you remain on the lake? Come up and live with us, and we will give you cattle. We are the rulers: the Atonga are under us, although they have broken off from us at present, and run away with our children.'[130]

Mbelwa, however, was less interested in what he could gain from the missionaries than in what he would lose if he failed to isolate them from his rivals. When Koyi and Sutherland established the pioneer station at Njuyu in 1882 he refused them permission to open schools, 'saying that

127 ibid. entry for 20 December 1878

128 Bandawe Station Journal entry for 16 December 1880, NLS 7910

129 By 'Tumbuka–Ngoni' I refer to those Tumbuka who had become members of the Ngoni state but still retained their cultural identity to a significant degree.

130 Kaningina Station Journal entry for 20 December 1878; Laws, February 1879 quoted in *FCSMR*, June 1879, 136

he himself must first be taught that he might judge our teaching'.[131] It is possible that his councillors were intrigued by Laws's claim 'that those nations which had received God's word had become great, while others rejecting it had been swept away', but they distrusted the mission's seditious anti-raiding doctrines, and feared that if their children attended mission schools they 'might despise the ignorance of their parents and refuse to undertake . . . forays'.[132] For a ruling elite as successful as the Ngoni had been in imposing their own social values on a heterogeneous subject population, there were obvious dangers in permitting aliens to compete for their subjects' allegiance. Visits to other chiefs were also forbidden, though Mtwalo established certain limited contacts with the missionaries. The only instruction officially approved was that given, unsuccessfully, to Mbelwa himself: 'Whenever he comes I get him on to the A B C,' wrote Sutherland sadly in December 1884, 'but before he goes any distance he tells me to . . . Get out of here . . . Give me cloth and so on.'[133]

The breakdown of this policy of isolation appears to have arisen out of the social tensions which I have already described. By the mid 1880s certain groups in Ngoniland were beginning to identify themselves with the mission. Although they were not allowed to open schools, the missionaries were not prevented from holding evangelistic services at their station, Njuyu, and these, while attended primarily by mission servants, began in August 1884 to attract a scattering of local villagers, most of them Tumbuka members of the Ngoni subject population. Others in groups of sixty or more came to work for three weeks or a month as labourers in the mission brickfield, and this became such a popular employment that by June 1885 the rulers at Hoho, the neighbouring village to the station, were protesting that only their dependants should be given work, and not those from a distance. Elmslie's medical work also appears to have made some impression, particularly his skill as a dentist.

Further consolidation of the mission's influence was provided in January 1886, when after the efforts of diviners had failed to break the long drought of that year, Elmslie was called upon by a deputation of Mbelwa's councillors to give his assistance. A missionary of an older generation would have leapt at the opportunity to demonstrate the superior powers of his God over those of the heathen. But Elmslie, a representative of a more sceptical age, was initially reluctant to give the

[131] ibid., November 1882, 325

[132] ibid., May 1884, 10

[133] Sutherland to Laws, 23 December 1884, Shepperson Collection

impression that he had any special rain-making powers and replied evasively about prayers that were used in connection with drought in South Africa and Scotland. Further pressure followed, and though Elmslie refused to hold a special meeting in Mbelwa's kraal, not wanting 'the Bible to be there because they have a superstitious belief about the mere book', he made some reference to rain in his normal Sunday service on 17 January. On the next day rain began to fall, with the result that for several years Elmslie became labelled, to his acute embarrassment, as one of the kingdom's rain specialists, able to prolong a drought if his wishes were not met.[134]

Mbelwa's motives in this affair must remain a matter of speculation, but it is important to recognise the existence, as in other centralised societies where the secular ruler was trying to consolidate his power, of tension between the royal authorities and religious officials, emphasised in the case of the Ngoni by the fact that most of the diviners, like most of the councillors, did not come from South Africa. Under Zwangendaba recently captured witch-finders of Chewa and Tumbuka origin are said to have used their power to kill off older established diviners of Thonga origin, while Zwangendaba himself is credited, in a story identical in all essential details to one told of Shaka among the Zulu, of deliberately sprinkling blood on the doorways of his kraal in order to trick the diviners into giving false judgement, and then slaying those who fell into the trap.[135] It is not impossible that Mbelwa in turning to Elmslie was seeking to reduce his dependence on a social group which he saw as a threat to the stability of his kingdom. Certainly in subsequent months, the missionaries regarded his alliance with Livingstonia as resulting largely from his desire for 'a safeguard for the future' against the councillors who, it was believed, were 'yearly increasing in power'.[136]

At all events, the rain episode, when taken with other developments, so increased the attractiveness of the mission to important new elements among the Ngoni that Mbelwa, whatever his original motives, could no longer continue with his policy of exclusion. The reaction of the Tumbuka subjects who, after January 1886, began to attend evangelistic meetings in crowds, was soon paralleled by the marked interest shown by some of

[134] The fullest description of these events is contained in a letter written by Elmslie to Cross, 8 February 1886, Shepperson Collection. For subsequent events see Elmslie to Laws, 22 November 1886, Shepperson Collection; Williams to Laws, 7 October 1887, NLS 7880

[135] Chibambo, 23; Elmslie, 23–4; Read, *Ngoni*, 179–80. See also William E. Rau, 'The Ngoni Diaspora and Religious Interaction in East and Central Africa', Unpublished seminar paper, UCLA 1970

[136] Williams to Laws, 7 October 1886, Shepperson Collection

the segment heads, anxious, both Elmslie and Williams believed, to win the support of the mission in any dispute with over-mighty councillors. In danger of arousing hostility against himself by refusing easy access to the missionaries, Mbelwa now changed his plans, and after a meeting with Mtwalo, gave permission in May 1886 for them to teach through the length of his land. His only advice, expressed through members of his council, was 'that instead of confining our work to the people around one station we would open stations at each of the principal divisions of the tribe'.[137]

The suggestion in principle was warmly welcomed by Elmslie, who only a year before had told the home committee of his desire to plant sub-stations throughout the more distant parts of the kingdom. The rapid expansion of European-manned stations elsewhere in northern Malawi meant, however, that no new recruits were available to supplement those already in the field. After Koyi's sudden death on 4 June 1886 had reduced the Ngoniland staff to two, Williams went to Chinyera, the out-station about five miles from Njuyu which he had temporarily opened the year before, and Elmslie started up a small school at Njuyu. But the key problem – the need to establish contacts with segments other than Mbelwa's – was not met, with the result that opposition against any school being established at once became apparent. In November 1886 Elmslie reported the current situation:

> Mombera does not now see that we can have a school simply on one side and though offer was made to open one at his place he did not seem willing for it as he is afraid of the jealousy of others, and until the chief is availing himself of the school the Hoho people will not send any children to be taught. If we could open a dozen schools in the country we could have one here but because we cannot do that we cannot have one.[138]

Only a tiny group of six or seven pupils continued to frequent the mission-house and receive lessons in secret.

Matters were now moving to a head. In December permission to open a school was once more granted, and once more antagonism against Mbelwa for monopolising the new asset was aroused. This time, however, the form it took threatened the security of the mission. If agents could not be spared for Ngoniland while Bandawe thrived, it was logical for sub-chiefs to seek to force the whole staff to come up to the hills. Little was done till August 1887, as Laws's visit the month before was opti-

[137] Elmslie to Laws, 10 May 1886, Shepperson Collection, Elmslie, 25 June 1886, quoted in *FCSMR*, December 1886, 365

[138] Elmslie to Laws, 5 November 1886, Shepperson Collection

mistically regarded as a prelude for more favourable changes. But after he had left empty-handed and particularly after Williams, now the only Lovedale man on the staff and a valuable go-between, had informed Mbelwa that he too, was to leave, the dam broke with spectacular force. If Williams went, all the missionaries should leave, Mbelwa declared as a prelude to his most important demand: either they come up to him from Bandawe and leave the Tonga to the mercies of the Ngoni, or they must evacuate the country altogether.[139]

Besides the central issue of desire for access to the mission several other factors were of importance – all concerned with the increasing power of the Tonga vis-à-vis the Ngoni. During the 1880s the African Lakes Company had extended its sphere of operations, setting up a central depot at Karonga in 1884 and a small store at Bandawe a year later. From the depot guns and ammunition were sold to Arab traders, in contravention of the company's stated policy, so it was believed, and these traders in their turn, the Ngoni contended, sold guns to the Tonga, thus building up the latter's supply of armaments.[140] Moreover, various incidents, notably the treaty negotiated by the ALC with Tonga chiefs in 1885, gave colour to the Ngoni belief that the British were prepared to protect the Tonga against them, and these were exacerbated by the fact that Tonga carriers sometimes taunted their former masters with boasts of their new-found power, and that Tonga raids occasionally took place on Ngoni villages, as well as vice versa. Underlying all was the feeling that the Tonga were gaining more than the Ngoni from the British connection; that they received more employment and hence more calico. As Elmslie declared, 'Jealousy of the Tonga is a big factor in the whole question and because it is so our difficulties are very great'.[141]

For two months, August to October 1887, the crisis continued to smoulder. Elmslie, already burdened by the need to care for his wife in the last stage of a difficult pregnancy, sent contradictory messages by every post to Laws at Bandawe. All the missionaries should leave Ngoniland, he declared in one letter; all those at Bandawe should join him in the hills he advised in another. 'We cannot save the Atonga by staying among them or by going away . . . There is ample room for us all here and it is as suitable a field as any on the west coast.'[142]

139 Elmslie to Laws, 10 August 1887, NLS 7890; Elmslie, 23 August 1887, in *FCSMR*, February 1885, 45

140 Bandawe Journal entry for 11 December 1885, NLS 7911; Elmslie to Laws, 10 August 1887, NLS 7890. Ngoni councillors also complained that the company agent Stuart had sold guns and gunpowder direct to the Tonga.

141 Elmslie to Laws, 24 August 1887, NLS 7890

142 Elmslie to Laws, 24 September and 15 September 1887, NLS 7908

Laws, however, remained firm. On 27 October 1887 he attended a great meeting with Mbelwa's councillors, and after much argument reached a compromise agreement: the missionaries would remain at Bandawe but would not interfere with what the Ngoni did at Chinteche, the northern focus of Tonga power. A station would also be opened at Mtwalo's head-village as soon as possible.[143]

To Elmslie, a fervent admirer of Laws who had first sparked off his enthusiasm for Africa, there was no question as to how the drama had been resolved. In a much quoted passage written years later, he declared that 'Living, as I did, with Mombera for six years before he died, I never knew of his having stopped a single war party from attacking the helpless Tonga around Dr Laws's station at Bandawe because of his belief in God; but over and over again because of his attachment to Dr Laws he refused to sanction war.'[144] But personal affection is a weak instrument at the best in bringing about profound political change, and though Elmslie drew the parallel of Laws's friendship with Mbelwa and Robert Moffat's with Mzilikazi, it is clear from his correspondence that the two cases were distinct. Mbelwa never gave any sign of manifesting that strange, almost physical, affection for the European which Mzilikazi so frequently indulged in. His interest in Laws arose directly from the fact that the missionaries in Ngoniland were young and inexperienced, and referred everything to their senior colleague. As no firm decision could be made in his absence, Mbelwa was naturally eager that he should attend major conferences.[145]

The strength of the agreement thus lay not in personal factors but in the extent to which it coincided with the pressures and changes in power in the political structure – and particularly in the growing isolation of the Jere from their councillors on the one hand and of Mbelwa from the segment heads on the other. Aware for the first time of the imperative need to widen their base, the missionaries began to make strenuous efforts to spread their influence among the more distant parts of the kingdom. In November 1887 Elmslie made a pioneering visit to Ng'onomo and Mtwalo in their villages, while Williams went to Mperembe's. Some delay followed during which Mtwalo sent several messages regarding the proposed residency. In July 1889, however, Elmslie visited Mtwalo again and got his ready consent for a station to be built near him, and in August

143 See reports in *FCSMR*, March 1887, 76 and in Laws to Smith, 8 November 1887, quoted in *Scottish Leader*, 27 January 1888, cutting in NLS 7906

144 Elmslie, *Wild Ngoni*, 94

145 See Sutherland to Laws, 17 June 1885; Williams to Laws, 2 October 1886, Shepperson Collection

this was finally established under the artisan McCallum, close to Mtwalo's head village of Ekwendeni. Within a month of his arrival McCallum had over 140 pupils at school. By 1895 Ekwendeni had become Livingstonia's largest Ngoniland station.

The mission's success came at an important moment in the history of the Ngoni. If one were to accept the supposition that all Ngoni groups depended inevitably for continued integration upon the assimilation of a steady supply of captives from beyond their kingdom, they might all have been expected to continue raiding till they were eventually checked and crushed by superior forces. In fact each group differed from the other, in part according to the extent to which they had assimilated local peoples, and each, even before the European conquest, was capable of adapting institutions and customs to new functions, given that the pressures to change were sufficiently large and that alternative functions actually existed.

For the northern Ngoni, pressure to change was provided, as we have already seen, by the mounting capabilities of the people beyond their frontier to repel attacks. Despite the assurance from the mission that an attack on Chinteche would not involve them in a collision with the British, they still hesitated to move. In November 1887 Elmslie reported that the season was now too late for any assault to be planned. Ng'onomo, the Ngoni war leader, refused to mount an attack without the support of Senga guns and unless the Tonga could be lured out of their stockade, and without his support those sections of the Ngoni nearest to the Tonga would take no action.[146] The year after, Ng'onomo went north to raid for cattle. Gradually the project faded out of mind and the Tonga were left in peace.

The failure to attack Chinteche did not, of course, mean the end of all Ngoni raiding. Because the missionaries, and later other Europeans, usually approached the Ngoni from Tongaland, there is a tendency to regard Ngoni–Tonga relations as the only ones of importance. But the Ngoni were surrounded by a variety of people – the Tumbuka, Henga and Ngonde to the north, Chewa to the south, Senga in the Luangwa valley to the west, and these latter in particular continued to be subjected to Ngoni raids well in to the 1890s, despite Chibambo's claim that raiding had completely ceased in Ngoniland by 1893. According to Fraser, a more reliable witness on this point, national raids had ended by the time of his arrival in the country late in 1896, but attacks by members of an

146 Elmslie to Laws, 10 December 1887, NLS 7890; 26 December 1887, NLS 7891

age regiment within a single segment, notably those of Mperembe and Ng'onomo, continued along with independent raids by groups of young men acting without orders.[147] These were small affairs, however, when compared with the nation-wide assaults of an earlier period, and they were largely restricted to areas where few Europeans had penetrated and none settled, an important consideration in the 1890s when the *pax Britannica* was slowly being imposed on those regions frequented by the British.

Meanwhile, through Livingstonia, new functions and opportunities were beginning to emerge as alternatives to those integral to a raiding economy. The young men of military age were clearly those most deeply affected by the constraints placed upon their traditional activities, for many of them sought military success as a means of achieving upward social mobility, and looked to the continuance of warfare in order to integrate themselves successfully within their society. During the 1880s it was men of this age-group who most insistently demanded of Mbelwa that he should give his authority for raids, attempting on one occasion to refuse to permit him to enter his new village till the order had been given.[148]

One possible alternative appeared to lie, as Mbelwa himself at one time seems to have recognised, in the educational facilities offered by the mission. As early as 1886 he told Elmslie that while small boys would have to be kept from school in order to herd the cattle, 'he could send us scores of idle young men' instead.[149] Mbelwa's acceptance of the missionaries, however, was motivated, if my analysis is correct, not by any desire to utilise them in strengthening the state structure, as in Buganda, or by establishing favourable contacts on a popular level with a larger society, as with the Tonga, but rather by the wish to remove a source of internal conflict by making the material assets of the mission widely available, and perhaps in the hope that with stations in every part of the kingdom, it would act as an integrating force in a splintering polity. The consequence was that the initial impetus towards education was relatively muted. Scholars at Njuyu amounted to nearly ninety in March 1889, and further schools were opened at Chinyera, Mlima and Ekwendeni, so that by 1890 attendance in the whole of Ngoniland stood at the 500 mark, and at an average of nearly 600 three years later. At Njuyu, however, Elmslie was forced to follow the example of many other missionaries in Central Africa

147 Chibambo, *My Ngoni*, 53; Fraser to Dr Smith, 20 October 1896, NLS 7880; Fraser, *Primitive People*, 41.

148 *FCSMR*, September 1887, 271. Elmslie, *Wild Ngoni*, 166–7

149 Elmslie to Laws, 15 October 1886, Shepperson Collection

in providing presents for those who came regularly, while at Ekwendeni attendance fell by a half within two months of opening.[150]

A crucial weakness of the mission's educational work was its failure to provide worthwhile benefits for those it wished to attract. In the absence of opportunities within the Ngoni state the only immediate beneficiaries were the small band of teachers – forty of them in 1893 – employed at rates of up to five shillings a month. Other Ngoni worked as labourers in the service of the mission, and one, Chitezi, received a contract to make and deliver bricks for mission buildings, though the rate at which he was paid – four shillings per thousand bricks – cannot have permitted him to accumulate considerable capital. Given the low esteem in which agriculture was held by the Ngoni proper, and the absence of local markets, peasant production was a virtual non-starter. Hence, as with the Tonga, though with far greater geographical obstacles to overcome, enterprising Ngoni – deprived of their military function – came to regard wage labour beyond their homeland as the only viable economic alternative. In 1894 it was reported that a large number of carriers employed on the expedition to seek a suitable site for the Livingstonia Institution came from Ekwendeni. They formed the vanguard for a mass exodus of labour which by 1904 was to rival even that from Tongaland. New ladders for the ambitious were being created. Advancement was no longer to depend entirely on prowess in war.[151]

As in other parts of the country, missionary influence where it penetrated deepest did so primarily among individuals without significant political status and among those most intimately connected with the mission's work. The first pupils at Njuyu, two of whom became the first Ngoni converts, in April 1890, were three sons of a Nsenga diviner, Mawelero Tembo, Makera Tembo and Chitezi. According to their father in a statement reported and possibly embellished by Elmslie, 'We were nothing till you came – you have made us forget we are slaves as we are all treated alike by you.'[152] Several other early pupils at Njuyu were Tumbuka subjects – Elmslie argued that they were quicker to learn than

150 Elmslie to Laws, 24 November 1888, NLS 7891; McCallum to Laws, 10 December 1889, NLS 7892

151 Livingstonia Mission Report, July–December 1894, 14

152 Quoted in Elmslie to Cross, 8 February 1886, Shepperson Collection. An alternative explanation would be that the first converts came from among individuals who were professionally interested in religion, and thus who were particularly susceptible to crises of belief. In this light the evangelist Mawelero Tembo can be seen as playing a very similar role within the context of the Church as that performed by his diviner father in the previous generation

the true Ngoni; while at Ekwendeni, even during the first days of teaching when curiosity was at its height, the children of Chief Mtwalo were among the small number not attending. The first pupils became in their turn the first teachers, and then the first converts. When Steele in 1892 performed the second baptismal service in Ngoniland, eight of the nine converts were teachers, and the ninth was the wife of Mawelero Tembo.[153]

Even in the 1890s, however, the ambiguity in attitude of Ngoni authorities was beginning to wear thin. If members of the Jere clan were among the most resolute in opposing missionary advances as likely to destroy the integrity of the kingdom and undermine military values, they were also those most closely in touch with the missionaries – with the exception of the converts and teachers – and those whom the missionaries were most anxious to influence: 'if we can get teachers of a high "tshibango" [caste],' wrote Elmslie, 'so much the better'.[154] By July 1888 one member of the royal clan was serving as a cook at Njuyu. In November 1889 he became a teacher, and was baptised with the other teachers two and a half years later.[155] More significant, several of Mtwalo's children at Ekwendeni came under the mission's influence, notably Mzikuwola, who later took the name of Yohane, the eldest son of Mtwalo, though by a junior wife, and Muhawi, later known as Amon, the true heir. Both were attending school in October 1890 at the time of their father's death. In the succeeding interregnum the missionaries, under the misconception that Mzikuwola would succeed – or had succeeded – to the chieftaincy, quickly made him a teacher, a position not attained by his potentially more powerful half-brother till 1893. They also used their persuasion to such effect that Mzikuwola, though not yet baptised, began reading the Commandments to the people of his village, weighed his influence against the dispatch of war-parties, and only agreed to go out on a raid into the Luangwa valley in 1891 on the private understanding with McCallum that he personally would kill no one.[156] Though only eleven converts existed in Ngoniland in 1892, the close alliance forged by the missionaries with some members of the ruling sector ensured that when the breakthrough did come it should have the effect of perpetuating existing privilege rather than of replacing it by a new political order.

[153] Steele to Laws, 4 May 1892, NLS 7896

[154] Elmslie to Laws, 17 July 1888, NLS 7891

[155] ibid.; Elmslie to Laws, 22 November 1889, NLS 7892; Livingstonia Mission Report, 1893–4, 8.

[156] W. H. J. Rangeley, 'Mtwalo', *Nyasaland Journal*, VI, 1952, 65–8; McCallum to Laws, 27 December 1890, NLS 7894, 17 March 1891, 2 May 1891, NLS 7895; Steele to Laws, 13 January 1892, NLS 7896

North and south of the Lake: the Maseko Ngoni and the Ngonde

Livingstonia's success in northern Ngoniland throws into sharp relief the comparative failure of the mission in southern Ngoniland and at the north end of the lake. In both areas the mission's inability to establish strategically-placed bases in the pioneer years contributed to its lack of success. In both areas too, the mission failed to expose internal divisions among the Maseko Ngoni and the Ngonde of the same type as she had exploited successfully in northern Ngoniland.

On the surface, the Maseko Ngoni were even less of an homogeneous unit than were their kinsmen in the north. Following the death of the regent, Chidionga, in about 1876, the new young chief, Chikusi, was threatened by the secession of the regent's son, Chifisi. Disputes between the two erupted into open warfare in the 1880s, which continued off and on until the death of Chikusi's successor Gomani at the hands of the Protectorate forces in 1896. Both parties sought allies among the powerful, gun-owning Yao chiefdoms to their east and looked eagerly for aid to any other potential source of power. Both too suffered from the failure of the Maseko Ngoni to effectively assimilate their Chewa subjects. As Linden has noted: 'This clash of matrilineal Chewa with the patrilineal Ngoni must have generated more tensions within society than the assimilation of the patrilineal northern Tumbuka by the Mbelwa Ngoni in the North.' Chewa wives brought to their marriages strong ideas on family structure, which were increasingly to influence Ngoni cultural patterns.[157] When Laws visited Chikusi in 1878, he discovered that it was only among chiefs and councillors that Chingoni was spoken. Seven years later, Albert Namalambe observed that the Maseko 'are not like the people of Mombera. . .All the people speak Chinyanja and Chikusi knows Chinyanja well indeed'.[158]

Given these apparently favourable circumstances, the missionary response was painfully slow and hesitant. Livingstonia and Blantyre, the latter with more justification, perhaps, as the Maseko Ngoni occasionally raided into the lands of their parishioners in the Shire highlands, both claimed southern Ngoniland as being within their respective spheres of influence. Plans for forward advance from Blantyre, however, were thwarted in the mid 1880s by the refusal of the Church of Scotland subcommittee to sanction an increase in expenditure, and it was not till 1893 that two maiden ladies, Miss Bell and Miss Alice Werner privately

157 Ian Linden, 'The Maseko Ngoni at Domwe, 1870–1900' in Pachai, *Early History of Malawi*, 247

158 *FCSMR*, March 1879, 66; August 1886, 240

financed and themselves set up a small outstation, Panthumbi, aided by the African deacon, Harry Kambwiri.

Meanwhile, in 1887, the Free Church had founded its own first station in southern Ngoniland. Laws, who visited Chikusi late in 1886, noted that his village, high on the bleak, treeless Ncheu plateau overlooking the lake, was not ideally suited for a new base. But he recognised that 'at present to begin work in such a place without a station near the chief's headquarters would frustrate all our efforts to bring the gospel to the people owning the sway of Chikuse'.[159] However, the crisis in northern Ngoniland a year later prevented him joining the inexperienced Dr Henry on the latter's pioneering expedition. The result was that Henry, who disliked what he saw of the plateau, which he compared to a Scottish moor, complete with Scotch mist, turned instead to the Livlezi valley, about thirty miles from the chief kraal, an area populated largely by Chewa living under the general suzerainty of Chikusi but not incorporated fully in the Ngoni kingdom. There he built a school, attended in August 1889 by between 50 and 60 pupils, the number according to Elmslie being accounted for by 'a distribution of gifts to all who promised to attend school and church'. A few miles away he established two outstations, each manned by a single European.[160]

Despite the vigour with which these activities were organised, they had no significant effect upon the rulers of the kingdom, the chief and his councillors and personal following. To the geographical remoteness of the mission was added the comparative political homogeneity of Chikusi's state. His Chewa subjects exerted an increasingly strong cultural influence on the kingdom but the state remained a unitary one, where Chikusi's dominion after Chifisi's defection, was virtually unquestioned. Mbelwa's kingdom, by contrast, was of a segmentary nature with a number of semi-autonomous chiefs challenging the power of the paramount. As Henry admitted, external political relations disposed Chikusi to be friendly to the whites. Anxious for support in his war with Chifisi, now allied to the Yao chief Mponda, he told Henry in February 1890, 'that I should give him medicine to kill his opponents' and when this was refused, sent messengers to Dr Scott at Blantyre asking him to help.[161] But when he was again rebuffed no internal purchase existed to make his people wish to prolong their link with the Europeans. Failing to win

159 ibid., April 1887, 110

160 ibid., May 1888, 134–6; January 1888, 12–13; Elmslie to Laws, 15 March 1890, NLS 7893

161 Henry to Laws, 23 October 1889, NLS 7892; 10 February 1890, NLS 7893; *LWBMS*, August 1890

active British support, Gomani, who succeeded Chikusi in August 1891 turned instead to his old enemy, Mponda and by paying him heavily in slaves and ivory, succeeded in wooing him from his allegiance to Chifisi's successor, Kachindamoto, and in driving the latter down to the lake.[162]

A further consequence of his entanglement in a hostile trading system was that his relations with Europeans quickly deteriorated. By August 1892 rumours were reaching Livlezi of plans being hatched between Mponda and the chief's elder brother to destroy Livlezi station and thus open up an uninterrupted line of communications between the lakeshore villages and the plateau. Reports of British progress in the wars fought against the Yao were received with increasing alarm at Gomani's village, culminating in the circulation of the rumour in 1895 'that HM Commissioner would come and tie the chief up', and subsequently the mission, an emblem of European influence too little known on the plateau to be distinguished from the protectorate government, itself became an object of suspicion. Barriers were placed against pupils attending school and pressure was put upon the young men of the valley to go up and settle with the chief.[163] By 1893 the pull of the European economy was also having its effect. Some Ngoni sought employment in the Shire highlands as low-paid labourers, but Gomani, anxious to retain his military power, retaliated by forbidding his warriors to leave the kingdom and by sending his regiments into action against Kachindamoto. As the shortage of labour became more marked in the Blantyre district, planters complained bitterly at Gomani's action and the administration became more hostile. Nemesis in the shape of Johnston's tiny army was at hand.[164]

The same lack of foresight appeared in Livingstonia's attempts to establish a sound base at the northwest corner of the lake. The country there was divided roughly into two main districts, the lakeshore plain the home of the Ngonde, and on the further side of the Songwe river, of their Nyakyusa cousins, and the foothills to the west where lived Nyiha, Lambya and Wandya peoples.

Mweniwanda's, the village near which Bain settled in 1884 was situated within this latter district. Standing on a flat featureless plain, damp and marshy in the rainy season, its only merit as a pioneer station was its proximity to the unfinished, barely discernible Stevenson's Road. The station was 'foolishly isolated' from the lake, and its inhabitants, accord-

[162] *BCAG*, 14 December 1894

[163] Livingstonia Mission Report, July–December 1895, 3–4; January–July 1895, 1.

[164] *BCAG*, 28 June, 26 September, 14 December 1894; Stokes, 'Malawi Political Systems', 369

ing to Bain, were 'the "riddings" of 5 or 6 tribes whose only resemblance is that they are all alike faint-hearted and feeble'.[165] Within a radius of three to four miles at least three different languages were spoken; food supplies were hard to come by and, a final indignity, the proximity of the African Lakes Company depot meant that the station tended to be regarded 'as a mere appendage of the company' and the Sabbath, to Bain's horror, was frequently profaned by the arrival of carriers and the selling of ivory.[166]

It was not surprising, therefore, that Bain decided to move further east into Ngonde country in 1885. His departure was delayed, however, first by the sickness and death of two members of the staff early in 1887 and then by the outbreak of the 'Arab war' in the same year. During the 1880s, several Swahili traders, notably Mlozi, Kopa Kopa and Salim bin Najim, had begun to sell ivory on a considerable scale at the ALC's depot at Karonga. Because of the unreliable performance of the company's steamers, long delays often occurred in the arrival of European trade goods and the Swahili, therefore, built permanent stockaded settlements a few miles away from Karonga at which they could accommodate visiting caravans. As in Manganja country, thirty years earlier, the demands of traders for food supplies put great strains on the indigenous agricultural community. Quarrels between the Swahili and their Ngonde hosts culminated in July 1887 with the killing of an Ngonde headman. The Ngonde responded by demanding that Fotheringham, the Lakes Company's agent at Karonga, should honour the treaties made by the ALC two years earlier and lead an army against the Swahili.[167] Although he refused, Fotheringham's natural inclination was to support the Ngonde, especially after the quick successes of the Swahili who, by 13 October, had taken possession of the country to a depth of twelve miles from the lake and on 1 November sacked the village of Kyungu, the Ngonde paramount chief. The Swahili, under their leader Mlozi, went to considerable lengths to avoid antagonising the whites who supplied a convenient market for their ivory. But Fotheringham feared that their advance would strike a blow at the independence of the company which would jeopardise the whole position of western trade in Central Africa. According to Bain: 'If the white men remain it will be only by permission of the Arabs and

[165] Bain to Laws, 2 June 1887, NLS 7890

[166] Cross to Laws, 7 April 1887, NLS 7880; Cross to Laws, 26 December 1889; Bain to Laws, 30 May 1885, Shepperson Collection

[167] Bain to Laws, 12 August 1887, NLS 7890. Useful accounts of the background to the Arab War can be found in Wright and Lary, 'Swahili Settlements', 561–70 and in H. W. Macmillan, 'Notes on the origins of the Arab War' in Pachai, *Early History*

on payment of powder, cloth and caps.'[168] Fortheringham therefore gave sanctuary to Ngonde fleeing to the station and went to the aid of Ngonde villages near to Karonga. By the end of November, the Swahili–Ngonde war had become a Swahili–European one, exalted in the eyes of the whites involved into an anti-slavery crusade. Company agents were joined by a miscellaneous collection of adventurers – South African mercenaries, a big-game hunter, a medical missionary and a love-sick Indian Army officer (Frederick Lugard). The Swahili in their turn made use of Henga mercenaries, who had entered Ngonde country as refugees from the Ngoni about 1881 and who subsequently employed Ngoni tactics in raids for food on various Nyakyusa villages.[169]

One effect of the war was to bring missionary work almost to a standstill. Chirenje (Mweniwanda's) lost one missionary in October 1887, when Fotheringham persuaded Bain to join him at Karonga, and the other in April 1888 when Cross departed to act as surgeon for the expedition raised to fight Mlozi. Henceforth it was left in the hands of a small group of untrained African agents, with only occasional fleeting visits of inspection by Europeans. By February 1889 it was so much neglected that Bain doubted whether the inhabitants could even understand the Sabbath services held there. War and hunger forced many neighbouring Wandya to flee elsewhere. Others took refuge in the mission stockade under the leadership of the Free Church agent, Pemba, only to be driven out by Robert Gossip in August 1890.[170] By 1910, all that remained of the station was 'one school poorly attended and two lonely graves in the bush'.[171]

Meanwhile Bain, after a brief rest at Bandawe, had returned north in August 1888 and as part of his new policy of breaking away from the company and following a distinctly missionary line, prospected up into Nyakyusa country, eventually fixing on a site in Ukukwe at Kararamuka's village, in the hill country near Tukuyu, later to become the central station of the Rungwe district of Tanganyika. In 1890, following the publication of the Anglo-German agreement delimiting the Nyasa–Tanganyika boundary along the line of the Songwe river, the Free Church home authorities made much of the fact that this agreement involved 'cutting in two our Mission field and stations'; an opinion corroborated by the historian J. Scott Keltie, who claimed that 'British missionaries had

[168] Bain to Laws, 13 October 1887, NLS 7890

[169] Wright and Lary, 563–4. See also F. D. Lugard, *The Rise of Our East African Empire*, London 1893, vol. 1, 66–76

[170] Gossip to Laws, 11 August 1890, NLS 7893

[171] *FCSMR*, June 1910, 258

been at work for years' in what became the German sphere.[172] In fact the mission's influence north of the Songwe was virtually non-existent. Kararamuka attempted to involve Bain in local politics but was rebuffed by the missionary, who eventually departed from Ukukwe in April 1889 after a bare eight months' residence. Cross followed him to the village in September, but after a few days decided that the danger of attack there from Arabs was too great to risk the settlement of a white missionary, and therefore quickly withdrew. Once negotiations with Germany were in the air the Home Committee grasped the political importance of having some representative at the north end, and Robert Gossip was sent up in August 1890, only to reach Ukukwe after the Anglo-German agreement had been signed, and only shortly before the sub-committee decided to restrict Livingstonia's activities to the British sphere.[173]

The most suitable new site now appeared to be Karonga, where Cross, during six months in 1889 had taught three hundred Ngonde refugees, and where the ALC agent, Kydd, assisted in building a school outside the Company's stockade in 1891. At first, however, Cross was sent on a new tour of exploration which took him, in clear contravention of his instructions to go no further than the south bank of the Songwe, on to the north, German side at Uwandali. Routed from there early in January 1892 he turned to Ngerenge, some thirteen miles north west of Karonga, not far from Kyungu's traditional capital of Mbande. This too proved to be imperfectly situated, for it was isolated from the main trade routes into the interior, and yet near enough to Karonga to be supervised from there. When Laws in 1894 got wind of a plan for Roman Catholic White Fathers to occupy Karonga he sent George Aitken to take the site before them. When he was joined by Cross in 1895 Karonga was already becoming the centre of missionary activity in the district with services being held in four outlying Ngonde villages. Thirteen years after James Stewart first started work at the north end, with a trail of four abandoned stations left behind, the mission at last set down to evangelistic and educational work.[174]

[172] Dr Smith to Sir Percy Anderson, 20 June 1890, NLS 7774; J. Scott Keltie, *The Partition of Africa*, London, 1895 (2nd edn), 264

[173] Bain to Laws, 23 March 1889, Cross to Laws, 5 September 1889, NLS 7892; Smith to Ewing, 27 May 1890, NLS 7774; Gossip to Laws, 5 November 1890, NLS 7894. See also S. R. Charsley, *The Princes of the Nyakyusa*, Nairobi, 1969, 98–9

[174] Cross to Laws, 18 September 1891, NLS 7895, to members of the Livingstonia sub-committee, 23 August 1894, NLS 7878, to Smith, 2 November 1894, NLS 7878; Livingstonia Mission Report, January–June 1895, 21; July–December 1895, 22

If the extraordinary vicissitudes suffered by Livingstonia explain her poor progress at the north end up to 1894, the tardiness of her later development there must be seen largely in the light of the character of Ngonde society. On a superficial level it might have been expected that the Ngonde, attacked and defeated by the Arabs and their Henga supporters, would have proved as susceptible to missionary influence as the Tonga at Bandawe. But even after the Karonga station had been firmly established the reverse appears to have been true. At the end of 1894 Ngerenge and Karonga between them boasted a total of three Ngonde communicants and some 150 pupils attending school. Three years later it was noted that the Ngonde were 'leaving themselves behind', most of the people attending school in the Karonga district being members of the minority Henga community who 'come to school to get sufficient education to enable them to be successful traders'.[175] By 1911, Henga teachers, using the Henga language, virtually monopolised Livingstonia's educational work in the north as well as carrying out the bulk of its evangelistic teaching there. A mission report noted the contrast in emphatic terms:

> The Henga are a keen, vigorous, progressive people; the great majority of the church members are from amongst them; their schools well attended, the pupils alert, and the boys and girls in about equal numbers. The Gonde, on the other hand, are slow to move, extremely conservative, and suspicious of the new movements going on all around them.[176]

As late as 1925, D. R. Mackenzie was still claiming of the Ngonde:

> They have never attached themselves to the Europeans as many of the surrounding tribes have done. . .Educationally, too, they are less advanced. . .Nor have they supplied, in any numbers, the trained assistants in mission work who form one of the principal successes of Missions among other tribes.[177]

One reason for this would appear to lie, paradoxically, in the comparative isolation of the Ngonde and their freedom from external attacks. The Arab raids were savage and destructive, but they were of short duration, beginning in 1887 after the first European had settled at Karonga, and continuing sporadically from 1888 when the Company went on to the offensive with their Ngonde and Nyakyusa allies, exerting pressure on the Arab stockades rather than themselves being besieged. Some years earlier, at the time of Zwangendaba's march north, the

[175] ibid., 1894, 10; 1899–1900, 17

[176] ibid., 1911, 38

[177] D. R. Mackenzie, *The Spirit-Ridden Konde*, London, 1925, 37

Ngonde suffered even more severely, when after successfully repulsing the Ngoni on three occasions they were finally forced to submit.[178] But here again the period of submission was comparatively short. After Mbelwa had led his followers south into Henga country Ngoni pressure slackened off, and though one spectacular raid took place on a village near Karonga in 1893, the main targets of the Ngoni were the Tumbuka and Henga further south. In the same way attacks by Bemba marauders across the Tanganyika plateau frequently disrupted the economy of the Mambwe, Namwanga and Wandya, but affected the Ngonde hardly at all.[179] Kerr Cross specifically commented on the amazing contrast between the people of Mweniwanda's country and the Tanganyika plateau on the one hand and the Nyakyusa in the hills to the north-east on the other: 'While the one [the Wandya etc.] live in stockaded villages and drag out a miserable existence the other are a free noble people, unconquered, fearing no enemy, and stalk about amid their banana groves and herds of cattle.'[180]

It is true that the Ngonde were considerably more exposed than their Nyakyusa kinsmen, hidden from unfriendly neighbours by mountains on three sides, the lake on the other. But it is evidence of their considerable political security that while almost all the peoples of the Tanganyika plateau lived behind stockades, often hidden in thorn thickets, the Ngonde lived in open villages that were the admiration of all travellers who visited them. Entering a Ngonde village near the lake shore in December 1882, Frederick Morrison was

> put . . . in mind of Paradise . . . O how pretty. For cleanliness and beauty I never saw aught to equal it. The houses were not packed together as in most villages, each one had its own little court, which contained the cow house, poultry house and dwelling house. Houses were round and about seventy-five inches high to wall top with a very steep roof. The wall tapered out towards the top and the bamboos of which it was made were all ornamented between each other by nicely-shaped pieces of hard clay . . . There are also a few very large trees in the village, under these were numbers of cattle seeking shelter from the sun, a few of them had bells round their neck, the bells were made of two pieces of iron, placed in such a position that when the cow moved the pieces struck against each other. I passed a place where a woman was busy milking. I stopped to have a look and was presented with a good drink of milk . . . I had

178 G. Wilson, *Constitution of Ngonde*, 28–9; Mackenzie, 175–6

179 *Central Africa*, April 1893, 50–1; Roberts, *Bemba*, 142–51

180 Cross to Laws, 26 September 1888, NLS 7891

> a very long walk through a number of houses and courts and must say that for cleanliness they could not be surpassed.[181]

Bain found villagers of Wandya origin 'a cowardly and terror striken people', dominated by the Bemba, but the Ngonde, he told Cross, were 'a truly noble people'. On the eve of the Arab war he described them as 'vigorous and united', and for that reason argued that the mission should settle among them.[182]

Thanks to these conditions, the Ngonde managed to retain substantially undamaged a social and economic system of considerable self-sufficiency well into the British era. Whereas the economic resources of most African societies were meagre and their eagerness to acquire European merchandise correspondingly great, the Ngonde were blessed, though less fruitfully than the Nyakyusa, with a fertile soil upon which fixed, as opposed to shifting, agriculture was practised, where banana groves flourished and where thriving herds of cattle were maintained. Salt, iron and pots, among a variety of wares, were traded to the Ngonde in exchange for food prior to the 1880s, but little ivory was sold, even to Mlozi after he had established his stockade, with the result that the ending of the ivory trade only marginally affected Ngonde economic and political structures.[183]

The religious position of the Kyungu was also a barrier to penetration; though not, it was to be proved later, an insoluble one. Although the Kyungu, thanks to his control of the ivory trade had emerged from religious seclusion before his first contacts with Europeans to play the part of a secular ruler, he remained the spiritual paramount for his people, holding in his person their health and unity. If the Kyungu was wounded Ngonde as a whole suffered. In the pre-European era his nobles might put him to death to preserve the strength of their land. His power was based as much on his religious as on his economic position. Droughts, comparatively infrequent in Ngonde, were believed to result from the action of a Kyungu living or dead; when they occurred, his nobles and sub-chiefs visited him at his capital, Mbande, from all over the country, bringing gifts and soliciting aid.[184] To an extent greater than in any other society the mission worked among, Livingstonia in forwarding the claims

181 Morrison Diaries entry for 16 December 1882

182 Bain to Laws, 2 June 1887; Cross to Laws, 7 April 1887, NLS 7890

183 D. Kerr Cross, 'Crater Lakes North of Lake Nyasa', *Geographical Journal*, v, (January–June 1895), 116; Christopher St John, 'Kazembe and the Tanganyike–Nyasa Corridor, 1800–1890', in Richard Gray and David Birmingham (ed.), *Pre-Colonial African Trade*, London, 1970, 208–10; Kalinga, 'Ngonde of Northern Malawi', 146–50, 201

184 G. Wilson, 29–35; Mackenzie, 69–8

of Christianity on the Ngonde was striking at the basis of the traditional ruler's power and of the unity of the tribe.

But perhaps the greatest strength of Ngonde society lay in its lack of friction with the Europeans. Elsewhere, the chief barriers against missionary progress were provided by economic or social activities – the slave trade, raids for captives – which were opposed as much by the advancing colonial forces as they were by the mission. Where peaceful influence failed to reform them, military powers were becoming increasingly available as a sure alternative, and once they had disappeared the need for new functions and opportunities, supplied in many cases through the mission, became much more apparent. The Ngonde, however, were allies rather than enemies of the Europeans, warriors who had no fundamental need to go to war, traders whose political institutions undoubtedly suffered in the long term by the cutting off of the east coast ivory trade, but who appear to have made a short-term transition without strain. Eventually the attractions of wage labour in a European-based economy, reinforced by the practical necessity of meeting hut tax demands, would seduce almost all young men away from home for a while. But that was for the future. In the 1890s the continuing vitality and completeness of Ngonde village life militated against change.

5

Popular Christianity and the making of a new elite, 1891–1914

The extension of British colonial rule to northern Malawi took place through a series of small wars fought between 1891 and 1898 and resulted in the establishment of a network of tiny government stations – five in all for the whole area north of Kasungu by 1905. Most of the agricultural societies connected with the mission accepted the transition comparatively easily. Ngonde headmen, having actively supported the forces of Harry Johnston in their final attack on the Arabs at Karonga in 1895, witnessed without demur the establishment of a government post there. Tonga chiefs who signed treaties with the ALC in 1885, repeated the performance for Johnston four years later. Some of them petitioned for the appointment of a British magistrate to the country in 1894 and again in 1897 – an indication perhaps that with the mission's withdrawal from the field of secular politics an opening still remained for a neutral third party to be used in settling disputes.[1]

For the northern Ngoni, however, as for all the intruding peoples of Malawi, the extension of British power offered a challenge to which they could accommodate themselves only with difficulty. Despite the striking changes effected through missionary contact in the 1880s, the revolution in their society was not complete when H. H. Johnston took up the reins of administration. With the death of Mbelwa in August 1891 and the subsequent growth of disunity within the kingdom in the four years' interregnum prior to Chimtunga's accession to the paramountcy, the likelihood of direct confrontation appeared to most observers to be great.[2] A marked increase in sporadic raiding expeditions took place in 1892 and

[1] Johnston to Salisbury, with enclosures, 3 January 1896. *Correspondence respecting Operations against Slave Traders . . . 1896*, Cmd. 7925; West Nyasa Note-Book; Johnston to Rosebery, 14 March 1894, FO 2/66; Edwards to Johnston, 31 March 1897, Johnston Papers JOI/I/I

[2] Rangeley, 'Mtwalo', 67–8; Steele to Laws, 13 January 1892, NLS 7896; *Central Africa*, August 1896, 136

1893, and these led even some of Livingstonia's agents to demand the destruction of the Ngoni kingdom.[3] That this was avoided in the early 1890s can be accounted for largely by circumstances beyond the control of the Ngoni – the remoteness of their homeland from the seats of administrative and economic power and the fact that, unlike their southern cousins near Dedza, they placed no obstacle in the path of labour recruitment for European plantations. A further factor was the necessary embarrassment involved for any colonial regime in intervening forcibly in an area where mission stations were already well established. This latter point, according to Johnston, was uppermost in his decision, after the defeat of the north-end Arabs, not to turn against the Ngoni at once but to deal with the Chewa chief Mwase Kasungu instead.[4] And when Mwase Kasungu had been defeated and his headman Chabisa had fled to Ng'onomo for protection, it was only Elmslie's opposition to the plans of the Collector at Nkota Kota for a punitive raid and his ability to get Ngoni chiefs to send letters to the Consul-General professing friendship that persuaded Johnston not to intervene unless directly provoked.[5]

In the breathing space thus provided the Ngoni witnessed repeated demonstrations of the superiority of British arms, not only in the campaign against the Arabs and Mwase Kasungu, but also against Gomani's Ngoni in 1896 and against Mpezeni's Ngoni two years later. Whether the lesson to be drawn from the expeditions was the futility of armed resistance or the need to resist on a wider scale than before was not at once apparent. While some chiefs, notably those in close contact with the mission, favoured conciliation, others, headed by Ng'onomo looked instead to the re-establishment of links between the various Ngoni groups, and particularly with Mpezeni.[6] But even at this stage Ng'onomo combined defiance with a desire to negotiate and in 1897 sent a present of ivory to the Collector at Nkota Kota as a token of his friendship.[7]

With the defeat of Mpezeni he repudiated any connection between them and turned decisively to a British alliance. So great was now the apprehension of the northern Ngoni that when Major Harding's expedition landed at Bandawe in June or July 1898 many feared that the administration had designs upon them and sought to escape by fleeing to

[3] See the remarks of Kerr Cross, *Central Africa*, April 1893, 50–2

[4] *Report . . . on the Trade and General Condition of the British Central African Protectorate*, 1895–6, Cmd. 8254, 13

[5] Elmslie to Dr Smith, 24 June 1896, NLS 7879; Swann to Laws, 14 February 1897, Laws's Papers. Johnston's reply is quoted in Fraser, *Primitive People*, 239

[6] Swann to Laws, 14 February 1897, Laws's Papers EUL

[7] *Aurora*, June 1898, 24

the lake and west to the Luangwa valley.[8] In involving themselves in a wage economy the young men of warrior age were implicitly rejecting raiding as a primary occupation, a point clearly made in the 1890s when, following Mpezeni's request to join him against the whites, a section among them proved to be the most resolute opponents of the resumption of warfare.[9]

The fact that direct conflict was averted, even at this period, only by the missionary presence is striking evidence of the importance of European attitudes in determining whether or not African societies would openly resist their advance. Hitherto the absence of European economic interests among them had gone far to explain why the northern Ngoni were left undisturbed. From 1898, however, a trickle of gold-prospectors and cattle-dealers, anxious to recoup losses they had suffered in Southern Rhodesia, began to push into the northern highlands. They were followed, though at a distance, by British administrative agents, who having established a government post at Nkata Bay in 1897, circumscribed the Ngoni's freedom of action by refusing to recognise their rights of suzerainty over Tumbuka subjects spreading south in search of new land. From 1903 Ngoni and Tumbuka alike were authorised to bring their disputes direct to the *Boma* (government office) at the lake. The next year parties of Yao policemen were sent deep into Ngoniland to collect taxes and to burn the villages of those who would not pay.[10]

The inevitable reaction to the extension of the trading frontier came in 1899 when the activities of the notorious trader, W. R. Ziehl, in commandeering cattle without payment so enflamed the Ngoni against him that only the swift intervention of Donald Fraser prevented an expedition being sent in pursuit. Five years later further friction resulted from the attempt of police to raise taxes within the watershed of the Rukuru, and once again Fraser's intervention was required to dissuade the police from intervening further.[11] By this time land under Ngoni control had become so wasted that thousands of them, headed by Tumbuka subjects, were beginning to move south beyond the boundaries previously established by H. H. Johnston. It was this move which created the conditions in which on 2 September 1904 an agreement between the Ngoni and the new Commissioner, Alfred Sharpe, was finally achieved.

At a time when the positive effects of resistance are being rediscovered

8 ibid. August 1898, 32

9 Elmslie to Hetherwick, 27 March 1915, Hetherwick Papers

10 *Aurora*, April 1901, 4; Monthly Report, Nkata, January 1904, MNA NNC3/4/1; Fraser, *Primitive People*, 240

11 *Aurora*, June 1899, 21–3; Fraser, *Primitive People*, 103–11

it is well to emphasise the substantial benefits gained by the Ngoni from negotiation. On a purely negative side the 1904 treaty ensured that the transition of power would take place as painlessly as possible. Taxation was not to be commenced before January 1906; none of the old quarrels between the Ngoni and other peoples was to be pursued further; no Tonga or Yao police were to be used in Ngoniland; Ngoni police were to be recruited as far as possible; and six chiefs, headed by Chimtunga were to receive subsidies. More positively, the major interests of the Ngoni were largely respected. Cattle, Sharpe promised, would not be confiscated for offences; no sudden scattering of subjects beyond their chiefs' control would be allowed; the Ngoni would be free to hunt on the bend of the Rukuru river. Above all, land would be found for those who wanted it beyond the limits of their own now exhausted domain. The Ngoni people would be preserved as a nation rather than destroyed.[12]

Such a settlement could hardly have been achieved if the extension of British rule had not been accompanied by the expansion of the colonial economy. The importance of the demands for labour from the ALC in the late 1880s cannot be over-emphasised. They provide the crucial attraction triggering off the first wave of migration from the lake. From 1891, however, this narrow base of economic activity was considerably widened. The number of European settlers increased from 57 in July 1891 to 237 by March 1894 and land under settler cultivation rose from 1600 to 5700 acres by 1896. At the same time, cultivated products – at first coffee and, after 1904, cotton and tobacco – slowly replaced gathered products – notably ivory and wild rubber – as the major items for export.

South of the lake, to which this activity was almost entirely confined, Yao and Manganja cultivators were able to compensate to some degree for the gradual decline of the ivory trade – still worth perhaps £37 000 in 1893 – by taking an auxiliary role in the plantation economy.[13] Some successfully grew food supplies for the labour forces of the Shire highlands; others collected wild rubber, oil seeds and beeswax for sale to Indian traders. Others grew cotton with some government support, especially in the Upper and Lower Shire districts from 1904.[14]

[12] The only full record of the agreement that I know is to be found in the Mzimba District Book dated 24 October 1904. Another less detailed account appears in Sharpe to CO, 14 October 1904, CO 525/3

[13] See *Report on First Three Years Administration . . . of . . . British Central Africa*, 1894, 16

[14] *Report on . . . the British Central African Protectorate*, 1895–6, Cmd. 8254, 4; 1897–8, Cmd. 9048, 10–11; 1902–4, Cmd. 2242, 13; 1905–6, Cmd. 2684, 10–12; P. T. Terry, 'The Rise of the African Cotton Industry in Nyasaland, 1902–18', *Nyasaland Journal*, xv (January 1962), 60

Further north, however, indigenous producers were hampered by the lack of local markets for foodstuffs, resulting from the almost complete absence of European economic concerns with the exception of the ALC's rubber estate at Vizaro and a few scattered plantations. They also found that the unsatisfactory soil of much of the north and the poverty of communications made the development of successful cash crops difficult to achieve. North of the Dwanga river, much of the western hinterland was made inaccessible to lake transport by the steep scarp of the Vipya plateau which plunges to a narrow litoral. With the silting up of the Shire river, even those areas linked to the lake could derive little benefit from water communications as long as rail transport was lacking from the south end. But after 1905, the British metropolitan government regarded Nyasaland as being more important as a producer of labour for the southern African mines than as a producer of raw materials and hence showed little interest in helping to finance a development which would have the indirect effect of raising the price of labour by providing migrants with a viable alternative in their own country.[15] The result was that Nyasaland, unlike British West African territories, was called upon to pay the full price for the construction of its own railway. In the absence of adequate funds, the line from Port Herald to Blantyre was completed only in 1908 and was not extended to Chindio on the lower Zambesi till 1916. Not until 1936 was a rail link established between the lake and the coast.

In favourable areas, lakeside dwellers such as the rice-growing Chewa of Nkota Kota and the Ngonde of the north were able to surmount these obstacles and become cash crop farmers. The Ngonde traded cattle to the Shire highlands in the 1890s only a few years after the rinderpest epidemic of 1892, which wiped out up to ninety per cent of their herds, and later grew cotton successfully until its cultivation was banned in 1927. Elsewhere African producers, whether Ngoni, Tonga or Tumbuka, were forced to turn to the escape route of migrant labour in order to acquire the increasingly diverse goods that now were in demand. The imposition of hut taxes from 1897 in Tongaland and from 1906 among the Ngoni undoubtedly intensified the search for paid employment as did the decision of the government from 1903 to allow labour recruitment to take place for the Transvaal mines. But these latter developments gave strength to an existing movement rather than creating it from scratch. While firm figures are impossible to provide it is clear that large numbers

[15] B. S. Krishnamurthy, 'Economic Policy, land and labour in Nyasaland, 1890–1914' in Pachai, *Early History of Malawi*, 396–7; Leroy Vail, 'The Making of an Imperial Slum: Nyasaland and its Railways, 1895–1935', *JAH*, XVI, 1, 1975

of Tonga – anything between two and five and a half thousand in 1894 – were working in the Shire highlands years before the imposition of tax, and more had begun the long trek into southern Africa in search of higher wages. By 1903 the collector at Nkata Bay was commenting on the yearly exodus of Tonga to Salisbury, while a year later they were going 'by the hundred' for work south of the Zambesi. By 1909 Hetherwick was calling attention 'to the state of affairs in Atonga Country where hardly an able-bodied man can be found . . . all the men having left for South Africa.'[16] It is a significant feature of this early migration that in contrast to the situation in the Central Province, very few Tonga workers were recruited by the Witwatersrand Native Labour Association in the government-sponsored tours made by its agents in 1904 and 1905. Despite the often perilous conditions found on the long overland route between Chinteche and Fort Jameson (Chipata) and from there to Salisbury and further south, most Tonga preferred to retain a certain freedom of choice as to where they worked and for how long. They thus retained a degree of personal initiative within a predominantly alien culture.[17]

As for the Ngoni, wage labour provided the only available alternative to an indigenous economy in the process of collapse. The rinderpest epidemic which destroyed most of their cattle in 1893 was only the most dramatic of a series of blows affecting local economic patterns.[18] Equally important was the end of raiding – marked by the disappearance of stockaded villages among the agricultural people of the lake shore from about 1900 and the gradual scattering of dispersed groups of Tonga and Tumbuka away from places of sanctuary.[19] In the Henga valley, near Khondowe, the new centre of the Livingstonia Mission, the process was particularly marked. In the mid 1890s, so one missionary commented, 'the population in this locality was thin and very unevenly distributed . . . From Kondowi to within three hours travelling of Ekwendeni, a journey

[16] *BCAG* 23 May 1894, 4; Laws to Smith, 10 September 1894, NLS 7877; C. Knipe to acting Governor, Zomba, 11 January 1903 in *Correspondence relating to the Recruitment of Labour in the Nyasaland Protectorate for the Transvaal and Southern Rhodesian Mines*, 1908, Cmd. 3993; Annual Report of Collector, West Nyasa District, 1902–3, MNA NNC3/1/1. Laws to Hetherwick, 21 July 1904, Hetherwick Papers. Summary of Proceedings of 4th Session of the Legislative Council, 2–5 November 1909, *Nyasaland Government Gazette*, 101

[17] Monthly Reports, West Nyasa, August, November 1904; December 1905, MNA NNC3/4/1; Annual Report, Collector West Nyasa, 1903–4, MNA NNC3/1/1

[18] Laws to Smith, 10 September 1894, NLS 7877

[19] Livingstonia Mission Report, 1901, 17, 1902, 46

of over two days, not a single hut was to be seen.' From 1898 to 1901, however,

> a rapid increase of redistribution of the population proceeded. The Poka left the perches which they had dug out for themselves on the steepest slopes of the Nyika Plateau to build on the flats, forming along with the Henga who were making back for their old home in the Rukuru plain a long straggling of villages parallel to the path going to Ekwendeni . . . The visible population of 1895 was more than doubled.[20]

New settlement patterns resulted in the interpenetration of natural and managed ecosytems, the ideal environment for animal diseases, and the game population increased as government regulations were enforced to reduce the use of firearms by Africans.[21] In 1910, fear of sleeping sickness was so great in Northern Rhodesia, that the whole of the basin of the Luangwa valley was declared a prohibited area for travellers. By 1924, belts of tsetse fly had cut off Ngoniland from the south, thus preventing the sale of Ngoni cattle, which were now at least as numerous as before the rinderpest epidemic.[22]

In these conditions it is not surprising that the Ngoni, as early as 1899 were said to have transferred their early interest in employment under the mission into a preference for the main industrial centres of labour. Workers by 1901 were reported to be departing in all directions, from Salisbury to Tanganyika, and in such strength that the missionaries believed that the introduction of a labour tax would not significantly alter the numbers involved. In 1902 it was accepted that young men of working age would spend most of the year out of their own locality.[23]

In instrumental terms, the mass migration of workers was probably of less importance to Livingstonia than the opening up of a limited number of opportunities for skilled employment in the administration and under traders and planters. Most work in the mines, plantations and armed forces could be accomplished as well without a mission education as with one. Indeed, many government agents and settlers in the 1890s shared a prejudice against African Christians and advised each other: 'Whatever

20 Livingstonia Education Diary, Report for 1904

21 See John Iliffe, 'Ecological Crisis and Economic Change in Sukamaland, Tanzania', 1870–1970, unpublished paper, Institute of Commonwealth Studies, London, 1975

22 Livingstonia Mission Report, 1910, ix and 2–3; Norman H. Pollock, *Nyasaland and Northern Rhodesia: Corridor to the North*, Pittsburgh, 1971, 321

23 *Aurora*, December 1899, 45; August 1901, 28–9; Livingstonia Mission Report, 1901, 15; 1902, 31

you do, don't have boys from the Missions.'[24] Yao Muslims from the lake were regarded in conventional colonial circles as being better soldiers and servants than Tonga educated at Livingstonia.

Despite these attitudes, Nyasaland provided somewhat greater opportunities for Africans with education than did the countries immediately to the south. The number of white artisans was severely restricted, both by the lack of mineral resources to attract them into the country, and by deliberate Government policy. As late as 1921 missionaries, planters and government officials between them provided 647 out of the Protectorate's 876 male employed Europeans. There were only thirty-two European clerks in the country, twenty-seven storekeepers, eight mechanics and three printers.[25] This gap Johnston had hoped to fill by attracting Indians, not only as peasant farmers and traders, but in intermediary posts as well 'such as store clerks, telegraph operators and hospital assistants'.[26] In practice while Indian traders spreading northward from Port Herald ousted the ALC from many outlying districts, and established their ascendancy over trade with Africans, the same lack of financial resources which prevented the significant encouragement of African agriculture also made it impossible for the government to bring in alien colonists on a large scale. A further hindrance was the complaint of many missionaries, expressed most fiercely by Hetherwick, that: 'Only a Christian man can govern Africa, and we cannot have Hindus caste or no caste, Brahmins or Mahommedans set over the development of a people whom Providence has entrusted to our discipline and training.'[27] Together, these led to Sharpe's conclusion of 1909: 'There is practically no opening nor demand in Nyasaland for either indentured or unindentured Indians.' The census of 1921 revealed only 563 Asians in the country, 82 more than a decade earlier. Of those employed all but 105 were in trade, and only 30 were clerks.[28]

With neither Europeans nor Indians to hand, posts of middle-grade administrative responsibility fell open to Africans in Malawi earlier and in greater numbers than anywhere else in Central Africa. As early as 1897 Law noted that 'from many quarters, comes the demand for natives who can be put in positions of trust and responsibility of a subordinate nature'.

[24] Quoted in J. Wordsworth Poole to his father, 13 May 1895, MNA PO1/1

[25] Census of the Nyasaland Protectorate for 1921

[26] *Report on First Three Years Administration ... of ... British Central Africa*, 1894, 30; Johnston to Kimberley, 1 June 1895, FO 2/88

[27] *LWBCA*, January 1895

[28] Sharpe to Secretary of State for Colonies, 10 March 1909, CO 525/28; Census of the Nyasaland Protectorate, 1911 and 1921

Two years later a traveller from Southern Rhodesia contrasted the situation in Mashonaland, where an African mechanic was unknown, to that in Malawi where Africans were employed in a variety of trades. The government by 1905 employed Africans in a range of positions as clerks, interpreters, typists, telegraphists, and mechanics, and reported that they were 'after a year or two's training, almost as competent as the Indian Babu and much cheaper'.[29] The circumstances were being created in which Hetherwick on 20 February 1925 boasted of the success of the missions in meeting European demands for educated skilled labour without recourse to India or China:

> All the great Industrial and other undertakings, buildings, Railways, shipbuilding, road making, transport driving etc., have been accomplished by native skill under white supervision. Had Kenya adopted this policy they could have been saved their present troubles.[30]

He did not add, as he might have done, that wages for Africans in Nyasaland remained notoriously low so that most men of ambition eventually gravitated elsewhere.

In this situation Ngoni, Tonga and Tumbuka turned towards Livingstonia to obtain those skills which would enhance their value in the labour market. Only the Ngonde, so much better off economically in their own locality, were indifferent to the wares missionaries had to offer. 'Karonga,' Alexander Dewar remarked in 1899, 'is unique in one way – the children having to be hunted up daily to come to school.'[31] By that year the small Henga minority in the district who had formerly allied themselves with the Arabs were attempting to utilise education for trading purposes with considerable success. Within a decade it was their language that was being largely used in local schools.

The Ngonde were the exception. In Tongaland the number of schools increased from eighteen in the first half of 1895 to 53 in 1898, while the average attendance rose from 1600 to perhaps 5000. The introduction of school fees in that year brought the expansion in students to a sudden halt – during the next decade they tended to average between 3500 and 4000, but the number of schools continued to increase – up to 107 in 1906.[32] In Ngoniland the rate of expansion was even more dramatic. From 1893 when 630 pupils were enrolled in ten schools the numbers expanded so considerably that by 1898 the highest number attending in

[29] *Aurora*, August 1897, 25; August 1899, 26; *Report on . . . the British Central African Protectorate*, 1904–5, 26; 1905–6, 28

[30] Hetherwick to Blackwell, 20 February 1925, Hetherwick Papers

[31] Dewar to Smith, 30 October 1899, NLS 7882

[32] Livingstonia Mission Report, January–July 1895, 7; 1898–9, 15; 1906, 38

one day was 4040. The introduction of school fees plus the absence of any European able to speak Chingoni at the central stations hindered the advance in the next three years, but in 1901 fifty-five schools existed with an average of 2800 pupils. A few years later the southern sphere organised from the new station of Loudon, opened in 1902, was divided for administrative purposes from that run from Ekwendeni. So vigorously did it thrive that in 1904 it alone maintained 134 schools with up to 9000 pupils.[33] By 1909 150 out-schools were open there with 12 000 pupils connected, and Fraser, the missionary in charge, questioned 'whether there is another mission in the world with so great school systems attached to one station as you will find in the Livingstonia Mission. The remark,' he added, 'could be made in another form. How many missions in the world are as inadequately staffed as the Livingstonia Mission?'[34]

Fraser's query indicates a certain unease about the rapid expansion of educational facilities and the consequent decline in standards which was more than reciprocated by older colleagues who did not share with him his belief in the value of influencing the wider community rather than the individual. Kerr Cross, for example, did 'not think the system of opening a number of junior schools without efficient teachers a wise one . . . It is in the nature of our work to lay hold on the individual more than on the crowd.'[35] Elmslie too deprecated the rapidity of growth. 'From what I see here,' he wrote to Laws from Bandawe, 'I am convinced that to say we have three or four thousand scholars in attendance is simply leading people at home to a wrong conclusion. I find that not 10% of all these make any progress at all, i.e. they never enter what is called Standard 1.' What was needed, he believed, was a reduction in the number of out-schools, 'so [as to] permit . . . those who are sent out to teach there getting continuous instruction for a period of years'.[36]

But though the missionaries deplored such unrestrained growth, their powers of checking it in this new phase were very limited. Sharing a horror of any assistance that might tend to lead to pauperism, they had insisted from the earliest days on a substantial degree of self-support in the educational system. Charges were made for New Testaments and for textbooks from the 1880s and school-fees were introduced at Bandawe in 1898 and in Ngoniland in a more desultory manner in the same year. This policy held back expansion, leaving the appeal of free education a cogent attraction for large sectors of the population. Where it was

[33] ibid., 1901, 14; 1902, 31; 1904, 31
[34] ibid., 1909, 23
[35] ibid., July–December 1895, 24
[36] Elmslie to Laws, 22 October 1892, NLS 7896

accepted, however, the demand for schools, even where they were to be erected and maintained at African expense, far exceeded the ability of the mission to provide teachers to man them. In several places schools were erected without any prior mission request, and long before teachers could be found. To reverse so strong a current when financial support was in the process of becoming an African responsibility was not impossible but it would clearly have been injudicious.[37]

From the mid 1890s this educational explosion was being accompanied by an even more dramatic change – the widespread adoption of evangelical Christianity. To some extent, the new movement can be seen as part of the same process as the growing demand for mission schools. Village schools often served as village churches; village teachers were frequently village evangelists as well. The demand for literacy – the central attraction of the early educational system – was in part a demand for access to the Bible. The content of village education, once the alphabet had been mastered, consisted of selected translations into Chinyanja and Chingoni of Matthew's Gospel, the Ten Commandments, the Lord's Prayer and 'Harry's Catechism', a popular late Victorian devotional work. The only reader in Chinyanja available to advanced classes at Bandawe in 1894 was the New Testament, 'which therefore takes a place along with Genesis as the textbook which all aspire to read'. Education for many bush school pupils was essentially a matter of memorising texts. The feature which distinguished village teachers by 1910 was their encyclopaedic knowledge of the Bible and their ability to quote extensively from it.[38]

What this suggests is that conversion to Christianity was in part a response to the widening of the social scale which resulted from involvement in the colonial economy. Along with Horton, it is possible to argue that as long as the economy of the Tonga remained essentially a subsistence one, their religious preoccupations could be met largely through the veneration of spirits – the underpinners of the microcosm. As increasing numbers of Tonga became involved in migrant labour, these lesser spirits ceased to be of religious relevance and instead the Tonga turned towards the Supreme Being who could be worshipped as readily in the mining compound of South Africa as in the dispersed settlements of their homeland. As the Yao example demonstrates, such an extension of social scale did not necessarily imply the extension of mission Christianity. For those Africans involved through long-distance trade with the Swahili coast, Islam provided a more acceptable solution to their religious require-

[37] Livingstonia Mission Report, 1898–9, 13–15; 1908, 25; 1909, 23

[38] ibid., 1894; McCallum, 'Report on Ekwendeni to 1889', NLS 7892

ments.[39] For the Tonga, Tumbuka and northern Ngoni, however, economic change was itself in part a consequence of mission activity; diplomatic alliances with Livingstonia had already been cemented. When to these were added a significant improvement in evangelist techniques and a marked change in the character of Christian appeal, the result could not be in doubt. For the first time, Christianity spread as a genuinely popular movement.

The technical improvement was essentially a linguistic one. In his six years at Cape Maclear, Laws learnt a highly-anglicised form of Chinyanja, which he later employed as the main *lingua franca* among the Tonga, despite the doubts raised by several missionaries as to the wisdom of this course of action. The pioneer African agents, Fred Zarakuti, Albert Namalambe and the others, also usually spoke Chinyanja with the result that the Tonga rarely heard the Gospel preached in their own language. By the mid 1890s, however, two new developments had taken place. Firstly, a new missionary, A. G. Macalpine, broke away from the prevailing pattern by learning Chitonga, which he began to use regularly in his services from 1894. Secondly, Tonga students were employed increasingly as evangelists and were responsible for most of the early conversions. It was to the pioneer Tonga elders, Yakobe Msusa Muwamba, Noa Chiporuporu Ng'oma and Stefano Mujuzi Kaunda, rather than to the European missionaries, that inquiries concerning Christianity were usually directed.[40]

At the same time, the advent of a new younger generation of missionaries headed by Donald Fraser injected into Livingstonia's evangelical work a dramatic, emotional element which had previously not been present. From its foundation at the tail-end of Moody and Sankey's first and most successful visit to Scotland, Livingstonia had constantly tended towards revivalism in its spirit and methods. Many of its missionaries were themselves converted by Moody, or by his Scottish lieutenant, Henry Drummond, and typical Moody practices – the use of a harmonium at services at a time when in Scotland instrumental music was still generally deplored, and the emphasis on public testimony by the newly converted – were taken over and widely employed. The older missionaries, Laws and Elmslie, were quick to pounce on what they regarded as excessive emotionalism, however, and it was not till the arrival of Fraser and his peers that revivalism was given free play.[41] Fraser, at the time of his

[39] See Horton, 'African Conversion'; Alpers, 'Islam', 194–6

[40] Fotheringham to Laws, 24 September 1892, NLS 7896; Macalpine, 'Account of experiences with the Livingstonia Mission', undated article, Macalpine Papers

[41] It is significant that while Henry Drummond was regarded with

appointment in 1896 was already a well-known figure in evangelical circles. An eloquent speaker with a brilliantly vivid personality, he had been a leading light in the Student Volunteer Missionary Movement in Britain during his years at Glasgow University and chaired with great success a major missionary conference at Liverpool only a few months before his departure to Africa.[42] On his way up to Malawi in 1896, he held testimony meetings at South African universities which strikingly demonstrated the power of his preaching. From Wellington, he wrote: 'At the close of my address many a head was bending on the desks in great distress. I asked all who were anxious to follow me to the wood and talk it over. Very many came and for an hour they asked questions, candidly stating difficulties. Then we had prayer, but sometimes the prayers was [sic] almost drowned by the sobs of the anxious.'[43]

In Malawi this type of appeal quickly met with sensational results. A year before Fraser's arrival in the country a significant popular movement began in Tongaland which took on some of the characteristics of a witchcraft eradication movement. 'The most striking feature in the past half year,' Macalpine reported in July 1895, 'has been the most remarkable awakening of the people around to a deepened interest in the Gospel message.' Six months later, 'The very remarkable religious revival . . . is still with us.'[44] Tonga were flocking in large numbers to church services, audiences of over 1000 being common at Bandawe, and, as has been noted, there were vast increases in school attendance. Many Tonga were also now eager for baptism. Catechumens awaiting admission to the church increased in 1895 to over 300 and to over 600 a year later, while the hearers' class topped the 1500 mark. More significant was the interest in Christianity aroused in villages whose only contact with the mission was through itinerant evangelists. In 1897 it was reported, 'A great movement towards Christianity began in the northern part of the district in March.' The same year crowds of 2000 were attending meetings addressed by Fraser, who had come down from Ekwendeni to dispense the sacraments.[45]

Meanwhile what Macalpine described as 'the wonderful Revival of 1895, a movement towards Christ, which changed the character and out-

veneration by many of the younger missionaries, Elmslie believed him to be 'a humbug but a slashing swell and . . . spittle licker to Lord and Lady Aberdeen'. Elmslie to Laws, 21 December 1890, NLS 7894

42 A. R. Fraser, *Donald Fraser*, 22–39

43 Fraser to Dr Smith, 19 August 1896, NLS 7879

44 Livingstonia Mission Report, January–July 1895, 5; July–December 1895, 8

45 ibid., 1897–8, 19, 22

look of Tongaland', was spreading far beyond its borders.[46] At Ekwendeni in May 1898 a five day 'communion season' was held which attracted congregations of between three and four thousand and gave rise to intense evangelical fervour. 'Among some of the teachers God seemed to be moving mightily', wrote Fraser.

> At one of the evening meetings with them, after I had spoken of backsliding and the need of re-consecration, we had a time of open prayer. Man after man prayed making broken confessions of sin, some were sobbing aloud, others gave way to severe physical emotion and became hysterical.[47]

Some teachers, in the tradition of John the Baptist, spent nights in prayer out in the bush, and were rewarded with visions of 'bright angelic forms' which Fraser, now thoroughly alarmed, attempted to dispel through medicinal doses at the dispensary. In 1892 there had been only eleven converts in Ngoniland. In 1898, 195 adults were baptised in a day, and a year later 662 Church members took communion watched by crowds six or seven thousand strong. Even at the newly-opened Institution at Khondowe the same fervour prevailed. There in December 1901 evangelical services were held, in which Laws took no part, and Scottish teachers and Africans alike 'drew very near to Christ'. 'Testimony after testimony of blessing received was given', and in the atmosphere of 'a small Keswick' pupils turned to staff at all hours of day or night with queries and requests for spiritual aid.[48]

The amazing scenes of mass enthusiasm which marked the visit of the popular evangelist, Dr Charles Inwood, to the Livingstonia stations in 1910 were undoubtedly prepared for by the tradition of emotional evangelism established in earlier years. The equal success of Eliot Kamwana, the Watch Tower preacher, a few months earlier may also have been linked to the patterns of worship which Fraser encouraged.

The question of the wider effects of the popular explosion on Livingstonia's relations with neighbouring peoples can be answered only with diffidence in a work based largely on written material. From the late 1880s missionary strategy was dedicated to the spreading of influence over a wide area rather than to the creation of closed enclaves. The distinction between German missionaries among the Nyakyusa who sought to organise their converts in mission villages, and the Scots in Ngonde who recommended that Christians should remain in their own homes to

[46] Macalpine, undated article, Macalpine Papers

[47] Fraser to Smith, 16 May 1898, NLS 7881

[48] Fraser, *Primitive People*, 93; Fraser to Smith, 7 June 1899, NLS 7882; Livingstonia Mission Report, 1898–9, 111; 1901, 36–42

influence their neighbours has been pertinently made by Monica Wilson.[49] No schools for the sons of chiefs were specially established and so no formal alliances with particular Christian groups or tribal elites were expressly created. In practice, however, the breakdown of the isolated position of the missionary elite led, particularly in Ngoniland where succession tended to follow fairly straight-forward rules, to the substantial identification of leaders within the traditional political structure with the newly-educated elite. In June 1897 Muhawi (later called Amon), now a mission teacher, officially succeeded his father Mtwalo as ruler over the Ekwendeni segment, while his half-brother Mzikuwola (or Yohane), also a teacher, became one of his sub-chiefs. Impressed perhaps by Elmslie's warning that without education the sons of chiefs and councillors would decline to the level of slaves and carriers Marau, a further segment head, requested the teacher Makera Tembo in 1895 to reside at his village, where his eldest son put away his wives and was baptised two years later. Mperembe, Mbelwa's half-brother, praised the work of the teachers, though gaining little himself from education, while Chimtunga, the new paramount, received a modicum of instruction and sent his own son to school. By 1900, when at least four members of the Jere clan, including Muhawi, were teaching at Ekwendeni Central School the cycle had begun whereby members of the royal clan passed from school to Institution and became teachers, before entering the tribal authority structure where the social pressures upon them and particularly the need to take more than one wife led to their suspension from church membership, as Muhawi was suspended in 1906.[50]

But whether missionary education was related to status, as to some degree it was in Ngoniland, or to earlier alliances made by the mission with particular villages, as was the case with the Tonga, the fact remained that the political importance of mission teachers grew significantly as the European presence became more intense. Ngoni chiefs and Tonga alike, who formerly had sought the alliance only of white teachers, now turned to Africans to act as intermediaries in their relations with the wider world. Mawelero Tembo and his colleagues threw their weight successfully against the dispatch of a military expedition following the coronation of Chimtunga in 1897; they were consulted on matters affecting the action of the administration, particularly on doubtful court cases where an

[49] M. Wilson, *Good Company*, 42

[50] Livingstonia Mission Report, 1897–8, 11–12; July–December 1895, 12; 1906, 24; Elmslie, 'Report for Ngoniland District', 1895, NLS 7878; *Aurora*, June 1897, 22; August 1902, 84; personal communications from Rev. Z. P. Ziba and Rev. Charles Chinula

adverse decision could lead to Government intervention; and one of their number, David Zinyoka, acted as interpreter when Sharpe in 1904 held discussions with Ngoni chiefs.[51] Moreover, they took a line on European intrusion that brought them into conflict from time to time with members of yet another new authority structure, the police, and which won them a reputation as trouble-makers among Government officials. In Tongaland between 1903 and 1905 the 'very great influence' of mission teachers was blamed for the failure of labour recruitment campaigns. In Ngonde mission teachers were criticised for 'spreading foolish and false reports about the civil police, to whom they attribute every imaginable crime'. In Ngoniland mission teachers personally expostulated with the trader, W. R. Ziehl, when he tried to seize cattle from individuals who refused to part with them, and after 1904 spoke on occasions to the local magistrate, H. C. McDonald about 'civil evils that were hindering progress' and 'plans for the people'.[52] No less than in the 1880s they attempted a secular role alongside their educational one; but whereas, before, their attempts at interference only underlined the isolation of their position, now and increasingly into the 1920s, they came to conceive of themselves and to be accepted as spokesmen to the colonial authorities and as representatives of their people.

Up to 1894 Livingstonia's activities were confined to the Tonga and Ngoni/Tumbuka stations; to the small Karonga settlement, and to the newly-established Institution on the Khondowe plateau overlooking the lake. In that year, however, fears of the movement of White Fathers south of Lake Tanganyika led to the dispatch of Alexander Dewar to Mwenzo in the heart of Namwanga country, a site that was chosen partly because of its proximity to Bembaland and partly because it was situated near the British South Africa Company station of Fife and on what was still believed to be an important trade route into the interior.[53] Similar fears of UMCA encroachments from Nkota Kota led in November 1897 to the founding by five Tonga teachers of a permanent school at Kasungu, the headquarters of Mwase, the leading Chewa chief.[54] And this was followed

[51] Livingstonia Mission Report, 1897–8, 12; *Aurora*, October 1902, 86; personal communications from Rev. Z. P. Ziba; *FCSMR*, January 1905, 25

[52] Annual Report of the Collector, Nkata, 1903–4, MNA NNC3/1/1; Sharpe to FO, 19 May 1902, FO 2/606; Donald Fraser, *The Autobiography of an African*, London, 1925, 203

[53] Livingstonia Mission Committee Minutes, 13 March 1894; Appeal to the Students of the Free Church of Scotland Missionary Union, Glasgow University, 1896, 1–5

[54] Livingstonia Mission Committee Minutes, entries for 20 July 1897, 8

in 1899 by the dispatch of nine Ngoni teachers into the Luangwa valley and the establishment of three schools in Senga villages as the prelude to what was to become the most extended and ambitious missionary operation ever undertaken by Livingstonia, leading to the occupation of large tracts of territory in North-Eastern Rhodesia.[55]

On one level the reasons for expansion appear to lie in the intricacies of European mission strategy. The decade from the mid 1890s was a period of great missionary advance in which powerful societies of all denominations – the White Fathers, the London Missionary Society, the Dutch Reformed Church and others – pushed rapidly into the 'unoccupied' areas of Central Africa staking out claims for spheres of influence which would effectively exclude their rivals. Faced with the prospect of losing its 'hinterland' to Tractarian or Roman Catholic bodies, Livingstonia – which had hardly been threatened by missionary rivals up to then – reacted with alarm. All along the line from Mwenzo to Ngoniland and Kasungu, Macalpine reported in 1904, teachers and preachers were being sent out 'to claim the country for Christ and save it from Heathenism and the Pope'.[56] Where special features existed, like the presence in the Bemba of a powerful people whose conversion might be expected to influence the attitudes of their scattered neighbours, the motive for advance was yet more clear-cut. The struggle for Bembaland is one of the dominant themes of missionary history in that area.[57]

A further incentive was provided by hopes of commercial expansion linked to expected changes in the communications network. Though subsequent events decisively disproved the prediction, missionaries and government agents alike generally believed in the mid 1890s that the Nyasa–Tanganyika corridor connecting the lakes was becoming a route of commercial importance which would be utilised by traffic from the Congo and from western Tanganyika. Mwenzo in prospect was visualised not as a rural backwater, but as 'an ever-widening sphere of influence' to which Europeans would be attracted as traders and Africans as carriers.[58]

February 1898; Prentice to Smith, 12 December 1897, NLS 7880; *Aurora*, April 1898, 13–14

55 Fraser to Smith, 15 November 1899, NLS 7882; *Aurora*, December 1899, 43

56 Diary of A. G. Macalpine, entry for 16 August 1904, Macalpine Papers

57 Robert I. Rotberg, *Christian Missionaries and the Creation of Northern Rhodesia 1880–1924*, Princeton, 1965, 31–6; Andrew D. Roberts, *A History of the Bemba*, Longman, 1973, 230–6; 244–69

58 Sharpe to FO, 14 October 1902, FO 2/601; Daly to Laws, 8 March 1897, NLS 7900; Appeal to Students . . . Glasgow, 1–4

So too, extension into the Marambo (the Luangwa valley) was believed at first to be extension into an area shortly to be opened up to new commercial influences. In 1898 and 1899 it was expected that Rhodes's railway north would run across the Kariba Gorge to western Tanganyika, passing through the Luangwa valley, thus bringing the Senga and Bemba into intimate contact with the outside world. It was only after the discovery of coal at Wankie in Southern Rhodesia that the decision was taken to carry the line by a more westerly route.[59] Even at the beginning of the twentieth century the old belief in evangelising where commercial prospects were most bright had not been entirely deserted by the Free Church Mission.

On a more profound level, however, it may be argued that the new wave of expansion sprang essentially from an impulse to extend the African Church only partly influenced by the missionaries. In 1897 Prentice and in 1898 Fraser toured the northern and southern spheres of the Luangwa valley respectively, making contact with Senga who lived in 'large stockaded villages, surrounded by thorn trees', visiting the Kamanga, and seeing evidence of Swahili dwellings among the Bisa. Volunteers were called for by Fraser at the sacramental meeting held at Ekwendeni in June 1899, and the response was so great that three schools were quickly established in the Senga villages of Kambombo, Tembwe and Chikwa.[60] By 1902 their number had increased to six, but this was eclipsed a year later when fifty-three senior pupils at the Institution, assisted by a small party of agricultural apprentices, spent their long vacation working from twenty-nine separate centres in the Marambo, spread over an area of 400 miles. In 1904, evangelists and teachers went out from all the major stations – Ekwendeni, Loudon, Bandawe and the Institution – not only to the Senga, but beyond into Bemba and Bisa country, where twenty-four teachers and one travelling evangelist were employed for three months working from seven major centres.[61]

In 1907 ten schools were being worked from Loudon among the Kundu, Bisa and Chewa, and nine among the Senga; Bandawe had thirty-five teachers spending six months of the year with the Senga;

[59] Overtoun to Laws, 19 August 1898, NLS 7901; *Aurora*, December 1898, 42; April 1899, 16; Leo Weinthall (ed.), *The Story of the Cape to Cairo Railway and River Route*, London, n.d., 11 and 33–9

[60] *Aurora*, October 1897, 37–8; August 1898, 31–2; December 1899, 43; Fraser to Smith, 4 August 1898, NLS 7881; 7 June 1899; 15 November 1899, NLS 7882

[61] Institution Education Diary, entry for 1903; Livingstonia Mission Report, 1904, 5–9, 32; Diary of A. G. Macalpine, entries for 17 July, 16 August 1904, 24–9 September 1905, Macalpine Papers

temporary settlements linked to the Institution had been established in Bembaland.[62] 'In the months of August, September and October, the Livingstonia Church sent away some men to the Bembaland to teach and to preach the great words of Jesus-Christ our Lord', wrote one of the students involved. 'The Bemba are very ready to receive Christ as their King. I witness this because I was one of them who went there. I and Samson were teaching and preaching in Chibeza village: the chief of the Biza people and many people came around our preaching of Jesus crucified.'[63]

In prospect the techniques of expansion were not regarded as essentially different from those used in the 1880s. Laws and Fraser were both convinced of the need for European supervision over the work of African teachers and all the plans for advance included provisions for the establishment of mission stations hard on the heels of the evangelistic and educational settlements considered proper for Africans to organise.[64]

In practice, however, the absence of European control was the major feature of the movement. By the late 1890s the bulk of Livingstonia's income was being spent on the development of the Institution. Plans for financial expansion were hindered by the growing scepticism felt in Scotland about the alliance between commerce and Christianity upon which Livingstonia seemed to have been founded, and they were further incommoded in 1904 by a court decision on the legitimacy of the United Free Church, placing its lands, property and funds at peril.[65] Home authorities in consequence showed little taste for western expansion. 'We feel very strongly,' wrote Daly the new committee secretary, 'that mission extension is the work of the natives themselves, and that the training of the Agents is the work of the European Missionaries.'[66]

The sequel differed from one district to another. At Mwenzo while European initiative pioneered the establishment of the station, African

[62] Livingstonia Mission Report, 1907, 31–2

[63] Quoted in Fergus Macpherson, *Kenneth Kaunda of Zambia*, Lusaka, 1974, 32

[64] Laws to Smith, 8 May 1898, Livingstonia Letters to Sub-Committee, NLS; Livingstonia Mission Committee Minutes entry for 29 June 1900

[65] In 1900 the Free Church of Scotland combined with Dr Laws's United Presbyterian Church under the title the United Free Church of Scotland. A remnant in the Free Church, the 'Wee Frees', refused to accept the settlement and raised an action seeking the total funds and property of the original Free Church. In 1904 the House of Lords found for the minority, though a year later legislation was passed reallocating the funds on a more equitable basis. As Livingstonia's own revenues were raised independently they were not directly affected.

[66] Daly to Fraser, 13 June 1902, NLS 7864

enterprise from 1898 was responsible for keeping it going. Though Dewar showed considerable energy in the early months in a range of manual activities, his main interest lay not with the Namwanga but with the Bemba on the far side of the Chambezi river. Frustrated by the refusal of porters to accompany him into Bembaland in November 1896, and by the failure of Laws and the home committee to sanction his plans for extension there, Dewar left the station in 1897 never permanently to return.[67] A year later, his successor McCallum withdrew about the time that in Bembaland Bishop Dupont of the White Fathers was achieving a significant political breakthrough at the court of the paramount, Mwamba.[68] Thereafter, for nearly three years responsibility for the district was vested in the remarkable Yohane (John) Afwenge Banda, a Tonga evangelist paid for by the Bandawe congregation, who had come up to Mwenzo in 1895. Even when the equally remarkable Dr James Chisholm took over the station in December 1900, Banda stayed on as his right-hand man. During the First World War he once again assumed control when Chisholm and the other Europeans were forced to withdraw.[69]

Elsewhere the African church preceded the European Mission. When Dr George Prentice was appointed to Kasungu in October 1900 Tonga teachers had been working there for almost three years. In the Marambo two or three European stations were sanctioned by the Livingstonia Committee in December 1904, and one was opened by Dr Boxer in 1905 in the southern sphere at Kazembe's. The withdrawal of Boxer, however, within months of arrival, owing to his wife's ill-health, left the field open to African teachers.[70] In the Chinsali district, David Kaunda, a Tonga evangelist brought up in Ngoni country, first preached to the Bemba in 1904. A year later he returned permanently to the area and in 1907 he reported: 'many are coming searching . . . They do not wish me to go away, but to make Chinsali as my home.'[71] Occasional visits to Chinsali

[67] *Aurora*, April 1897, 14; Laws to Smith, 4 October 1895, NLS 7878; Dewar to Smith, 8 January 1897, NLS 7880; Livingstonia Mission Committee Minutes, entry for 5 March 1897

[68] Livingstonia Mission Report, 1898–9, 110–11. For the White Fathers in Bembaland see Roberts, *History of the Bemba*, 246–54 and 259–69

[69] Macalpine, 'Experiences with the Livingstonia Mission', 47–8, Macalpine Papers; Dewar to Smith, 8 January 1897, NLS 7880, J. H. Morrison, *Streams in the Desert*, London, n.d. 74, 94–7

[70] Macalpine, 'Wayside Notes of a visit to the Foreign Mission Field of Bandawe Native Church', entry for 21 September 1905, Macalpine Papers; Livingstonia Mission Report, 1904, XI; 1905, XII–XIII; Daly to Laws, 2 December 1904, NLS 7865; Livingstonia Mission Report, 1905

[71] Livingstonia Mission Report, 1907, 55

were made from Mwenzo by Dr Chisholm, who baptised the first convert in that area in 1911, but otherwise Kaunda remained in control. So successful were his activities that in 1913, when R. D. McMinn established the first European-manned station at Lubwa, a band of church members, catechumens and hearers had already been built up, and schools were being carried on in forty-five villages by seventy-seven teachers, some of whom had been brought forward as far as Standards v and vi.[72] In the southern Marambo, 105 church members existed by the time that Riddell Henderson founded the station of Tamanda in 1912 and fifty-one schools were in operation.[73] Only in the Chitambo district where Livingstone had died was the pattern different. There the mission's plan for sending out another young Tonga teacher, Y. Z. Mwasi in 1905 was vetoed by local government agents who demanded that a European be sent instead. Teachers from Bandawe and Ekwendeni were employed by Malcolm Moffat when he began work in that area from 1907, but they lacked the exceptional freedom from supervision enjoyed by their compatriots elsewhere.[74]

At a time when scholars tend to downplay the concept of conversion, it is well to emphasise the revolutionary beliefs held by many of the pioneer evangelists. Armed with the Bible as a source of instant, though conflicting, authority, they were, in the judgement of one perceptive observer, 'as unstable . . . as liable to be tossed about by winds of doctrine as were Xtians of the early Churches'.[75] Nevertheless, they brought to their work a confidence which surprised the Scots. On his journey to Mwenzo in 1895, John Afwenge Banda reacted with 'calmness itself' to a Bemba raid in his vicinity and put heart into local villagers by 'singing hymns and telling the people to appeal to the true and only God'.[76] With the fervour of the newly converted, they made the evil of 'heathen' custom their major target. One evangelist in the Marambo asked the local magistrate 'to seize the dancers of a village because they refused to give up dancing when requested to do so'. Another informed Elmslie that if the people continued to tend their gardens on the Sabbath, 'I shall go and take their hoes, that they may not dishonour God's day.'[77] A common

[72] ibid., 1913, 49–50. See also W. V. Stone, 'The Livingstonia Mission and the Bemba', *Bulletin for the Society for African Church History* ii, 1968 and Macpherson, *Kenneth Kaunda of Zambia*, 2–49

[73] Livingstonia Mission Report, 1912, 30–2

[74] Macalpine, 'Wayside Notes'; Livingstonia Mission Report, 1907, 57–72; 1908, 52–3

[75] Institution Education Diary, annual report for 1903

[76] Dewar to Smith, 9 January 1896, NLS 7806

[77] *FCSMR*, April 1907, 169

complaint in north-eastern Zambia in 1908 was that 'The school-teachers have been trying too much to take chiefship on themselves of late.' At Kapayenze's village the government district messenger was struck and insulted by his Christian son when he sided with the headman against the teachers. It is hardly surprising that in one village in the Marambo the school was torn down and the teachers compelled to flee, while in another the teachers were driven out with clubs.[78]

Although Livingstonia's Nyasa missionaries lacked political authority, several of them assumed a measure of informal influence in the 1920s and 1930s, when their work became better known. It is not entirely fortuitous that David Kaunda was the co-founder of the first welfare association in Northern Rhodesia, or that his son, Kenneth, became first President of Zambia. Nor was their influence confined to Livingstonia's sphere. Such was the reputation of its teachers that by the first decade of the twentieth century, agents from Loudon were being employed by the South African General Mission on the lower Shire and others from Bandawe were working for the Dutch Reformed Church among the Chewa. Six agents previously stationed at Mweniwanda's had joined the Moravians in Rungwe; six more from Bandawe had been enlisted by the Berlin Mission. Several graduates from the Institution went to stations of the London Missionary Society in 1905 and three others went to the Plymouth Brethren on Lake Mweru in the same year. The seeds sown at the Overtoun Institution were blown all over East and Central Africa.[79]

[78] Evidence in Native Court, Fort Jameson, 7 April 1908, Lusaka NE/A/3/10/7; *FCSMR*, March 1904; Institution Education Diary, entry for 1905

[79] A. R. Fraser, 135; A. C. Murray to Laws, 28 March 1890, NLS 7893; Marcia Wright, *German Missions in Tanganyika, 1891–1941*, Oxford, 1971, 45–6; Institution Education Diary entries for 1905 and 1907

6
The Overtoun Institution

The founding of a central institution in November 1894 rivals the move to Bandawe, thirteen years earlier, as the most significant single event in the history of the Livingstonia Mission. In one sense it depended on conditions already in existence. Without the exceptional prior response in Tongaland and among the Tumbuka and Ngoni, the necessity for a centre of post-primary education would hardly have been felt. Without the existence of supporters as committed and as wealthy as Overtoun and Stevenson, the financial requirements of the new station would not have been met. And without the imagination and ambition of the Scottish missionaries, the experiment would never have been attempted.

In other respects, however, it marked a new departure from the previous pattern of development. The creation of an institution fifteen years before a counterpart was founded in the Shire highlands and twenty-four years before a rival was constructed in Northern Rhodesia, ensured more decisively than anything else, the continued pre-eminence of northern Nyasaland in the field of education. The Henry Henderson Institute at Blantyre was not founded until 1909; the Kafue Training Institute in Northern Rhodesia until 1918. Nor did its foundation lack political significance. Up to 1894 unity within the mission was confined largely to the Scottish agents – the African Church being divided into several separate spheres. Now, through the Institution, the academically most successful northerners, wherever they came from, were all brought together for a training that could last seven years or more. The contacts thus established gave the 'new men' a sense of shared experience and hence a unity of vision which would otherwise have been difficult to achieve. It is no coincidence that, when native associations became established in Nyasaland from the 1920s, the area of cooperation among northern associations closely paralleled Livingstonia's own field of work.

As with many other innovations at Livingstonia, the inspiration behind the founding of the Institution came from Dr Laws. By the beginning of the 1890s Laws had become convinced that the creation of a viable

Christian community in northern Nyasaland could be achieved only if African teachers, pastors and evangelists were given a more substantial training than that which individual missionaries had been able to provide. The expected influx of Europeans following the declaration of a British protectorate in 1889 was a further reason for action, for it surely would lead, Laws believed, to increased demands by Europeans for trained African labour and by Africans for new skills with which to grapple with the newly-intrusive economy. His conclusions were formulated in a memorandum which he drew up while on furlough in Scotland in 1892 and circulated among members of the Livingstonia Committee early in the following year. A 'strong well-equipped educational and intellectual centre' should be established, he argued, containing not only a college where teachers and pastors could be taught but also a number of industrial departments where all pupils might receive some manual instruction and where apprentices would be trained in a variety of technical skills. Supported by a small hospital – itself 'the embryo of a Medical School for Native Medical Missionaries in Central Africa' – the Institution should draw its pupils from among those 'giving promise of future usefulness' at the district stations, but should not confine itself solely to the training of agents for mission employment. It should conduct at least part of its operations – those in the senior technical department – on commercial, profit-making principles; should train a stream of clerks, storekeepers, and telegraph operators to be utilised in commercial and government concerns; and should employ English in the central school to facilitate contacts with European agencies.[1] The site eventually chosen at Khondowe overlooking the lake and in the shadow of the beautiful Nyika plateau, was selected in part, it was later suggested, for its isolation from the settler community.[2] But if Laws feared the corrupting influence of an immigrant society, his faith in the beneficial effects of capitalist-inspired economic change was unquestioning. Like the monastery builders of medieval Europe, whom Livingstone had admired, he foresaw his foundation as an instrument of economic transformation, a catalyst for commercial activity. The Institution, Thomas Binnie was later to hope, would become 'a great and important centre of population'.[3] On the one hand it would meet the requirements of the European businessman; on the other it would stimulate the growth of the African entrepreneur, and

[1] Robert Laws, 'Memorandum regarding the Organisation and Development of the Livingstonia Mission', printed in *The Livingstonia Mission, 1875–1900*

[2] W. P. Livingstone, *Laws*, 258

[3] T. Binnie to Laws, 22 October 1896, NLS 7896

consequently the prosperity of the African community. Whether the two functions were compatible was a question that had not yet been raised.

Laws's proposals for the Institution were a subject of controversy and debate from the first appearance of his memorandum until his retirement from the mission in 1927. For the businessmen in Scotland who formed the majority of the Livingstonia Committee the attraction of the scheme was immediate and clear. Impressed by Laws's sympathetic understanding of the requirements of European commerce, they sanctioned in April 1893 the establishment of a training institution somewhere in the hills, not on the lakeshore, and set up a building fund a few months later.[4] Instructions were given that the size of station boarding-schools should be limited so as not to compete with the school at the central station,[5] and Laws was authorised to search for a suitable site on his return to Malawi – a task he accomplished in October 1894 with the aid of Dr Elmslie and a band of porters from Ekwendeni.[6] In the same year Lord Overtoun and James Stevenson donated a total of £9000 to Institution expenses.[7]

In Scotland Laws's proposals met with admiring approval; in Malawi they were greeted with scepticism, and in some cases, with open hostility. Elmslie, probably the only colleague of Laws to have been shown his plans prior to the Committee's decision, regarded the scheme as ten years premature, though he did not condemn it entirely.[8] But other agents, particularly those from pioneer stations whose progress was adversely affected by the drain of resources to the Institution, were less disposed to be charitable. Resentful of the almost complete lack of consultation with the mission council, Kerr Cross accused Laws in 1894 of acting as if he were Pope, and complained that though the idea of the Institution was good, the timing had been disastrous. Three years later the sense of grievance had still not been dispelled. When Alexander Dewar was refused permission to advance from Mwenzo into Bembaland, he reacted with acidity. 'Put briefly,' he wrote in 1897, 'the Institution is to succeed should everything else have to lie dormant or even fail. It seeks to absorb men, money and material.'[9]

Further objections to the Institution scheme centred on more fundamental issues than those connected with the allocation of resources. No

[4] Livingstonia Mission Committee minutes entry for 11 April 1893
[5] ibid. entry for 13 March 1894
[6] Livingstonia Mission Report 1894, 12
[7] Livingstonia Mission Committee minutes, entries for 13 March and 14 June 1894
[8] Elmslie to Laws, 22 October 1892, NLS 7896
[9] Kerr Cross to members of the Livingstonia Committee, 23 August 1894, NLS 7878; Dewar to Smith, 8 January 1897, NLS 7880

sooner had Laws decided on a site than he set out to obtain huge tracts of land in the area, two to three hundred square miles in extent, in part so that all food and water requirements of the Institution, for fifty years to come, could be met from its own territory; in part so that it could carry out a major afforestation programme which would provide the mission with timber for its carpentry operations and ensure that it would eventually become financially self-supporting.[10] Had the Protectorate government been responsible for land in the north, there is little doubt that Laws's hopes would have been checked at the outset. As Harry Johnston informed him in July 1895, the government disapproved of large land grants being made to individual proprietors and sought to provide at least a minimum of protection for African rights.[11] But though Johnston had sovereignty in the north, it was Cecil Rhodes's British South Africa Company which owned the land that Laws now wanted. On his return to Africa in 1894, Laws met Rhodes at Cape Town and told him of his plans for economic expansion. With no likelihood that the company would utilise the territory, Rhodes listened sympathetically to the claims of the mission.[12] Not until October 1895 was Laws able to see Major P. C. Forbes, the company's representative in Malawi, but when he did so the interview, according to a colleague, 'was – this is private – almost unexpectedly favourable'.[13] The company reserved to itself all mineral rights of value, but otherwise was prepared to grant most that was asked of it – an area estimated at 196 square miles in September 1898, though in fact comprising 334 square miles.[14]

How far such grants might benefit the mission was a question that even Lord Overtoun found difficult to answer. It might be, as Laws was quick to point out, that much of the land required was only of marginal economic value; that much of it was at least temporarily unoccupied following the dispersal of Tumbuka and Henga in the wake of the Ngoni

[10] Laws to Major P. C. Forbes, 24 August 1895, NLS 7878; 10 January 1896, NLS 7879

[11] Laws to Smith, 12 August 1895, NLS 7878

[12] Laws to Forbes, 24 August 1895, ibid. There is a detailed if somewhat fanciful account of this interview in W. P. Livingstone, *Laws*, 266–7

[13] James Henderson to Margaret Davidson, 6 October 1895 in M.M.S. Ballantyne and R. H. W. Shepherd (eds.), *Forerunners of Modern Malawi*, Lovedale, 1968

[14] J. F. Daly to D. E. Brodie, 27 April 1911, NLS 7867. The absence of any accurate survey is the main reason why the amount demanded fluctuated so markedly. In August 1895 Laws considered that between 140 and 150 square miles were required by the mission. By 1906 he had extended the claim to nearly 300 square miles; in 1908 he was back to 164.

invasions.[15] All the same, even if missions such as the Church of Scotland's at Kibwezi in Kenya offered precedents for the acceptance of such grants, the outcome in a country as small as Malawi was fraught with uncertainty. By 1906 several members of the committee in Scotland had become 'seriously alarmed' that an estate of '100 square miles, proposed and negotiated for at the Institution, had grown to be spoken of as 200 or 300'.[16] 'While we wish to have sufficient land for agricultural purposes, for timber, water sources, and possibly stone and lime,' Overtoun explained to Laws, 'we all think that 100 square miles is the outside of what we should ask or take.'[17] More than that, it was suggested, might land the mission with embarrassing financial obligations and also 'involve us in trouble with the natives alienating them from the Mission and causing them to look upon the Missionaries as landlords and rulers'.[18] In 1908 Laws's critics directly clashed with his supporters at a meeting of the Livingstonia Estates Committee. Eight members voted for a motion sanctioning the acquisition by the mission council of 164 square miles of land (the minimum that Laws would accept), eight voted that no more land should be taken than could be 'held and used directly under the Institution's scheme of Education'.[19] The compromise eventually reached was a typically confused piece of mission committee planning. Under protest, the chairman, Thomas Binnie, agreed to accept the larger claim; at almost the same moment the company withdrew its original offer.[20] Not till 1921 was the transfer finally effected, and then only 50 000 acres were granted in five separate blocks – less than half what Laws had originally wanted, but more than enough to arouse the animosity of those Africans whose property rights had been disregarded.[21]

Meanwhile, Laws's building programme at the Institution had also provoked controversy. In the same way that James Stewart in 1861 had

[15] Laws to Forbes, 24 August 1895, NLS 7878; Robert Laws, *Reminiscenes of Livingstonia*, Edinburgh, 1934, 146–7

[16] Daly to Laws, 21 September 1966, NLS 7865; Lord Overtoun to Laws, 14 September 1906, printed in Livingstonia Mission Committee Minutes

[17] Overtoun to Laws, ibid.

[18] Daly to Elmslie, 21 February 1907, NLS 7866

[19] ibid. and Diary of A. G. Macalpine entry for 1 January 1909, Macalpine Papers

[20] Daly to Prentice, 12 April 1910, NLS 7866; to Chisholm, 10 February 1911, NLS 7867

[21] The amount transferred appears to have been 45 017 acres (Indenture between the British South Africa Company and the General Trustees of the United Free Church of Scotland, 24 February 1921, Liv. Corr. MNA). For some African reactions see evidence presented to the Native Reserves Commission, North Nyasa District, 1929, MNA J8/5/3

regarded the steam-engine and saw-mill as symbols of industrial advance, to be introduced into Central Africa as quickly as possible, Laws in the 1890s looked to piped water and the electric turbine to provide demonstrations of Christian industrial progress, more widespread and influential in their effects than could be construed from an estimate of their utilitarian value alone. A remarkable essay he wrote to commemorate Livingstonia's Jubilee expressed his philosophy in unmistakable terms:

> in the Mission work, science has become the handmaid of Christianity. The steam-engine of the little S.S. *Ilala* was its first demonstration; roads, the telegraph and telephone – electric light and power, water being used to saw wood and grind corn, water being laid down a valley and up a hill, the throb of the printing press turning out page after page of the Word of God in eight languages, the plough and wheelbarrow and other tools in the industrial departments here have all been of use in almost unbelievable ways in leading souls to Christ and building up the Kingdom of God.[22]

The consequence of such a belief was a lop-sided approach to mission development. All residents at the Institution in the first few years lived in a haphazard collection of temporary mud and wattle huts which were gradually replaced during the late 1890s by more permanent structures. So determined, however, was Laws to introduce sophisticated technical equipment to the industrial departments that the school and, particularly, the dormitories were seriously neglected. The contrasts thus created were frequently commented upon by mission observers.[23] A piped water supply was introduced at Livingstonia at the cost of over £5000 as early as January 1904. A water-driven turbine providing the station with electric light – only the second of its type in Central Africa – was put into operation in October 1905. A waggon road up the precipitous cliff from the lake was carried as far as the station – an extraordinary engineering feat – a few months later.[24] But while the building and engineering departments strained to equip Livingstonia with the latest advances in industrial science, the housing made available to pupils and apprentices was still of the simplest standard. As late as 1900 Elmslie reported that pupils at the Institution were sleeping two or three to a bed in wattle huts inferior in

[22] R. Laws, 'Present Position and Need' in *FCSMR*, October 1925, 449

[23] In 1903, for example, J. F. Daly, the committee secretary, informed Elmslie: 'The Institution as a manufacturing agency, is said to be coming into existence slowly, but the Institution proper, schools, church, hospital, etc., in which all interests centre, is said to be almost still to begin.' Daly to Elmslie, 15 May 1903, NLS 7864

[24] Accounts of the progress and completion of the various projects at the Institution can be found in the annual Livingstonia Mission Reports.

comfort to those of their own homes and 'unfit for habitation in the cold damp climate we have here'.[25] Lacking adequate clothing and dependent on food supplies so irregular that on two occasions – in 1897 and 1901 – classes had to be suspended and the students sent home, the first generation of pupils survived in conditions of acute discomfort. Frequent cases of pneumonia occurred on the cold windswept plateau leading in 1902 to the deaths of at least three pupils in residence.[26]

In the industrial departments the efforts of the missionaries met with only partial success. The policy at first pursued was to make the station a commercial centre stimulating the growth of the colonial economy. Laws justified the work of the mission to men like Major Forbes by stressing the contribution it made in encouraging Africans to take to continuous wage employment.[27] At the Institution he carried his philosophy into effect by giving jobs to 1200 labourers in 1901 and to more than 3500 in 1903 during the final stages of the construction of the road to the lake.[28] An ambitious apprenticeship programme was instituted in the 1890s which by 1904 was training 130 apprentices on five year contracts in such varied skills as building, carpentry, engineering, telegraphy and printing.[29] Attempts were made by Malcolm Moffat, the first agriculturalist at the station, to grow not only maize, wheat and vegetables for local consumption, but also coffee and Mlanje cedars to be sold for profit. Chairs, tables and doors were made in the carpentry department for sale to settlers and government officials. Several commissions were executed by the printing department for the ALC, the African Transcontinental Telegraph Company and other commercial concerns.[30]

But while initial attention was given to expanding the European-controlled sector of the economy, the plight of the peasant producer was not entirely forgotten. By 1904 it was widely apparent that although the Institution was intended to create the conditions in which European activity could flourish in the north, in fact commercial expansion was taking place elsewhere, leaving Khondowe uncomfortably isolated.[31] The

[25] Elmslie to Smith, 14 December 1897, NLS 7882; to Smith, 21 January 1900, Livingstonia Letters to Sub-Committee, NLS

[26] Livingstonia Mission Report for 1901, 4; Institution Education Diary entries for 16 May and 1 July 1898; 1 April 1901; 1902–3

[27] Laws to Forbes, 24 August 1895, NLS 7878

[28] Livingstonia Mission Report, 1901, 13; 1903

[29] ibid., 1904, 3

[30] ibid., 1900, 13–14

[31] 'We fear from all accounts that trade and traffic are leaving Lake Nyasa to pass up the valley behind your hinterland and that this will injure the prospects of trade for the Livingstonia Institution, thus making your

increased volume of labour migration from the Northern Province, indicated by the speed with which apprentices trained at the Institution were seized upon by commercial firms from Blantyre and further afield, demonstrated the need to put indigenous agriculture on a more prosperous footing. Nothing was to be gained, however, from the skills taught or the machinery introduced at the Institution, and little from the highly theoretical training given to agricultural apprentices from 1903, and admitted by the missionaries themselves to be of little value.[32] In 1908 Elmslie took advantage of Laws's absence on furlough to draw up a statement as chairman of the Institution Senatus which dismissed the possibility of a further expansion of trade taking place in the area around Livingstonia, and called for a reduction in the size of the industrial departments.[33] The next year an attempt at reform was set underway: steps were taken to limit the Institution's agricultural activities so that a market for peasant surplus could be created at Khondowe; cotton gins were introduced under mission control to stimulate the growth of cotton, as a major African cash-crop.[34]

But these activities were half-heartedly pursued and, like similar schemes to improve implements and methods of agriculture, gradually fell into disuse. By the 1920s some Livingstonia graduates had established themselves in their own villages as carpenters with the tools they had acquired during their training. Others had become traders, others still were modernising farmers.[35] But these were the exceptions. The public opinion of the Phelps-Stokes Commission in 1924 was that the major omission of the Institution lay in 'the need of relating the splendid industrial training to village handicraft and the extension of agricultural influence to the gardens and fields of the people'.[36] The opinion of W. P. Young, one of

electric works, large workshops, etc., etc., too big for any trade likely to be secured by Livingstonia.' Daly to A. Chalmers, 4 October 1904, NLS 7865

[32] 'Report of the Council's Sub-Committee on Organisation and Expenditure', printed in Livingstonia Mission Committee Minutes, 1909, 5

[33] Minutes of the Institution Senatus, Appendix to 6 June 1908, Livingstonia Papers

[34] 'Report of the Council's Sub-Committee on Organisation and Expenditure', 8; Livingstonia Mission Report, 1910, 7; *Livingstonia News*, February 1911, 2; Minutes of the Institution Senatus, 11 April and 11 July 1911, Livingstonia Papers

[35] R. Laws 'Co-ordination of Technical and Literary Training'. Report of Native Education Conference, 1927, 20–3. Report by Alex. Caseby on the Agricultural Department, 1923, NLS 7885; Laws to Lyall Grant, 2 July 1915 (copy) Hetherwick Papers

[36] Jesse Jones, *Education in East Africa*, 208

Laws's subordinates, as recorded by the secretary of the Commission, was much more damning: 'He feels that the Institution is not serving the native life so much as the European planters. The apprentices are trained with electric saws, etc., appliances which they can't possibly use in the villages. Their brick-work is only useful for brick latrines!!!'[37] Livingstonia's economic role was still primarily one of providing trained artisans for European employment with the drawback (as far as the Nyasaland settler community was concerned) that most of her graduates preferred to work in Tanganyika or in Northern Rhodesia rather than in the Shire highlands where wages were notoriously low.[38]

Looking at the economic impact of Livingstonia in the thirty years before the visit of the Phelps-Stokes Commission it is difficult not to conclude that Laws's long-term plans were based on false assumptions. In one sphere, indeed, the aim of the mission was triumphantly accomplished. In so far as Laws wished to use the Institution as an instrument for the furtherance of the colonial economy, his plans met with considerable success. Quite how many workers from the industrial departments moved into employment elsewhere it is impossible to determine. Apprenticeship records at the Institution have not been preserved; many workers were casual labourers employed for particular tasks and then dismissed.[39] What one can say, however, is that the hopes entertained for the new institution in December 1894 by 'all employers of labour in this country who have up to the present time found it almost impossible to obtain anything which could be called skilled labour' were largely realised.[40] From October 1897 when the first two pupils of telegraphy were sent off to work for the Telegraph Company at Zomba, the flow south of specialised workers was unremitting.[41] By 1899 the number of sawyers, journeymen, printers and agricultural workers leaving the Institution was so great that the task of keeping trained workmen beyond their apprenticeship was considered impossible.[42] Five years later, men trained in the industrial departments were scattered from Katanga in the

37 Journal of Dr J. W. C. Dougall, entry for 26 April 1924, Edinburgh House

38 Statement by Major I. C. Sanderson and Mr J. D. Milner, Report of the Native Education Conference, 1927; Annual Report of D C Karonga for 1927, MNA NNK2/1/1

39 I would estimate the number of apprentices and trained workers from the Institution who went into employment before 1914 as between 250 and 500

40 *British Central African Gazette*, 14 December 1894

41 Livingstonia Mission Report, 1897–8, 6

42 ibid., 1897–1900, 8

west to Chinde in the east and in the south to Salisbury and the gold-fields in southern Africa.[43]

Where demands arose from the government they were promptly met by the mission. In February 1904 the secretary of the British South Africa Company at Fort Jameson (Chipata) wrote to Laws telling him of his need for typists as well as for a man to do tracing in the survey department.[44] A year later a commercial course was organised under Cullen Young in which instruction was given in typing, book-keeping and shorthand.[45] So vigorously did it thrive that in 1913 the British South Africa Company Board in London gave a grant of £75 for five years to train clerks for government service in Northern Rhodesia.[46] The total number subsequently recruited is difficult to estimate, but it seems likely that by the mid 1920s at least fifty Institution graduates had been so employed. 'The work of both the Nyasaland and Northern Rhodesian Governments is largely being done by those black men trained at a college established by Dr and Mrs Laws', Clements Kadalie wrote with pardonable exaggeration in 1921.[47] Medical assistants were trained earlier and probably better at Blantyre, but when employers had vacancies for skilled telegraphists or clerks up to the late 1920s, it was to the Overtoun Institution that they most frequently turned.[48]

Anxious to create new patterns of work in Central Africa, Laws and his colleagues established a code of time-discipline at the Institution almost as draconian as those imposed in the factories of Manchester during the early years of the Industrial Revolution. Apprentices, fresh from their villages, were called upon to work an eleven hour, five and a half day week, with evening classes an obligatory extra. 'Every apprentice,' the regulations laid down, 'must be punctually in his place and ready for work at the ringing of the bell, both in the morning and after meals; and must continue steadily at work during the appointed hours.' All work done by the apprentices was recorded in a time-book supplied for the purpose; no wages were paid for time not thus accounted for. An apprentice who was late or who loitered at his work was fined in accordance with the time he had wasted; the amount of the fine was calculated on

43 ibid., 1904, 4

44 Richard Goode to Laws, 4 February 1904, Lusaka NE/A/3/10/7

45 Livingstonia Mission Report, 1905, 9

46 Daly to W. P. Livingstone, 3 December 1913, NLS 7868

47 Newspaper cutting from *Cape Times*, 1921, Aberdeen University

48 See statement by A. T. Lacey in Record of Oral Evidence heard by the Royal Commission on Closer Union, March–August 1938, vol. III. Foreign and Commonwealth Office Library

the same scale as overtime was paid. As the missionaries, in addition, attempted to enforce a vigorous code of moral conduct in the industrial departments, the pressure on apprentices was very considerable. Men were dismissed for making or drinking beer, polygamy, 'immorality' and for 'being a bad influence'. It is not surprising that some forty per cent of the apprentices registered their disapproval by leaving the station before completing their indentures.[49]

Although Livingstonia cannot be regarded as being principally responsible for the growing poverty of northern Malawi, there is little doubt that the economic activities of her agents contributed to the emergence of a colonial slum. Laws's policies in the 1890s were based on two dubious assumptions: the first, that Africans could benefit from contact with almost any kind of European economic activity; the second that skills acquired for use in the European-dominated sector could be utilised almost as effectively by African peasant farmers. 'If natives are fit for doing the work required by the Europeans,' he was later to write, 'they will be able to do the simpler work required by their fellow natives.'[50]

By the 1920s the falsity of these beliefs had been demonstrated beyond reasonable doubt. Far from inspiring an agricultural revolution among local Tumbuka farmers, the experiments undertaken on Livingstonia's estate had merely convinced them of the rightness of traditional methods. Hampered by the poor soil of much of the plateau, the mission's agricultural experts had staggered from one disappointment to another. Coffee had failed as an export crop and wheat as a crop for local consumption. The import of oxen had been brought virtually to an end by the presence of tsetse fly in the Henga valley and of east coast fever by the lake. Many of the trees planted by Laws had died. The Institution had become a net importer of foodstuffs, and provided less than a quarter of its own total requirements. Where new techniques like the introduction of ploughing had been attempted the inexperience of the European agents had been cruelly revealed. Ploughing, Moffat ruefully confessed in 1907, was a waste of money without heavy manuring. And manure in the quantity required was never available. 'In our fields without manuring, even after ploughing and hoeing we are unable to compete with native cultivation.'[51]

[49] Regulations for Apprentices, 1898, Lusaka, NE/A 3/10/7 Minutes of the Institution Senatus, entries for 18 and 29 November 1926

[50] R. Laws to Secretary, Native Education Commission, Salisbury, Southern Rhodesia, 17 April 1925, Livingstonia Corr. Box 1

[51] Report of the Council's Sub-Committee on Organisation and Expenditure, 1909, 6. See also A. Caseby, 'Livingstonia Mission Estate', 17 May 1927, Aberdeen University

And as traditional methods brought greater returns, the demonstration effects of the mission were predictably slight.

As the rate of labour migration accelerated in response to tax demands from the government, the problem of agricultural expansion became increasingly severe. Laws had hoped that returning migrants would transform themselves into rural entrepreneurs through the investment of hard-won capital and skill.[52] But with over 50 per cent of able-bodied men absent from the northern districts by the 1930s, surplus labour was unavailable and potential markets were small. By 1926 when the Assistant Director of Agriculture visited Livingstonia, the mission's agricultural policies had collapsed like a house of cards. With few exceptions, the skills taught in the Institution were not being utilised in the surrounding area. No commercial cash-crops were being exported; few significant improvements in agricultural techniques had taken place, even among tenants on the mission's estate.[53] Where innovations could be detected, like the introduction to the Henga valley of such crops as bananas, cassava and mangoes, it was not Livingstonia that had inspired them, but the intermingling of Henga refugees with lakeshore people back in the 1870s.[54] It is true that the Institution was still the principal local metropole in the area; the only significant market for maize and vegetables; the only local employer of labour with the exception of the Department of Public Works. All the same, it acted within a wider economic context in which the function of the Northern Province had been transformed into that of a supplier of various forms of labour. And it had actively participated in bringing about this transformation, even if the aims of its agents bore little relation to the results achieved.

The industrial departments constituted the limbs of the Institution; its heart lay in the central school. Started in a small way in December 1894 by Laws's formidable wife, a former elementary school-teacher in Scotland, the school owed much of its early character to James Henderson, who arrived at Khondowe in July 1895. Ignorant of Africa and lacking any practical experience of teaching other than what he had acquired in a year's course at Edinburgh's Moray House Training College, Henderson was in many ways a curious choice for the Institution's first headmaster.

52 Laws to Secretary, Native Education Commission, Salisbury, 17 April 1925

53 Paraphrase of a Report by E. W. Davy, Assistant Director of Agriculture, enclosed in CS, Zomba to Laws, 6 May 1926, Livingstonia Papers, Box 9

54 I have drawn this point from a very interesting unpublished thesis: R. E. Gregson, 'Work, Exchange and Leadership: the Mobilisation of Agricultural Labor among the Tumbuka of the Henga Valley', Columbia PhD, 1969, 91

But what the young Scotsman lacked in experience he made up in dedication as a teacher and in organising ability.[55] When Henderson took over the classes, five pupils were being taught in the Upper School and some thirty more (mostly workers and neighbouring children) in an elementary vernacular school conducted by Charles Domingo.[56] Within a year these two schools had been supplemented by a junior mixed and by a separate upper school for girls, and the number of boarders had risen to ninety-six.[57] By 1899, the basic framework of the educational departments, which was to last on into the 1920s, had become established. In April of that year 232 pupils were taking full-time courses, forty more than the average over the whole period up to 1914.[58] Half of these – a sizeable minority girls – were being educated in the Junior School, entry to which required no previous training. Eighty-six more, many of them students from Bandawe and Ekwendeni, who had been specially chosen for the Institution on the basis of their performance in district school classes, were placed in the Middle School. Above this came the Upper School or Normal Department where twenty-four pupils in Standards IV, V and VI were being trained as certificated schoolteachers. And above this again was the Theological course in which were enrolled two putative ministers in April 1899 – Charles Domingo and Yakobe Msusa Muwamba, both of whom were to complete the course successfully in September 1900, though neither were to be ordained.[59]

Aside from the main full-time classes, three other types of school were conducted from the central institution. Evening classes were attended by between seventy and 120 apprentices and out-workers, though Henderson complained that the time available was too short for the subjects undertaken, and that in consequence little real knowledge was acquired. For a month in the year a Continuation School was run for district teachers who wished to refresh their knowledge, and improve their qualifications. Finally, like the other stations, the Institution acted as the central co-ordinator of a network of village schools, only four in number in 1899, but increasing rapidly in the next few years as large numbers of Henga

[55] For further details on Henderson see Ballantyne and Shepherd, *Forerunners of Modern Malawi*, vii–x:

[56] Institution Education Diary, 22 July 1898, Livingstonia Papers

[57] ibid., 26 April and 12 June 1896

[58] According to the Education Diary and the annual Livingstonia Mission reports there were 167 full time pupils at the Institution in 1897, 232 in 1899, 223 in 1901, 177 in 1904, 218 in 1907, 188 in 1909 and 168 in 1912. The average over the whole period 1897 to 1913, was 189.

[59] Institution Education Diary, 28 April 1899; Roll Book of the Institution, entries on Domingo and Muwamba

moved back into their homeland from the Karonga region where they had formerly taken refuge from the Ngoni.

One principle dominated the organisation of the educational departments. Like his mentor, Laws, Henderson regarded the immediate function of the Institution as the production of school teachers for the district stations.[60] In consequence he organised the school work on a pupil–teacher basis with almost every pupil from the Middle School upwards spending at least part of his time giving instruction to others. The result was that by 1900 the small Scottish staff taught only a tiny proportion of the total number of classes conducted in the Institution district. Six African certificated teachers, four of them members of the theology class were responsible for most of the teaching in the Middle, Junior and Evening Schools. Pupils from the Normal Department gained practical experience by assisting the certificated teachers in the junior and evening classes. Pupils from the Middle School opened temporary village schools during their vacations. And pupils from vacation schools were appointed as monitors when full-time village schools were eventually established. Among the Africans resident at the Institution no more than two or three were not receiving instruction in some class; no more than a handful were not giving instruction in another.

It is a measure of the success of Henderson's methods that, in 1903, a new stage in the educational development of the Institution was reached. In the previous eight years, so the headmaster explained, 'the Institution had to adapt itself to meet immediate urgent needs; and its main concern was to provide trained Christian teachers qualified to deal with large numbers and to bear responsibility to a distance beyond the range of frequent supervision'.[61] The graduation from the Normal Department of thirty-six trained teachers in October 1902 meant that these needs were largely satisfied, for though the mission could undoubtedly have benefited from the employment of more skilled teachers, it had not the money to pay their salaries. 'The way,' therefore, now seemed open, Henderson argued, 'for bringing on the other courses which under the past circumstances have had either to occupy a secondary place or wait altogether.'[62]

The consequent expansion of the Institution as a centre of post-primary

[60] Henderson, like most of his colleagues, was sometimes annoyed by Laws's autocratic ways, but this did not affect his appreciation of the man. 'For the doctor I have the highest respect and admiration', he wrote in September 1895. 'His skill and practical knowledge are extraordinary and his good sense remarkable', *Forerunners of Modern Malawi*, 52

[61] Institution Education Diary, 'Ninth Year, 1903'

[62] ibid.

training illustrates both the irrelevance of much that was taught by the Scottish missionaries, and also the sincerity of Henderson's attempt to introduce his pupils to what he regarded as the richness of 'Western civilisation'.[63] In the three years before his appointment in 1906 as Principal at Lovedale, in succession to Stewart, and in the three years following, the Institution aspired to educational heights that were not to be matched in Malawi till the introduction of the first government secondary school nearly forty years later. Above the Normal Department which attracted over seventy pupils in 1907, four new courses were introduced, one for evangelists who did not wish to take the full, exacting theological course, one in commerce to provide training in store and office work, one in medicine for dispensers and hospital assistants, and one in arts, devised in 1901 for those students who had completed the Normal course and who were judged to be too young to go on to the theological course immediately.[64]

Though the arts course attracted only half a dozen students in as many years, its programme indicates the extent of Livingstonia's educational ambition. Taken over a three-year period, it involved the study of English language and literature, history, logic, philosophy, psychology, mathematics, ethics and sociology. The examination papers covering the first year's work provide evidence of the range of material covered. A successful student by October 1903 could give 'an outline of the developments of Greek philosophy that led to the recognition of Psychology as a separate science' and could discuss 'pain in the processes through which it is supposed to lead to purposive action'. He could give a brief criticism of the Chinese language, explain why Norse possesses a special interest for English-speaking people and discuss the different ways in which Old English poetry differs from the poetry of modern times. He knew what changes were brought about in England by the Norman Conquest and could name three translators of the Bible and the author of the 'Vision of Piers Plowman'. He had a detailed factual knowledge of 'Pilgrim's Progress' and a rudimentary understanding of the basics of Greek and Latin, gained in special classes held by Henderson out of school hours.[65]

In later years the handful of graduates who passed unscathed through this intellectual minefield were to look back on their time with Henderson

[63] Report of the Nyasaland United Missionary Conference, Livingstone, 1901

[64] Institution Education Diary, entry for 1903; Livingstonia Mission Report, 1903, 1, 9; Minutes of the Investigation Senatus, 9 August 1901, Livingstonia Papers

[65] Examination Papers for the Arts course, April and October 1903, Livingstonia Papers Box 4

with the pride and affection that comes from having taken part in an ambitious and risky experiment.[66] But for Henderson's successors, the Rev. D. R. Mackenzie and the young Glasgow graduate, Peter Kirkwood, the experiment was not one that they wished to prolong. Kirkwood's personal view, expressed soon after his arrival at the Institution, was that 'the code for Central Africa would be more beneficial if less ambitious'.[67] He witnessed with good grace the graduation in 1907 of Lamek Mankwalwa Banda, the first pupil to receive the certificate of the arts course, but was probably not unduly disappointed when his own departure on furlough early in 1909 meant that the arts course was temporarily closed.[68] Six months later Laws's absence in Scotland provided the opportunity for a more permanent step to be taken. The Mission Council in September recommended that the arts course be abandoned entirely, 'on the grounds that it is out of touch with the general educational needs of the country', and added that the Institution should concentrate on two main tasks – the one that of training evangelists, theology students and medical assistants in the College; the other that of instructing prospective teachers in the Normal Department.[69] Candidates should be allowed to enter Standards IV to VI whether or not they wanted to become teachers, it was reluctantly agreed. But as no pupil was to be accepted without the personal recommendation of the missionary to the district from which he came, church membership was retained as a qualification for entry.[70] Compared with the education offered anywhere else in Malawi, the courses taught in the Normal Department continued to be highly ambitious in the subjects they covered. Compared with what had taken place before 1909, however, the Institution experienced a lowering of aspiration and probably a decline in the standard of teaching provided.

It is at least arguable that the main historical significance of the Institution up to 1914 concerned the creation of new forms of social differentiation among Africans, based on educational privilege. The formation of an educated elite began in the late 1870s, when men like Albert Namalambe became full-time workers for the mission, but was accelerated by the creation of a central college which offered Africans limited access to skills

[66] Personal communication with Messrs E. A. Muwamba and Hancock N'goma, June 1966

[67] Livingstonia Mission Report 1906, 12

[68] Institution Education Diary, entry for 1907: Minutes of Institution Senatus, 9 February 1909. Banda, a Chewa from Kasungu returned to the Institution in 1922 for a two-year course and later became one of the first African pastors in the DRC Mission

[69] Livingstonia Mission Council minutes, entry for 18 September 1909

[70] ibid., 14 October 1911

not otherwise available. As the prestige of the Institution in government and commercial circles grew, so the opportunities open to its graduates widened, and so their status shifted from that of an intelligentsia sharing a common intellectual background but without economic power to that of a genuine – if modestly rewarded – elite, capable of maintaining a partial monopoly over the limited range of privileged positions open to Africans of talent within a colonial society.

Fortunately for rival aspirants, the Livingstonia elite was a small if influential body. Although 850 pupils are recorded as having been admitted to full-time classes at the Institution up to January 1915, something between a half and two thirds left or were dismissed within a couple of years of their arrival and only some 350 completed their courses successfully and went out into the wider world as fully-trained Livingstonia graduates.[71]

What must be noted about this little group is the breadth of its social vision and the limited area from which most of its successful members were drawn. Like Kiungani, the UMCA college on Zanzibar, which it in some ways resembled, the Institution was instrumental in creating a strong sense of corporate identity. Forced to use a common language in school – Chinyanja, later Tumbuka, in the elementary classes, English in the upper forms – Tonga, Tumbuka and Ngoni pupils were brought together in classroom and dormitory and shared the responsibility of vacation teaching.[72] The background of the pupils became more variegated as the reputation of the Institution spread, but their sense of identity did not weaken. 'I found a lot of other boys who had come from Bandawe and from Ngoni, and from Karonga, a great number of young men', Donald Siwale, one of the first students from Mwenzo was later to recollect. 'We learnt together . . . and I still remember them.'[73] By 1907 the Tonga, Tumbuka, Henga and Ngoni pupils who formed some three quarters of the Institution population had been joined by Chewa sent from the Dutch Reformed Church station at Mvera, by Ngonde from Karonga, Namwanga from Mwenzo and by Phoka and others from the Institution district. At least twenty pupils had been sent by the London Missionary Society from south of Lake Tanganyika; five more had come from the Garanganze Mission on Lake Mweru; one had come up on his own from Blantyre, and two former soldiers, James Inyati and Yakobi

[71] Figures calculated from the Institution Roll-Book

[72] For the Kiungani comparison see John Iliffe, *Tanganyika under German Rule*, Cambridge, 1969, 176–8

[73] I owe this reference to Dr Andrew Roberts who kindly lent me a tape of his interview with Mr Siwale in July 1970.

Sibanda, had trekked all the way from Salisbury, Rhodesia, to 'seek an education which [they] found . . . impossible to obtain in [their] own land'.[74]

To some extent the new contacts may well have accentuated and perhaps even created a sense of tribal identity. Later, in the 1920s, the graduates Edward Bote Manda and Charles Chinula acted as advisors to local chiefly authorities – Manda expounding the case of the Tumbuka Chikulamayembe dynasty with the enthusiasm which Chinula reserved for propagating the claims of the rival Ngoni leader, Chief Mbelwa.[75] But if the Institution in some ways fostered, albeit unwittingly, the new-style tribal divisions of the twentieth century, it also helped to create bonds of trust among people of diverse origin who would not otherwise have been associated together. Interest associations like the Literary Society (founded in 1902) or the Young Men's Christian Association presided over by the Shona ex-trooper, James Inyati, were organised on a non-tribal basis and brought together pupils from different backgrounds.[76] If Chinula and Manda were divided in the 1920s on questions of local politics, they were united in their knowledge of each other and in their links with such fellow-graduates as Levi Mumba in Zomba, Donald Siwale in Mwenzo, Y. Z. Mwasi near Bandawe and a score of others situated in positions of influence and relative privilege.[77] It would be idle to suggest that a Livingstonia leaving certificate had the social weight of an old school tie. But for the first generation of graduates it did provide both a source of pride and also a passport to continuing privilege, as the story of the Muwamba family demonstrates. Yakobe Msusu Muwamba, the first graduate from the theology course, was followed to the Institution in January 1896 by his two sons, Ernest Alexander and William. The boys returned to the Bandawe district in the care of Macalpine after their father's sudden death in October 1900, but in December 1905 they re-enrolled at the Institution with bursaries provided by the mission. The subsequent career of Ernest Alexander Muwamba followed the standard pattern for a successful Institution graduate. Having passed extra Stan-

[74] The arrival of Inyati, who had 'served with credit through the Mashonaland rebellion' and of Sibanda is recorded in the Institution Diary on 10 September 1900. All other information is drawn from this Diary and from the Institution Roll Book

[75] See below pp. 287–9

[76] Livingstonia Mission Report 1902, 16; Institution Education Diary, entry for 1906. The YMCA was the successor of the Christian Endeavour Society which was founded in February 1903

[77] Interview with Rev. Charles Chinula, July 1964; Andrew Roberts interview with Donald Siwale, July 1970

dard VI, the successor to the arts course, in 1910, he taught for two years in the Bandawe district before following his relation, Isaac Clements Katondo Muwamba to Northern Rhodesia in search of better paid employment. His skill in writing legible English won him a clerkship at the Bwana Mkubwa Mine at Ndola in 1913 and then a job as clerk and interpreter with the Northern Rhodesian Government. Promotion to chief clerk followed, with a spell during the Second World War as acting district commissioner. He returned to his homeland in 1944, and in 1949 was appointed to the Nyasaland Legislative Council as one of its first African members. By that time he could confidently reflect on the influence of his family. One relation, Clements Kadalie, a contemporary at Livingstonia, had become the leader of the ICU in Southern Africa, another, Isaac Clements Katondo, had paralleled his own career as a senior clerk in Northern Rhodesia. The Muwamba family had become, by any definition, a part of the emergent Malawi bourgeoisie, soon, in the third generation, to produce a businessman, director of tourism and a doctor.[78]

In some respects, the Institution functioned as a haven for 'marginal' men – a refuge, for example, for Charles Domingo who, having been carried from his home on the Mozambique coast as a child in 1881, used the mission as a vehicle for personal advancement.[79] But for every Domingo there were more than a dozen Tonga and Tumbuka pupils who took advantage of the early contacts established by the mission in their area to obtain a disproportionate share of the places available in the Normal School. Though little more than 9 per cent of the population of the Northern Province was described as Tonga in the census of 1921, Bandawe provided 33 per cent of the full-time pupils in 1896 (forty-two out of 127), including 70 per cent of those in the Upper School[80] (fourteen out of twenty). In later years, the proportion of Tonga as part of the total population of Livingstonia declined, but the more advanced classes continued to be largely the preserve of students from stations established for a number of years. In 1901, for example, it was noted of pupils passing

78 Personal communication from Mr E. A. Muwamba, June 1966. For details concerning the present generation see Bridglal Pachai, *Malawi: the History of the Nation*, 275

79 W. P. Livingstonia, *Laws of Livingstonia*, 194–5

80 Livingstone Mission Report 1896–7, 5; Nyasaland Protectorate census for 1921. For the purpose of this calculation I have taken the Northern Province to consist of the following districts: Dedza, Dowa, Marimba, West Nyasa, Momberas and North Nyasa. It need hardly be said that the 1921 census figures must be regarded with the greatest caution but there is no reason to suppose that they seriously over-estimated the proportion of Tonga in the north.

from the Institution that in almost every case those who entered from remote districts where no stations were established dropped off after one or two years. Those who came from erratically-occupied stations like Mwenzo and Karonga also tended to leave early, and only those from a background of fully organised educational work where the training at the Institution was a step forward from the level already reached at the local boarding school, were likely to stay on to complete the Upper School course and perhaps enter the theological, commercial or medical departments.[81] Though Bandawe and Ekwendeni provided less than half the boarders in 1900, four fifths of the pupils in the Upper School (fifty-one out of sixty-four) and all the theological students (five) came from those two stations.[82] Even in 1912 they provided six of the eleven students in Standard VI.

What these students took from the Institution depended largely on the nature of the education they had received. Ambitious in the subjects it covered, the syllabus followed in the Central School was so neglectful of African experience as to open it to a charge of cultural imperialism. Instead of learning about the history or geography of their own homeland, Standard V pupils in 1903 were questioned on the names of the capes on the east coast of Scotland and the west coast of England, on the shortest sea route from Glasgow to Inverness and on the right of James I to the Crown of England. In earlier classes they might have been told of the longest rivers and the largest lakes in Africa, of British possessions and South African towns.[83] But what they would not have acquired was a sympathetic understanding of Malawi's past or an accurate knowledge of her economic potential.[84]

How far this programme amounted to a deliberate campaign of indoctrination is a difficult question to answer. On the one hand it can hardly be denied that Laws attempted to use the educational system to further the cause of the colonial economy. The hours of manual training to which the students were subjected, he wrote, resulted from his wish to

[81] *Aurora*, August 1901, 30–1

[82] 'Educational Report for the year opening 4 June 1900', Livingstonia Letters to the Sub-Committee, NLS V.31

[83] Institution Examination Papers, 1903; Livingstonia Papers

[84] This generalisation is particularly true for the period in which Henderson was Headmaster. In later years Laws gave Economics lectures on 'the needs and conditions of the country' and Scottish missionaries generally became more aware of the importance of local history. 'What could be more inappropriate,' asked Hetherwick in 1910, 'than having a class engaged for a whole year's work on a bit of English or Scottish history.' Report of the Third Nyasaland Missionary Conference, 22

develop 'in the character of the pupil habits of thrifty, patient, diligent and persevering industry'.[85] When he insisted that English should be spoken not only in the classroom but in the dormitory and dining-room as well, he did so in the belief that widespread knowledge of the 'language of the Empire' was a necessary precondition of colonial stability.[86] When he lectured to the Normal course, the topics he selected – 'the development and function of government . . . The use of money, the evil of debt' – were designed to lead students 'to think more deeply and widely of the responsibility laid upon them as Christian teachers and leaders of their fellow countrymen from barbarism to civilization'. A talk on 'the necessity for and use of taxes', for example, reached the predictable conclusion 'that taxation formerly under native rule was much heavier than now under British rule'.[87]

On the other hand, if Livingstonia's syllabus was culturally biased, it did provide a foundation for independent inquiry. By itself the heavy emphasis on reading and studying the Bible which characterised all classes in the Institution, may not have been of political importance. But when detailed knowledge of the Bible is wedded to the Free Church belief, expressed by Henderson, that 'our most urgent duty is to . . . bring people directly to the sources of their faith and to habituate them to an inner life in which there are no intermediaries', then the significance of the subject becomes much greater.[88] Armed with an independent source of authority, students in the Upper School brought a critical cast of mind to bear on debates in the literary society and on Laws's lectures on civic affairs. No doubt the emphasis on the acquisition and regurgitation of facts found throughout the Institution acted initially as a disincentive to critical discussion.[89] But it is clear that as the students' command of spoken English improved, discussions on such issues as the nature of education or the future of Africa were conducted with increasing assurance.[90] What is more, the

85 R. Laws, 'Memorandum regarding . . . the Livingstonia Mission', 11

86 Livingstonia Mission Report 1896–7, 11; *Aurora*, February 1897, 4; Laws to Administration Secretary, Northern Rhodesia, 14 July 1913, Livingstonia Papers, Box 1

87 Institution Education Diary, annual report 1907

88 ibid., annual report 1903

89 Among many complaints concerning the fact-oriented nature of the Institution's system, one written, probably by Kirkwood, in 1912, is particularly vivid. An 'over-loaded timetable' he wrote, 'tended to lead our students to look upon education as mere knowledge getting, and set them to the fish-like task of constant gulping'. Institution Education Diary, report for 1911–12.

90 ibid., report for 1910–11

absence of African topics from the syllabus did not imply the exclusion of all that was potentially inspiring. Joan of Arc and William Wallace were among famous men and women studied in the Upper School history class and these two, the teacher noted without comment, caught the imagination of her pupils more than any of the others.[91] Just as the Bible with its emphasis on the equality of all men before God, could be used to challenge the inequalities implicit in colonialism, so the simplest history lesson could provide useful ammunition for budding critics of a colonial regime.

In certain respects the great majority of Livingstonia graduates of the first generation were trapped in a web of cultural assumptions from which they never effectively broke clear. Even Edward Bote Manda, a pastor and schoolteacher whose radical comments at the Institution are still vividly remembered by his former pupils, tamely followed the mission orthodoxy in committing himself in the 1920s to the view that before the arrival of Laws 'the country . . . was naked in spirit, intellect and body' and that 'men who once were brutes are now changed into sensible human beings'.[92]

In other respects, however, the Institution's influence was politically liberalising. As the work of Clements Kadalie, Levi Mumba and Charles Domingo all demonstrate, able graduates from the Normal course before 1914 were able to speak and write English with an assurance matched by few other Africans north of the Limpopo. Equipped with at least Laws's views on 'the needs and conditions of the country',[93] they had heard debates on 'the development of native trade and industry' and taken part in discussions on legal systems and the need for penal reform.[94] If Edward Bote Manda had been their teacher they would have been inspired by the story of the emancipation of American slaves.[95] Had they been taught by Henderson they would have been told of the importance of individual judgement.[96] Like Manda, they would often have assumed that progress in Malawi was a matter of cultural adaptation to colonial

[91] Livingstonia Mission Report 1913, 7

[92] E. B. Manda and Chas. C. Chinula to R. Laws, 12 October 1925, Livingstonia Papers, Box 1. Manda's sentiments are partly explained by the fact that he was writing to congratulate Laws on his fifty years in Central Africa, but it is still significant that he should wish to express his congratulations in this form

[93] Institution Education Diary, report for 1910–11

[94] ibid., 1903

[95] David J. Cook, 'The Influence of Livingstonia Mission upon the Formation of Welfare Associations in Zambia, 1912–31' in Ranger & Weller, *Themes in the Christian History of Central Africa*, 107

[96] Institution Education Diary 1903

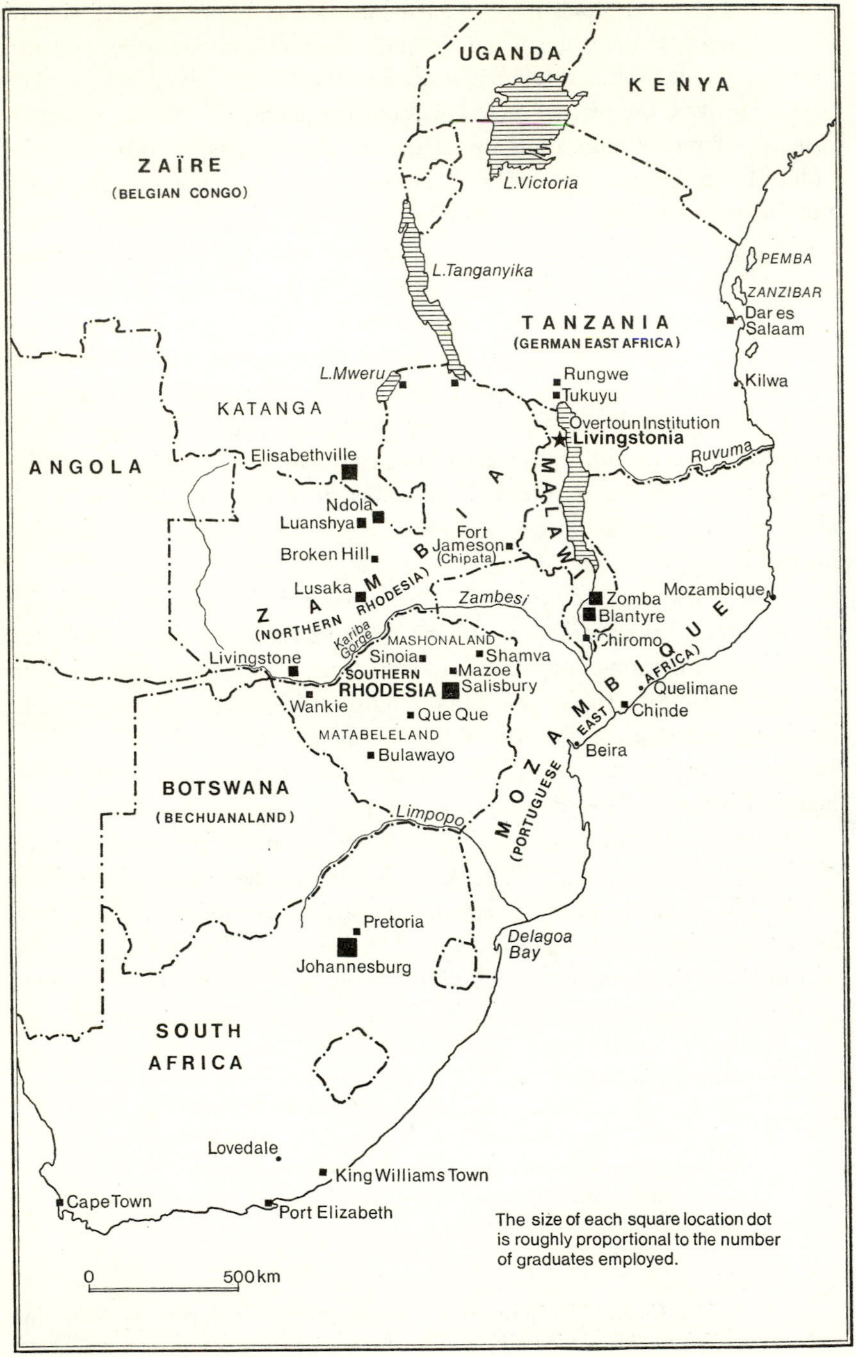

UGANDA
KENYA
L.Victoria
ZAÏRE
(BELGIAN CONGO)
L.Tanganyika
PEMBA
ZANZIBAR
Dar es Salaam
TANZANIA
(GERMAN EAST AFRICA)
L.Mweru
Rungwe
Tukuyu
Kilwa
KATANGA
Overtoun Institution
Livingstonia
Ruvuma
ANGOLA
Elisabethville
MALAWI
Ndola
Luanshya
Fort Jameson (Chipata)
Broken Hill
ZAMBIA
(NORTHERN RHODESIA)
Lusaka
Zambesi
Zomba
Blantyre
Mozambique
Kariba Gorge
MASHONALAND
Chiromo
Livingstone
Sinoia
Shamva
Mazoe
SOUTHERN RHODESIA
Salisbury
Quelimane
Wankie
Que Que
Chinde
MATABELELAND
Bulawayo
Beira
MOZAMBIQUE
(PORTUGUESE EAST AFRICA)
BOTSWANA
(BECHUANALAND)
Limpopo
Pretoria
Johannesburg
Delagoa Bay
SOUTH AFRICA
Lovedale
King Williams Town
Cape Town
Port Elizabeth
The size of each square location dot is roughly proportional to the number of graduates employed.
0
500 km

Map 4. Malawi in South Central Africa

norms. But, again like Manda, they might also have believed that the colonial structure was imperfect and could be usefully reformed through African pressure.[97]

In the absence of significant commercial opportunities in the Northern Province, the Livingstonia elite looked for employment mainly to the mission and to European-controlled occupations in other parts of South and Central Africa. Some Tonga, including a handful of Institution graduates, turned from 1902 to independent trading in the West Nyasa district, usually without notable success.[98] Other former pupils found jobs in Nyasaland with the Lakes Company and as telegraph operators, storemen and clerks; and more still used a spell of teaching in the service of the mission as the prelude for employment in metropoles as far apart as Cape Town and Dar es Salaam and in jobs as varied as customs officer and drill sergeant.[99] Salisbury and the small gold mines on the line of rail in Southern Rhodesia were the most favoured centres of work, followed by Johannesburg and the larger mines on the Rand and by Elisabethville and the copper mines controlled by the Union Minière Company in Katanga. But at least one former pupil, the Tonga, Andreya Kateta, reached Chicago in 1902 in circumstances which are still unclear,[100] a second, Simon Muhanga, worked in four separate centres in Northern Rhodesia before returning to Karonga, others scattered into Bechuanaland, Mozambique and Tanganyika, and several obtained jobs with the British South Africa Company Administration in Northern Rhodesia. When Clements Kadalie trekked south from Livingstonia in 1915 on the first stage of a journey that was to make him the best known trade unionist south of the Sahara, he trod in the footsteps of well over a hundred former pupils who had pioneered the route from the early years of the century.[101]

For many, however, including nearly 70 per cent of those who studied

[97] The influence of Manda's ideas can be gauged from the following passage written by Dr H. Kamuzu Banda to his uncle, Rev. H. M. Phiri on 21 April 1946; 'When I was a boy you used to tell me what the leaders at Khondowe such as Mr Edward Bote Manda and others planned to do just before the war started in 1914. The things you used to tell me about the meetings which had been planned at Khondowe then are still in my mind. Now I think what Mr Edward Bote Manda and others wanted to do can be done by African Congress.' I owe this reference to Dr Roderick Macdonald

[98] Annual Report of Resident, West Nyasa District, 1902–3, MNA NNC3/1/1

[99] Institution Roll Book

[100] According to a note in the Roll Book, Kateta completed his studies in a college in Chicago and later married an American

[101] Clements Kadalie, *My Life and the ICU*, London, 1970, 32–6

over two years at the Institution, the mission itself became at least a transitory centre of employment.[102] Out of 286 students who entered the Institution in the first three and a half years of its existence, ninety-four were still in Mission service in 1905. Most of these were district teachers who tended to work for Livingstonia for a couple of years before going elsewhere in search of higher wages. But some like Charles Domingo and Y. Z. Mwasi taught in the Institution's middle and lower classes and looked to the mission for internal promotion; others were medical assistants under Dr Laws; others again were administrative assistants like Levi Mumba, later to be the first President of the Nyasaland African Congress, who worked for several years at the Institution prior to the First World War.

The point to be stressed is one of considerable importance. Despite the drain of manpower from the north, several of the best educated members of the new elite remained permanently or semi-permanently in their homeland and within the mission network. The influence of migrants in terms of the exchange of ideas and experiences played no small part in the development of political organisations in the Northern Province, but as will be shown, the dominant role remained with the local residents. Though a vicious form of economic underdevelopment had been established in the Northern Province by 1914, the province still possessed and retained the highest percentage of the educated and politically adept to be found in the whole country. It is from these two facts that much of the pattern of subsequent political events derive.

[102] 216 of the students who entered the Institution between July 1895 and June 1901 stayed there for 2 years or more. Of these 139 (64.35%) are recorded in the Institution roll book as having worked for the mission.

7
Church and State, 1891–1914

The Scottish missions and the colonial occupation

When acting-consul Buchanan declared a protectorate over the Shire highlands on 21 September 1889 he set in motion a chain of events leading to the arrival of Harry Johnston, first Commissioner and Consul General, at Chiromo in July 1891, to the subsequent establishment of British rule over the whole of what was to be called Nyasaland, and consequently to a transformation in the conditions under which missions in the country worked. Hitherto, missionaries, even when they attempted to stand aloof, had participated actively in the local political scene as equals and sometimes as subordinates, to the neighbouring authorities. Now, though they might continue to participate with far fewer obstacles and uncertainties than before, their political actions tended increasingly to be defined in relationship not to African politics but to those of the colonial regime. The closer the political interests of the missionary lay to those of the administrator, the more likely it was that Africans would regard the one as an extension of the other.

In Malawi these interests were only partly complementary. In contrast to the situation south of the Zambesi where, according to Cairns, 'total missionary failure' led LMS agents after thirty years of fruitless toil 'to the vision of the Chartered Company as an instrument of God to crush the Matabele and provide missionary access to a haughty warrior nation',[1] both Blantyre and Livingstonia had established substantial contact with local peoples in the quarter century before occupation, and were reluctant to see destroyed all that had been carefully built up. From the earliest days they had sought British Government support, first to reinforce the anti-slave trade campaign and reduce the difficulties involved in missionary participation in civil jurisdiction, and latterly to keep out the Portuguese and Arabs. Attempts had been made unsuccessfully to obtain consulships for E. D. Young and James Stewart, CE, and Dr Stewart as

[1] Cairns, *Prelude to Imperialism*, 242

early as August 1877 had produced a scheme, remarkably similar to that later formulated by Harry Johnston, for the appointment of a commissioner with a steamer on the lake and a small armed force.[2] The Church of Scotland's Foreign Missions Committee on 25 October 1884 and again in March 1885 had appealed to the Foreign Secretary (then Lord Granville) to prevent Portuguese encroachments in the Blantyre district, and had joined with the other churches the following year in an attempt to limit Portuguese influence to a line south of the Ruo river.[3] And these actions had been merely the prelude for a vigorous campaign waged in 1887 and 1888 by the missionaries and their powerful supporters in Britain for government action against the 'north-end' Arabs and the Portuguese, which culminated in April and early May 1889 in a series of public meetings held in Aberdeen, Glasgow and Edinburgh, and the presentation to Lord Salisbury of a monster petition signed by over 11 000 ministers and elders of the Scottish churches.[4] When Salisbury by an ultimatum of January 1890 forced the Portuguese to withdraw their troops from the Shire his 'firmness' was lauded as 'magnificent'.[5] 'The news of the British Flag being hoisted on the Ruo and the Shire Hills declared under British protection has greatly delighted us', a Church of Scotland official enthused.[6]

But if the missionaries welcomed the imperial government, they had little desire to see it act in an imperial manner. When Dr Stewart presented his original plan for government support he remarked that 'The general principle of the plan is the same in the Indian Protected States where a B.R. [British Resident] had been appointed.'[7] Some form of indirect rule appears to have been wanted, with the government preventing other powers moving into the Malawi regions, but leaving the existing political situation largely undisturbed. Loose talk in the early years of forming British protectorates or spheres of influence was converted by the stony insistence of the government that it could not intervene

[2] Livingstonia sub-committee minutes, entry for 30 June 1880, NLS 7912; 'Replies to questions proposed by Capt. Elton' 23 August 1887, Stewart Papers ST1/1/1

[3] McMurtrie to Salisbury, 6 January 1886, NLS 7548; to D. C. Scott, 23 September 1886; to Rankin, 23 December 1886, NLS 7534

[4] The best account of this campaign appears in *The Scotsman*, 16 and 19 April, 18 May 1889 and *The Times*, 18 May 1889

[5] McMurtrie to D. C. Scott, 13 February 1890, NLS 7534

[6] Maclagan to D. C. Scott, 21 November 1889, NLS 7550. For a comparable response from the Free Church see Dr Smith to Sir Philip Currie, 22 January 1890, NLS 7774

[7] 'Replies to questions proposed by Capt. Elton'

in a dynamic political capacity into the negative policy that '*as missionaries* we ask *to be let alone* in Nyasaland and do not press for a British sphere of influence there'.[8] When Horace Waller on behalf of the three missions involved, approached Lord Salisbury on 2 March 1887, he told him that:

> The object of the missionaries was *not* to gain protection from personal danger, or to be able to rely on military force against native barbarism; on the contrary their sole desire was to save the settled tribes among whom they were settled from the vice of demoralization which must result if the Portuguese were to push on to the lake.[9]

A year later, Professor Lindsay, a distinguished Free Church leader, took the same view: 'The missionaries did not ask for interference directly on their behalf. If free entrance was given by the Zambesi, the missionaries and trading companies would do the rest.'[10] Even in the moment of greatest peril in 1889, the missionaries did not request a British protectorate.

Further friction was consequent upon the historical antecedents of the administration. In 1885 the African Lakes Company, frustrated by frequent robberies on its trade routes, and alarmed by Portuguese territorial claims, attempted to clarify its political position. Treaties were made with Makololo, Yao and Tonga chiefs, and with several others on the Nyasa–Tanganyika plateau, and the British Government was requested either to take up the rights ceded by the chiefs or to grant a charter to the company enabling it to begin governing itself.

Among missionaries with experience of John and Fred Moir, the company's managers, the almost unanimous opinion was that they were completely unsuited for such responsibilities. 'They cannot govern Mandala store,' J. A. Smith, himself a former company employee, wrote, 'and how they are to govern the country they are pretending to be anxious to take over is a problem to be solved.'[11]

Livingstonia, however, was so closely identified with the ALC, particularly in Scotland where Dr Moir, father of the joint managers, was a member of the Livingstonia sub-committee along with the two leading directors, James Stevenson and John Stephen, that criticisms sent home tended to be muted, and a joint policy on political questions was usually agreed upon. On Laws's advice in 1885 the committee instructed their

[8] Smith to Munn Ferguson, 8 April 1889, NLS 7773

[9] Memo. of meeting between Rev. R. H. Penney, Rev. Horace Walter and Lord Salisbury, 2 March 1887, NLS 7873

[10] Quoted in *The Manchester Guardian*, 19 May 1888

[11] J. A. Smith to Laws, 14 December 1885, Shepperson Collection

agents to assist the company in obtaining treaties, and when, a year later, the question of a charter was raised with the British Government, the mission firmly supported the company's claim.[12]

Blantyre in contrast was restricted by no such identity of interests. The missionaries regarded as 'ridiculous' the prices charged by the company for the carriage of goods, and blamed the death of at least one of their colleagues on the deficiencies of the company's passenger service. When the proposal to grant the company the power of forming a protectorate was first produced, Hetherwick protested strongly to Consul Hawes, basing his case on 'the manifest incapacity of the Lakes Company as at present constituted for undertaking such administration'.[13] In Scotland, D. C. Scott took steps to dissuade the UMCA from supporting Moir's scheme, and the Foreign Missions Committee followed this up by informing the Foreign Office of its disapproval.[14]

During subsequent years the Blantyre missionaries hardened in their opposition to chartered company rule, while those from Livingstonia remained sympathetic towards it. Partly as a result of Blantyre's protests, the ALC directors in 1886 decided to shelve their plans for a protectorate. They were not discarded totally however, and in September 1888 suspicions were once more aroused by a chance indication that John Moir regarded the treaties as still valid.[15] A year later in 1889 Cecil Rhodes put forward a plan for absorbing the ALC into his much more powerful organisation, the British South Africa Company, and offered up to £9000 a year to finance the government of the regions north of the Zambesi. Livingstonia officials, who had been urging the ALC to act for nearly a year, were delighted at Rhodes's initiative. Only a month before the first offer was made, Dr George Smith in April 1889 had suggested that 'The true solution' of the impasse created by the British Government's refusal to intervene 'is for the F.O. to give a charter to a strong Company there like Mackinnon's further north.'[16] Rhodes's company, presided over, it was hoped, by Lord Balfour of Burleigh, was regarded as a satisfactory outcome of all that the missionaries had been campaigning for.[17] Its

12 Livingstonia sub-committee minutes entry for 13 March 1885, NLS 7912

13 Hetherwick to Hawes enclosed in Hawes to FO, 30 March 1886, FO 84/1751

14 Maclagan to Hetherwich, 23 December 1885; Maclagan to Lister, 20 July 1886, NLS 7584

15 FO to Hawes, 24 July 1886, FO 84/1751; 'Proceedings of Informal Meeting assembled at Blantyre', 24 September 1888, Lugard Papers, s.35

16 Dr Smith to Munn Ferguson 8 April 1889, NLS 7773

17 Balfour, Parliamentary Secretary to the Board of Trade from 1889 to 1902 and Secretary of State for Scotland from 1895 to 1903, was the leading

charter, Smith believed, in an obvious reference to the company's political powers, 'is skillfully drawn so as not to excite the attention of Portugal and Germany'. A. L. Bruce, Livingstone's son-in-law and a director of the ALC, described it to him approvingly as 'a telescope intended to be drawn out so as to cover the territory north of the Zambesi, up to Tanganyika in due time'.[18]

Among Church of Scotland representatives, the response was less enthusiastic. Some officials, notably McMurtrie, the F.M.C. convenor, had so despaired of British Government action in 1888 that they had looked for a new Rajah Brooke to carve out his own Sarawak in Malawi as an independent British domain.[19] To these, Rhodes's intervention came at a highly opportune moment. At Blantyre, however, the missionaries stood firm to their original principles. Along with their announcement in the September issue of the *Blantyre Mission Supplement* of the declaration of a British Protectorate, a warning note was struck: 'The legislation to follow may be either wholly in Government hands or in the hands of a Chartered Company under Government supervision. We hope for the former and protection of native rights and missionary appeal.'[20] The confidential publication in July 1890 of Johnston's memorandum on the administration of British Central Africa by a chartered company, leaked secretly to the missionaries by John Moir, did nothing to still their suspicions. The missionaries, in Johnston's words, immediately 'took flame at the idea of being governed by a wicked Company', and between August and October opened up a formidable verbal attack in their monthly magazine.

> A large Company aided by Government, is welcome indeed [the supplement for August declared]; but the relegation of all interests, missionary, trader, settler and especially native interests, to the sole judgement of a large monopolizing Commercial concern is not and never has been considered help at all, certainly not protection.[21]

A whole year before the new government was established, the mission was ranged strongly against it.

politician representing Church of Scotland interests in Parliament at this time. His position in the government made it necessary for him to refuse Rhodes's offer

[18] Dr Smith to Cross, 24 October 1889, NLS 7774

[19] McMurtrie to Cleland, 25 October 1888, NLS 7534. James Brooke, the 'White Rajah', was an ex-naval officer, who took service with the Sultan of Brunei in 1841 and became ruler of Sarawak in full sovereignty in 1846

[20] *LWBMS*, September 1889

[21] ibid., August 1890. For Johnston's comments on the missionaries see Johnston to Rhodes, 7 June 1893, Salisbury CT1/16/4/1

Part of Blantyre's suspicions undoubtedly arose from its estimate of the new commissioner. Johnston antagonised the mission firstly in 1889 by conceding the whole Shire highlands, including Blantyre, to Portugal in the draft treaty he concluded in Lisbon in April of that year. The Free Church, after an initial spasm of opposition, came quickly to recognise that an agreement which left almost the whole of its sphere of influence within the British zone was 'a compromise of a very important missionary and imperial character'. Dr George Smith warned Laws that 'As missionaries we must keep out of politics, but must not politically oppose any *modus vivendi* which will relieve the present strain you and your colleagues and the traders are bearing so nobly'.[22] And the Foreign Missions Committee, after receiving a personal statement from Johnston, resolved on 14 May not to oppose the agreement if various British rights were recognised in the Portuguese sphere.[23] Henceforth, the church's relations with the Commissioner, if distant, were correct.

Blantyre agents, however, not unnaturally regarded Johnston's agreement as a betrayal which could not be obscured even by Lord Salisbury's rejection of the draft treaty and the final solution achieved in June 1891. Further doubts were raised by Johnston's initial intention, quickly abandoned, of cooperating with the Arab traders and using them as government agents, perhaps, it was feared, in order to 'play them off against the missionaries'.[24] Relations too were embittered as a result of the Commissioner's friendly warning to McMurtrie, made on his return from Malawi in 1891, that the high death rate among Blantyre missionaries was caused by their use of a polluted water supply. Scott indignantly repudiated the suggestion, all the more painful to him because it suggested the negligence of his brother-in-law, Dr John Bowie, who had himself recently died. But though the charge was allowed to drop, the fact that it had been made at all continued to rankle.[25]

To these 'historical' reasons for the particular intensity of Blantyre's opposition to the colonial administration three further factors must be added.

In the first place, the Blantyre missionaries by 1890 had developed a radical philosophy for Africa which was to bring them into conflict with the metropolitan authorities of their church.[26] Around Scott a small circle

22 Dr Smith to Laws, 9 May 1889, NLS 7773

23 Minutes of the Foreign Committee of the FCS, entry for 14 May 1889. Church of Scotland Offices, Edinburgh. For the circumstances surrounding the abortive treaty see Hanna, *Beginnings*, 135–8

24 McMurtrie to Walker, 19 February 1891, NLS 7534

25 See McMurtrie to D. C. Scott, 16 March and 10 August 1891, NLS 7534

26 Andrew C. Ross 'The Foundations of the Blantyre Mission, Nyasaland',

of like-minded followers had formed themselves: Willie Scott, his brother, John Bowie, Alexander Hetherwick and Henry Scott among them, several of whom were related to him by marriage or by birth. By and large they came from the professional middle classes in contrast to Livingstonia's ordained men who were generally of upper-working or lower-middle class backgrounds: the Scott brothers were the sons of an Edinburgh accountant; Bowie's father was Secretary of the Philosophical Association in the same city. Macvicar was a son of the manse. Well educated and talented – all had been to one or other of the Scottish universities, and several, including Hetherwick, David Scott, Bowie and Macvicar, had done brilliantly there – they had the assurance of men confident of their ability to make their way in any walk of life, who had deliberately turned aside from the mainstream of promotion. What drew them together appears to have been a certain independence of spirit, a radical, deeply critical approach to the Western world that came out less in their conventional political attitudes than in their social ones. Willie Scott, for example, had no sympathy with socialist political doctrines, and believed that legislation had little value in bettering the condition of the working classes, while his brother, in choosing the mission staff, looked particularly for 'the traditions of a gentle, well-bred courteous home'.[27] But in Scotland they had both deeply concerned themselves with the working-class condition and were frustrated by the failure of their church to respond in the same vein. Willie Scott, according to his biographer, 'was terribly dissatisfied with Church life as it showed itself throughout the city [Edinburgh]. He had no sympathy with the system . . . which forces the minister to devote most of his time to the congregation, and leave the "mission hall" in the charge of an assistant or a missionary.'[28] As for Clement Scott he extended his criticism of the official organs of the Church of Scotland, and of contemporary methods of worship, to an attack on various aspects of the Western world and a defence of many African institutions in comparison. His ambition, he admitted in November 1888, was 'to see in this land native power established in thorough sympathy with superior civilization and permeated by it'.[29] But that did not mean that Western civilisation was superior in all respects.

Religion in Africa, Centre of African Studies, University of Edinburgh 1964, 105–7

[27] W. H. Rankine, *A Hero of the Dark Continent*, Edinburgh 1896, 79–80; *LWBMS*, May 1891

[28] Rankine, 79–80

[29] *LWBMS*, November 1888. For a more extended study of Scott's policies see Ross 'Foundations'

> The great Kaffir race which *possesses* Africa [he wrote years after he had left Blantyre], has a deep sense of rule and authority, of religion and personal liberty, of home and country. Its monarchy is twentieth century in character; its religion the worship of one God; its personality far more exacting in politeness, mutual respect, recognition of the duties of friendship and of every relationship in life, than our own; its home-ties deeply and pathetically real, and bereavement rends its heart with a sorrow understood only of a few.[30]

Livingstonia missionaries by comparison, though several of them had a first-hand knowledge of working-class life unrevealed to the Blantyre men, were much less radical in their attitudes; much more prepared to accept and even propagate the values of an industrial society. Laws was always anxious to act in support of the government and, as he declared in April 1888 over the contentious problem of the continuance of the north-end war, 'felt himself unable to approve of any line of policy which Her Majesty's Government could not recognise as within the rights of British subjects to carry out'.[31] It was entirely typical of their different attitudes that whereas Scott regarded the British assumption of political control as a threat to African rights, Laws saw it as a challenge, leading 'to an influx of Europeans, and to a demand for educated natives to assist them in commercial and artisan work'.[32] Scott's reaction was to raise the banner of opposition in defence of African interests; Laws's to found the Overtoun Institution in order to provide Africans with the facilities to cope successfully themselves with the new conditions.

Secondly, the two missions differed on the type of settlements they had founded. Both, as we have seen, were theocratic in origin; but whereas at Livingstonia attempts had been made for several years to rid the mission of its temporal powers, at Blantyre the missionaries still gloried in their responsibilities. Ten years after Duff Macdonald's departure, Elmslie noted that 'The plan of a colony is still in force at Blantyre in a modified form.' D. C. Scott, in Ross's words, 'became a chief among chiefs and had to go to many Mlandu with his neighbours such as Kapeni and Mpama'.[33] The growth of a small community of British settlers in the

30 D. C. Ruffelle Scott, '*Living Stones*' *Sermon upon the Church of Scotland Blantyre Mission in British Central Africa*, Edinburgh, 1901, 5–6

31 Quoted in John Buchanan to FO, 13 April 1888, FO 84/1883

32 Laws 'Memorandum on the Organisation and Development of the Livingstonia Mission', 1892

33 Quoted in cutting from *The Scottish Leader*, 26 March, n.d., NLS 7906; A. C. Ross, 'The Origins and Development of the Church of Scotland Mission, Blantyre, Nyasaland 1875–1926', Edinburgh PhD 1968, 111–12

Shire highlands prior to 1890 further encouraged the expansion of the missionaries' temporal aspirations. Hetherwick, it was claimed in March 1886, 'appears to have the opinion that the Blantyre Mission from being the first to settle here is considered by many to be the centre of the English population and would be held responsible by the natives for any action taken by the European community at present living in the neighbourhood'.[34] Two years later, D. C. Scott was suggesting 'that very soon something like a conference of the interests in the country should be formed and that the harmonious and mutual understanding hitherto existing in the community should be formulated into something like contracts and safeguards'. 'It was not to *make* a State that Sir Harry Johnston was sent,' the missionaries were later to claim in a sentence succinctly summarising Blantyre's fundamental complaint, 'but to deliver from Portuguese occupation a state already made.'[35]

The third and perhaps the most important distinction was the geographical one. The financial resources available to Johnston's government were so meagre that it was impossible for him in 1891 and subsequent years to attempt the pacification and active administration of the whole of the Protectorate. Instead, he restricted his activities to the districts of white settlement in the Shire highlands and attemped to put down slave trading, as he explained to Lord Salisbury, 'along our narrow and precious line of communication between the Shire and Tanganyika'.[36] Livingstonia's sphere of work was thus hardly affected by the introduction of government: the first administrative post among the Tonga was not established till 1897 and among the northern Ngoni till 1904. Blantyre, Domasi and Mlanje, however, came within the range of the Commissioner's activities from the start and were the scene of several military expeditions sent against Yao chiefs; while the Blantyre district, in addition, was the first in which taxation was imposed. The effect of the administration upon the work of the two missions was thus quite different in their separate areas. In the neighbourhood of Livingstonia's settlements the growth of British power, witnessed from a distance, coincided with a marked growth in popular interest in the mission and particularly in education. Near the Blantyre settlements, however, the increased interest in mission teaching was more than counterbalanced by the damage done to existing mission–Yao ties, by the uprooting of villages formerly friendly to the mission, and by the distractions resulting from a sharp expansion in the number and

[34] Hawes to FO, 20 March 1886, FO 48/1751

[35] *LWBMS*, May 1888; August to December 1897

[36] Johnston to Salisbury, 25 February 1892, *Papers relative to the suppression of slave-trading in Nyasaland*, 1892, Cmd 6699.

size of European plantations in the highlands. In 1894, for example, the teacher, J. A. Smith, commented on the damage done to Blantyre's schools by the removal of a neighbouring chief's village on the orders of the administration and also by the tendency of children to abandon their education in favour of paid work on the plantations.[37]

The result was that each major society developed its own distinctive approach towards the government. At Blantyre, the missionaries' ingrained suspicion of Johnston, and of his ties with Rhodes, flared into such open hostility that by 1893 Johnston was seriously considering the advisability of deporting Scott and Hetherwick from the country.[38] He was also devising elaborate counters against their attacks by founding the *British Central Africa Gazette*, 'as a means of providing an alternative source of local news' to the mission's magazine, and, so he told Rhodes, by 'effecting a religious cleavage at Blantyre' through the clumsy expedient of donating over £35, largely from administration funds, to the UMCA in the name of Rhodes and his principal BSAC advisers, and by offering to finance the building of an Anglican Church at the Scottish mission's headquarters.[39]

How far the missionaries' opposition arose, as Johnston and Sharpe both asserted, from an unwillingness 'to accept the fact that they are no longer a Political Power in the country'; and how far it sprang, as a recent commentator has suggested, from a 'difference of attitude towards the African and his society' is still a subject of controversy.[40] That the political circumstances of the mission played a part cannot easily be denied. Time and again – in the case of Malamia at Domasi, of Mitioche at Chiradzulu, of Malungu at Ndirande and of Chikhumbu at Mlanje – the attacks on Yao chiefs which aroused the greatest mission hostility took place within an area where Blantyre had already established a degree of local influence. Scott's rebuke to missionaries using the government's law courts; Hetherwick's queries as to Johnston's authority to raise taxes, were both not so much the criticisms of an opposition party as of a would-

[37] FMC report in General Assembly Papers of the Church of Scotland 1895, 120

[38] Sharpe to FO, 31 October 1894, FO 2/67

[39] Johnston to Rhodes, 7 June 1893, Salisbury CT1/16/4/1

[40] Sharpe to FO, 31 October 1894, FO 2/67; A. C. Ross 'The African – a Child or a Man', in Brown and Stokes *Zambesian Past*, 339. Among modern writers, both Roland Oliver, *Sir Harry Johnston and the Scramble for Africa*, London, 1957, 209–13 and Ake Holmberg, *African Tribes and European Agencies*, Göteborg, 1966, 283–310 agree substantially with Sharpe's opinion.

be rival sovereign power.[41] Nor was the mission entirely justified in claiming that the sole weapons it sought to use in bringing 'Central Africa into obedience to civilization' were those 'of peaceful argument and respected "presence"'.[42] No more bellicose support for the continuation of the north-end war was received than from Blantyre; while when the mission at Domasi was threatened by Kawinga in 1895 it was D. C. Scott who called on the administration's armed assistance and W. A. Scott who assisted in the subsequent expedition. Much was written in *Life and Work* of the constitutional nature of African society in order to point the need for constitutional methods in dealing with it; but when the needs changed, the despotic character of African society was signalled out instead.[43]

Yet these contradictions – inevitable perhaps in a protest movement whose heart was stronger than its head – should not be allowed to obscure the very real concern of the missionaries in building up the Protectorate on the foundations provided by African political authorities, and with their consent, rather than of smashing those authorities as a prelude to the introduction of European rule, as Johnston undoubtedly desired. While Johnston successfully played off various conflicts of interest between African rulers in Malawi in order to establish his rule by force, Scott and his friends insisted that 'No attempt at government or administration would be successful in Africa any more than elsewhere that does not carry chiefs and people along with it', and publicly attacked 'the formula of *divide et impera* which we have seen advocated as an effective African policy'.[44] Given the destruction of indigenous political systems inevitable when an aggressive policy of 'pacification' was followed without the resources available to speedily achieve its ends, it is understandable that Scott should condemn the new administration so heartily. In essence the two policies were irreconcilable.[45]

The different reception given by Livingstonia to the government goes far to explain why for Johnston, as for a series of his successors, Laws was 'the greatest man who has yet appeared in Nyasaland'.[46] At Blantyre in

[41] *LWBCA*, October 1898; Hetherwick to Dr A. Scott 13 June 1893, NLS 7534

[42] *LWBCA*, February 1897

[43] D. C. Scott to Buchanan, 17 May 1888, Lugard Papers, s.34; Sharpe to Kimberley, 7 and 28 February 1895, FO 2/88; *LWBCA*, May and November 1892

[44] *LWBMS*, October 1892; Shepperson and Price, 17–18

[45] For a critical examination of Johnston's policies see Stokes, 'Malawi Political Systems'

[46] Johnston to FO, 17 March 1890, FO 84/2051. Hetherwick, by contrast,

1892 the very existence of laws and regulations in the Protectorate was queried: at Bandawe in the same year the missionaries went out of their way to utilise the magisterial authority of the state in settling inter-African disputes and in dealing with cases brought direct by the mission against its neighbours.[47] Almost every punitive expedition undertaken by Johnston was criticised by Established Church missionaries in the belief, so they wrote in *Life and Work*, that 'the British Government could rule and develop this whole African Empire in all questions really native *without striking a blow*'. Laws, though he was informed of the occasional case where the government acted in too high-handed a manner, exerted most of his diplomatic skills in restraining hot-headed colleagues – Cross at the north end, Govan Robertson at Livlezi – from calling down vengeance on the Arabs and southern Ngoni respectively at a time when the administration was anxious for peace.[48]

Back in Britain the same contrast prevailed. Free Church authorities shared with those of the Established Church a suspicion of Johnston's ambiguous dual role as Commissioner for the Protectorate and Administrator of the British South Africa Company's territories; they resented his attempt to assign spheres of influence to each mission, partly because '*that* was a question solely for the Churches concerned to be settled on purely *spiritual* grounds', and more, because he would have excluded Livingstonia from southern Ngoniland – as she was later to exclude herself; and they rose in well justified protest against his proposed poll tax of 12s, reduced before implementation to 6s and later to 3s.[49] But that was as far as they would go. George Smith warned Laws, at a time when deputations to the Foreign Office were at their most popular that 'we must not let ourselves be dragged by Clement Scott into condemning Johnston's administration as he tries to get his committee to do'.[50] He and Laws were ready to explain to Salisbury the injustice of excessive taxation and the need for it only to be levied after full explanation had been made.

was described as 'a loathsome little brute' by one member of the administration. Wordsworth Poole to his mother, 2 September 1895, MNA POI/I

47 Hetherwick to Johnston, 7 December 1892, Blantyre Mission Papers, MNA; Sharpe to Johnston, 17 December 1892 enclosed in Johnston to FO, 2 January 1893, FO 2/54

48 *LWBCA*, December 1894; Laws to Govan Robertson, 18 April 1895, NLS 7878

49 Livingstonia Mission Committee minutes entry for 17 November 1892; Dr Smith to Bruce, 9 February 1891, NLS 7774; Livingstonia Mission Committee minutes entry for 16 December 1891, NLS 7899

50 Dr Smith to Laws, 18 March 1892, NLS 7899

But they refused to join the Established Church in its protest against Johnston's burning of villages, until, as Lindsay wrote, 'it should be clearly shown that this burning was not done to put down the slave trade'. As early as February 1892 Laws was sending back to Britain 'reliable facts and views as to Mr H. H. Johnston's actions and policy of a nature less unfavourable to these than rumour had led us to believe'.[51]

Even on the question of the introduction of British South Africa Company rule, Livingstonia's support for Blantyre in its most successful campaign was barely nominal. The 1891 agreement, whereby the Protectorate was administered by the Foreign Office with the help of a subsidy from the British South Africa Company, was a highly fragile compromise which could not last for long. Scott and Hetherwick believed, with considerable justification, that Rhodes was anxious to turn the paying agency into the ruling one and they therefore scrutinised Johnston's actions with considerable concern in the years up to November 1894 when the Treasury agreed to take over financial responsibility for the Protectorate.[52] But while the Blantyre missionaries argued that there were compulsive moral objections to the extension of company rule – the fundamental inability of a financial concern, whose major responsibility was to its shareholders, to deal fairly with the varied interests of the protectorate; the danger inherent in the spread of South African attitudes and policies to Malawi – Laws appears to have regarded Rhodes's scheme without positive disapproval. Indeed he may have sympathised with the Free Church official who wrote to him at the time of the withdrawal of the company's subsidy, expressing his fears at what a Foreign Office dominated future would bring.[53] Laws's major concern in the mid 1890s was to obtain possession of a vast estate, over 100 square miles in extent for the Overtoun Institution. Johnston, in his capacity as commissioner, was reluctant to authorise such a large land grant, though he made it a general rule to facilitate missions acquiring small sites, almost wherever they wanted them. To Rhodes however, who owned the land in question, and to his agent Major Forbes, Laws's request dovetailed not untidily with their own policies south of the Zambesi, of making enormous land grants to missions in order that they might play a full part in opening up the new territory to the international economy. Rhodes responded favourably to Laws's initial request for land, made in a private interview at Cape Town in November 1894, and Forbes was also

[51] Lindsay to Laws, 18 March 1892, NLS 7899; Dr Smith to Fotheringham, 4 February 1892, NLS 7775

[52] For further details see Oliver, *Sir Harry Johnston*, 224–44; Holmberg *African Tribes*, 297–310

[53] J. F. Daly to Laws, 18 January 1895, NLS 7900

sympathetic. 'The Major told me that he is prepared to grant sites and farms wherever we may have stations or in localities where we may in the future open out', Elmslie wrote in 1897. 'He said that Rhodes had asked him to report on the missions in Matabeleland and in Nyasaland. He had felt bound to put our mission first in influence and extent of operations.'[54] From 1895, when Johnston intervened in the land question to accuse Livingstonia of conferring fewer benefits on the settler community of Nyasaland than Blantyre and the UMCA, Livingstonia's relations with the company were warmer than with the Protectorate government. The company paid part of the salary of the medical missionary, Dr Chisholm, at Mwenzo from 1899 and also gave grants towards the training of African clerks and artisans at the Institution. In return Livingstonia provided the administration of North-Eastern Rhodesia with many of its best trained African employees.

Livingstonia's attitude should not be misconstrued. An unwillingness to attack the government did not imply a desire to identify with it. On the contrary, the Scottish Presbyterians, torn by the typical mission dilemma of being anxious to encourage the extension of industrial civilisation, but repelled by the conduct of the secular pioneers of that culture, resolved the problem increasingly by making the distinction between them and other Europeans as clearly defined as possible. Even in the 1880s the behaviour of elephant hunters near Bandawe had caused the missionary-in-charge to refuse to allow ALC employees to reside there, except in cases of sickness. With the added influx of settlers from 1890 the gulf between what the mission preached and what other Europeans practised noticeably widened. For all the shortcomings of certain ALC agents they included among their number, as Laws was well aware, several devout evangelists who faithfully acted in the tradition of the lay missionary. 'We have had worship every night,' wrote one ALC engineer, 'and on Sundays a service in the forenoon for ourselves and a native service at night for the boys.'[55] Less could be expected from members of Rhodes's company; less still, in the early days, from officials of the administration, who despite Johnston's efforts to attract 'honest, fearless, energetic, cultured gentlemen', were more often of the rough diamond frontier variety.[56] Time and again in the early 1890s reports reached Laws of behaviour by individual officials

[54] Elmslie to Smith, 16 June 1897, NLS 7880

[55] Kydd to Laws, 11 December 1886, Shepperson Collection. Frederick Morrison's Diary provides abundant evidence of similarly pious behaviour.

[56] H. H. Johnston, 'England and Germany in Africa', *The Fortnightly Review*, 1 July 1890, 127

which, it was said, 'will hinder us dreadfully in our work'.[57] One consequence was the decision to keep mission schools well clear of ALC depots; another, influenced by the previous difficulties into which the mission had fallen as a result of her help in obtaining the 1885 treaties for the company, was to give only limited assistance in extending the power of the *Boma*.[58] Coillard in Barotseland, J. S. Moffat among the Matabele, might act as middlemen in furthering the advance of colonial rule. In Ngoniland, Elmslie by 1889 was determined to have nothing to do with it.

> The Consul's movements are full of interest and especially his proposed visit to Mombera [he told Laws in September of that year]. I hope he wont come here and if he does come I can predict his non-success . . . No communication will be had with him except through us and I would refuse to be the medium: and if treaties such as the A.L. Co. tried to get settled were presented I would like Bain with the chiefs at the north advise the Angoni to decline them if I were asked concerning them. You may not be able to see how such affects us, but I assure you it would do harm to our work. From past experience I would respectfully say that if the Atonga are to be treated with, do not allow the Mission to show connection with it in the way of having them signed on the station.[59]

Elmslie's advice illustrates the major importance of local, political perspectives in explaining the different ways in which individual missionaries responded to the advance of colonialism on the ground. During the 1890s at least three different attitudes existed among Livingstonia's agents. To those like Elmslie, who worked in northern Ngoniland, the priority was to preserve the Ngoni from a major confrontation with the British at a time when missionary contacts appeared to be bearing fruit. Elmslie anxiously warned against the extension of the Arab war towards Ngoniland in 1889 and tried to dissuade Johnston from making treaties with Mbelwa and Mtwaro, because 'no treaty binding them to peace with surrounding tribes will hinder the warriors from going out'. Forced against his will to mediate between the administration and Ngoni rulers in 1896, he strongly opposed any attempt to punish the Ngoni for harbouring the refugee Chibisa. Fraser intervened successfully to reduce friction between Ngoni warriors and white adventurers in the last years of the century. He and Stuart accompanied Sharpe at the famous conference in

57 Gossip to Laws, 6 September 1890, NLS 7894
58 Gossip to Laws, 4 June 1891, NLS 7895; Harkness to Laws, 12 January 1885, Shepperson Collection
59 Elmslie to Laws, 23 September 1889, NLS 7892

1904, at which the absorption of northern Ngoniland into the Protectorate finally took place.[60]

To missionaries working in marginal areas, such conciliatory attitudes appeared dangerously mild. Viewed from the Ngonde angle at Karonga, the Ngoni were a vicious, marauding people, whose suppression was to be desired. 'It is to crush and render impossible atrocities of this character,' Kerr Cross wrote in 1893 of an Ngoni raid in his vicinity, 'that the domain of British civilization must be extended in Central Africa.'[61] As an ally of the Ngonde, Cross threw himself into the crusade against the 'north-end' Arabs, with a fervour which Alfred Sharpe found positively embarrassing. In 1892, during a period of peace, Cross 'kept alive the feeling of insecurity . . . by constantly asking the Arab people, "When was war coming?"'.[62] In the same way, the missionaries at Livlezi resented Ngoni and Yao raids on the district in which they worked and despaired of changing conditions without military intervention. To Dewar in 1895, Johnston's administration 'more properly might be called a Maladministration', not because its policies were harsh, but because they were not harsh enough. Insufficient action had been taken, he argued, in punishing Ngoni thieves who stole goods consigned to the mission. The administration had delayed too long, Govan Robertson believed, in failing to attack slavers from Mponda's. In March 1895, Sharpe, the acting commissioner, was forced to warn Robertson that he would remove him from the district 'if I hear of you or your people mixing yourselves up again with those slavery questions'.[63]

As secretary of the mission council, Laws's perspective was naturally broader than that of many of his colleagues. Unlike the Ngoniland missionaries, he does not appear to have believed that any advantage would accrue from refusing assistance in extending colonial rule. Against the advice of Elmslie he witnessed the treaties signed by Johnston with Tonga headmen in 1889. At the same time, with the major exception of the Arab war, Laws was not prepared to encourage military intervention. In 1889 he became convinced that the Arab attack was a premeditated one, aimed at establishing their dominance over the lake, and for this reason he supported the company in its military adventure. He made

[60] Elmslie to Laws, 20 September, 21 October 1889, ibid.; Elmslie to Smith, 24 June, 1896, NLS 7879; Fraser, *Primitive People*, 239–42

[61] *Central Africa*, April 1893, 50–1

[62] Sharpe to Johnston, 17 December 1892, enclosed in Johnston to FO, 2 January 1893, FO 2/54

[63] Dewar to Dr Smith, 12 January 1895; Sharpe to Govan Robertson, 28 January 1895 (copy), NLS 7878

clear, however, that Cross would not be allowed to serve as a military combatant and later reproved Robertson for seeking to use force in rescuing runaway slaves.[64]

The sequel, in the late 1890s and early twentieth century is highly revealing. At Blantyre, a spirited defence of the rights of those who could not speak for themselves was converted almost insensibly into a demand for the right to determine their future. For all Scott's admiration for African culture and forms of political organisation, his philosophy contained an authoritarian edge: the God-ordained function of the African disciple was to serve; of the European missionary to advise and instruct: 'The relationship is almost that of sonship and the master has to be the father.'[65] Hetherwick, as early as 1888, took the doctrine further when he asked, 'What now does Africa need?' and answered 'she could not tell you; she does not know her needs . . . It is only the missionary who knows Africa's needs.'[66] Along with the demand for church representation in state affairs ('the natives would find their place because the Church speaks for them') went the request that the state should act decisively in stopping Yao initiation dances, in banning African beer – often the only means by which a trader could accumulate capital – in preventing the free movement of labour and in a host of other petty restrictions, designed to shape African society to the mission's liking by legislation from above.[67] The same tendency brought Hetherwick, the most intelligent and articulate critic of Johnston's land settlement policies, into substantial if paradoxical identification with the views of European traders and planters. Hetherwick was keenly aware of the dangers implicit in the growth of the European community at Blantyre. 'A Europeanised atmosphere is not conducive to missionary sympathies', he declared in 1910. 'It is hostile in its background and fatal to that intercourse between the native and the European missionary which is essential to all true mission life and work.'[68] Yet drawn by the logic of common opposition to the administration, Hetherwick attacked the introduction of formal labour regulations on the grounds that they 'threatened to press very heavily on the planting interest if not to extinguish it in many places' and condemned Johnston

64 Laws to Govan Robertson, 18 April 1895, NLS 7878

65 Quoted from pamphlet enclosed in Scott to Laws, 14 November 1882, Laws's Papers. See also 'The Kaffir Race and Language' in *CSHFMR*, September 1892, 587

66 Quoted in Cairns, *Prelude*, 95. See also Rankine, *Dark Continent*, 232

67 *LWBCA*, October 1896, October 1894, November 1899

68 Presidential address, Proceedings of the Third General Missionary Conference of Nyasaland, 1910, 4

for implying that some planters ill treated their workers. He also supported the Chamber of Commerce in its endeavours to have a higher rate of tax imposed on those who did not work under a European employer for at least one month in each year, a measure which Laws, for all his greater tolerance of government, firmly opposed.[69]

As for Livingstonia, its missionaries' independence from European planters must be weighed against Laws's respect for governmental authority. 'His official position has absolutely vetoed any little tendency he had to be an agitator', Fraser wrote of Laws at the time of the latter's appointment to the Legislative Council. 'He is now only a defender of the Government's difficulties.'[70] It is certainly true, that on a number of issues, missionaries forcefully disagreed with government policies. Eighteen months after he had attacked officials of Johnston's administration for failing to punish Ngoni thieves with sufficient severity, Dewar, in September 1896, fiercely criticised the behaviour of the Collector at Ikawa Boma in the BSAC's sphere, for setting fire to a village near Mwenzo and shooting one of the villagers.[71] At Bandawe, Macalpine advised Tonga headmen against the payment of the new labour tax in 1902, and criticised the attempts to force labour from the Tonga as a punitive measure.[72] Dr Innes publicly complained about 'petty thieving' by African policemen in the Karonga district in 1908, and Laws threw aside his scruples in 1913 to protest in dignified and forceful language against the proposed enactment of a piece of racialist legislation aimed at protecting white women against sexual assault by Africans.[73]

On fundamental issues of principle, however, missionary assumptions were remarkably similar to those of colonial officials. Because they opposed the use of forced labour, Livingstonia's agents attacked the introduction of a labour tax but they accepted the assumption that the African had a duty to repay the colonial government 'for the protection and privileges he enjoys' under its rule and they agreed that various moral benefits resulted from employment under Europeans. At the meeting of the Mission Council in 1900, there was 'a general feeling that the native is not showing the earnestness he might do in giving something greater in the way of labour in return for all the benefits he is deriving from the

69 Krishnamurthy, 'Land in Nyasaland', 163–4. *LWBCA*, January 1897; January–March 1902; *Aurora*, April 1902, 64–6

70 Fraser to Hetherwick, 23 February 1914, Hetherwick Papers

71 Henry S. Meebela, *Reaction to Colonialism*, Manchester, 1971, 91–2

72 Sharpe to FO, 19 May 1902, FO 2/606. Sharpe to FO, 14 October 1902, FO 2/607; Daly to Macalpine, 8 October 1902, NLS 7864

73 Laws to Acting Chief Secretary Zomba, 18 September 1913, Livingstonia Letter Book, 1912–23; *Livingstonia News*, August 1908

settled government, the missions, and the trading and planting industries'. All missionaries, it was felt 'look – or ought to look – upon the commercial and agricultural enterprises in the country as the complement to their work, because of the opportunities they afford for the regeneration of the native in those phases of his life and character which their special work does not so fully reach'.[74] Charles Domingo expressed the alternative view in 1911: 'The three combined bodies, Missionaries, Government and Companies, all gainers of money – do form the same rule to look upon the native with mockery eyes . . . Therefore the life of the three combined bodies is altogether too cheaty, too thefty, too mockery.'[75]

Compared to the political activities of other missions in Central Africa, those of the Scottish missions in Malawi are outstanding for their pugnacity and integrity. But even their public voices diverged from the language of African protest.

Presbyterian attitudes

The establishment of the colonial administration was accompanied by the proliferation of Christian missions in Nyasaland. In 1886 the Christian monopoly which Blantyre and Livingstonia held over the Malawi regions was dented by the foundation of a UMCA station at Likoma Island on the lake. Two years later came a northward thrust from the Dutch Reformed Church, partially disguised by the fact that the first agent, A. C. Murray, was instructed 'to form as far as possible one mission with that of the Free Church', and collaborated closely with Laws and his colleagues from his base at Mvera.[76] It was thus not till 1892 with the founding by Joseph Booth of the Zambesi Industrial Mission at Blantyre that the challenge to the Scottish missions' hegemony began in earnest.[77] The next year friction over business arrangements, and a difference of opinion on the question of church development led the DRC missionaries to break from Livingstonia by setting up their own executive council. And this was followed in turn by the founding of a further five smaller missions within the space of the next eight years, all but one associated with Booth at some period, and by the introduction of two Roman Catholic missions, the

[74] *Aurora*, August 1901, 28–9; April 1902, 64–6; June 1900, 25; October 1899, 36

[75] Quoted in Shepperson and Price 163–4. See also pp. 210–18 below

[76] A. C. Murray to Laws, 5 April 1888, NLS 7891. This mission was founded through the initiative of a hundred members of the Ministers' Missionary Union of the DRC. From 1903 it came under the direct control of the Cape Synod.

[77] For Booth, his background and early activities in Central Africa see Shepperson and Price, 18–36

Montfort Marist Fathers and the White Fathers, in 1901 and 1902 respectively.[78]

For Livingstonia the direct consequences of the missionary expansion were comparatively slight. The smaller missions, anxious to become self-supporting as quickly as possible through the cultivation of plantations, were driven to the Southern Province, most of them within a thirty mile radius of Blantyre, the one part of Malawi where the transport system was sufficiently advanced to permit much hope of commercial success. Apart from a minor storm provoked by Booth's success in inveigling workers from Bandawe by the promise of higher wages, they excited little initial resentment against them from the Free Church.

But while the multiplication of missions left Livingstonia's sphere of influence virtually unimpaired, it did bring into focus the qualities which distinguished the Free Church mission from other Christian bodies in Central Africa and contributed to the special role that it played in the history of the Nyasaland Protectorate. These distinctions should not be overemphasised. All missions in the 1890s recognised that the prime task of religious conversion could not be achieved without the introduction of at least a modicum of Western education; all that were Protestant shared Henry Venn's ideal of a self-governing, self-supporting native church. Where they differed most markedly was on the type of society they wished to create and on the means at their disposal for carrying those wishes into effect.

On both points Livingstonia was well qualified to make a significant contribution. Thanks to the backing she received from Scottish industrial interests, the financial resources at her disposal were considerably greater than those that any other mission could command in Malawi, at least up to 1900. Missionary financial statistics are notoriously unreliable, but in round figures it would appear that her annual income up to 1881 was about £3000 compared to £2500 for Blantyre; that it increased to £4000 annually in the next decade, and then rose sharply to £7000 from 1893. It rose again in the last three years of the century by which time it was exceeding that at Blantyre by over £2000 a year as the following table demonstrates:[79]

[78] The smaller missions are considered in a conveniently summarised form by R. L. Wishdale, *Sectarianism in Southern Nyasaland*, London, 1965, 12–15. For a history of the Roman Catholic Church in Malawi, including an account of the abortive White Fathers mission at Mponda's in 1889 see Linden, *Catholics, Peasants and Chewa Resistance*

[79] Figures taken from FMC reports General Assembly papers of the Church of Scotland 1875 to 1901, from Appeals on behalf of the Livingstonia Mission 1876, 1886 and 1891, and from Livingstonia Mission Reports, 1896 to 1900

Expenditure on	*Livingstonia*	*Blantyre*
1897–8	£8555	£6447
1898–9	£10082	£6028
1899–1900	£8475	£7149

Livingstonia was thus able to employ a larger European staff than Blantyre, though by 1907 at least it was being outstripped in this respect by both the UMCA and the Dutch Reformed Church, and could place more stations under European control; six in 1894 at a time when Blantyre only had three. Reliance on the generosity of a few wealthy men also meant that special needs could be entered for with exceptional speed. Livingstonia's pioneer party was able to take a steamer with them to the lake; Blantyre could not afford to purchase one until 1894. Livingstonia could go ahead with the building of the Overtoun Institution, though by 1906 more than £16 000 had been spent on it; at Blantyre lack of funds delayed the building of the Henry Henderson Institution till 1909.

Moreover, Livingstonia agents approached their task with a determination to revolutionise the society in which they worked which contrasted markedly with the attitudes demonstrated by members of the UMCA or the Dutch Reformed Church. The UMCA, with a recruitment policy which ensured that almost every missionary would have his own private income, was almost exclusively staffed by what an observer described as 'charming, and devoted priests and laymen of great culture and refinement'.[80] With their public school and largely Oxford or Cambridge backgrounds these sons of country parsons and small-town solicitors were often ignorant of or repelled by the dynamic, self-assured world of Victorian industry. They thus sought in Africa, not to transform societies, but to insert Christianity into them with as little disturbance as possible. 'It is not our wish to make the Africans bad caricatures of the Englishmen', wrote Bishop Smythies. 'What we want is to Christianise them in their own civil and political conditions; to help them to develop a Christian civilisation suited to their own climate and their own circumstance.'[81] The missionaries 'were a religious body, not educationalists', the Rev. G. B. Hand declared in 1919. The UMCA 'did not want to advance education beyond a certain point generally. Boys were apt to get swollen heads through over education and were consequently spoilt.'[82]

Similarly, the Dutch Reformed Church mission, the most flexible and imaginative in Malawi where matters of staff deployment were concerned,

[80] R. C. F. Maugham, *Nyasaland in the Nineties*, London, 1935, 48

[81] Gertrude Ward, *The Life of Charles Allan Smythies*, London, 1898, 4

[82] Conference on Education, 1919, MNA S1/1494/19

was debarred by two important distinctions compared with the Scottish missions, from playing as dynamic a role in matters of social change. Its agents in the first place were predominantly of rural stock. 'Some of the missionaries were farmers in South Africa before they entered mission work' declared the Phelps-Stokes Commission; 'all without exception have grown up on farms as boys'.[83] Compared with the emphasis placed by Livingstone and the Scottish missionaries, with their largely urban background, on 'Commerce and Christianity' their slogan was that of 'the Bible and the Plough'. Again, the doctrine to which they ascribed of 'the natural diversity of races', while it implied much genuine concern with improving the conditions of the existing society and raising the moral and physical standards of African villages, ensured that no attempt would be made to revolutionise that society itself. The aim of the mission in J. L. Pretorius's words, was the creation of 'a Bible-loving, industrious and prosperous peasantry'. It was to that end that while a vast number of elementary schools were formed, attempts to develop secondary education were resisted, and English was only introduced into the training school for teachers at Mvera (in 1904) because otherwise the pupils would have refused to continue to attend.[84] Immense concern was taken to develop agricultural techniques 'which the Natives can themselves imitate successfully in their own homes', and to introduce handicrafts which could 'fit the men and women to become home workers', but no attempt was made to teach techniques of value at European centres of work.[85]

It is this situation which explains the educational dominance of the Scottish missions even at a time when in terms of the number of pupils or of schools they were far surpassed by other missions. More important even than the influence of Livingstonia's industrial supporters was the fact that the leading policy makers in the field, the ordained and medical missionaries were largely representatives of that industrial culture and in sympathy with its aims, at least in the first generation. With the exception of a few sons of ministers like Bain, Fraser and Innes, they came in general from urban lower-middle- or upper-working-class families and had experience of working-class occupations: Laws, the son of a cabinet maker, worked for a time as an apprentice to that trade; Steele, an orphan from the Buchanan Institute, Glasgow, worked in a shoe shop run by his brother; Black, the son of a village schoolmaster, spent some time as a

[83] Thomas Jesse Jones, *Education in East Africa*, 212

[84] J. L. Pretorius, 'The Story of the Dutch Reformed Church Mission in Nyasaland' *Nyasaland Journal*, x, 1957, 11; M. W. Retief, *William Murray of Nyasaland*, Lovedale, 1958, 97

[85] *Education in East Africa*, 212–13

joiner before entering an architect's office.[86] Such backgrounds were conducive of a certain scepticism about society at large. Laws's father denounced to his famous son 'The world at home and abroad . . . and the Madened [sic] desire for Wealth, Power and Pleasure leading many to ruin and filling our newspapers with suicid [sic] death and lunacy.'[87] But if the foibles of the upper classes or the excesses of the 'irreligious poor' were to be condemned, the virtues of 'the pawky hard-headed, middle class elements of their nation', which Hector Duff believed the missionaries to typify, were clearly to be advanced to Africa as part of their most solemn Christian duty.[88] Donald Fraser's comment on Laws's hackneyed dictum that to teach an African to lay a line of bricks in a straight line was a great step towards civilisation, is highly pertinent in this respect. 'It is the carpenter's precise idea of civilisation', Fraser wrote. 'Perhaps Dr Laws's training in his father's cabinet-maker's shop had more to do with his missionary idea than all his university degrees.'[89]

The negative side of such a doctrine was the attempt to imprint the pattern of Scottish social reform upon the sometimes intransigent contours of African village life. Almost all Free Church missionaries were interested in Home Mission work in Scotland and some had practical experience in the toughest areas of their homeland: Laws in the smallpox and fever hospitals of Glasgow, Black as a district missionary for the Free Barony Congregation, Cross at Pollockshields and Prentice in the Cowgate in Edinburgh. The concepts they developed among the suppressed industrial proletariat of Scottish cities, and from the social doctrines of Thomas Chalmers and his disciples, deeply coloured their whole approach to social problems in Africa. With Chalmers, the architect of Free Church social policy, they distrusted any form of general or permanent assistance for the needy as tending to sap the independence of the individual, and looked to personal effort alone to achieve social improvement.[90] 'The missionaries,' according to Laws, 'greatly object to do anything, which might tend to pauperize the native and seek . . . to inculcate the benefit of

[86] Basic background details on Livingstonia's ordained missionaries are contained in William Ewing, *Annals of the Free Church of Scotland, 1843–1900*, Edinburgh, 1914; and J. A. Lamb, *The Fasti of the United Free Church of Scotland, 1900–1929*, Edinburgh, 1956

[87] R. Laws, 7 May 1888, Shepperson Collection

[88] Hector Duff, *African Small Chop*, London, 1932, 55

[89] Article in the *Scots Observer*, 27 August 1927, cutting in Laws's Papers.

[90] The policies of Chalmers are discussed in Stewart Mechie, *The Church and Scottish Social Development, 1780–1870*, London, 1960, 47–63; and in Lawrence J. Saunders, *Scottish Democracy 1815–1840*, Edinburgh, 1950, 208–21

honest labour.' 'If a people see that it is not necessary to make an effort towards self-help,' wrote Fraser, 'they succumb at once to pauperism.'[91] Drunkenness, a major cause of concern in Scotland in the 1870s, was regarded with much less justification as a similar evil in Central Africa. Livingstonia's church members were totally banned from drinking beer; Lutherans and members of the Dutch Reformed Church were merely discouraged from taking too much.

More positive was the emphasis on social revolution arising inevitably in the eyes of the missionaries from the replacement of 'feudal' ties by economic ones, and the consequent creation of a premium in the values of an industrial society which would weaken the control of the master over his slaves, the polygamous husband over his wives, and the despotic chief over his subjects, and thus allow new classes to appear. 'The elevations of the common people,' Laws declared, 'will react upon the chiefs . . . and as the people, by working with us or by raising our produce acquire habits of industry and forethought, a self-respect and independence of character will arise which will procure them more liberty.'[92]

Compared with the emergence of an African commercial middle class envisaged by missionaries in Nigeria in the 1840s, the ambitions of Livingstonia agents a generation later appear disappointingly modest. Africans participating in the new economy would be more likely to be carpenters or joiners, than sophisticated traders, they believed. More likely still they would be employees in European concerns. Laws who took pride in the mission's role as a labour bureau, never ceased to emphasise 'the many situations in the country requiring educated natives. The missionaries should be able to provide native christians to fill them.'[93] It was in part to meet such demands that some instruction in manual labour was given in all classes at the Institution and that skills like brick making and printing were carefully taught.

To many observers these policies, easing the way for colonial development, were the main justification of the mission's educational work. To Major C. A. Edwardes, the sight of girls being taught English at Livingstonia 'called up visions of House-keepers and female servants in the days to come'.[94] But for Livingstonia's agents to have accepted such a limited perspective would have been to betray the educational traditions to which they owed their own advancement. Despite their often poverty-stricken

[91] Robert Laws, *Woman's Work at Livingstonia*, Paisley, 1886, 30–1; Donald Fraser, 'Self-support of the Native Church', *Aurora*, August 1902, 79.

[92] Laws, 18 March 1878, quoted in *FCSMR*, July 1878, 165.

[93] *Aurora*, October 1899, 33; *Third Missionary Conference*, 25

[94] Edwardes to Johnston, 31 March 1897, Johnston Papers JO1/1/1

backgrounds, every one of the twenty-three ordained or medical missionaries sent out before 1900 had gone either to a university or its equivalent, the Royal College of Physicians and Surgeons in Edinburgh.[95] They were products of a Scottish educational system which with all its faults did permit some boys of ability and perseverance from working- or lower-middle-class backgrounds to get a comparatively cheap education to qualify them for the professions, particularly medicine and the church. Moreover, while they came from every part of Scotland, with Glasgow predominating numerically – nine of the twenty-three had been to university there – Aberdeen, with five university graduates headed by Laws, provided the distinctive culture of the mission – a culture to which Laws planned to give symbolic shape by topping his institution with a replica of the crown of King's College. And of all parts of Scotland Aberdeen and the north-east was the one where the educational tradition was most vigorous and effective and the chances of the poor student were most bright.

One consequence was the intellectually bracing, though sometimes alarmingly ineffective approach which Laws brought to his evangelical work. A doctor even more than a missionary, Laws shared with his contemporary Henry Drummond a determination to demonstrate that 'the principles of Revealed Religion are based upon the laws of the natural world, and the same operations are common to both'.[96] When faced by questions dealing with the creation he turned not to Genesis but to the specimens of lava he had brought from Vesuvius. The causes of day and night were explained 'by the spherical form of the earth and its revolutions round the sun'. Science, for Laws, was 'the handmaid of Christianity', and though he believed in saturating his students with the Bible, he totally rejected a fundamentalist interpretation of its contents.[97]

A second consequence was the devotion to education as a positive means of advancement that runs strongly throughout the mission's history. Even in the 1920s when all the canons of orthodox colonial policy

[95] It is instructive to compare this figure with the 'Fewer than thirty-five' missionaries who had received a university education in the whole of Zambia up to 1924 (Rotberg, *Christian Missionaries*, 161). By the same token, seventeen of the 76 agents appointed to Livingstonia before 1900 had medical degrees, compared with nine out of 362 agents in the UMCA

[96] Quoted from a contemporary review in the *British and Foreign Evangelical Review* of Drummond's most popular work, *Natural Law in the Spiritual World*. A sardonic introduction to Drummond is provided in Carswell, *Brother Scots*, 1–53

[97] Livingstonia Mission Journal entry for 30 January 1876. *Missionary Record of the United Free Church of Scotland*, October 1925, 449

leaned towards the Jeanes School type of training with the pupil associated as far as possible with his traditional background, Laws never wavered in his defence of academic education: 'To discard or even lessen the literary training would be to block the way for advancement of native leaders and means the reduction of the natives to a class of helots.' Twenty years earlier his colleague, James Henderson, had defended the right of Africans to obtain as good as possible an education in a more poetic vein. 'We cannot justifiably treat them as mere flotsam of existence interesting only as spiritual salvage,' he told the Nyasaland Missionary Conference in 1900, 'for they as well as we have the promise of the life that is now.'[98]

A desire to revolutionise African society implies a distaste for existing institutions. If James Henderson differed from many of his contemporaries, it was not because he was more appreciative of African culture, but because he rejected a policy of selective giving. 'Our peoples, if not physically moribund like the indigenous races of Australasia, are as really perishing in their stagnation from progress and their utter inefficiency for the great ends of mankind', he told the missionary conference of 1900. 'It is not possible to stem the tide of Western civilization if we desire it; but there is a more excellent way. Christ is in the civilization more than we at all realise, so let us give it to them, keeping none of it back.'[99]

Houses that were square rather than round, funerals conducted without signs of visible emotion, marriages blessed with a feast of tea and scones and culminating in the singing of 'Auld Lang Syne' in Chinyanja were all symbols of progress as defined by Presbyterian Scots.[100]

It is one of the ironies of Livingstonia that a Presbyterian, Free Church mission should have been organised on highly centralised, autocratic lines. The Free Church in Scotland was a decentralised body with semi-autonomous parishes controlled by a minister supported, and to some degree supervised, by a committee of lay elders. In Malawi, however, Laws was sole head of the mission from 1877 until the formation of a mission council, composed initially of medical and ordained missionaries alone, in 1886. As the stations were far apart, this body met infrequently, and in practice many important decisions continued to be taken by Laws, in his capacity as treasurer and organising secretary of the council. As late as 1894, George Smith, the secretary of the Foreign Missions Committee, informed him:

98 R. Laws, 'The Co-ordination of Technical and Literary Training in the Education of Natives of Nyasaland', *Report of the Native Education Conference ... held at Zomba, May 1927*, Nyasaland Protectorate, 1927; *Nyasaland Missionary Conference*, 1901, 48

99 ibid.

100 See Morrison Diary entry for 8 February 1883

> You are head not only of the Institute but of the whole mission and I have never publicly or privately taken any other view. I would give you 'Home Rule' in the best sense out there and, personally, make you Dictator – an office I wish you would always practically take to yourself. You would find obedient subjects at home and abroad.[101]

Despite protests, Laws as treasurer of the council retained the responsibility of allocating funds to different stations, and also frequently bypassed the council entirely.[102] It was not until J. Fairley Daly became secretary of the Livingstonia Committee in Scotland in 1904 that some attempt was made to check whether statements submitted in the name of the council by Laws reflected the views of all of its members, or only of its organising secretary.[103] When African elders were elected to the new Kirk Session at Bandawe in 1895, Scottish Presbyterian practice was being followed rather than the practice hitherto existing in Malawi. Laws worked actively for the establishment of the Livingstonia Presbytery, but in the absence of a democratic tradition within the mission, the Church was also autocratically organised. The centralisation of authority which contributed towards the efficient running of the mission was to be a source of discontent for African leaders.

[101] Smith to Laws, 10 February 1894, NLS 7889

[102] See draft minute of the Livingstonia sub-committee for 27 January 1890, NLS 7895

[103] Daly to Elmslie, 21 February, 1907, NLS 7865

8

The origins of independency

On 7 January 1909 the resident missionary at Bandawe was given the disturbing news by one of his African elders that Eliot Kenan Kamwana, a Tonga evangelist connected with the Watch Tower Bible and Tract Society, was actively proselytising in the West Nyasa district. Macalpine's comment that 'A certain section may easily be misled by him, especially if he deludes them with a counterfeit baptism for which the ignorant here have something like a *craze*' was abundantly justified by subsequent events.[1] When Macalpine left the district on furlough early in April, some 7000 adherents were said to have been baptised. By the time that Kamwana was deported to Zomba some two weeks later, the number had risen to over 9000, including many from Usisya beyond Tongaland, and from as far away as Nkota Kota.

The rise of Watch Tower, the first separatist movement in the north, and one which marked, in the words of Shepperson and Price, 'the beginning of the newer type of African reaction to Europeans in Nyasaland',[2] dramatically illustrates the tensions which grew into the relationship between Livingstonia and some members of those societies with which she came into contact by the first decade of the twentieth century. In contrast to the situation in South Africa described by Sundkler,[3] independency in Malawi arose in an area remarkably free from the more obvious friction consequent to white rule. No brooding memories of humiliating defeat in battle at the hands of the British invaders could stir the Tonga in 1909, for they had not been defeated, but had willingly and peacefully placed themselves under British protection. Nor had their relationship with the administration – consisting in the West Nyasa district in 1897 of one collector with an assistant and twenty untrained Yao askaris – been a peculiarly unhappy one. Unlike the Yao and the Manganja in the Shire highlands, the Tonga suffered little alienation of land before 1909, the

[1] Macalpine Diary entry for 7 January 1909. Macalpine Papers

[2] Shepperson and Price, *Independent Africa*, 154

[3] B. G. M. Sundkler, *Bantu Prophets in South Africa*, London, 1948

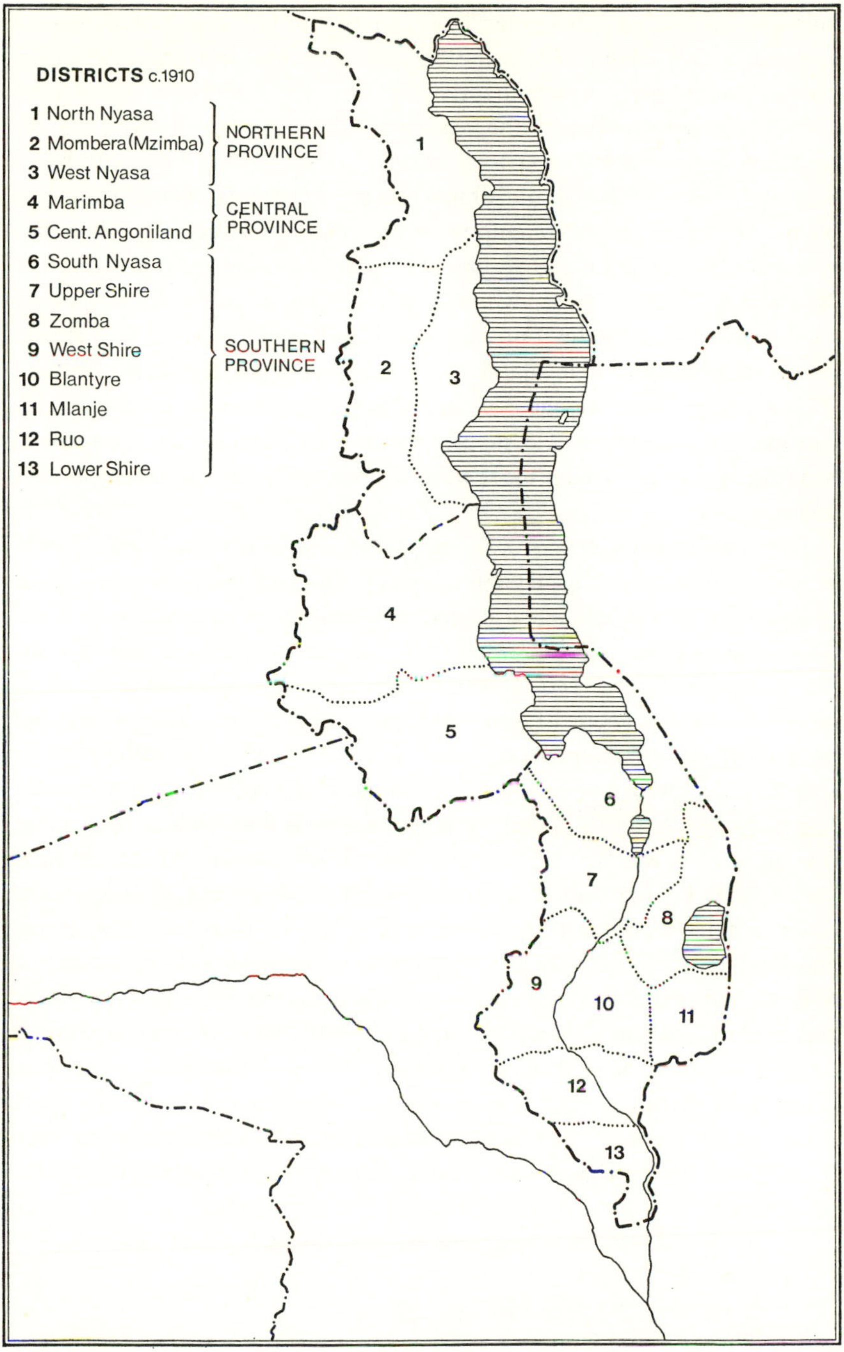

Map 5. Provincial and district boundaries of Malawi c. 1910 based on B. Pachai (ed.), *Early History of Malawi*, Longmans, 1972.

only foreign landlords being the Lakes Company at Vizaro, Livingstonia, and one or two white hunters and planters. Hut tax, introduced in 1899, though undoubtedly a popular grievance was not responsible as in other areas for driving an unwilling male population out to work. Like the northern Ngoni, the Tonga took eagerly to work in a European-based economy, years before administrative pressure was placed upon them to do so. The increases in tax empowered in 1901 provoked disturbances a year later, which led the government to dispatch a company of troops to Nkata Bay.[4] But in 1907, when the preaching of a Kunda prophetess against hut tax and the Europeans was followed by quite widespread unrest in Malawi, Tongaland was one area completely unaffected.[5] Though Kamwana was able to use the tax question to strengthen his support, the evidence would suggest that it was a less important agent in focusing grievances than the contradictions inherent in Livingstonia's policy.

The revolutionary effects of Livingstonia's influence on Tonga society have been fully noted in previous chapters. By the late 1890s a new social group, that of the mission teachers, was emerging as a major political force; the position of the society vis-à-vis her neighbours was sharply changing, and thousands of Tonga were becoming involved in the hazards of an industrial economy. On top of these changes, the waves of religious enthusiasm which swept Tongaland from 1895 to 1898 and again for several years from 1903 indicated a communal concern not just for the material benefits to be gained from contact with the mission, but for the less tangible rewards which lay in church admittance. The year 1903 would long be remembered, Dr Boxer believed, as one of 'the richest times of spiritual harvesting at Bandawe'. African Christians held weekend services in all the principal villages, and the sound of hymns was said to have replaced that of dancing.[6] At village after village the attendance and interest gradually increased until the people were coming 'according to their houses', one missionary reported.[7] By 1906 Sabbath services were being held in ninety-eight village centres attended each week by more than 14 000 hearers.[8] Vast and emotional audiences flocked to the mass conventions which Fraser had started. Hundreds of Tonga sought com-

[4] Sharpe to Hill, 3 April 1902, with Pearce to Sharpe, 27 March 1902, enclosed FO 2/605

[5] Nyasaland Protectorate Report for 1907–8, cmd. 3729, 22; West Nyasa Monthly Report, August 1907, MNA NNC3/4/1

[6] Livingstonia Mission Report, 1903, 23

[7] *FCSMR*, October 1903, 457

[8] Livingstonia Mission Report, 1906, 32

fort and stability in a changing world in the certainties which appeared to lie in baptism.

It was at this point that the contradictory character of Livingstonia's policy appeared. Although they aimed to change the social and economic conditions of a society as a whole and followed religious policies which had wide popular effects, the missionaries shrank from mass conversion. They rejected, too, in practice if not in theory, the evangelical concept of instantaneous conversion through Grace, and believed that admission to the church could be granted only to those who had served lengthy apprenticeships, whose characters could be fully attested, and who were thoroughly instructed in their beliefs. Baptism, they believed, in the words of a recommendation adopted by the first Nyasaland Missionary Conference of 1900, should:

> be not granted unless the candidate has been under definite religious instruction throughout a period of at least two years, during which the missionary has had means of ascertaining as to his life and character, and that instruction should include as a *minimum* a course of teaching on the Lord's Prayer, the Ten Commandments, the Sacraments, and the Apostles' Creed with the relevant passages of scripture.[9]

Further caution was required, the missionaries felt, because of the changed social situation in which they were working. As late as 1895, Christian converts had had their faith tested by threats of injury to themselves and their friends, and by the self-imposed isolation which was inevitably the lot of those who attempted to break from the customs of the wider community. But with the spread of the popular movement the profession of Christianity became 'cosy and comfortable', and it was feared that many were being tempted to become church members for social reasons alone, having 'a form of godliness without knowing the power thereof'.[10]

The missionaries, in consequence, attempted to test the sincerity of applicants' beliefs by making compulsory the educational training and financial self-support which they had always tended to regard as integral features of the true Christian community. If church members were to be properly instructed in their faith it was necessary, Macalpine decided, that they should receive education. In 1899 he gave orders that no candidate for the baptism class should be recognised who was not attending school. Elmslie took the policy a stage further at Ekwendeni, where he announced in 1902 that: 'There are several hundreds in the Catechumen's

9 Proceedings of the Nyasaland Missionary Conference 1900, 67

10 Fraser, 'Growth of the Church', 238; Livingstonia Mission Report, 1899–1900, 12

classes who have been kept back repeatedly during the last three years for no other reason than that they may if they desire learn to read the Gospel and they do not.'[11] And four years later, even admission to the catechumen's class was made conditional on the ability to read.[12]

At the same time, the financial demands of the mission sharply increased. In 1898 school fees had been demanded for the first time at Bandawe. The sum required was only threepence a term, but Government hut taxes had been started in the same year, and 'many people,' Macalpine believed, 'think they are now in for a fleecing'.[13] Two years later church privileges were being refused to Christians who would not pay sixpence a year for the schooling of their children, and in 1908 the compulsory purchase of portions of the Scripture was also enforced.[14] Church contributions were made an additional source of revenue, and in 1910 Laws took what he admitted to be the extreme step of refusing to pass for baptism a man who 'as a Catechumen had given nothing that year to the cause of Christ'.[15] Church membership and some measure of economic prosperity were becoming virtually inseparable.

Administrative problems also added to the candidates' frustrations. Before the popular movement got under way, it had been easy for the missionary to know and teach personally every member of his little flock of about a hundred souls, many of whom were directly employed by the mission. But when vast numbers came seeking baptism, this was no longer possible. The European missionary withdrew gradually into a supervisory role as 'overseer or bishop'[16] and thus lost the face-to-face relationship which had been one of the greatest assets of the early church. As Charles Stuart commented in 1902: 'We do not seem to get into close enough touch with the people in their village life, meeting with them mostly, as we do, in school and church and in the ordinary work of the station.'[17] Many new classes for catechumens and hearers were set up,

[11] ibid., 1902, 28

[12] ibid., 1906, 25

[13] ibid., 1898–99, 15

[14] Proceedings of the Nyasaland Missionary Conference 1900, 54; Livingstonia Mission Report, 1908, 37

[15] Laws to Hetherwick, 16 November 1910, Hetherwick Papers

[16] The phrase is that of Donald Fraser (Proceedings of the Nyasaland Missionary Conference 1910, 56). He so frequently emphasised the new episcopal role of the missionary that Hetherwick began to address him as 'The Bishop' (A. R. Fraser, 133; Hetherwick to Fraser, 18 June 1908, Hetherwick Papers).

[17] Charles Stuart to the sub-committee, 30 October 1902, Livingstonia Mission Report, 1902, 73

with extra grades being inserted through which the candidates had to pass, and the task of watching the behaviour of candidates devolved on African deacons and elders, none of whom had the power to baptise. The inevitable consequence was that long delays took place before classes were examined: the hearers in Usisya and Ruarwe districts had to wait for two years before Elmslie visited them.[18] In the absence of direct knowledge of the applicants, the tests were also made more searching. In 1902 Elmslie turned back sixty of the 140 candidates for a preliminary catechumen's class. Two years later at Bandawe, Macalpine baptised only 151 out of the 900 who had applied.[19]

Eliot Kamwana's experience was typical of that of many of his compatriots. Anxious to use the skills he had acquired at the Overtoun Institution as a pastor rather than simply as a teacher, Kamwana was bitterly disappointed when he was refused admission to the church by Institution elders in 1901, largely, it seems, because the period of probation had been arbitrarily extended as too many Tonga were requesting baptism.

His reaction, like that of several of his fellows, was to seek church privileges from more sympathetic hands. Leaving the Institution, which he had joined from the Bandawe central school in March 1898, Kamwana turned to the Plainfield Seventh-day Adventist Mission, founded by Joseph Booth at Thyolo, where he was quickly admitted to full church membership. For two years he taught English to Standard I at Thyolo before leaving for South Africa in 1903. His subsequent experiences moulded his vision of colonial society. From 1904 he worked as a hospital assistant in the Main Reef mine near Johannesburg and preached in the mining compounds to his Malawi compatriots. Three years later, in answer to a call from his old mentor, he moved to Seapoint, Joseph Booth's new base in Cape Town, where with some half-dozen other Malawians, he was instructed in the complexities of Watch Tower doctrine. Six months more, and his training was judged to have been successfully completed. Supplied with his passage by Charles Taze Russell, the American founder of the Watch Tower Society, Kamwana returned to Malawi in 1908. His arrival in the West Nyasa district in mid-September precipitated a new wave of religious enthusiasm.[20]

18 Elmslie to Livingstonia sub-committee, 25 October 1902, in Livingstonia Mission Report, 1902, 69

19 ibid., 1902, 69; 1904, 39

20 Most of this information is drawn from Kamwana's own statements made on 5 July 1915 under cross-examination to the Commission inquiring into the Chilembwe Rising, CO 525/66. See also Shepperson and Price, 153–4

The frustration experienced by those members of Tonga society whose entry into the church had been delayed and impeded was not the only source of friction west of the lake. During the first few years of the century, increasing tension also centred round the attempts of some graduates from the Institution to obtain greater responsibilities than the missionaries were prepared to concede to them. Few defections among church members in good standing resulted, but the authority assumed by the Scots was subjected to critical questioning.

The origins of African leadership in the Livingstonia Mission can be dated from the arrival at Cape Maclear in October 1876 of the four Lovedale-trained assistants, Shadrach Ngunana, Isaac Williams Wauchope, Mapas Ntinili and William Koyi, who had been selected by Dr Stewart to fill the part played on the Nigerian coast by Sierra Leoneans in evangelising on a larger scale and more economically than Scottish agents were believed capable of doing.

Unlike the interpreters recruited earlier by E. D. Young at Cape Town, the Lovedale men were regarded as the agents of the mission rather than its servants or dependants. Every one of them, with the exception of William Koyi, was a second-generation Christian, and all were educated up to the level of the artisans, and in some cases beyond.[21] They were paid at comparable rates to their Scottish colleagues – £45 plus rations in 1876; £130, all in, in 1883.[22] And though their social position was ambivalent – two of them acted as waiters at a special dinner held by the Europeans in 1877[23] – they lived in the same types of houses as did the Scots, and jealously preserved their right to be consulted when decisions were taken, and to perform evangelistic work as well as manual labour.[24]

Despite the early loss of two of the most able of the evangelists in 1877 – Wauchope, invalided home following a nervous breakdown, and Ngunana, who died of consumption in June – the value of the Lovedale assistants was not at first disputed. Like the Scottish artisans, they sometimes intervened too vigorously in local quarrels beyond the station: Ntinili earned a rebuke from Laws on this account for setting fire to a neighbour's hut which burned down several others.[25] At the same time,

[21] Stewart, *Lovedale Past and Present*, 125–7, 283–5, 379–83. At least one of the Scottish artisans, Thomas Crooks, was illiterate, but all the South Africans could read and write

[22] It is interesting to note by way of comparison that artisans were being paid £90 plus £30 for rations in 1881, and £150, all in, in 1884

[23] Letter from Ngunana, 29 November 1876, quoted in *Lovedale Past and Present*, 21

[24] Dr Stewart to Smith, 8 June 1880, NLS 7876

[25] Minutes of Livingstonia sub-committee, entry for 4 April 1881, NLS 7912

Ngunana proved his worth as a teacher at the Cape Maclear school in the few months prior to his death, while Koyi demonstrated an ability to converse in Chingoni, which he used to excellent effect both in 1878 on the expeditions to Chikusi and Mbelwa, and also from 1882 as the pioneer agent among the northern Ngoni. His success as 'a connecting link in colour and language' between the missionaries and the Ngoni was so great that Laws in 1879 appealed for more agents while on a visit to Lovedale, and the Home Committee offered bursaries to pay for the training of additional black South Africans destined for Livingstonia.[26]

From the 1880s, however, pressure developed within the mission to get rid of the Lovedale men, or at least to reduce them to a subordinate position. Criticism was not in the main focused on their inefficiency, real or imagined, but rather on what in other circumstances would have been regarded as a major asset – their affinity with potential converts, and their refusal to reject entirely the attitudes and assumptions of local Africans from beyond the mission station. As early as 1878, Ntinili had been criticised for ceasing to board at Cape Maclear,[27] and later, in 1885, Koyi's work in Ngoniland was praised by his new colleague, W. A. Elmslie, with the proviso: 'There is a danger in knowing the people too well and while Koyi is invaluable here there is not that respect shown to him which should be and which is a factor in raising the people from their low condition.'[28]

Following Koyi's death on 4 June 1886, the latest arrival, George Williams, a London Missionary Society convert from Bedford in the Cape Province, became the natural target of censure.[29] Williams, who took up residence in Ngoniland in 1884, was, as Elmslie admitted, a 'thorough evangelist', possessed of a real gift for teaching the Bible and capable of carrying out 'successful work' single handed in the outstation he had opened at Chinyera.[30] What he lacked was that dignified reserve, 'the whole bearing of a European', without which, his companion believed, no missionary could effectively operate.[31] Elmslie, who was convinced that 'we are here to show the natives something higher than what they have not only in thought but in daily life', complained in March 1887 of

[26] Laws, 23 August 1818, quoted in *FCSMR*, March 1879, 66; ibid., August 1879, 193; Dr Smith to Dr Stewart, 3 January 1883, NLS (1. 2–572)

[27] Cape Maclear Journal entry for 2 September 1879, NLS 7909

[28] W. A. Elmslie to R. Laws, 9 June 1885. Shepperson Collection

[29] Details of Williams's career are supplied in *Lovedale Past and Present*, 381–3

[30] W. A. Elmslie to Laws, 7 January 1887; 14 March 1887, NLS 7890. Elmslie to Dr Smith, 29 May 1885; *Free Church of Scotland Monthly Record*, October 1885

[31] Elmslie to Laws, 7 January 1887, NLS 7890

Williams's lack of manners. When rebuffed by Laws, who reminded him that Christ's manners may also have been open to criticism, he accused him instead of spending too much time in villages among Africans who were not working at school.[32] The list of charges he presented in September 1888 vividly illustrates the cultural gap which divided the two men from each other. Williams, it appears, had permitted Ngoni visitors 'to make a door of his open window'. He had allowed his servants to 'empty their slops standing on the verandah', and he had re-employed a young man dismissed from the station for stealing meat. His greatest error had been to enter into the social life of his neighbours instead of issuing rebukes from a distance, as Elmslie was accustomed to do. On 16 November 1887, he had gone to a beer party at Chitezi's. On 31 December he had attended a 'hoeing for beer', and Elmslie suspected it was not the first. 'Mr W.,' he told Laws, 'had neither actively nor passively resisted heathen practices and has given his direct sanction to many of them by attending and taking part in them e.g. beer drinking and "Ukutomba" [coming of age of girls] dances and marriages within reach'. His conclusion was: 'It is utterly fruitless to endeavour to raise the morals of the people if personal countenance of and participation in such scenes are manifested by those that preach the pure Gospel of Christ.' Either Williams should be refused reappointment to Ngoniland when his contract expired, or Elmslie himself would be forced to resign.[33]

What had most vexed Elmslie was less the individual conduct of the Lovedale assistants than their aspirations to positions of responsibility and to educational skills equal or even superior to those held by some Europeans. In contrast to the opinions more commonly expressed at Livingstonia, he believed:

> that such men are spoiled by the estimate they know the authorities of Lovedale have of them . . . because though they may read and write well they have not the moral or mental attainments which go to the formation of a sound character and though they may be recognised and treated as Christian brethren it does no good to put them in a false position.[34]

In 1886 the Home Committee disregarded his plea, made before Koyi's death, that 'when a renewal of Agents takes place . . . I would prefer Europeans'.[35] But in 1888 the opposition proved more malleable. In

[32] Elmslie to Laws, 18 September 1888. Livingstonia Papers; Elmslie to Laws, 14 March, 20 May, 15 September 1887, NLS 7890

[33] Elmslie to Laws, 18 September 1888. Livingstonia Papers

[34] Elmslie to Laws, 1 July 1888, NLS 7891

[35] Elmslie to Laws, 10 May 1886, Shepperson Collection

October Elmslie launched a further attack on the employment of Lovedale assistants. 'Away with Hebrew and Greek for such men', he wrote. 'Send them out fit for associating with other people or give them simply a position such as Don or Albert [Namalambe] have if they show like ability or interest in their work.'[36] Williams's departure from the mission a few days later showed that Elmslie's argument had been accepted. By 19 December George Smith, the secretary of the Home Committee, was attempting to have the salary formerly paid to Williams transferred to a Scottish artisan.[37] No further appointments from Lovedale to Livingstonia were made, and whereas, in 1887, J. C. White (later Lord Overtoun) had written of his increasing conviction that the evangelisation of Central Africa should be undertaken principally by men like Koyi, by 1889 the official view had become: 'that African evangelists have no advantage in health, economy of expenditure or efficiency over Scottish artisans'.[38]

In part, this change of policy resulted from personal factors such as Elmslie's notorious propensity to get himself embroiled in quarrels with other mission agents, white as well as black,[39] and the long-drawn-out struggle between Stewart and Laws, and their followers, for control of Livingstonia. So proprietorial was Stewart's interest in the mission, even after he had returned to Lovedale, that in 1880 he deliberately delayed sending Koyi and Mapas Ntinili back to Malawi while the central site was still situated at Cape Maclear.[40] Efforts were made to settle the rates of pay and the responsibilities of the evangelists at Lovedale alone, and Stewart attempted to use the lever of their presence as a means of getting teachers from Livingstonia sent down for training under him.[41] In rejecting their assistance, Laws was tacitly following the same policy that he pursued in establishing a separate printing press at Livingstonia, and subsequently a separate institution. He was demonstrating the independence of the mission and reducing its ties with the south.

But more serious factors were also involved. It can hardly be a coincidence that the decision to exclude Africans from major positions of

36 Elmslie to Laws, 16 October 1888, NLS 7891

37 Dr Smith to F. N. Henderson, 19 December 1888, NLS 1.4.521

38 J. C. White to R. Laws, 11 July 1887, NLS 7773; Dr Smith to Thirkield, 14 October 1895, NLS 7776

39 Details of his epic quarrel with Dr Kerr Cross are provided in Cross's letter to members of the Livingstonia Committee, 23 August 1894, NLS 7878

40 Dr Stewart to Laws, 31 August 1880; 1 February, 31 May 1881, Livingstonia Papers

41 Dr Stewart, 8 June 1880, in Livingstonia sub-committee minutes, 22 July 1880, NLS 7912; Stewart to Laws, 20 October 1883, Livingstonia Papers

responsibility at Livingstonia came at the same period that they were being denied opportunities of advancement in church and state on the west coast of Africa, and were experiencing difficulties in maintaining educational standards in the south.[42] The disillusionment of missionary or trading groups in schemes for the 'regeneration' of African societies from within was being followed in the 1880s by the growing popularity in Britain of quasi-scientific, social Darwinist theories which stressed the cultural inferiority of non-Western peoples.[43] It was being followed, too, by the extension of European formal rule, which disrupted the old relationships of equality between Christian mission and African ruler, and led not only to the increased ease with which the missionary could dispense with African allies in the political field, but also to a disenchantment with African leadership as such.[44] Though the different time scale in West Africa, and the absence of any local Africans in positions of importance before the 1880s, makes the parallel only partly applicable, there is a sense in which the rejection of the Lovedale men had the same effect as the failure to provide an African successor to Bishop Crowther in Nigeria in ensuring the growth in later years of tension within the local church.

One symptom of this tension was the differing attitudes that developed between certain white and black Christians towards African institutions and customs. Despite the lip-service they paid to the creation of a genuinely indigenous church, the early missionaries of Laws's and Elmslie's generation had sufficient confidence in the virtues of Western society to reject any major compromise with habits or beliefs which ran counter to their own. Even Macalpine, while he acknowledged 'the large use which the Apostles made of popular customs and institutions in the organization of the Christian Church', argued that it was often so difficult to separate the good from the bad that 'sometimes . . . the best way is simply to cut the Gordian knot and make a clean sweep altogether'. Under his influence, church members in Tongaland in 1895 banned beer drinking in any form, along with slavery and polygamy, however defined.[45]

With the arrival of Fraser, however, a new, more sympathetic element was added to existing mission policies. Fraser represented that section in

[42] Ajayi, *Christian Missions*, 233–73; David Kimble, *A Political History of Ghana 1850–1928*, Oxford, 1965, 87–108; Shepherd, *Lovedale*, 243–4

[43] P. D. Curtin, *Imperialism*, London, 1972, XVI–XVII

[44] This process has been described for Nigeria by Ajayi, *Christian Missions*, 233–5, and by James Bertin Webster, *The African Churches among the Yoruba, 1888–1922*, Oxford, 1964, 4–41

[45] Proceedings of the Nyasaland Missionary Conference, 1900, 17–20

the evangelical movement in Britain associated with the Keswick Convention which rejected the desire to dominate, while accepting the need to identify the church as closely as possible with its African environment.[46] From the early years of the century he worked against the prevailing puritanical and negative attitude of the young church, in which Christianity tended to be defined in terms of a series of prohibitions, and 'To become a Christian' in his own words, 'meant to give up polygamy and beer drinking and dancing'.[47] Instead, he emphasised the extent to which existing religious beliefs of the Tumbuka and Ngoni – in life after death, in one God or in revelation from on high – approximated to those of Christianity.[48] What was desired, he argued, was a movement which would 'turn the emphasis of one's teaching from the negative Prohibitions of Christianity to the glorious fullness of its gifts'. To that end, from 1897, he encouraged the writing of Ngoni hymns, often composed to local tunes; introduced new more elaborate forms of liturgy and symbolism than could be found in the Free Church in Scotland (though his steps in this direction were timid when compared to those of D. C. Scott at Blantyre); and began the experiment of fusing on to the Christian marriage ceremony traditional obligations connected with the payment of dowry.[49]

It was at this point that Fraser's opponents began to muster. Elmslie, already suspicious of the mass conventions which his colleague had introduced in Ngoniland, fought tenaciously against any attempt to dilute the purity of the nuclear family, 'the unit of the Church', and the symbol, as Professor Ajayi has pointed out, of Western individualistic society against the communalism represented in polygamy.[50] A major issue was the custom common in many central African societies, of widows remarrying with their deceased husbands' brothers. After several unsuccessful attempts, Fraser in October 1911 did manage to push through Presbytery a motion

[46] For a discussion of those influenced by the alternative narrow, guilt-ridden, tradition of Keswick see Webster, 43–5, and Ayandele, *Missionary Impact*, 213–14

[47] Donald Fraser, 'The Church and Games in Africa', *International Review of Missions*, x (1921), 110–17

[48] Fraser, 'Heathenism' Proceedings of the Nyasaland Missionary Conference, 1910, 30–4

[49] A. R. Fraser, 168–78, Donald Fraser, 'Progress in Ngoniland', *Aurora*, June 1897, 22; J. Martin, 'Visit to Ngoniland', *Aurora*, December 1902, 98–9; Fraser, *Primitive People*, 224–5, 275. Scott's reforms are discussed in Ross, 'Foundations'

[50] Elmslie, 'Marriage and Divorce', Proceedings of the Nyasaland Missionary Conference, 1910, 57. Ajayi, *Christian Missions*, 107–8

legalising the custom. But a year later Elmslie counter-attacked, and succeeded in having the motion annulled.[51] Attempts by Fraser to introduce a school marriage, distinguishable from the normal marriage in church by the absence of legal provisions as laid down by the state, was likewise rejected. Livingstonia came to demand of her church members and catechumens that they be married under the provisions of the Christian Native Marriage Ordinance of 1912, which contained the penalty for those lapsing into polygamy of up to five years in gaol.[52]

The expectations aroused in the early stages of Fraser's reforms were thus never fully realised. Many church members remained puritan zealots, loud in their condemnation of 'idleness, beer-drinking and dancing', and fierce in their denunciation of the playing of games, the love of high wages or the desire for fine clothes.[53] Several more, however, including a high proportion of the most talented students from the Institution, turned against the mission's policies as being intolerably confining. African dances, condemned outright by most missionaries, for fear that the harmless would lead to the obscene, had their African supporters. Charles Domingo read a paper at a conference in Blantyre in 1902 praising some aspects of them.[54] Six years later at Loudon, Charles Chinula, then a teacher, and a strong believer in purifying rather than destroying customs, was secretly encouraging his pupils to take part in dances at the school house, unknown to the resident missionary.[55] Polygamous marriages were also supported. Confronted by the fierce penalties contained in the Marriage Ordinance, large numbers of catechumens and members courted suspension in the years immediately prior to the First World War by marrying outside the church.[56] When faced with accusations derived from a foreign code of morals they reacted with vigour. As early as 1900 a certificated teacher in the theological class defended what the missionaries described as 'a fall from the highest position attainable here to almost the

[51] Presbytery of North Livingstonia, minutes for 20 October 1911 and 18 October 1912. W. A. Elmslie to A. J. Hetherwick, 18 May, 15 December 1912. Hetherwick Papers.

[52] Hetherwick to Elmslie, 13 June 1912; Laws to Hetherwick, 11 May 1913, Hetherwick Papers. Livingstonia Mission Council minutes, entry for 14 August 1913

[53] See the reports of native Christian conferences at Blantyre (*LWBCA*, October–December 1901, 14) and at Livingstonia (*Livingstonia News*, April 1908, 11–14)

[54] *LWBCA*, October–December 1901, 14

[55] Interview with Rev. Charles Chinula, Loudon, 25 July 1964

[56] Laws to Hetherwick, 11 May 1913, Hetherwick Papers; Livingstonia Mission Report, 1913, 20; 1914, 2

lowest possible . . . by propounding an Antinomian law of Christian liberty, which he did in a long paper submitted to the session'.[57] New modes of intellectual response were appearing, exemplified most remarkably by an article written by Levi Mumba, defending 'The Religion of my Fathers' from ignorant and prejudiced attack.[58] Enough of the spirit of cultural revolt was abroad to turn many of those suspended on disciplinary grounds towards Kamwana in 1909, and to permit the rapid circulation of the magazine, *Watch Tower*, even among teachers who remained loyal to the Church.[59]

A second source of friction had its roots in the excessive caution shown by the mission in granting authority to local Africans. Following the removal of the Lovedale men, a measure of self-government devolved on local congregations through the establishment of Kirk Sessions on Presbyterian lines at Bandawe in 1895, and in Ngoniland two years later, and through the formation of the Presbytery of North Livingstonia at Khondowe in November 1899.[60] An elaborate programme for the training of pastors was instituted, containing provision for a three-year course in theology and church history to be taken following completion of the arts and Normal courses. And this was paralleled by the transfer of considerable responsibilities to such men as Makera Tembo and Mawelero Tembo in Ngoniland, who were left in charge of the stations at Elangeni and Njuyu from 1895 and 1896 respectively, and to David Kaunda and John Afwenge Banda in Zambia.[61]

But as with reforms of church policy, the expectations aroused by the devolution of authority were greater than the powers devolved. Church government, while ostensibly opened up to significant African participation, remained before 1914 a largely European concern. Missionaries not only carried a disproportionate influence into the session meetings, where Elmslie by stating his opinion to be 'the law of Christ' was able to silence opposition, they also took many decisions without reference to their African colleagues.[62] Mission finance and matters of jurisdiction concerning Europeans both remained questions for the mission council alone to decide, and from 1912 a regulation was in force, aimed in the first instance at silencing Fraser, which prevented any European proposing

[57] ibid., 1900, 5–6

[58] Published in *IRM* XIX (1930)

[59] Livingstonia Mission Report, 1909, 4 and 7

[60] ibid., January–July 1895, 5; 1897–8, 12; *Aurora,* December 1899, 42, 45; Presbytery of North Livingstonia, minute for 15 November 1899

[61] Livingstonia Mission Report, July–December 1895, 12–13; January–June 1896, 18; 1896–7, 10–11; Elmslie to Dr Smith, 30 November 1896, NLS 7879

[62] Morrison, *Streams in the Desert*, 47–8

serious matters of legislation to the Presbytery without discussing them first in the mission council.[63] It is indicative of the small degree of influence possessed by Africans that not one was invited to attend any of the three Nyasaland Missionary Conferences held before 1914;[64] nor was any consulted on the establishment of Livingstonia's first vernacular newspaper, *Makani*, in 1906.[65]

As for the employment of trained pastors, the repeated suggestion of officials in Scotland that 'experienced native workers should be placed in charge of . . . old established work, so as to enable the Europeans to open up new stations and break new soil'[66] was frequently evaded by the missionaries at Livingstonia, who believed 'that the African is most efficient as an evangelist when guided and controlled'.[67] Congregational self-support was made the standard for local self-government, and the ordination of Africans was postponed again and again, 'not' according to James Henderson 'because of difficulties about those who ought to be ordained as about those to whom they would be ordained. We do not see such congregations as we are forming are yet in a position to have a native pastor ordained to them.'[68] Charles Domingo, 'a first-class preacher, very highly educated and of unblameable character', in the opinion of the Scots, finished his Livingstonia theological training in 1900, and was licensed in 1902.[69] Yet in 1908 when he left the mission following a quarrel with Fraser at Loudon, he had still not been ordained.[70] Yesaya

[63] *Aurora*, December 1899, 45. Elmslie to Hetherwick, 5 December 1912, Hetherwick Papers. Mission Council Minutes entry for 17 October 1912. For a more detailed discussion of the distribution of power within the Church see pp. 243–9

[64] Hetherwick's comment was: 'A Conference on Native Church affairs without the presence of any native seems to me to be like the play of Hamlet without Hamlet.' (Hetherwick to Laws, 12 May 1914, Hetherwick Papers)

[65] T. Cullen Young, 'The Native Newspaper', *Africa*, XI (1938), 66

[66] Daly to Binnie, 15 December 1911, NLS 7867

[67] Donald Fraser, *The Future of Africa*, Edinburgh, 1911, 206. This was an opinion shared by almost every other missionary of the time. See Laws to Dr Smith, 8 August 1898. Dewar to Dr Smith, 30–1 October 1899, Livingstonia letters to sub-committee NLS (v.31)

[68] Livingstonia Mission Committee Minutes, entry for 27 March 1894. James Henderson to Hetherwick, 15 February 1904, Hetherwick Papers

[69] Presbytery Minutes, entries for 2 November 1900 and 22 October 1902; Fraser to Hetherwick, 12 November, 1908, Hetherwick Papers

[70] In separate interviews with me, two contemporaries of Domingo, the Rev. Charles Chinula and the Rev. Z. P. Ziba both argued that it was frustration at not being ordained that caused Domingo to leave the mission. According to Ziba, the final break took place in the following way. Fraser told

Zerenje Mwasi, a Tonga, was clerk of the Session at Khondowe by 1901, completed the theological course in 1902, and was licensed in 1906.[71] Not till 1914, thirty-nine years after the foundation of the mission and three years after Blantyre had taken the same step, did he, along with two evangelists from Ngoniland, Jonathan Chirwa and Hezekiah Tweya, became one of Livingstonia's first African ministers.[72] 'Let us be ordained before we die!', the cry of the Ngoni, Daniel Mtusu during the First World War,[73] might easily have been repeated by many of his compatriots. And even when ordination took place, the authority of the African pastor was subordinated to that of his missionary colleague. By February 1915 Mwasi's attempt to assert his independent role at Bandawe had led to his suspension by Dr Turner and to the assembling of a special meeting of Presbytery to adjudicate between them. The decision arrived at, deeply humiliating to a man of Mwasi's spirit, was that he should be allowed to resume work in March only on condition that he agreed to 'obey the instructions of the minister in charge as to how he is to carry on his work, and where he is to work, and whatsoever other directions he may receive for the furtherance of the work of the Bandawe congregation'.[74] The extent to which the position of Africans had changed since the heyday of the Lovedale men can be illustrated from the fact that even in 1920, the senior African assistant at the Overtoun Institution, Uriah Chirwa, was being paid little more than a third of what George Williams had received in 1888, £48 per annum as compared to £130.[75] Though Kamwana's first campaign was then only a memory, the changed circumstances which the contrast implies, played no small part in creating the climate of opinion which he was able to exploit.

To these domestic frustrations two more specific sources of tension can be added. The first, upon which Elmslie was insistent in his emphasis, was the susceptibility of Nyasa migrant labourers in Southern Rhodesia and South Africa to the appeal of independent sects.[76] This appeal can be

Domingo: 'Charles, you are under my rule'; to which Domingo replied, 'No, I am under you in your house but I am not under you in the session.' When they met again, after a short interval, Domingo asked for Fraser's blessing, but was refused, and the break was completed.

71 Livingstonia Mission Report, 1901, 9; 1902, 15; Presbytery Minutes, entry for 11 May 1906

72 ibid. entry for 18 May 1914. There is a photograph of the three, taken shortly after the ceremony in W. P. Livingstone, *Laws*, 289

73 Fraser, *Autobiography*, 206

74 Presbytery Minutes entry for 18 February 1915

75 Livingstone, *Laws*, 364

76 *Livingstonia News*, October 1909, 72

explained partly by the failure of Livingstonia, and indeed of all Malawi missions, to extend their essentially rural work to the urban areas where migrants flocked. During the 1880s, Livingstonia agents had actively encouraged the Tonga to take to wage employment. In the early years of the twentieth century, enough of the beliefs behind this policy survived to make them differ from their Blantyre colleagues in refusing to condemn outright the exodus of workers to the south. Laws, though he objected to Africans being forced to work in a particular occupation, could not agree, he told Hetherwick, 'to any measure which would prevent the native from selling his labour in the dearest market should he desire this'. Both he and Fraser, while condemning the conditions prevalent in the Johannesburg mines about 1904, believed that 'from the open life at Salisbury and other districts . . . often good has been the result'.[77]

But if the Livingstonia missionaries espoused the rural community ideal less strongly than did many of their compatriots, they were just as reluctant in practice to provide facilities in urban areas which would keep the Church abreast with the changing pattern of employment. By 1904 Laws had been alerted to this problem which he attempted to surmount in a variety of ways. Friendly, though overworked Protestant missionaries, some of whom were unable to speak any Nyasa dialect, were contacted in Salisbury, Johannesburg, Bulawayo and Livingstone. Members going to Blantyre were provided with letters of introduction to Hetherwick. An occasional pastoral letter was circulated among migrants. Three evangelists were sent in 1906 to work among Nyasas in the Rhodesian and South African mines.[78]

But these hastily conceived measures were ineffective in grappling with the social and spiritual problems which confronted the migrants. Some European pastors, notably the Rev. M. Cochrane of the Presbyterian Church at Salisbury, and some Livingstonia-trained evangelists, Walter Seremani and Edward Chamaranda at Mazoe, were successful in making limited contact with Nyasa congregations. But these were the exceptions. Faced by the bleak environment of the mining compound and the settler farm, migrant Nyasas scattered as far afield as Chiromo, Broken Hill and Bulawayo had, by 1907, established literally dozens of independently organised, self-supporting congregations, the precursors of the larger-scale religious and political organisations that operated in the mining

77 Laws to Hetherwick, May 1903; Fraser to Hetherwick, 18 May 1904, Hetherwick Papers

78 Laws to Hetherwick, 28 December 1904; 14 January 1905, Hetherwick Papers. Livingstonia Mission Report, 1906, 2, 7 and 33; Overtoun Institution Senatus Minutes, entries for 9 January and 10 July 1906

areas by the 1930s.[79] Distant from European control such congregations, though by no means deliberately antagonistic to the Scots, were important as nurseries of African initiative. Even when Livingstonia retained links with her church members, as at Mazoe, it was they rather than the missionaries who took the final decision concerning the employment of Institution-trained evangelists. Of the two sent to work under Cochrane in 1906, one, Nathan Gondwe, had to be recalled a few months later because the congregation objected to his ignorance of English.[80] Where, as on the Rand, no such links existed, the *de facto* independence of the congregations was virtually complete. Ministered to by evangelists – among them for three years Kamwana – whose authority derived solely from the approval of their fellows, the migrants were exposed to a variety of sectarian influences.

Little evidence exists at present on the initial contact of Nyasas with such bodies as the black American African Methodist Episcopal Church (active in South Africa from 1898), but as early as 1904 according to the Missionary Superintendent of the Presbyterian Church of South Africa, several northern Malawians had been drawn into the Ethiopian Church movement.[81] Two years later Kamwana, while still a part-time unaffiliated evangelist, would appear to have made contact with Ethiopian Church leaders in Pretoria and King Williams Town.[82] And by the same date, Joseph Booth had begun to instruct the first of at least seven Nyasas at Cape Town in 'the rather confused combination of Watch Tower teachings and Sabbatarianism to which he then adhered'.[83] In contrast to later manifestations of Watch Tower, there seems little reason to characterise the initial outburst in Malawi in 1908 as a social movement of the semi proletarianised.[84] What it did reflect, however, was the improved access to new religious ideologies that migration to South Africa provided and

[79] An interesting description of one of these little congregations is contained in a letter written by an Institution graduate to Laws from Chiromo in 1905, printed in the *FCSMR*, August 1906, 361

[80] Overtoun Institution Senatus Minutes, entry for 12 February 1907

[81] Laws to Hetherwick, 28 December 1904, Hetherwick Papers

[82] See his evidence to the Chilembwe Rising Commission of Inquiry, 15 July 1915, CO 525/66

[83] Kenneth Lohrentz, 'Joseph Booth, Charles Domingo and the Seventh Day Baptists in Northern Nyasaland, 1910–12', *JAH* XII (1971), 465

[84] Sholto Cross, 'The Watch Tower Witch-Cleansing and Secret Societies in Central Africa' Conference on the History of Central African Religious Systems, Lusaka 1972

the new experience of religious independence that resulted from worshipping in a compound church.

It is one of the ambiguities of Watch Tower that a movement linked to the creation of the new southern African economy may also have been connected with internal Tonga rivalries, whose origins date back at least to the establishment of the pioneer Livingstonia station in the area in 1878. What was at issue was the selective nature of the mission's contacts with her neighbours, or rather the fact that certain villages, notably Marenga's close to Bandawe, gained much more from the association than did outlying villages at Chinteche, or even a close neighbour of Marenga's like Chifira. Such differences, it has been noted, exacerbated rivalries in the 1880s, when Marenga's success in gaining wealth and protection through her proximity to Bandawe was deplored not only by the rulers of more exposed villages, who gained less in economic or political terms from the presence of the mission in Tongaland, but also by those like the Muwamba family at Chifira, who regarded themselves as senior to the rulers of the neighbouring villages of Chimbono and Marenga, but found that the association of Marenga with the mission made his village appear the most important in British eyes.[85]

With the spread of the popular religious movement from the mid 1890s, the grievances of those who felt themselves to be under-privileged are likely to have gained in intensity. All Tongaland, it is clear, was affected by the wave of religious enthusiasm; but whereas near Bandawe, a core of church members had already been established by the time it began, other areas had a shorter history of missionary involvement and were thus more likely to be penalised by the long probationary period imposed by the mission and less accustomed, as well as less able, to make the financial sacrifices involved. Whether Watch Tower can thus be regarded as a substitute to which the less fortunate turned in a bid to partake of those benefits which had formerly flowed from Livingstonia alone, cannot be determined with complete certainty from the fragmentary evidence at present available. But that this is likely can be seen from the marked distinctions in attitude between those who believed they had gained from Livingstonia's presence and those who had lost.

Although enthusiasm for Watch Tower conversion was experienced in every part of the region in 1909, the vigorous response in the northern district of Usisya, where 2000 were said to have been immersed, and in the southern district of Dwambazi suggests that outlying regions had

[85] This is well illustrated by the fact that Marenga (or Mlenga Mzoma) was appointed a Principal Headman in 1917, while Chikuru, the headman at Chifra, was not. van Velsen, 'Administration'. See pp. 77–80 above

more than their fair proportion of converts.[86] While Marenga's remained the centre of mission activity and of loyalty to the government, Chifira, the home of Kamwana, as well as of Clements Kadalie, became the headquarters of the new movement. Its position as a source of discontent lasting well on into the 1920s centred on the low place which was assigned to it in the colonial spectrum. As Kadalie was later to remark, when noting his own concern to pursue studies in America, 'Tell me, is there any young man among Marenga's people busy with this defensive plan? I at once say "No"; they are quite satisfied with the present situation.'[87] Marenga, the headman, was appointed a teacher at Livingstonia and subsequently a school inspector. Mankambira at Chinteche, itself a centre of Watch Tower, was converted by Kamwana in 1909.[88] New inequalities were being articulated in a new religious guise.

The response to Watch Tower can thus be seen as an attempt to reintegrate a society which had been divided against itself by Livingstonia's influence. Nyasas admitted into the mission church became at once members of an international community, linked by many ties to the parent body in Scotland, but also part of a privileged elite who rejected, frequently contemptuously, the communal rituals that were integral to their local society. The attraction of Kamwana's alternative lay in the fact that he opposed to this Free Church elitism the promise of membership of a Christian community, which was open to all who accepted his message and were publicly baptised. Following Watch Tower orthodoxy, he preached the corruption of established governments and historic churches and prophesied the coming millennium in October 1914, when the true believers would come into their own. In one sense he thus gave to the disadvantaged the hope of a salvation which unbelievers would not share. In another, by promising, so it was believed, free books and free schools, he offered a solution to what had become the insoluble problem of Free Church educational dominance.[89] Most of the converts he made in 1909 were drawn from that sector of society which was frustrated by its failure to get into the church and refused, or perhaps was unable to pay the financial price of admission.

> So far as the religious element was concerned [wrote Elmslie] it was no doubt a revolt against our strict system of admission. It could not have succeeded at all had there not been widespread general

86 *Livingstonia News*, April 1909, 24; August 1909, 52

87 C. Kadalie to A. Muwamba, 21 April 1923, MNA s2/71/23

88 West Nyasa District Note-Book

89 R. D. McMinn, 'The First Wave of Ethiopianism in Central Africa', *Livingstonia News*, August 1909, 56–9

> knowledge of scripture truths, and there was a desire to get a Church standing without having to undergo the prolonged probation we prescribed.[90]

Those immersed, he thought, were primarily 'hear[er]s whose entrance to class had been deferred for various reasons, and catechumens in the same position; then crowds of heathen received without instruction or examination who answered to the cry "free education and books and no *sonko* to the church"'.[91] Livingstonia school fees fell away, church collections in Tongaland were more than halved, and a number of suspended teachers joined the new movement, and provided it with much of its leadership. But hardly a member of the Bandawe congregation in full status turned to Kamwana.[92] Watch Tower was less important for the inroads that it made upon the existing church community than for the alternative path it provided for those who had been seeking entry.

How far the Watch Tower movement drew upon indigenous religious traditions among societies west of the lake, how far it arose from a situation created specifically by Livingstonia are difficult questions to answer. Witchcraft-eradication movements, cleansing their adherents from sin, have recurred among many central African societies, and though the evidence for their existence in northern Malawi before the 1920s is slender, the success of the Kayayi cult in Ngoniland sometime before 1904, when doctors promised everlasting life through the sale of their medicines, suggests that aspects of such beliefs may well have been present in precolonial days.[93] It is tempting to see in the massive response to Kamwana's message of regeneration, through baptism, leading to salvation at the millennium in 1914, elements of an eschatology related to non-Christian beliefs, and appealing to members of a society seeking freedom from guilt at a level deeper than the Scots had been able to plumb. In the strict sense, as Sholto Cross has demonstrated, witchcraft-eradication movements and Watch Tower, with its emphasis on the imminence of the second coming, and the limited numbers to be saved, were ideologically distinct.[94] But if Kamwana's message was a new one, it is possible that the terms in which it was presented may have contained some familiar overtones. No attempt

[90] Livingstonia Mission Report, 1909, 4

[91] Elmslie to Hetherwick, 12 July 1912, Hetherwick Papers

[92] Livingstonia Mission Report, 1909, 34–40; *Livingstonia News*, October 1909, 68; Diary of A. G. Macalpine, entry for 9 January 1909, Macalpine Papers

[93] Fraser, *Primitive People*, 198–200. A similar opinion, applying more generally to Central Africa, has been expressed by T. O. Ranger, 'Mchape and the study of Witchcraft Eradication', Conference on the History of Central African Religious Systems, Lusaka 1972

[94] Cross, 'The Watch Tower'

to expose witches, or to destroy anti-witchcraft devices seems to have taken place during Kamwana's brief, six-month preaching tour but, according to an observer, many of the 9000 baptised believed that the act of immersion cleansed them from all sin.[95] And such an act of communal purification, one may argue, would involve an attempt to eradicate witchcraft.

Although most accounts of Kamwana have depicted him as a proto-nationalist pioneer, whose militant policies constituted a serious threat to the colonial regime, it may well be that this view involves a misreading of the nature of his political impact.[96] There is no dispute that, as a disciple of Russell, Kamwana taught that established governments and historic churches were instruments of the Devil which would be swept away at the approaching millennium when the faithful came into their own. But it is by no means clear how far he carried those generalised denunciations of secular government into specific attacks on the colonial system in northern Malawi. As late as February 1909 indeed, one close and interested observer, the local Resident at Chinteche, reported that though he had kept a careful watch on Kamwana for fear that he was preaching sedition, 'I have not found the slightest evidence on this point.'[97] And Kamwana himself in 1915 explicitly denied that he had ever preached that there would be no more taxation, or that white people would leave the country, though he readily admitted his belief that during the Second Advent secular powers would be swept away.[98]

Where evidence has been produced, it has come not from Kamwana's writings, but from the accusations made against him by the Scottish missionaries at Bandawe. A. G. Macalpine and R. D. McMinn were alarmed by the rapid expansion of his following late in 1908, and solicited evidence from their African agents which they presented to the government in the following March. According to their accusations Kamwana had not only prophesied the disappearance of British rule in October 1914, but had condemned the introduction of taxes and predicted the establishment of an African state. McMinn purported to quote fiery statements made by Kamwana at large meetings held throughout the district.

The advent of Christ was to take place at the end of 1914. The

[95] *Livingstonia News*, August 1909, 57–8

[96] Rotberg, *Rise of Nationalism*, 66–9, John McCracken, 'African Politics in twentieth-century Malawi' in T. O. Ranger (ed.), *Aspects of Central African History*, London, 1968, 195; B. Pachai, 'The State and the Churches in Malawi during early Protectorate rule', *Journal of Social Science*, University of Malawi, 1, 1972, 13; Shepperson and Price, 153–9

[97] West Nyasa Monthly Report, February 1909, MNA NNC3/4/1

[98] Evidence presented to the Nyasaland Rising Commission of Inquiry, 15 July 1915, CO 525/66

> whites were all to leave the country. There would be no more oppression from the tax gatherers. 'Those people there' (indicating the Residency on the hill) 'you soon will see no more; for the Government will go. In the meantime do not let your hearts be troubled; for the white men whom I represent will not only educate you freely, but will provide money for taxes.'

McMinn claimed that Kamwana had impressed the uneducated with his boastful talk: '"I have baptised 7000 whites in the South; I have dined with Members of Parliament. We shall build our own ships, make our own powder and make or import our own guns etc.", i.e. when the revenue is in our own hands.'[99]

McMinn's evidence – or at least those parts which present Kamwana in a militantly political light – has been the basis for much historical generalisation, but it was gathered by hostile witnesses at a time of emotional upheaval and hence should not be accepted without question in the absence of corroborative testimony. Ten years later, after all, similar comments on Watch Tower leaders made by McMinn's colleague, Riddell Henderson, were dismissed out of hand by government officials as 'the vague sort of general accusation' to which missionaries frequently resorted.[100] Given the element of doubt, it is necessary to refer back to Kamwana himself. What likelihood is there that he acted in the aggressively political manner attributed to him?

The answer to this question must begin with the recognition that during his time in South Africa Kamwana gained an intimate view of the uglier side of the colonial system which may well have coloured his social attitudes. His years as a hospital assistant on the Rand coincided with the government's ill-fated labour recruitment experiment when Nyasa miners died at the rate of over 120 per thousand per annum.[101] At Cape Town in 1908 he not only imbibed the teachings of his radical mentor, Booth, but passed the gruelling test of public disputation at open air meetings with hundreds of the city's toughest and most sceptical whites.[102] As we know from his submission to the Commission of Inquiry in 1915, his belief in millennial solutions was strongly tempered with concern for the physical welfare of his people. Among the African grievances that had

99 McMinn, 'The First Wave of Ethiopianism in Central Africa', *Livingstonia News*, August 1909, 56–9. See also Livingstonia Mission Report, 1909, 33–5

100 West Nyasa District Report, February 1919, MNA s2/1/19

101 S. M. Pritchard, 'Memo, on Mortality among Tropical Natives', 25 July 1906, in *Correspondence relating to the Recruitment of Labour in the Nyasaland Protectorate for the Transvaal and Southern Rhodesian Mines*, 1908

102 J. Booth to J. Chilembwe, 10 December 1911 [copy], CO 525/61

contributed to the rising he listed: 'Little wages, no liberty or franchise. Overtax, injustice, no pension nor allowance for children, wife or parents of the dead soldier in the war.' The reforms he suggested were of a wide ranging, though of a distinctly unrevolutionary nature: 'Jealousy and hatred of particular classes of Europeans should stop. Pension and allowance for the children, wife or parents of the dead soldier in the war should be considered. Liberty should be given to some extent. Native tax collectors and policemen should stop to extort and ravish in the Districts. There should be no respect of persons in Judgement.'[103]

But though Kamwana possessed the angry commitment that undoubtedly could have led him to political action, his behaviour prior to the Chilembwe Rising in January 1915 suggests that his religious beliefs carried him in another direction. After his deportation to South Africa in 1909 he demonstrated the independence of his views by secretly returning to the West Nyasa district a year later, only to be arrested and deported once again.[104] While detained at Mlanje in 1914 he corresponded with John Chilembwe, but warned him against active opposition to the government.[105] When Chilembwe called upon him on 23 January 1915 to join his rising, he reported the matter to the local Resident.[106] For Kamwana, colonial institutions may have been corrupt, but it would appear that he believed with Pastor Russell that active involvement in overthrowing them was wrong and that the faithful should await the intervention of God.

In the absence of hard evidence concerning Kamwana's political involvement it seems reasonable to conclude that he was subjected to inflated accusations of the same type as those made against Watch Tower leaders in both Zambia and Malawi in the 1930s – accusations which historians now tend to discount. If this is so, the sharp division which George Shepperson has detected between militant Watch Tower in the prewar period and accommodationist Watch Tower subsequently is surely overemphasised.[107] Watch Tower in 1909 may have been more of a safety valve than has often been imagined.

[103] Written evidence submitted by Elliott Kamwana to the Nyasaland Rising Commission of Inquiry, CO 525/66

[104] *Livingstonia News*, December 1910, 93

[105] In his correspondence with Chilembwe, Kamwana stated his belief 'that the present powers to be will be swallowed up by the war which is in process', but he also told him 'that wisdom of the Scriptures is better than knowledge of war'. Evidence by Kamwana to the Commission of Inquiry, CO 525/66

[106] Evidence of Mr C. Grant, 1st class Resident, Mlanje District, ibid.

[107] George Shepperson, 'The Politics of African Church Separatist Movements in British Central Africa, 1892–1916', *Africa* 24, 1954, 245

In what ways, then, was Kamwana's movement of political significance? Firstly, Kamwana himself, however remote his solutions from practical reality, was a man of courage and tenacity whose readiness to stand up to Europeans made him in the eyes of many of his compatriots a symbol of African independence. It was in this guise that he entered the pantheon of saints and martyrs of independent Watch Tower churches in Northern and Southern Rhodesia during the 1920s.[108] Secondly, to paraphrase T. O. Ranger, the 'tones of bewilderment, bitterness, fatalism and desperate hope' which echo through the fragmentary and distorted comments of the Scottish missionaries may well represent the authentic voice of many of the lakeside Tonga confronted by the harsh realities of colonialism in the years before the First World War.[109] In this sense, Watch Tower is of importance as a manifestation of popular feeling – though it should be emphasised that this feeling was of a profoundly different character to the popular radicalism of the 1950s associated with the nationalist movement.

Not only Kamwana and his leading assistants but also the overwhelming majority of Watch Tower adherents in the country ignored appeals for help in 1915 and remained quiescent during the Chilembwe rising. 'The small Watch Tower community has remained thoroughly loyal and law-abiding throughout the year', the Resident for the West Nyasa district reported early in 1916. He argued that the body should not be suppressed, for it had 'given no trouble during the past five years' and possessed no anti-European element in its teaching.[110] It may be true, as Ian and Jane Linden have argued, that the millennial expectations contained in Watch Tower encouraged certain of Chilembwe's supporters to seek the New Jerusalem through violent action. But for the majority Watch Tower teaching functioned more as an obstacle than as an incentive to revolt. Indeed, the evidence suggests that but for the influence of Russell's doctrines, more Malawians would have joined Chilembwe's army.[111]

Kamwana's deportation marked the beginnings of a new phase of religious independency in Malawi. Deprived of its prophet, the Watch Tower movement in the West Nyasa district experienced a crisis of leadership. Undeterred by threats of government persecution, adherents at Cape Town determined to reinforce their northern outpost, and success-

[108] See Taylor and Lehmann, *Christians of the Copperbelt*, 238–46

[109] T. O. Ranger, *The African Voice in Southern Rhodesia*, London, 1970, 214

[110] Annual Report on West Nyasa District for year ending 31 March 1916, MNA, NNC3/1/1

[111] Jane and Ian Linden, 'John Chilembwe and the "New Jerusalem"', *JAH*, XII, 4, 1971

fully appealed for volunteers. Two of Booth's Tonga pupils, Hanson Tandu and Gilbert Chihayi, were sent back to their homeland in September 1909, where they were joined a month later by the white South African, Pastor Brink.

The arrival of these reinforcements failed to avert the mounting crisis. Chihayi led several evangelists into Ngoniland where they preached with a zeal which, as one Livingstonia missionary conceded, 'Our own teachers might quite well copy'.[112] But Tandu was arrested as a deserter from the King's African Rifles and Brink, exhausted by the rigours of the journey from Broken Hill across the Luangwa valley, was carried on a stretcher to Bandawe and died at the District Residency thirty hours later.[113] When William Johnston, a Glasgow joiner acting on behalf of the Watch Tower Bible and Tract Society, visited the West Nyasa district in August 1910 he found the congregations confused and demoralised. By refusing to provide extra financial support or to sign the labour certificates which would have reduced their holders' tax liability by half, Johnston emphasised the other-worldly nature of the doctrine he preached and dashed the hopes of the Nyasa adherents. He thus opened the breach which was soon to lead to the separate establishment of Seventh Day Baptist churches.

Like many other religious innovations in Malawi, Sabbatarianism in the Northern Province can be traced to the influence of Joseph Booth. Despite his conversion in Scotland in 1906 to the Watch Tower movement, Booth did not abandon the sabbatarian beliefs to which he had been converted in 1898. He handed some of them on to the group of Nyasas he instructed at Cape Town, though not all of these were persuaded by his teaching. Kamwana gave no sign of sabbatarian influence during his sensational visitation of the West Nyasa district, subsequently declaring 'I was [not] and will not be a teacher of the Sabbath', but Chihayi, though he regarded himself as a loyal Watch Tower evangelist, in 1909 did his utmost to popularise the cult of Saturday observance.[114]

In 1910 Booth jettisoned his allegiance to Pastor Russell and visited the Seventh Day Baptist congregation at Plainfield, New Jersey, which had sponsored one of his earlier ventures in Malawi, the Plainfield Industrial Mission. Using Kamwana's conversions as a lever, he succeeded in raising from the Americans some 50, later 100, dollars a month which he

112 Livingstonia Mission Report, 1909, 18

113 ibid., 36–7; *Livingstonia News*, October 1909, 75, 90; Fraser to Hetherwick, 18 October 1909, Hetherwick Papers

114 Kamwana to Charles A. Green, 27 June 1911; Booth to Pastor Timon Achirwa, 24 September 1911, University of Malawi

sent in £5.00 contributions to selected Nyasa Watch Tower leaders.[115] Disillusioned by Johnston's refusal to provide assistance, several quickly defected to the Seventh Day Baptists, including Hanson Tandu, who had now been released from prison. The pastors who had allied themselves to the sabbatarian movement, Tandu explained to Booth in March 1911, 'are all thinking about the money they have received from you last month'. Among the minority who remained loyal to Watch Tower were several who 'are wishing to write and state their feelings. Their feelings are that they cannot prolong with Russell seeing that from 1908 till then Russell has not sent a copper to them. They are indeed grumbling upon him for not sending them sustenance.'[116]

Any assessment of the early years of the Seventh Day Baptists in northern Malawi must lean heavily on the evidence provided by Charles Domingo, the outstanding leader of the movement and its most effective propagandist. Domingo, after Yakobe Msusa Muwamba, was the most impressive of Livingstonia's early converts. Educated at Lovedale for two years, as well as at the Overtoun Institution, he passed the examination for theological students in September 1900 and worked for six years as a teacher at the Institution, winning a glowing reputation as a sensitive instructor of children and as the soloist in the College choir. In 1907 he was transferred to Loudon to prepare for the ministry as an assistant under Donald Fraser, but a year later he broke with the mission and departed for the Shire highlands.

During the next two years Domingo subjected himself to a rigorous course of self-education. In December 1908 according to Hetherwick, he was living at John Chilembwe's Providence Industrial Mission. In January 1909 he informed Fraser that he had been called by God to work among his own people on the lower Zambesi at Vincente. Later in 1909 he made contact with Pastor Russell and began a comprehensive study of Watch Tower doctrines.[117] In 1910 he turned to the path he was to follow for the next six years. Correspondence with Booth convinced him of the merits of Seventh Day observance and when he returned to northern Malawi, it appears as a Watch Tower evangelist to the Dwambazi district, it was the Seventh Day message he was most anxious to propagate.[118] By

115 *Independent African*, 157, 160; Lohrentz, 467. In 1911 exchange rate was $4.866 to the £.

116 H. Tandu to Booth, 11 March 1911, University of Malawi

117 Hetherwick to D. Fraser, 1 December 1908; Fraser to Hetherwick, 12 January 1909, Hetherwick Papers; Chief Secretary, Zomba, 22 May 1916, Circular letter, Unclassified, MNA

118 Domingo to Booth, 10 April and 19 September 1911, University of Malawi

December of that year his position had clarified. Based at Chipata in Ngoniland as a Seventh Day Baptist pastor, he was busy constructing, on the foundations laid by Chihayi, a network of congregations and schools which were to form the nucleus of the new church in that area. Under his supervision, Ngoniland by 1912 had become the centre of Sabbatarianism in Malawi.

The difference between Kamwana and Domingo reflects and indeed overemphasises the difference between Watch Tower and the Seventh Day Baptist movement. Kamwana was a prophet, a charismatic preacher who enjoyed an emotional relationship with his enormous body of followers. As he indicated in the evidence he presented to the Chilembwe Commission, he had little interest in the establishment of schools, which he regarded as 'not my work', and the practical consequences of his teaching were thus largely confined to the formation of congregations of believers. 'Education in the college and seminaries has bad effect on natives mind or any people', he once declared. 'Knowledge is power. But [there are] very few who can use knowledge properly for general interest.'[119]

Domingo, on the other hand, was one of a group of pastors which included Gilbert Chihayi, Hanson Tandu, Amon Malinda, Andrew Amuhone and Jacob Chigowo, who were all virtually independent of each other and met only infrequently at district conventions. His success was based less on charismatic appeal than on organising ability and considerable powers of statecraft. Unlike Kamwana, he was almost obsessively concerned with remodelling his adopted homeland on 'progressive' European lines. 'Nyasa country [is] now 36 years old,' he wrote in 1912, '[and] should start to rise up as our fellow country Japan is.'[120]

For most of their members, the dividing lines between the two movements were blurred, and over the years there was considerable shifting of allegiance between them. Yet though Seventh Day Baptists made considerable use of Watch Tower literature, in their ultimate aims the two faced in different directions, the one inwards towards spiritual preparation for the imminent millennium, the other outward towards the bettering of the secular world. With the exception of Domingo himself, Cullen Young noted:

> I cannot think of any case of a teacher deserting his old work for the new. Little boys and girls to whom the promise of free books and the flush of mistaken nationalism embodied in the 'our own schools'

[119] Written evidence submitted by Elliott Kamwana, CO 525/66

[120] Quoted in Shepperson, 'African Church Separatist Movements', 240

war-cry combined to paint a too tempting prospect were the main body of the movement.[121]

Like Watch Tower, the Seventh Day Baptists made converts among the less privileged members of the community who either could not afford the school fees that Livingstonia levied, or else lived at a distance from those schools she had started. But whereas for Kamwana secular education was a potentially dangerous irrelevance, for Domingo it provided an important avenue for African advancement. His aim, he informed Booth in 1912, was 'to train Boys and Girls not only to read and write but to be strong men and women possessing higher faculties'. 'We are not so full of ambition to have University or College,' he admitted, 'but more a station, and there start to scholarise the Nyassalanders.'[122]

It is an error to assume that independent religious movements in northern Malawi developed as a kind of apostolic succession from Kamwana to Domingo. Despite the heavy defections of 1910, Watch Tower retained a core of members in the West Nyasa district, ministered to by Timon Chirwa and Jordan Ansumba, the only evangelists who did not secede to the Seventh Day church. This band of the faithful was heartened by Kamwana's brief and illegal visit to the Dwambazi district late in 1910 and, particularly around Chifira and in the Dwambazi, Sanga and Usisya regions, survived successfully into the First World War.[123] In August 1914, fifty-one Watch Tower churches still existed in the district with a total membership of about 1000.[124] New communities had also grown up in various northern centres between Karonga and Kasungu, and others had been formed in the Upper Shire, West Shire, Blantyre and Lower Shire districts. Moreover, Tonga migrants, inspired perhaps by Kamwana himself on his journey between South Africa and Malawi in 1910, had carried the Watch Tower message to Southern Rhodesia.[125] Small congregations, composed predominantly of clerks, 'boss boys' and the like, were set up at the Globe and Phoenix mine near Que Que, the Eldorado mine near Sinoia, and at Salisbury, Shamva and other centres. The creation of these congregations gave Watch Tower the

121 Livingstonia Mission Report, 1911, 24

122 Domingo to Booth, 17 March 1911 and n.d. Malawi University Library

123 Tandu to Booth, 11 March 1911; *Africa Report*, March 1911, ibid.; *Livingstonia News*, December 1910, 93

124 Governor of Nyasaland to S. of S. for Colonies, 6 March 1916, MNA S/2/49/19

125 The suggestion that Kamwana was personally responsible for bringing Watch Tower to Southern Rhodesia is made in a statement by the Clerk in Charge, Que Que to the Native Commissioner, Gwelo, 15 May 1917, Salisbury N3/58

character of a labour sect and insured that the movement would be difficult to suppress. Returning migrants smuggled Watch Tower literature into Malawi from 1916 in defiance of a government edict forbidding its circulation, and waited patiently for the return of Kamwana from the Seychelles to which he had been deported in the wake of the 1915 rising. By the time of his return in 1937 Watch Tower had become an important social movement in areas far remote from its place of origin.[126]

As for the Seventh Day Baptists, the expectations aroused in 1910 were never fully realised. Domingo and his colleagues could not create an effective church school system in the poverty-stricken Northern Province. Many of their adherents had been unable to afford the school fees that Livingstonia charged, and had welcomed the Watch Tower message that it was against God's law to sell books or to charge scholars for the lessons they received.[127] In theory Domingo rejected this belief and argued the necessity of self-support:

> If people in a country do not wish to help oneself there can be no liberty and Independency, but will always beg, beg, beg and if a people behave thus laziness conquers and not a bit of bread can be found among its families. . . They'll be great stupids tho' education possesses them.[128]

In practice, however, self-support was an unattainable ideal. So little cash circulated in the Northern Province that church donations were usually made in the form of flour and beans, and the levying of school fees was bitterly resisted. The pastors were forced back on what scanty and intermittent alms their 'ambassador' Booth could collect for them from America, and anxiously complained when provisions from South Africa were delayed or when donations were not forthcoming. By 1912 salaries for teachers and bricks for churches had become alike impossible to raise, slates, pencils and syllabus cards were at a premium; food and clothes for scholars were unobtainable luxuries. In 1911 Domingo complained that his paper, envelopes and postage stamps were finished, that the very table he wrote upon was borrowed from his brother-in-law, a member of the Presbyterian Church.[129] His wife, Sarah, and his two young children moved from Chipata to Dwambazi in search of food; workmen building his storeroom went unpaid.[130]

[126] For Watch Tower after the First World War see Ranger, *African Voice*, Meebelo, *Reaction to Colonialism*, 133–85 and S. W. Cross, 'The Watch Tower Movement in South Central Africa 1908–45', D. Phil. Oxford, 1973

[127] *Livingstonia News*, February 1912, 10

[128] Domingo to Booth, July 1912

[129] ibid., 9 June 1911

[130] ibid., 17 March 1912

Seen against this background of grinding poverty, the achievements of the Seventh Day Baptists were not inconsiderable. It is true that Domingo's vision of a central boarding school modelled on Tuskagee, the famous American Negro college, faded into nothing. Most of his teachers had only the most rudimentary grasp of English; school materials were in woefully short supply. Yet at least in those schools personally supervised by Domingo respectable standards were maintained. In 1912 at Chipata pupils were trained in English reading, Vernacular reading, Translation, Dictation, Writing and Arithmetic. Domingo gave lessons in singing and there was also instruction in manual work. N. O. Moore and Wayland Wilcox, American Seventh Day Baptists, who were sent from Plainfield to inspect the Malawi Churches in 1912, were critical of much that they saw, but they noted approvingly of Domingo that he 'had a well planned and organised school'.[131]

The publication of the investigators' report in November 1912, however, brought Baptist expansion to a halt. Influenced by Elmslie and Macalpine, they asserted that only two thousand converts had been made – not the ten thousand that Booth had claimed – and that these were people 'already living under Christian influence', many of them suspended from Livingstonia's church. Booth travelled to Plainfield to reply to the charges, but his lengthy defence was not accepted. Financial support to Cape Town was therefore halted, though Domingo did receive occasional contributions direct from America for at least another two years.[132] In 1915 three Seventh Day pastors were working in the Mombera district where seven had operated previously. Domingo himself, according to one witness, was 'in very poor circumstances – almost in rags'. But he had just rejected the offer of a clerkship at the local *Boma*, saying defiantly that 'God would provide for him'.[133]

For most members, adherence to the Seventh Day Baptist church provided the dual attraction of access to an esoteric knowledge from which the Scottish missionaries were excluded, along with the satisfaction of being part of a tight-knit, comprehensively-organised community where African leadership could be abundantly displayed. The members' self-confidence was bolstered by the aggressive anti-Catholicism of the sect: one popular chorus, sung at a four day convention held at Chipata, went: 'Down falls Pope, Down falls Pope, *With his Sunday in hell*'. Their frustration at the lack of individual opportunity within the colonial system

[131] N. O. Moore, 'Seventh Day Baptists and Mission Work in Nyasaland, Africa'

[132] ibid. and E. Shaw to Domingo, 8 December 1914

[133] Laws to Hetherwick, 8 March 1915, Hetherwick Papers

found an outlet in membership of a community of believers where all, at least in theory, were equal. Domingo preached that the veil of the temple had been rent in two so that everyone could enter the holy of holies. 'While in the days of the Israelites *only* the *high priest* entered. But now-a-days every believer *is permitted* to enter.'[134] In theory, by rejecting the pacifism of Watch Tower, Seventh Day adherents left open the option of militant involvement in creating the just society, though in practice members from the north took no part in the 1915 rising, even in support of their fellow-sabbatarian, Filipo Chinyama from Ncheu.[135] Their political importance, therefore, lies less in the threat, real or imagined, that they posed to the government, and more in the nature of the community they created and the aspirations it expressed.

Domingo's personal significance is of a different order. Despite his contacts with Booth and the contributions he made to the latter's *African Sabbath Recorder*, he was an isolated figure, lacking a political organisation through which to spread his ideas. Yet in the letters he wrote between 1910 and 1912 a body of political thought exists, rooted in the soil of northern Malawi, which provides a searching criticism of the British colonial system.

It is a measure of Domingo's isolation from intellectual circles in Africa that though he had made some study of the writings of Edward Blyden, he was entirely uninfluenced by ideas of cultural nationalism. His beliefs, rather, were grounded on the authority of the Bible, and started from the premise that all races are essentially equal. 'What is the difference between a black man, and a white man? Are we not of the same blood, and all from Adam?'[136] But if Africans were potentially equal with Europeans, the opportunities open to them were by no means the same. Domingo drew on his experiences of subordination at Livingstonia to convict the Presbyterian missionaries of un-Christian behaviour. Though Christ had dwelt only three years among His disciples 'and *after these times left whole Responsibility to them*... White fellows have been here for *nearly 36 years*, and *not one of them* sees *a native as his Brother*, but as *his boy*, tho' a native is somehow wiser than he in managing God's work.'[137]

For Domingo, this failure in brotherhood derived not from some fundamental lack of sympathy among all whites – Booth was an obvious exception – but rather from the link between racialism and colonialism which

[134] Domingo to Booth, n.d. but approximately 1 November 1911

[135] See *Independent African*, esp. 212–13 and 291–5

[136] Domingo to Booth, 19 September 1911

[137] ibid.

he observed in the Nyasaland Protectorate. The appeal which some of the other pastors made for a resident American missionary he regarded with open alarm. 'The call for a white Resident *to come and rule over us* is altogether too weak', he emphasised in a letter to Booth. 'Many white fellows become Xtians when they are in Europe, and as soon as they taste Nyassaland coffee they turn-tail, and are unable to acknowledge their way of travelling within the truth of God. Even the very (so called) Reverends do loose their GOD's title (Psalms CXI.9) when they come to Nyassaland.'[138]

Armed with this perception, Domingo elaborated the most crucial part of his argument. Discounting the occasional criticisms made by Livingstonia missionaries of the government, he asserted that the various dominant institutions in Malawi – economic, religious and administrative – shared a common identity of interest which, in sum, was the colonial society. Despite its self-identification as an outpost of God's kingdom, this society was, he claimed, essentially non-Christian and could be condemned for its failure to live up to the spirit of God's laws. His analysis has become deservedly famous:[139]

> There is too much failure among all Europeans in Nyassaland. The Three Combined Bodies: Missionaries – Government – and Companies or Gainers of money do form the same rule to look on a Native with mockery eyes. It sometimes startle us to see that the Three Combined Bodies are from Europe, and along with them there is a title 'CHRISTNDOM'. And to compare or make a comparison between the MASTER of the title and His Servants it pushes any African away from believing the Master of the title. If we had power enough to communicate ourselves to Europe, we would have advised them not to call themselfs 'CHRISTNDOM' but 'Europeandom'. We see that the title 'CHRISTNDOM' does not belong to Europe, but to future BRIDE. Therefore the life of The Three Combined Bodies is altogether too cheaty, too thefty, too mockery.

It is the strength of Domingo's analysis that he was able to move from theoretical discussion to an illumination of practical problems, and from there back to generalities again. Taking up a problem that confronted all Seventh Day believers – how they could observe their Sabbath while working on European estates – he began by informing Booth 'how the Nyassaland Europeans are as *cruel as anything*'. But, as he recognised, the real exploitation of Africans lay not in the harsh behaviour of a few

[138] Domingo to Booth, 20 September 1911

[139] ibid. A slightly edited version of this passage was published by Joseph Booth in *The African Sabbath Recorder* and is quoted in full in *Independent Africa* – 163–4

individuals, but was inherent in the tyranny of the system as a whole. The argument is succinctly developed in the following passage:[140]

> Suppose it is arranged that such Brothers should *keep on* working on The Sabbath Day, and observe it while they are near the Church of the Sabbathers: It would mean not keeping the Sabbath at all, but *just breaking* it. If it arranged that they should try to *fight on* i.e. *refusing to work* on The Sabbath Day called Saturday; they will be *dismissed* from the employment, and will *fail* to get some money to pay for their *hut-tax*. The *native police will come*, and arrest them; they will be severely punished for their *disobedience &* Christianity will not sweeten them. If they are arrested, they will be *thrashed* with chikoti, and at the *same time* will get a heavy work which, they will even *have to work* on the *denied Sabbath* of God.

His conclusion was that the Apostles had been persecuted by the heathen, but now a so-called Christian society was punishing men for their Christian beliefs.

The weakness of Domingo's analysis, a weakness made inevitable, perhaps, by his ignorance of socialist thought, is that though his Scriptural model isolated some of the failings of colonial society, it provided no meaningful alternative. Two possible courses were open to him: the one chosen by John Chilembwe – the role of the symbolic martyr, which neither personality or intellect befitted him to adopt, and the path he did choose to follow in attempting to create a truly Christian African-dominated community within the wider colonial society. The limitations in such an approach have already been demonstrated. Not only did Domingo lack the kind of resources which would have enabled him to provide an educational system comparable to Livingstonia's, the type of system to which he aspired was one which simply paralleled the Free Church's rather than providing an effective alternative. There was the same narrow emphasis on scholastic skills, the same readiness to train students in techniques they could use effectively only within the export sector of the economy, the same insistence on learning by rote with slate and chalk, and the same authoritarian discipline. The ironic effect, illustrated by Donald Fraser's comments to the 1915 Commission of Inquiry, was that Domingo's actions helped to legitimise the colonial system instead of confronting it with a practical challenge. Despite the hostile probings of the Commissioners, Fraser stoutly denied that there was anything pernicious in the doctrines Domingo preached, or that his schools were particularly inefficient. 'From what I met from Domingo,' Fraser stated, 'he is most respectful. And from what I could learn of his doctrines

[140] Domingo to Booth, 16 April, 1911

he is teaching the gospel from the Bible simply, and some peculiar things such as the Seventh Day Baptists preach.'[141]

The solitary intellectual, lacking the support of a body of like-minded comrades, is particularly prone to temptation. Domingo took no part in the Chilembwe Rising, but he attracted government suspicion in 1916 when it was discovered that he had endorsed Booth's African Congress petition, and was deported to the Southern Province. In 1919 his domestication began. Allowed to return to Ngoniland in that year, he was recruited into government service and was sent as a clerk to the Mzimba *boma*. His restless spirit had not been entirely caged: as late as 1927 he tendered his resignation from government service in order to rejoin the Seventh Day Baptists. But tempted by offers of higher pay he changed his mind, and in 1934 was one of only two first-grade clerks in the Northern Province – and completely uninvolved in politics.[142]

His epitaph had been written more than twenty years earlier. In 1911 Joseph Booth informed Chilembwe: 'Pastor Charles Domingo sees the need and great possibilities for Africa as I do more than any other living man thus far.'[143]

Fraser's public support for Domingo illustrates the speed with which Livingstonia missionaries recovered their self assurance following the confusion into which they had been thrown by Kamwana. In 1909 Livingstonia had faced a crisis which threatened to undermine her special position in the Northern Province. The missionaries had drawn consolation from the knowledge that Kamwana attracted few church members to his community, and that most of the teachers who joined him had already been suspended from Livingstonia on disciplinary charges. But set against this was the indisputable fact that within a few months Kamwana had baptised well over twice the total number of Christians admitted into the Livingstonia church in the Bandawe region since its foundation there in 1878.[144]

For at least a couple of years Watch Tower and the Seventh Day Baptists between them provided not only the bulk of Christian adherents but the most dedicated evangelists in the north and the most confident theologians. Teachers and evangelists working for Livingstonia had their

141 Evidence of Rev. Donald Fraser before the Nyasaland Rising Commission of Inquiry, CO 525/66

142 PC to Resident, Mzimba, 18 February 1927, MNA NN1/20/3; Annual Report of PC Northern Province, 1934, MNA NN2/1/3

143 Booth to Chilembwe, 10 December 1911 (copy), CO 525/61

144 Kamwana claimed to have personally baptised 9126 converts. According to official figures, Livingstonia had baptised 3986 in the Bandawe district up to the end of 1909.

services interrupted by sabbatarian zealots and were drawn into doctrinal disputes for which they had little stomach. Copies of the magazine, *Watch Tower*, passed from hand to hand at the Overtoun Institution and were avidly read by students in training.

By 1915, however, Livingstonia had regained the initiative. Following the baptism of a large number of new converts in 1909 a major evangelical campaign was launched which came to a climax in August and September 1910 with the visit to Malawi of the Rev. Charles Inwood, a powerful evangelical preacher. In packed, emotionally-charged revivalist meetings at Loudon, Bandawe, Ekwendeni and the Institution, Inwood, through his interpreters, called forth an hysterical fervour from his congregations surpassing in intensity anything that Kamwana had generated. At Loudon his impact was so great that the whole congregation of 2500 burst into public confession of sin, while at the Institution everyone present broke into tears: 'Many were so overpowered that they were unable to rise. Strong men and women had to be carried out like helpless babes.'[145] In 1911 at Loudon rumours spread 'that fire was to come from heaven to burn up all who concealed their sins'. Laws on his return from furlough in April was believed to be bringing an army which would fall upon and slay all Watch Tower adherents.[146]

As the years passed, the relative ineffectiveness of the independent churches became more marked. Numbers fell so that in 1915 Watch Tower and the Seventh Day Baptists together had a total membership of only some 2500. The limited nature of their impact on Livingstonia can be deduced from the table below.

	(A) *Adult Baptisms*		(B) *Schools*		*Average School*
	Bandawe	*Loudon/Hora*	*Bandawe*	*Loudon/Hora*	*Attendance Bandawe*
1902	37	228	49	49	
1904	213	315			
1906	191		129	112	
1908	197	293			5618
1909	572	652	138	150	
1910	225	214	140	168	
1912	135	130			
1913	110	183	130	194	5865

Apart from the rapid increase of adult baptisms in 1909, explained by the readiness with which the missionaries admitted new members to the church in the aftermath of Kamwana's success, the statistical profile of Presbyterianism remained largely unchanged. In contrast to the decline

[145] Rev. Charles Inwood, *An African Pentecost: the Record of a Missionary Tour in Central Africa*, London, 1911, 41–60

[146] *FCSMR*, September 1911, 410; *Livingstonia News*, February 1911, 19

in church attendance which took place within the Roman Catholic Church in Malawi at this period, Livingstonia's church membership continued to grow, though at a slower rate than in the years before 1909, even in the two districts most directly affected by Independency. In 1901 there had been only 1576 communicants in the Livingstonia church; in 1915 there were 10 203. From 1910, the number of new adult baptisms fell away, but school attendance figures, which reached their peak at Bandawe in 1908, maintained a steady level up until the First World War.

Livingstonia in 1915 was only one among a number of churches in the Northern Province; it was no longer the sole fount of Christian truths, but an authority whose claims were sharply challenged by others. At the same time, as all the available statistics demonstrate, it was far and away the dominant religious and educational body in the north. Confronted by the dual threat of German invasion and of government interference – the latter provoked by the active involvement of several Presbyterians in the Chilembwe rising – it faced the future with a considerable measure of confidence.[147]

[147] For Presbyterian responses to the Chilembwe rising see *Independent African*, 363–80

9
Church and school, 1914–40

The First World War was a watershed in the history of the Livingstonia mission. Despite the financial problems which had plagued it in the previous decade, Livingstonia in 1914 was still one of the best organised missionary societies in Central Africa; the proud possessor of the most advanced post-primary Institute in the area; the respected exponent of ideas for African development along industrial lines, which still had their enthusiastic supporters. Ten years later, in 1924, her position had drastically altered. Parallel to the decline of educational standards at the Institution went the fall in Livingstonia's proportion of schools in Nyasaland, from over 30 per cent before the war to only 16 per cent after.[1] At the same time, a serious crisis of confidence affected the mission authorities, which made some of them question the validity of much that had been done at Livingstonia in the previous fifty years. As the administrative and financial system was put under pressure, more responsibility fell into African hands, so that whereas before 1914 church government was largely a European concern, by the mid 1920s Africans were seriously involved at a number of levels. In one sense, therefore, the First World War accelerated the process by which Livingstonia became simply one mission among many, dwarfed in the number of schools and converts it possessed by such comparative upstarts as the White Fathers and the Dutch Reformed Church. In another sense, the process of significance was the emergence of a new group of African leaders – leaders who, in some cases, were to use their experience of authority in the church in the wider sphere of political action.

The impact of war

The outbreak of war was a major blow for Livingstonia, resulting in the

[1] The figures contained in the Report of the Third Nyasaland Missionary Conference demonstrate that Livingstonia possessed 39% of schools in the Protectorate (446 out of a total of 1116) in 1910. In 1924, however, the Phelps-Stokes Commission reported (Jones, *Education in East Africa*, 200) that she ran only 401 schools in Nyasaland out of a total of 2521.

disruption of much of her work. The two northern stations, Karonga and Mwenzo, both situated close to the border with German East Africa, were the first to suffer its impact. Anxious to place the British on the defensive from the outset, Colonel von Lettow-Vorbeck, the brilliant German commander, sent small skirmishing parties across the frontier in August 1914, one of which was repulsed at Karonga early in September. At Mwenzo, however, no British reinforcements gathered in response to the German probe; much of the population fled and Dr Chisholm decided to follow. By 6 September, he had moved to the village of Kantongo, some twelve miles to the south, leaving John Afwenge Banda behind him to care for the station as best he could. 'I am telling you that Mwenzo is a lonely place', Banda reported. 'All people are away to Tenga (Musitu), some away in the bush, except Chikandu and Aaron of Hospital these are with me.'[2]

Chisholm subsequently joined the British expeditionary forces, and though he returned to Mwenzo in 1916, he did so not as a missionary but as a surgeon at the military base hospital. Banda, who died in that year, was replaced by the Reverend Jonathan Chirwa, from Ngoniland, but as most teachers had been recruited for war work, the village schools were not restarted. As late as November 1918 von Lettow's success in eluding his British pursuers resulted in Mwenzo being overrun once again and its hospital being ransacked for supplies.[3]

If Mwenzo suffered most dramatically from the war, the other stations were not far behind. The British military authorities at Karonga, following their somewhat fortuitous success in the September battle, requisitioned the mission buildings as a hospital and relegated Mackenzie to his office.[4] For over a year, Mackenzie attempted to run schools and church services, but once the build-up of forces got under way, prior to the invasion of German East Africa, he was forced to admit defeat. So many Karonga teachers were recruited as guides, interpreters and recruiting sergeants that in April 1916 he closed down the schools altogether and took employment under General Northey as a transport officer on the route to Fife.[5] Two months later, he reported that the war had swept past Karonga

[2] Reproduced in James A. Chisholm, 'The Flight from Mwenzo', *FCSMR*, January 1915, 9. For a general survey of the East African campaign as it affected Nyasaland and North-Eastern Rhodesia see C. P. Lucas, *The Empire at War*, London, 1921, vol. IV, sections II and III

[3] *UFCFMR*, 1916, 44; 1918, 17; *FCSMR*, March 1919, 46

[4] Laws to Ashcroft, 18 November 1914, Livingstonia Letter Book 1912–23, MNA

[5] D. R. Mackenzie to Laws, 23 January, 26 and 30 April, 30 May 1916. Liv. Corr. Box 5, MNA

but the population was still heavily employed in carrying loads.[6] There were demands for porters in every district in the north, which continued until the end of 1918.

For most stations, it was these demands, rather than any threat from the Germans, which constituted the real source of upheaval. Despite the withdrawal of pupils from Mwenzo and Karonga early in the war, classes at the Institution continued without a break until February 1916 when the Senatus decided that the teachers should be released for government service.[7] Meanwhile the few Scots left at the station had increasingly turned their energies to the production of food supplies and camp furniture for the military bases at Karonga and Fife. Once the invasion of German East Africa began, Laws became an important contractor for provisions. By 1917, the Institution store was doing flourishing business but all higher classes were closed, as were the schools in the Livingstonia district.[8] Teachers from Ekwendeni and Loudon were also sent into military service by the local missionaries, and in 1918 a final band was collected together at Bandawe and marched off to join the Forces.[9] By that time, over half the Scottish agents had been recruited to war work in some capacity, and stations as large as Bandawe and Loudon were staffed by a single man.

The decline in Livingstonia's resources was accompanied by a new demand upon them. Following the British occupation of south-west Tanganyika, the German agents of the Moravian and Berlin Missionary societies who worked in that area were deported to Blantyre. Laws respected the work of the Moravians, with whom Livingstonia had established close links, and was determined that it should not go to waste. When he received a request for aid from the distinguished Moravian, Oscar Gemuseus, he wrote to the Governor of Nyasaland, asking whether responsibility for the Moravian sphere could be temporarily vested in the Scots.[10]

He was initially repulsed, but responded by reopening negotiations. Blantyre and the UMCA were brought into the discussions, a provisional programme of partition was agreed upon and, in October 1917, following a visit he had made to New Langenburg, to interview the senior political

[6] Mackenzie to Laws, 1 June 1916, ibid.

[7] Institution Senatus minutes, entry for 9 February 1916, MNA

[8] *UFCFMR*, 1917, 11; 1919, 30. Between 1917 and 1919 annual profits from the Institution store averaged £1319.

[9] Resident's Monthly Report, West Nyasa district, 28 February 1918, MNA NNC3/4/2

[10] Laws to J. Reid, 12 March 1917, Livingstonia Letter Book, 1912–23

officer, Hector Duff, Laws was able to announce that progress had been made. No European missionaries were to be allowed into the occupied territory, but in the Langenburg district, west of the Livingstone mountains, African agents would be admitted instead. The suspicion of unsupervised mission teachers, prevalent among British administrators following the Chilembwe Rising, had been overborne by the more urgent fear that, left to themselves, the Moravian congregations would provide sympathetic audiences for pro-German propaganda.[11]

Livingstonia's African church responded with considerable vigour to its greatest missionary challenge since the initial occupation of the Marambo. Small sums of money were raised by the Presbytery and from various congregations; a respected Tonga evangelist, Yoram Mphande, was chosen as the leader of the expeditionary party; three more evangelists and two carpenters were recruited, and on 28 November the pioneer party set off by boat to Mwaya and from there to New Langenburg and Rutenganio where the mission was initially to be based.[12] Laws's instructions to his agents were typically precise and clear. After reaching New Langenburg, Mphande was to report to the local Resident and learn from him where they could work. At Rutenganio, the carpenters were to repair the church and school while the others made habitable one of the smaller houses and prepared gardens of vegetables and maize. Schools were not to be opened at first, but church members were to be sought out and hearers' classes begun. 'In all your dealings with the people, be sure to be respectful to headmen and old people', the agents were enjoined. 'To live like Christ among the people must be your effort every day.'[13]

In her study of German missions in Tanganyika, Marcia Wright has chronicled the success of the Livingstonia men.[14] The Moravian Christian communities, deprived by the military authorities not only of their German, but also of several of their African leaders, were naturally suspicious of alien intruders and initially subjected Mphande and his colleagues to considerable harassment. As time passed, however, the Nyasas succeeded in gaining the confidence of the local congregations. By March 1918, Mphande had visited eight stations and received the names of 908 church members.[15] Reinforced later in the year by six teachers from Blantyre he

[11] Laws to Dr F. Innes, 9 October 1917; Memo. from H. L. Duff, 3 October 1917, ibid.

[12] Laws to Chisholm, 18 October 1917; to Ashcroft, 19 December 1917, ibid.

[13] Laws, 'Instructions to Native Agents going to work in Occupied Territory', 22 November 1917, ibid.

[14] Marcia Wright, *German Missions in Tanganyika*, 145–6

[15] Laws to Reid, 6 March 1918, Livingstonia Letter Book

established excellent relations with the Moravian church leaders still at liberty, two of whom attended a Livingstonia Presbytery meeting in 1920 to thank the church for sending him to them.[16] When European missionaries were eventually allowed into the territory in 1920, D. R. Mackenzie discovered that Mphande was regarded as 'friend and minister of all, the final court of appeal in all Church matters'.[17]

Mphande's exploits help to demonstrate the dual impact of the war on Livingstonia's Christian communities. As the demand for *tenga tenga* men (carriers) increased, the confidence established between Scottish and African agents diminished. Unlike the Moravian, Gemuseus, who wrote to Laws in August 1914, deploring 'this dreadful war', and calling for a local truce, most of the Scots were convinced that what was taking place was 'a fight between the Devil and all that makes for the wellbeing of man' and were eager to become involved.[18] The result was that whereas before 1914 the terrible suffering of the porters would undoubtedly have provoked a storm of criticism from the missionaries, during the war conditions were accepted as being undesirable but almost inevitable.[19] Despite the virtual breakdown of *tenga tenga* arrangements at Karonga early in 1916, the missionaries at Ekwendeni, Loudon and the Institution sacrificed their African teachers to a war which Nyasas did not regard as their own. The return to their homeland of the ragged, starving survivors deepened resentment and caused the number of deserters to increase. Many of the Tonga who were invalided home to the West Nyasa district in 1917 brought back stories of 'ill-treatment, frequent floggings and loads far in excess of their strength', but Dr Turner at Bandawe, though aware of conditions, was still prepared to gather his employees together in 1918 and commit them in one group to military service.[20]

[16] Livingstonia Presbytery minutes, entry for 20 July 1920

[17] *FCSMR*, November 1920, 196

[18] O. Gemuseus to Laws, 26 August 1914; Liv. Corr. Box 1, MNA; Elmslie to Hetherwick, 15 December 1914, Hetherwick Papers

[19] Mackenzie's studiedly moderate criticisms can be compared with the much sharper comments made by the Resident at Chinteche, A. Siberrad. Mackenzie's strongest comment on the situation at Karonga in 1916 was his request that Laws should 'quietly draw Mr Macdonald's attention to the fact that there are among the Angoni who have come here a few old men who are not really fit for work' (Mackenzie to Laws, 23 January 1916, Liv. Corr. Box 5). Siberrad, by contrast, bluntly informed his superiors of 'the intensely unsatisfactory' conditions at Karonga, which had resulted in the invaliding home of a number of carriers, 'many of whom appear to be in a starving condition' (Resident, Chinteche to Chief Secretary, Zomba, 26 April 1916, NNC1/1/1 MNA).

[20] Resident, Chinteche to Chief Secretary, Zomba, 16 November 1917,

Deprived of the support of those whom they had regarded as their natural protectors, the teachers turned to other outlets to express their resentment at being called to pay the price for an alien war. The Chilembwe Rising provoked no active response in the North, but one chief, Chimtunga, paramount of the Ngoni, was deprived of office and deported for his refusal to recruit, while in Tongaland in 1917 a Watch Tower adherent, Sam Amanda, was imprisoned for his publicly-expressed opposition to the carrier system.[21] Hymns sung at Watch Tower assemblies in 1919 were full of references to the losses sustained. 'Fire burns in Sodom. Your children are thrown into it. The white man too gave their teacher and they are finished', went one version, vividly conjuring up the plight of the village children and of the mission teachers, consumed by the flames of war. 'The white men say the war is finished, where are your children?' asked another, sung at Guru's village, which added ominously: 'You may shave your heads', meaning 'you may go into mourning'.[22]

But while the war exposed the vulnerability of Livingstonia's African agents, it also provided them with opportunities to lead. In different ways, all three pastors ordained before 1914 were able to break from the shackles of European control and establish their authority over local congregations. Jonathan Chirwa spent two years at Mwenzo virtually unsupervised and from there made occasional visits to the Moravian congregations in the Mbozi district. Hezekiah Tweya was sent to Karonga in 1917, following the temporary retirement of Mackenzie, and worked there for some nine months before the Presbytery ordered his return to Ngoniland. Yesaya Zerenje Mwasi, though he was not moved from the West Nyasa district, was called in 1916 by the Sanga congregation to serve exclusively as its pastor.[23] At the same time, a group of evangelists also participated in active church leadership. Apart from Yoram Mphande, who was ordained as a pastor at Kyimbila in Tanganyika in 1924, at least six men were burdened with major responsibilities.[24] One of these, Andrew Mkochi, spent over a year at Chinsali before being ordained as Livingstonia's fourth African minister. Another, George Nyasuru worked successfully among the Berlin Missionary Society congregations in the Livingstone mountains

NNC1/1/1; Monthly Report for the West Nyasa district, February 1918, NNC3/4/2

21 A. R. Fraser, *Donald Fraser*, 226–9; Resident, Chinteche to Chief Secretary, Zomba, 2 May 1918. MNA NNC1/1/1

22 Resident, Chinteche to Chief Secretary, Zomba, 3 July 1919, MNA S2/11/19

23 Livingstonia Presbytery minutes, entries for 20–1 October 1916; 5 November 1917; 17–19 July 1918; Laws to Ashcroft, 19 December 1917, Liv. Letter Book, 1912–23

24 *UFCFMR*, 1924, 95

with only periodic supervision from European missionaries. Two more, Patrick Mwamulima and Mark Makwanga, supervised the Karonga district during the seven years prior to the return of a permanent missionary in 1923.[25] Such men remained agents of the Livingstonia mission, but they were just as independent of European control in practice as Charles Domingo had been working for the Seventh Day Baptists a few years earlier.

In part, the crisis which faced Livingstonia resulted from financial problems which had emerged several years before the outbreak of the war. By the turn of the nineteenth century, the mission's expenditure amounted to some £8500 a year. The extension of her work into Northern Rhodesia and the opening of the Institution, caused it to rise to £10 000 by 1906 and to £12 200 by 1914.[26]

Income and Expenditure of the Livingstonia Mission, 1902–14

	1902	1904	1906	1908	1910	1912	1914
Income	£7480	11 282	9341	11 866	11 109	11 244	12 380
Expenditure	£8766	11 359	10 848	10 692	11 194	11 094	12 274

Income also rose, but with the deaths of several of the mission's most prominent supporters – James Stevenson in 1903, Lord Overtoun in 1908, and Thomas Binnie in 1910 – the task of raising funds from a limited group of business men gradually became untenable. In 1905, Fraser attempted to broaden the base of popular support by appealing for the creation of a Livingstonia Auxiliary within every congregation in Scotland. But a year later only one third of the congregations were actually giving for Livingstonia.[27] As early as 1901, the Livingstonia Committee faced up to the inevitable by offering to place the mission under the full control of the Foreign Missions Committee of the United Free Church of Scotland. Its own financial problems prevented the Free Church from acceding to the request, but when the offer was repeated in 1908 the Church reacted more favourably. Spurred on by J. F. Daly, the Secretary of the Livingstonia Committee, the Foreign Missions Committee agreed

25 Livingstonia Presbytery minutes, entries for 21 October 1916, 17 July 1917; *UFCFMR*, 1921, 41; ibid. 1923, 108; Mark Mwakwanga to Elmslie, 26 May 1921; to Laws, 21 April 1923; P. R. Mwamulima to Laws, 9 April 1923, Liv. Corr. Box 5, MNA

26 Livingstonia Mission Reports, 1902–14. The figures for 'Income' relate only to money raised in Britain and do not include money raised through the Institution and Station Buildings Appeals. Likewise the figures for 'Expenditure' relate only to the General Fund and not to the Institution and Station Buildings Fund

27 Livingstonia Mission Report, 1905, xv; *FCSMR*, October 1906, 447

that Livingstonia should become eligible for a share in certain general legacies and bequests for foreign missions though her financial responsibility and administrative work continued separate as before.[28] By 1910, however, it was evident that this measure was ineffectual in coping with Livingstonia's problems. Sweeping aside a variety of well-meaning proposals, the Church implemented a temporary scheme, whereby the Foreign Missions Committee appointed the Livingstonia Committee but accepted suggestions from Livingstonia officials as to one half of the members.[29] Four years later, the long-awaited amalgamation took place. Livingstonia was placed on the same footing as other missions of the Church without a separate Scottish administration, but with eight representatives for a limited period, on the larger African sub-committee.[30]

Despite the fact that amalgamation was seen as the short-term answer to the mission's financial problems, Livingstonia came closer to administrative and economic ruin in the years after 1914 than at any time before. With the outbreak of the First World War, donations from Britain sharply declined and the financial state of the mission became precarious. In the four years, 1917 to 1920, the battered Mwenzo station received only £274 from abroad.[31] Laws asked the heads of all stations 'to use as strict economy as possible', and maintained essential services at the Institution only through the handsome profits he made at the Khondowe store.[32] By 1920, there were fewer Scots at work than there had been at Cape Maclear some forty years earlier.[33] Most of the stations, according to Fraser, were 'either desolate or undermanned'.[34] Back in Scotland, the new African sub-committee struck at least one observer as being less knowledgeable concerning Livingstonia than its predecessor, and less capable of rescuing the mission from her precarious position.[35]

Although the material damage suffered by the Livingstonia stations was quickly repaired in the post-war period, the church and educational network took longer to recover. As early as 1900, James Henderson had warned his fellow missionaries that educational work was in danger of

28 J. L. Fairley to J. Hastings, 22 January 1903, NLS 7864; J. F. Daly to A. Callender, 2 July 1907; to Elmslie, 29 November 1907; 24 December 1908, NLS 7866

29 Daly to Laws, 1 June 1910, NLS 7867

30 Liv. Miss. Report 1913, vii; *FCSMR*, May 1914, 207–8

31 Chisholm to Ashcroft, 11 January 1920, NLS 7885

32 Laws to 'The Missionary in Charge, Livingstonia Mission Stations', Liv. Letter Book, 1912–23

33 *FCSMR*, October 1920, 185

34 Fraser to Hetherwick, 3 March 1919, Hetherwick Papers

35 M. Moffat to Laws, 14 April 1920, Liv. Corr. Box 7, MNA

out-stripping its resources.[36] With the expansion of congregations at Loudon and Kasungu during the war, the problem became more severe. It increased with the doubling of the number of communicants attached to Livingstonia in the decade after 1915,[37] and was accentuated by the enlarged territorial responsibilities falling to the mission in Tanganyika, particularly from 1920, when Scottish missionaries began to take over the German stations.

For a short period, it appeared that full recovery might be possible. Swept up in a wave of post-war euphoria, delegates to the General Assembly of the United Free Church resolved in 1920 that no work in any part of the mission field was to be abandoned. A major fund-raising campaign, coordinated by Fraser, was launched with the cooperation of the other Scottish churches, with the result that, by 1924, the income of the Foreign Missions Committee was some £40 000 higher than it had been ten years earlier; Livingstonia's own income from Scotland had risen to nearly £24 000.[38] The rise in income, however, was accompanied by inflation and a fall in exchange rates abroad. In 1922, it was reported that the FMC's reserve was practically exhausted. Two years later, its deficit was over £15 000. By that time, the demand for retrenchment had become insistent. Livingstonia in the 1930s was to receive more from Scotland than any other United Free Church mission in Africa. But she was to do so in conditions where the need to save was constantly proclaimed and where expansion was regarded with disfavour.[39]

A major consequence of this financial crisis was the withdrawal from outlying work which took place in the mid 1920s. Ignoring the wishes of local Christians, the mission authorities in 1921 offered Kasungu and Tamanda, both stations situated among Chewa speakers, to the Dutch Reformed Church Mission, which was working in a largely Chewa area. At first the Dutch missionaries were reluctant to accept. A few months earlier, they had been refused permission by the colonial government to take over the Berlin Missionary Society's sphere, as the German agents had wanted. They were therefore reluctant to help Livingstonia divest herself of responsibilities in one area, so that her work in Tanganyika could be expanded further.[40] By 1923, however, the take-over scheme

36 Proceedings of Nyasaland Missionary Conference, 1900, 48

37 According to figures contained in the U. F. Church F.M. reports the number of communicants rose from 10 203 in 1915 to 20 365 in 1925

38 *UFCFMR*, 1920, 6; 1924, 7 and 18–19; Agnes Fraser, *Donald Fraser*, 243–9

39 *UFCFMR*, 1922, 9; 1924, 8; 1925, 7; 1928, 14

40 Livingstonia Mission Council minutes, entry for 15 July 1921; Prentice to Ashcroft, 5 September 1921, NLS 7885

had been accepted in principle. Despite the protests of Kasungu's Kirk Session, which was alarmed both by the paternalistic attitudes of the Dutch and the low standards of education that prevailed in their schools, Livingstonia's Mission Council sanctioned the plans in August and handed over the stations in the following year.[41]

The transfer of Kasungu was followed by the loss of the new Tanganyikan field. When D. R. Mackenzie took up residence at Rutenganio in May 1920, it had seemed likely that Livingstonia would retain permanent control over the German sphere. Three further Scots were brought into the territory, and by 1923, two stations had been reopened in addition to Rutenganio, at Iosko and Itete. Church sessions had been elected in several congregations and the question was being actively canvassed as to whether they should make up a Presbytery within the new Church of Central Africa Presbyterian.[42]

From 1924, however, the likelihood of a German reoccupation became increasingly great. Frank Ashcroft, the Secretary of the Foreign Missions Committee, agreed with Prentice that the Tanganyikan stations should be 'returned to their *original* and surely still *rightful* owners'.[43] When he met representatives of the Moravians and Berliners in Germany, he assured them that the Free Church occupation would be regarded as temporary, and that, as far as possible, Lutheran practices and hymn books would continue to be used – a decision which scandalised the Scots in the field.[44] Further meetings with J. H. Oldham at Edinburgh House cleared the way for the German return, and in 1925, the first Berliners came back, to be followed over the next two years by most of the Moravians. 'The Presbyterians bowed out with grace,' the historian of the German missions concludes, 'having established an excellent record in reconstructing and encouraging congregations towards self-government, rebuilding a flourishing central and bush school system and setting a standard of medical work which the Germans could not sustain.'[45]

Back in Malawi, control and supervision remained difficult to re-establish. The schools in the Luangwa valley were so irregularly visited by missionaries that no guarantee could be made to the Northern Rhodesia Government in 1922 that they would be inspected even twice in a year.[46]

[41] Prentice to Laws, 1 September 1923. Liv. Corr. Box 7, MNA; Riddell Henderson to Ashcroft, 14 October 1923, NLS 7886; Livingstonia Mission Council Minutes, entry for 9 August 1923

[42] *UFCFMR*, 1921, 40–1; *FCSMR*, April 1924, 163

[43] Prentice to Daly, 24 January 1922, NLS 7885

[44] *UFCFMR*, 1923, 14

[45] Wright, *German Missions*, 158

[46] T. C. Young to Ashcroft, 26 May 1922, NLS 7885

In the absence of courses at the Institution, certificated teachers were in desperately short supply. In 1921, Elmslie reported that only twenty-seven existed out of 575 teachers in all in the three major districts.[47] Even when classes were reopened in that year, the two unqualified women instructors, Miss Irvine and Miss Petrie, were unable to provide more than minimally adequate training.[48] So difficult was it becoming to find teachers that Elmslie questioned whether the standard demanded of them should not be deliberately lowered.[49] 'I may be narrow minded and old-fashioned,' a representative of the new post-war generation of missionaries informed Laws in 1926, in a statement that strikes against everything that the pioneers struggled for,

> but I don't believe that the poor people at home who support us do it that we can take over the Government's responsibilities, but so that we can teach the people to read the Word of God. A wider education is good and necessary, but it is not our first concern and I can't see the justice of trying to accomplish it on resources barely sufficient to fulfill our primary responsibilities.[50]

But what the mission failed to provide, the colonial government of Nyasaland was unwilling or unable to substitute. Demands that it should take an active part in the provision of educational facilities had been made by Scottish missionaries from 1898, but it was not until 1907 that the first block grant of £1000 was paid. Even then it was so divided, Mackenzie complained, that Livingstonia received 'little more than one-fourth of the grant, although we carry on more than two-thirds of the schools in the Protectorate'.[51] In 1920, the total sum disbursed was raised to £2000, and this figure was increased to £3000 in 1924. In that year, as the statistics collected by the Phelps–Stokes Commission showed, nearly seven times as much was being spent on African education by the Government of Uganda, twelve times as much by the Government of Kenya, and ten times as much by the settler Government of Southern Rhodesia, where the African population was probably smaller than that of Malawi. Little more than one per cent of Nyasaland's admittedly meagre revenues were being allocated to African education.[52] In 1925, Living-

47 Elmslie to Ashcroft, 8 May 1922, NLS 7885

48 *UFCFMR*, 1921, 80

49 Elmslie to Laws, 28 February 1921, Liv. Corr. Box 9, MNA

50 J. R. Martin to Laws, 28 November 1926, ibid.

51 *Livingstonia News*, June 1908, 19–20; D. R. Mackenzie, 'The Reorganisation of Educational Work', October 1909 in Minutes of the Livingstonia Mission Committee

52 Jones, *Education in East Africa*. According to the Report of the Department of Education of the Nyasaland Protectorate, 1960, the proportion of

stonia received £500 in local government grants. In the same year, her sister mission of Calabar in eastern Nigeria was paid £7796 by the Nigerian government.[53] It is in the contrast between these two figures that the fate of educational development in the two countries can be seen most clearly.

The educational debate

While the effects of the war and its aftermath were intruding themselves on the mission, changes were also taking place in the character and aim of her work. For over forty years, Laws had succeeded in moulding the educational policies of Livingstonia to his belief that one of the prime duties of the mission was to educate Africans to a level where Christians would be able to take a major role in the administration of their own country. To that end, the greater part of the mission's resources had been channelled towards the Institution in the years prior to the war. By the 1920s, however, the same change in the climate of opinion in Scotland which had led to the breakdown of Livingstonia's financial and administrative system, was making officials look with greater sympathy towards the new beliefs of Fraser and his younger colleagues in 'mass education . . . rather than the intensive education of a few'.[54] Fraser, one of the most eloquent exponents of the new educational orthodoxy associated with T. J. Jones and the Phelps-Stokes Commission, was principally concerned at Loudon with the development of village schools designed to 'purify and develop all that is best, and to create a richer personality and nationality'.[55] Fraser regarded the Institution as overly foreign in its aspirations and achievements. Those who admired it, he argued, 'responded to a little bit of Europe rather than to a sublimated Africa whose genius they could not understand. A broad road avenued by cedar trees, electric power, running machinery were a far better witness of civilization for the British visitor than progress in African arts.'[56] His comments on a report by the home secretary, Ashcroft, made in 1923 demonstrate the extent of his disagreement with Laws's philosophy. Both men accepted the importance of the village school; both were convinced that some form of post-primary training was necessary in a Central African context. But, whereas Laws worked from the assumption that training in European

government spending on education ranged between 1.058% in 1926 to 4.5% in 1946. In 1960, by comparison, 15% of government expenditure went on education

53 *UFCFMR*, 1925

54 Donald Fraser, *The New Africa*, London, 1927, 163. See pp. 128, 227 above

55 ibid., 138. Ashcroft's report is printed in *UFCFMR*, 1923, 133

56 *The Scots Observer*, 27 August, 1927, Laws's Papers

skills was a necessary precondition for African development, Fraser believed that such development would be positively harmful if it resulted in the destruction of village communities. Confronted by Laws's alleged ambition of creating 'a great industrial centre', at Khondowe, he commented that 'to realise such a dream I would not lift a little finger'. Ashcroft, he noted, 'has been immensely impressed with the pelton wheel sawmill to which he would like to go back again and again, the engineering department with its coils of wire, motor bikes etc. (incidentally, with a loss of £844 in 10 years), the carpentry department with its 70 apprentices unable to cope with the orders – (what about the journeymen?)'. But he had not asked 'what relation has the whole immense activity and the whole output to tribal life? What relation have all the machinery and the industrial departments to education?'

Fraser believed that 'The answer is not "none"', but he hinted that in practice it was very little. To call the Institution, as Ashcroft had done, 'a great educational centre' was 'not convincing . . . a factory is an "educational centre" if it trains apprentices'. He admitted that 'The service that the Institution has given to the country in training skilled artisans has been immense', but argued that 'a more direct and larger contribution to the social conditions of the people could be made.'[57]

With Booker Washington and Jesse Jones – the most respected exponents of the craft-centred Tuskegee tradition – he looked to the training of agricultural teachers 'who, after the fashion so successfully used in the Southern States of America among the negroes and in South Africa, will through practical demonstration as well as by lessons in the villages and schools teach better methods of agriculture and of caring for the stock, both small and great'.[58] But, unlike Jones, he did not regard as the purpose of such an education the creation of second-class citizens, docilely contented with their lot. 'The "contented and loyal" phrase is scarcely the purpose', he informed R. F. Gaunt, the first Director of Education in Nyasaland, when commenting on his Educational Memorandum of 1927. 'Education must necessarily rouse discontent with poor conditions and the restlessness of awakening national consciousness.' His aim, rather, was 'to push further the present unique opportunity for Nyasaland becoming a self-contained colony, where the small trades and industries will be in the hands of the natives and not of Greeks, Indians or Chinese'.[59]

[57] D. Fraser, 'Remarks on Mr Ashcroft's Report on his visit to Livingstonia' n.d., Liv. Corr. Box 1, MNA

[58] ibid. See Kenneth King, *Pan-Africanism and Education*, Oxford, 1971, 5–57

[59] Fraser to R. F. Gaunt, 25 May 1927, Edinburgh House

The test as to the respective strengths of Laws's and Fraser's policies centred round Laws's plans for rebuilding the Institution. The resumption of classes following the war had exposed the inadequacies of the existing accommodation and had made most missionaries accept the need for new classrooms and dormitories. But the plan which Laws prepared in 1922 and elaborated over the next four years, bore little relation to the Institution's immediate requirements. The dignified, if somewhat heavy, two-storied building which he visualised, sheathed up to the first floor in stone, and dominated by a replica of the tower and crown surmounting King's College, Aberdeen, was not designed simply as a school for teachers. 'We are not building for today, but for coming centuries', Laws wrote to the Glasgow architect who advised him. 'I hope that this will yet be known as the Overtoun College of the University of Livingstonia – a dreamer's dream some may say, but not a few of my laughed-at dreams are realities today.'[60] Drawing students from Northern Rhodesia and Tanganyika as well as from Nyasaland, the Institution would serve as a centre of post-primary training for East Central Africa south of Kenya. 'We have the opportunity now of moulding the future and higher education of Central Africa and of securing that it shall be on an enduring Christian foundation', Laws informed the Foreign Missions Secretary in 1926. 'Hence I implore the Committee not to set aside the plans proposed and throw away the harvest of past years now ready to be garnered.'[61]

For five years, Laws's scheme hovered on the brink of acceptance. In 1925 it was provisionally approved by the Foreign Missions Committee and in the same year it won the praise of Sir Herbert Stanley, the Governor of Northern Rhodesia, who promised to use the college for the higher education of students from his own territory. Sir Charles Bowring, the Governor of Nyasaland, was another early supporter. In October 1925, Bowring laid the foundation stone of the new buildings at the mission's jubilee celebrations. Later in the year he wrote to Laws expressing his hearty approval: 'Livingstonia appeals to me enormously as a training centre because of its comparative isolation and at the same time easy accessibility. The students are away from the many temptations of town life, and yet within easy reach by the lake and in touch by telegraph.'[62] In 1926 Bowring brought Laws's plans to a meeting of the Governors of East African Protectorates in the hope that the government of Tangan-

[60] Laws to A. Balfour, 17 April 1926, Liv. Corr. Box 1, MNA. See also Livingstonia Mission Council Minutes, entry for 7 October 1922

[61] Laws to Ashcroft, 12 August 1925, NLS 7888; Laws to Ashcroft, 23 December 1926, Liv. Corr. Box 1, MNA

[62] Quoted in ibid.

yika would agree to send some students to Livingstonia. A month or two later he carried the plans back to Britain with the aim of enlisting the support of the Colonial Office.

But while, to governors, Laws's plans were of genuine interest, to mission officials they were increasingly a source of embarrassment. Alarmed by the rapid rise in the estimated cost of the college buildings – from £20 000 to £35 000 in four years – the Buildings Committee in Scotland decided in 1926 to reject Laws's plea that the plans should be accepted as they stood. Instead, the committee drew on an earlier comment made by Fraser to question whether Blantyre was not better situated than Livingstonia for such a college and to ask whether the buildings required could not be of more modest proportions. Laws's reply emphasised the extent of the demand for higher education with which Blantyre and Livingstonia between them would soon be barely able to cope. But the committee was not convinced and only reluctantly agreed to a compromise. In 1927 it informed the mission council that while plans for the whole building would have to be postponed, those for the west wing could be executed at a cost of £8000.[63]

Meanwhile, Laws had run out of allies. The subject of one of the most successful of mission biographies, he was now a legendary figure to the church-going public in Scotland. But although his career was one at which churchmen marvelled, it was Fraser to whom they listened.[64] As the disabilities of old age took their toll, Laws's influence over his missionary colleagues slackened. In September 1924, members of the mission council informed the Home Committee of the necessity of appointing a colleague and successor to him as principal of the Institution. A year later, on 8 October 1925 (fifty years after Laws's arrival in Malawi), they met to decide the issue. Fraser was no longer eligible as he had recently accepted the influential post of joint secretary of the FMC in Scotland; but his protégé, W. P. Young, was proposed and was elected by a large majority. In a frank minute, the mission council suggested that Laws

[63] Laws to Ashcroft, 5 August 1926, NLS 7889; Laws to Ashcroft, 23 December 1926, Liv. Corr. Box 1, MNA; Livingstonia Mission Council Minutes, entry for 12 July 1927

[64] Some indication of the interest that Laws aroused in Scotland can be drawn from the fact that in 1923 W. P. Livingstone's biography, *Laws of Livingstonia* was the book most frequently borrowed from the United Free Church Lending Library in Edinburgh. However, the runner-up was Donald Fraser's *African Idylls*, and Fraser, Moderator of the Church in 1921 and one of the joint Foreign Mission Secretaries from 1925, was much closer than Laws to expert opinion at Edinburgh House and in the Colonial Office. See *FCSMR*, February 1924, 53.

should give up his administrative duties at the end of his five-year period of service, a view that the Committee in Scotland endorsed by formally calling on Laws to resign.[65] In September 1927, following a sudden illness, he left Malawi for good, to spend his remaining years in Scotland, stubbornly campaigning for the college which he had come to regard as 'the crown of my life work'. His death in August 1934 closed a chapter in the mission's history.[66]

With Laws departed to Scotland his proposals were laid to rest. Unless they received substantial government support, the Scottish committee was unwilling to act, but Bowring, as he revealed in February 1928, was unable to obtain Treasury assistance, and refused to use local funds.[67] As for W. P. Young, his views were similar to Fraser's. 'I do not really see that anything is to be gained by sending out another European builder', he wrote in February 1928. 'It is expensive (we would have to build a house for him), but far more important than any consideration of that sort, it is making the College here like the Church, a purely European thing quite unrelated to Africa.'[68] The news that no grant would be forthcoming from Northern Rhodesia, where Sir Herbert Stanley had been converted to Phelps–Stokesian policies, he received with muted satisfaction. The lesson to be drawn, he told Ashcroft, was that, 'in the very undecided state of things politically and educationally just now, we have no right to bind ourselves to building anything more than a worthy central Institution for the Tumbuka–Henga speaking area. That is emphatically our job; anything more at present is mere speculation.'[69] A year later in 1929, Laws's scheme was officially abandoned. Work on the west wing should be halted, the mission council advised, and a single-storey building constructed in its place. At a cost of £8000, this would provide Livingstonia with all that the missionaries wanted, a training institution for primary teachers rather than a regional centre for secondary education.[70] Young's comment in 1931 summarises the change in policy that had taken place at the Institution since the days when Henderson was headmaster.

> More than thirty years ago, this Institution was offering courses in general education which were far beyond anything we offer today.

65 Livingstonia Mission Council Minutes, entries for September 1924 and 8 October 1925. Laws to Ashcroft, 5 August 1926, NLS 7889.

66 *FCSMR*, November 1927, 464, 467

67 C. L. Bowring to Laws, 21 February 1928, NNA s1/470/28

68 W. P. Young to Ashcroft, 25 February 1928, Liv. Corr. Box 1, MNA

69 W. P. Young to Ashcroft, 2 March 1928, ibid.

70 Young to Ashcroft, 24 July 1929, ibid.; Livingstonia Mission Council Minutes entry for 8 July 1929

> For during those thirty years there has been – in a good sense – a down-grade movement in that we have been brought more and more to emphasize the fundamental importance of sound training in the vernacular school and the development of an ordered system built on it.[71]

With the educational debate behind it, Livingstonia embarked on a number of new educational projects in the 1930s. On his return to Nyasaland in 1922 after eight years away from the country, four of them spent on military service in France, W. P. Young had become convinced that the Institution was 'not serving the native life so much as the European planters'.[72] His conclusion was that agricultural, rather than literary or technical education must be given priority if rural conditions were to be improved. As headmaster of the Institution school, prior to Laws's retirement, he had refused to issue English dictionaries to his pupils on the grounds that 'the passion for learning English' led to 'the danger of a lop-sided and too intellectual education'.[73] Now as Principal of the college, his influence extended further. In 1931, he informed the governing Senatus of the Institution of the need to abandon the apprenticeship scheme and instead to seek out new priorities:

> Most important of all, we ourselves ought to put the raising of the level of common life in the villages first in our consideration of training, and we ought to be giving a lead towards improvements in houses, furnishing, sanitation, gardens and crops. With all these changes and developments in African life, we ought to review the training given in the Institution in relation to the needs and desires of the village community, so that our training may be more directly aimed both at raising the level of common life and at giving the African real opportunities for development and employment along sound lines.[74]

The printing, engineering and stonework departments were of use to the mission, not to Africans; they could be reduced in size and the print-

[71] Livingstonia Station Educational Report, 1931, Liv. Corr. Box 2, MNA

[72] Quoted from the diary of J. W. C. Dougall, 26 April 1924, Edinburgh House. Born in Edinburgh in 1886, Young was the son of a minister. He was educated at Glasgow Academy and the University of Edinburgh and was appointed to Livingstonia in 1910. He served with distinction in France during the war, first as a combatant and subsequently as chaplain. He then became Secretary of the Student Christian Movement before returning to Livingstonia as headmaster of the Institution School in 1922.

[73] W. P. Young, 'A Schoolmaster in Africa', *FCSMR*, September 1927, 403–5

[74] 'Memorandum on the training at the Institution', Senatus Minutes, entry for 13 April 1931

ing press transferred to Blantyre. The building and carpentry departments taught valuable skills; they should be expanded and made more efficient.

An improvement in agricultural techniques was a central need, he recognised, without which a 'peasant proprietor class' could not be created in the north. Some preliminary work had already taken place. At Loudon, Fraser had introduced community gardens, connected with village schools, from the early 1920s. And this action had been followed at the Institution in 1924 by the establishment of a course for agricultural demonstrators, expanded in 1927 to include practical training in handicrafts and carpentry as well as the study of agriculture and forestry.[75]

Young's ambition was to set this training on a firm foundation by establishing a demonstration farm and school in an area where, unlike Khondowe, the soil was sufficiently fertile for crops to be successfully grown. His plan was for a farm-school, sited at Karemteta in the Henga valley, which would provide local farmers with advice on new crops as well as training pupils in simple building and carpentry techniques. It would thus contribute, so he hoped, to the creation of a 'progressive' agricultural elite who would settle on up to forty acres of land, individually owned, and employ labour on a wage basis in order to harvest cash crops.[76]

But though the mission had once influenced change, events now were to pass her by. Despite the element of fantasy contained within it, Laws's scheme had emerged out of a tradition of genuine achievement and had attracted a measure of financial support in Scotland. Young's proposals, on the other hand, were unrelated to the mission's earlier successes and failed to evoke the same kind of response. Although Jesse Jones praised Livingstonia to the President of the Carnegie Trust in 1929 his colleague, C. T. Loram, made it clear that Carnegie money was available in Malawi only to the government-run Jeanes Schools scheme, and that were funds to be set aside for private ventures, they would go to the DRC at Mkhoma, whose agricultural projects were of proven quality.[77]

By the end of 1931, Young had reluctantly discarded the Karemteta scheme as being no longer a practical proposition, but had failed to uncover a suitable alternative. Livingstonia's agricultural training remained,

[75] Fraser, 'Remarks on Mr Ashcroft's Report on his visit to Livingstonia', n.d., Liv. Corr. Box 1; Liv. Mission Council Minutes entries for 23 September 1924 and 12 July 1927

[76] W. P. Young, 'Proposals for a community School in Farming and Crafts', 10 October 1930, enclosed in Fraser to Oldham, 1 December 1930, Nyasaland Education General Corr., Edinburgh House

[77] T. J. Jones to Dr F. P. Keppel, 26 September 1929 (copy); C. T. Loram to Young, 9 January 1930. Liv. Corr. Box 2, MNA

as he admitted, 'the worst part of our work', yet efforts to improve it were uniformly unsuccessful.[78] Young was aware that without active state intervention in the provision of markets and the improvement of communications, there was little hope of creating the self-sufficient rural community that he aspired to build. But he blindly ignored the importance of the migrant labour system to the economies of southern Africa and hence the unlikelihood of the Nyasaland government taking measures that would seriously threaten its continued operation. He was also unaware of what Leroy Vail has recently demonstrated – that owing to the interference of the British Imperial Government a significant proportion of Nyasaland's limited revenues were being spent by the 1930s on unproductive railway ventures in Mozambique.[79]

By the time of his retirement in 1938 the results were abundantly clear. Not only had no model farm been established, it had become accepted that agricultural demonstrators, working on an individual basis, were incapable of reducing the incidence of rural poverty. School gardens, much praised as a 'basis for teaching' up to 1936, had been officially discredited by educational experts. For most children, the superintendent of education in the Northern Province warned, the cultivation of a 'garden of maize, beans and potatoes', resulted in 'boredom and an intense dislike of the so called agricultural lesson'. Mats and baskets made in village schools were thrown away after the inspector's visit, 'or worse still, became targets of ridicule for the skilled, uneducated craftsmen in the villages'.[80]

The immensity of the problem was indicated in the Report on Emigrant Labour, made by a Government Commission of which Young was a member, in 1935.[81] So little cash entered the five northern districts through the sale of agricultural produce, the commission reported, that hut-tax demands from the government and communal obligations could be met only through extensive emigration. At least forty-five per cent of adult males were absent from the Mzimba district and sixty per cent from West Nyasa.[82] Some peoples, notably the Tonga, were able to adapt their economy to the demands of labour migration, with a fair measure of success, but in general the absence of so many males from their homeland had a stultifying effect on cash-crop production. In 1937, no economic

[78] W. P. Young to McLachlan, 5 November 1931, Liv. Corr. Box 1

[79] Vail, 'The Making of an Imperial Slum'

[80] Report of the Education Department, Nyasaland Protectorate, 1937, 18–19

[81] *Report of the Committee appointed . . . to enquire into Emigrant Labour, 1935*, Zomba, 1936.

[82] Richard Gray, *The Two Nations*, London, 1960, 120–1

crops were grown by Africans in the Mzimba or West Nyasa district, and cotton was cultivated only to a limited extent around Karonga.[83]

As for the mission's land-utilisation policy, W. H. Watson concluded in 1947 that it was 'largely unsuccessful. Primitive ways of agriculture are still followed, little rotation of crops, burning of top cover, hoeing vertical slopes, indiscriminate tree-cutting all flourish.'[84] At Bandawe, the longest established of the stations, soil erosion was a major problem. 'The errors of the past have unfortunately become a torrent of cumulative trouble for the present', the new agriculturalist reported. If preventive action was not rapidly taken, the stations, rather than being self-supporting in foodstuffs, would become increasingly barren.[85]

Livingstonia's failure to bring about the expansion of agricultural production was only one among several setbacks suffered by the mission in the 1930s. W. P. Young was prepared to sacrifice the introduction of secondary education for improvements in the efficiency of village schools, but there is reason to doubt whether substantial improvements in this sphere took place. At the High School of the Institution, converted into a teacher-training college in 1931, an average of 115 students, almost all from the northern region, were instructed each year in the mysteries of primary school teaching.[86] But with the wages paid to Grade III certificated teachers averaging only some £9.00 a year (three times less than the wages paid to comparably qualified government clerks in Tanganyika) the attraction of other employment was considerable and the wastage rate correspondingly high.[87] Over eighty per cent of pupils leaving the High School with first class certificates in 1925 went to jobs other than teaching, and by 1939 the proportion had not improved. Out of all the teachers from the West Nyasa district trained in the High Sschool during the previous three decades, only one was still in mission service.[88] In that year the number of schools in the Loudon and Bandawe districts was only half

[83] Eric Smith, *Report on the Direct Taxation of Natives in the Nyasaland Protectorate* . . ., Zomba, 1937, 19–21

[84] W. H. Watson to Paterson, 1 March 1947, Liv. Corr. Box 1, MNA

[85] R. C. Wood to the Principal, the Overtoun Institution, 1 September 1940, ibid.

[86] According to the Annual Returns for the Overtoun Institution, 1931–9, numbers attending the High School fluctuated between 165 in 1931 and 87 in 1938, with the average number being 115

[87] See A. L. Lacey to Acting Chief Secretary, Zomba, 24 July 1930, enclosed in Governor Nyasaland to Secretary of State for Colonies, 30 August 1930, CO 525/138/33499/1930

[88] W. P. Young to Oldham, 21 June 1927, Edinburgh House; Report of Edn. Dept., Nyasaland Protectorate, 1939, 12

what it had been in 1910, though the number in the Khondowe and Karonga districts had risen considerably. More teachers were employed by the mission in 1927 than in 1939, and whereas in 1910, some 24 500 pupils were attending Livingstonia's schools in Malawi, by 1938 the number had fallen to 23 000. The considerable expansion of elementary schools in the hands of the Roman Catholic missions and the Dutch Reformed Church meant that Livingstonia controlled less than ten per cent of the schools in the Protectorate, though in 1904 she had over sixty per cent. As for the quality of these schools, a memorandum written by a missionary at the Institution in the early 1940s, makes sombre but instructive reading:

> There is dissipation of funds due to too large spread. Undue responsibility has been thrust on Africans with insufficient education and training; teachers are trying to teach standards too high for their training: and undue results have been expected. All missions in the past have aimed at 'mass education': too many schools have been opened, with poor buildings, meagre equipment and ill-educated and untrained teachers. The results of this policy are seen now in a great spread of low-grade work. There is a superficial literacy, but there is excessive wastage and retardation, and a large percentage of examination failures. These results are seen in every type of school – Village, Central Station and Normal Schools. Higher education lags behind: and thinking Africans are disturbed by this state of affairs and resentful of it. We must give at least some the best education that we can: and we cannot expect public funds to be granted unconditionally to a system open to such criticisms.[89]

As the educational pre-eminence of Livingstonia was eroded, her leaders went onto the defensive. Young admired the rurally-based agricultural policies pursued in the Jeanes Training Centre, opened at Domasi in 1930, but he resented the fact that agricultural supervisors trained at Livingstonia were not granted the government certificates given to Jeanes-trained teachers and yet was reluctant to send northerners for training in the south.[90] At the same time, he opposed the government's policy of making Chinyanja (now Chichewa) an official language of the Protectorate, and fought a long, and ultimately unsuccessful, battle to prevent its introduction into the Tumbuka-speaking area in which Livingstonia worked.[91]

[89] 'Livingstonia – Mission Educational Policy', n.d., Liv. Corr. Box 7, MNA

[90] W. P. Young to Lacey, 8 April 1932, Liv. Corr. Box 2, MNA

[91] 'Statement on the Proposal of Government to enforce the teaching of Chinyanja in village schools after 1934 ...', July 1933, Liv. Corr. Box 2,

His greatest anxiety concerned the introduction of secondary schools. During the early 1930s Young developed a dual strategy in which he repeatedly expressed his belief in the need for some kind of higher education, while giving priority in practice to training in crafts and agriculture. His lack of any sense of urgency was strikingly demonstrated in the reply he made to the memorandum on higher education produced by Levi Mumba in 1932. 'While I think that the opportunity should be available for boys in this country to go further,' he informed Mumba, 'I certainly hold very strongly that money should be spent on the training of school-teachers, which the country needs, rather than in giving special advanced training to a few.' Some kind of Alliance School on the Kenyan pattern, providing instruction from Standards v to viii, might have to be established, he admitted to a friend, but 'I think this is very secondary to the crafts school idea'.[92]

In 1937 he agreed that 'secondary education was a definite need in Nyasaland', but suggested that 'the time was not quite ripe yet for such a full development' as A. L. Lacey, the Director of Education, was proposing.[93] He and his successor, W. C. Galbraith, were anxious to preserve the hold of the two Scottish missions over the higher reaches of education in Malawi, yet they were unwilling to act decisively in order to maintain this monopoly. The reluctance of the missions to accept the government scheme for a secular high school was matched by the government's reluctance to divert resources to a religious school largely financed by the State, as the plan prepared by the non-Catholic Federated Missions envisaged. Not until October 1940, fourteen years after the founding of the Alliance High School in Kenya, was the much-discussed secondary school established, and it was located not at Livingstonia, as Galbraith had wanted, but at Blantyre, across the way from the Church of Scotland mission.[94]

Students from the Northern Province were to fill a disproportionately high percentage of the number of places available to Nyasas in secondary schools in the 1940s, as they were to do from the mid 1960s at Chancellor College of the University of Malawi.[95] But whereas, up to 1914, northern

MNA. See also Herbert Young, Governor of Nyasaland to Dr Turner, 6 November 1933, CO 525/153/25352/1934.

92 Young to Levi Mumba, 15 March 1932, Liv. Corr. Box 2; Young to Oldham, 3 July 1932, Edinburgh House. See also p. 271 below

93 Miss B. D. Gibson to Dougall, 24 September 1937, Edinburgh House

94 W. C. Galbraith to Dougall, 26 August 1938, ibid.; Report of Edn. Dept. Nyasaland Protectorate for 1940, 3

95 It has been estimated that the Northern Province, the home of one fifth of Malawi's population, provided over two thirds of the first students taking a

Nyasas competed successfully with African neighbours from a variety of countries for positions requiring new educational skills, by the time of the Second World War, the opportunities available to them had been considerably reduced. As an educational centre, Livingstonia was beginning to live on her past; though as the centre of a network of Christian communities, her influence continued to be of importance.

The Christian community

At 7 p.m. on 15 November 1899 three Scottish ministers, Elmslie, Dewar and Macalpine, meeting at the Overtoun Institution, constituted themselves the North Livingstonia Presbytery of the Presbyterian Church of Central Africa. As temporary chairman, Macalpine read out a minute of the mission council which sanctioned the Presbytery's foundation and laid down guidelines which were to influence its development in subsequent years. 'The Council,' the minute stated, 'approve of the early organisation of the native Church into congregations and regularly constituted courts, viz: Kirk Sessions, Presbyteries and Synod.' Thus a variant of the part democratic, part oligarchic system of church government that flourished in Scotland was to be transposed to Central Africa. The council, however, also decreed: 'to the jurisdiction of such courts, the Native Church as such be subject but that the European agents and the financial arrangements of the missions continue subject, as at present, to their several home committees and local councils'. Though Africans were to be permitted a share of responsibility within the church, the mission's affairs were to remain the preserve of Scottish agents.[96]

It was against this background of theoretical rights and practical disabilities that a gradual devolution of authority from European to African took place in the 1920s. Up to the First World War, Scottish control of the church was virtually complete. The ordained missionaries came together with a representative sample of lay agents at annual meetings of the mission council, always held in the week preceding the most important meetings of Presbytery. There they discussed the Presbytery agenda in advance, and took many decisions without reference to their African colleagues. Control over Scottish-raised funds was defined as meaning

degree course at the University in 1965. Macdonald, 'African Education', 542–3

[96] The title 'North Livingstonia Presbytery' was used because the Scots assumed, wrongly, that the Dutch Reformed Church missionaries at Mvera would shortly form a separate 'South Livingstonia Presbytery of the Church'. Minute of the Presbytery of North Livingstonia, entry for 15 November 1899

control over the schools of the mission, educational policies, rates of pay and certificates of proficiency granted to teachers. Where questions were raised of the evacuation of one district, or the evangelisation of another, it was normally the council that took the decision. Plans for the Institution remained its prerogative up to the 1940s, and plans for the African Church were frequently discussed as well. Proposals for a central fund, raised entirely in Malawi, to provide the salaries of African ministers, were discussed in detail at council before they were sent to Presbytery, and even the ordination of the first three African pastors was delayed until council had approved the step.[97]

Meetings of Presbytery were also largely dominated by the Scots. African elders were elected to Presbytery from May 1900, and from 1906 formed the majority of its membership. But whereas these men were appointed for a single year and had little opportunity of gaining experience of its workings, the ordained ministers attended by right and monopolised the executive positions of president and clerk. From 1906 licentiates were also invited to attend all meetings – one of the first being Y. Z. Mwasi, who had also been one of the first African elders elected.[98] But these men, even when they became ordained pastors from 1914, were denied the status granted to European missionaries. Instead of being called to a congregation, as ministers were in Scotland, African pastors were appointed as assistants to the missionary in the district in which they worked, with final responsibility over them being vested in the hands of the Presbytery. Mwasi's attempt in 1915 to assert his independence from Dr Turner, the minister in charge at Bandawe, resulted only in his public humiliation and an official restatement of mission policy.[99] Hezekiah Tweya, according to Elmslie in July 1915, 'has no congregation of his own. He lives on the station with me and takes his work according to my guidance.'[100] Fraser confirmed that 'Our native pastors are not equal with the European minister.' Their supervision he regarded as 'a matter of tremendous importance'. For where Africans like Bishop Crowther had been allowed unsupervised control in the past, European

[97] Livingstonia Mission Council minutes, 1909–38. Vol. 1 of the Mission Council minutes, dating from 1899 to 1909, appears to have been lost

[98] Livingstonia Presbytery minutes entry for 11 May 1906

[99] ibid. for 13 February and 30 August 1915. It was agreed at the meeting on 30 August 'that a Licentiate or an ordained minister, until he is inducted to a charge of his own, is under the direction of the missionary in charge of the district in which he is appointed as the representative of the Presbytery and holding its powers'. See p. 199 above

[100] Evidence of Dr W. A. Elmslie to the Chilembwe Rising Commission of Inquiry, 12 July 1915, CO 525/86

intervention, so he asserted, had been eventually necessary, and the resentment which resulted from it had led to the creation of independent churches.[101]

External factors were as important as internal ones in changing this state of affairs. As I have demonstrated, a temporary reduction of European staff and in consequence an increase in the responsibilities open to Africans resulted from the impact of the First World War. Laws's reaction to the Chilembwe Rising was to seek to increase African responsibilities still further, for he had become convinced (in contrast to Fraser) that religious secession more commonly resulted from a denial of African authority than it did from granting that authority too soon.[102] The Sanga congregation's call to Y. Z. Mwasi in October 1916 symbolised the growth of African power. Once the Central Fund committee had been convinced that the congregation possessed the resources to pay Mwasi's salary, he became their individual minister with the same constitutional rights as those possessed by Europeans. Two years later, he was elected the first African Moderator of Presbytery, and in 1921 he was appointed temporarily as Clerk.[103] By that time, Africans were playing an increasingly vigorous role in Presbytery, and the opinions of Scots were occasionally being challenged. Six ordained pastors now formed a permanent nucleus in the body and several representative elders also possessed considerable experience. In that year Elmslie informed Laws of 'a growing discontent among native members of Presbytery' that they did not meet until Mission Council business had been transacted. He reported that the members 'think that we agree among ourselves as to what is to be said and done at Presbytery', and advised that 'we should sit in Presbytery first and then sit in Council'.[104] His advice appears to have been taken, for in 1922 Council abandoned its practice of reviewing Presbytery business in advance, though it continued to interest itself in Presbytery affairs.

As concessions were granted, African agents gained greater confidence and further demands were made. An important step was taken in 1926 when the council surrendered its exclusive control over the ordination of Scottish lay agents by agreeing that the ordination of A. C. Halliday should be considered first by the Livingstonia Presbytery.[105] This was followed in July 1927 by a demand from Mwasi that an African should

[101] Evidence of Rev. Donald Fraser, 13 July 1915, ibid.

[102] Laws to R. W. Lyell Grant, 2 July 1915. Hetherwick Papers

[103] Livingstonia Presbytery minutes, entries for 18 and 21 October 1916; 16 July 1918; 20 July 1921

[104] Elmslie to Laws, 21 March 1921, Liv. Corr. Box 9, MNA

[105] Livingstonia Mission Council minutes, entry for 22 July 1926

be appointed General Treasurer to supervise the financial arrangements of the Church. Influenced in part by the example of the pastor, Edward Bote Manda, who had been imprisoned for embezzlement in 1925, Laws opposed the motion; but with some European support it carried the day, and Y. M. Mkandawire was appointed to the office.[106] Five years later in 1933 Presbyterial control over ministers, which Fraser had regarded as a safeguard of major importance, was considerably weakened by the decision that henceforth pastors would be appointed to congregations for four years at a time rather than annually, as had been the case.[107] By that time fourteen pastors were active in Livingstonia congregations and Presbytery meetings were attended by as few as four Scottish ministers out of a total attendance of over sixty.

Only in the mission council did Europeans continue to dominate; and the influence of council, though still far-reaching, was less extensive than it had been previously. In 1921 it was approached by the respected teacher, later pastor, Yesaya Chibambo, who complained, 'that a native has no voice in the Mission work'.[108] The Council received the complaint sympathetically but responded with only the most minimal of reforms. To Chibambo's request, 'that ... some remarkable servants of the Mission should be encouraged to attend Mission Council', its members replied with a direct refusal:

> The Mission Council is elected by the Church in Scotland and are by it charged with the control and development of operations in the country. And as even all the European workers in the Mission are not members of Council, it is not in the mind of the Home Church that native workers, meantime, should be members of Council.[109]

Questions of the status and duties of employees were subsequently discussed at meetings attended by African ministers, and from 1926 a teachers' association was in existence, which considered the educational work of the mission, though it had no power to make policy or allocate funds.[110] No African was appointed to the mission council before the beginning of the Second World War. But whereas, in the mid 1920s, the mission council had transferred Kasungu to the Dutch Reformed Church, without consulting the Kirk Sessions of the congregations involved, in

106 Livingstonia Presbytery minutes, entry for 18 July 1927. For the case against Edward Bote Manda see Laws to Ashcroft, 19 November 1924, NLS 7887

107 Liv. Presb. minutes, entry for 17 July 1933

108 Y. M. Chibambo to the Mission Council, n.d., enclosed in Liv. Mis. Council minutes, 15 July 1921

109 ibid., entry for 15 July 1921

110 ibid., entry for 14 July 1926

the mid 1930s such conduct would have been unthinkable. The affairs of the African Church had become mainly the concern of the Livingstonia Presbytery, while the Council concentrated on such issues as the allocation of European staff, the grading of African schoolteachers, the rearrangement of classes and the wages to be paid to employees.

The union in 1924 of the Livingstonia and Blantyre Presbyteries in a Synod of the Church of Central Africa Presbyterian illustrates the ambiguities of church development in Malawi. The value of such a union had been stressed by Laws as early as 1893, and proposals were put to the Blantyre missionary, Hetherwick, who rejected them, in 1895 and were incorporated into the minute establishing the Presbytery of North Livingstonia in 1899. In 1903, Hetherwick revived the idea, much to Laws's satisfaction, and in 1904 the first detailed discussions between representatives of the two Presbyteries took place and proposals on union were tentatively formulated.[111] Problems arose over the theological basis of the church, the number and variety of missions with which it was to be associated, the disciplinary code to be established and the relations of European missionaries to what was always contemplated as an essentially African organisation. By 1914, however, all obstacles had been overcome and in May the decision to enter into union was officially sanctioned by the assemblies of the churches in Scotland.[112] The intervention of war prevented the Synod from being formally established, and subsequently delays resulted from the lack of transport facilities down the lake and from the attempt to bring in the Dutch Reformed Church before the transfer of the Kasungu district took place. In September 1924, the first meeting of the Synod was finally held, to be followed two years later by a second meeting at which the Mkhoma Presbytery of the DRC was formally admitted.[113] No further Synod meetings were held until 1933 and by that time the major characteristics of the church were already established. Each Presbytery retained its own constitution and took many decisions without reference to the General Synod. European ministers occupied a dual role in which they were recognised as full members of Presbytery but were not subject to its jurisdiction.

Decisions taken on the character of the union influenced the subsequent nature of the CCAP. As Ross has shown, Scottish missionaries both at Blantyre and at Livingstonia expressed a variety of different opinions from the 1890s on the character of the African church and the role of

[111] Liv. Presb. minutes, entries for 15 November 1899, 14 October 1903 and 6 October 1904; Hetherwick to Laws, 8 June 1904, Hetherwick Papers

[112] Laws to Hetherwick, 1 August 1914, Hetherwick Papers

[113] Laws to Ashcroft, 20 October 1926, NLS 7889

Europeans within it.[114] All believed that some form of union was desirable, but whereas Hetherwick and Laws wanted to preserve the Presbyterian basis of their church, D. C. Scott and, later, Fraser, were more concerned with the creation of a single, interdenominational body. Laws believed that Europeans should not be subject to the ecclesiastical control of the church. Hetherwick, like Scott, was anxious 'to keep the unity of the European and native elements' and thus hoped that 'the Church Synod formed by the union . . . should be our supreme court for all, both European and African'.[115]

By 1914, two major decisions had already been taken. The name agreed upon, 'The Church of Central Africa Presbyterian', was a compromise choice, which reflected the compromise in aims of the parties involved. 'The Presbyterian Church in Africa', the title recommended by a joint committee in Scotland, was regarded as emphasising the non-African, Presbyterian element too much; 'The Church of Central Africa', Fraser's choice, was viewed as ignoring that element entirely. By stressing the Central African ingredient, so Hetherwick wrote, they were emphasising that 'we mean it to be the Church of the land and the people'; by including 'Presbyterian' in the title, they were implicitly rejecting the LMS and the Moravians, whom Fraser had wished to involve.[116] As for the internal unity of the church, it was Laws's argument that came out on top. Despite Hetherwick's theoretical allegiance to the concept of 'ONE Church in Central Africa', his white parishioners forced him to accept the establishment of separate European and African congregations, each with their own Kirk Session, at Blantyre and Zomba. Their creation supplied a precedent to justify the decision that European members of the Presbytery should be subjected only to the jurisdiction of their church in Scotland.[117] Not until 1959 did Church of Scotland ministers enter fully into the ecclesiastical structure of the CCAP; during most of the intervening period Scottish missionaries (at least those in Northern Rhodesia), did not even take meals together with Africans at the biennial meetings of the Presbytery.[118] In some ways, the CCAP was to function as an instrument for African initiative; in others, up to the 1950s, it was to serve as a

114 Ross, 'Origins and Development of . . . Blantyre', 308–13

115 Laws to Hetherwick, 24 June 1904; Hetherwick to Laws, 9 August 1904, Hetherwick Papers

116 Hetherwick to Laws, 25 September 1912, Hetherwick Papers; Liv. Presb. minutes, entries for 26 September 1910 and 14 October 1912

117 Hetherwick to Laws, 9 August 1904; to J. W. Arthur, 5 October 1916, Hetherwick Papers

118 Ross, ibid., 309 footnote; Peter Bolink, *Towards Church Union in Zambia*, The Netherlands, n.d., 199n

monument to racial disunity. The advantage, at least in theory, of the independent status of Europeans, was that Africans were thus freed 'from domination by Western modes of thought, worship and organisation'. The disadvantage, according to an official report of 1936, was that such a division appeared 'to bring racial and political discrimination into Church life'.[119]

Though no formal division between Europeans and Africans was made in the Livingstonia Presbytery, elements of racial prejudice undoubtedly existed. Lay missionaries in the 1920s assumed that 'wherever a white man is on a station he ranks in all authority over the native', and bitterly complained when they were told that African pastors were their superiors in matters relating to the church.[120] Separate seating areas for Europeans were provided in the church at Lubwa and at other mission stations. 'By the same token, and in the interests of hygiene, white people would drink first from the Communion Cup.'[121] R. D. McMinn, a devoted missionary, loved and respected in Bembaland, 'had a strong colour bar as regards Africans' according to Rev. P. B. Mushinda, his colleague for well over thirty years. Though McMinn acknowledged that Mushinda was 'my right hand in my works' as late as the mid 1940s, he refused to eat or drink with him.[122]

By 1930, the Presbyterian Church in northern Malawi had emerged from its pioneer phase. The five historic stations – Bandawe, Ekwendeni, Loudon, Karonga and the Institution – remained the educational and medical centres of the mission, but they represented only a small part of the church's physical presence. Thirty-one congregations existed, the largest with over 1100 communicant members, the smallest with fewer than 290.[123] They were tended by some twenty ministers – thirteen of them African pastors – any one of whom might be called upon to take responsibility for a district as large as Argyllshire.[124] Helping the ministers were some thirty evangelists, long-standing Christians with considerable pastoral experience, plus the elders elected by each congregation.

The elders, though unpaid, played an active role in the church's life. In many districts they organised Sunday services, took them themselves

[119] Church of Scotland Foreign Missions Report for 1936, 27

[120] A. Halliday to Webster, 28 August 1923, NLS 7886

[121] Fergus MacPherson, 'Note on Paul Mushindo' in Paul Bwemba Mushindo, *The Life of a Zambian Evangelist*, University of Zambia Institute for African Studies Communication No. 9, 1973, xxii

[122] Philip Short, *Banda*, London, 1974, 39

[123] Annual returns of the Livingstonia Mission for 1930, Liv. Corr. Box 8, MNA

[124] J. R. Martin to Ashcroft, 24 January 1922, NLS 7885

and preached with 'fervour and devotional spirit'.[125] Most, according to Chisholm, were 'men of one book – *the* Book' and could provide chapter and verse for any Biblical reference.[126] They instructed candidates for Baptism, visited the sick, settled quarrels between church members and reported breaches of church law to the local Kirk Sessions.[127] Like their predecessors before 1914, they tended to define the church negatively as the sum of a series of social prohibitions. Grave discussions took place in Presbytery as to whether Christians from Blantyre and the Moravian sphere could be admitted into communion without first renouncing beer drinking, which these churches cautiously countenanced.[128] The Kirk Sessions frequently functioned as disciplinary courts, suspending members who accepted protective charms, or who were in breach of the marriage laws, who had drunk beer or who had sought advice from witch finders.

The leaders of the church, the African pastors, bore only passing resemblance to the simplified images of progressive moderniser or deferential parasite with which they have been labelled by modern historians.[129] Paid only £36 a year on average in the mid 1930s, they owned little else than a Bible, a few books, a couple of chairs and a table. Up to 1944, they were all first-generation Christians, middle-aged men, several of whom had spent over two decades as teachers and evangelists before being ordained as ministers.[130] Vernon Stone has argued that R. D. McMinn, the missionary in charge at Lubwa, was acting contrary to the general policy of the Livingstonia Presbytery in ensuring that David Kaunda was not ordained until March 1930, twenty-six years after he had first preached the Gospel at Chinsali.[131] But Kaunda's experience of unrewarded service was shared by many of his ministerial colleagues. Peter

[125] Martin to Ashcroft, 2 May 1922, ibid.

[126] *UFCFMR*, 1923, 103

[127] Wilson, *Communal Rituals*, 168–9

[128] Liv. Presb. minutes, entries for 18–19 October 1911, 18 July 1918

[129] See Chanock, 'Development and Change' in Pachai, *The Early History of Malawi*, 435–8

[130] The first second-generation Christian to become a pastor, the son of Rev. Peter Thole, was ordained as chaplain to the Nyasaland troops in the KAR in September 1944. See Duncan Campbell to Dougall, September 1944, Liv. Corr. Box 1, MNA

[131] Stone, 'Livingstonia Mission and the Bemba', 320. See also R. D. McMinn, 'A Devoted African Pastor', *Other Lands*, July 1933, 156. Kaunda's academic limitations may well have been a further obstacle to his ordination. A devoted evangelist and teacher, he was granted a Schoolmaster's Diploma in 1914 by special resolution of the Mission Council after his thesis had been referred on three occasions. Liv. Mis. Council minutes, entries for 21 August 1913 and 13 May 1914

Thole, for example, the most prolific and gifted of the church's hymn writers, completed Standard VI at the Overtoun Institution in 1901 and spent twenty-seven years as a teacher and school inspector before being inducted into the pastorates of Njuyu and Emcisweni in October 1928.[132] Charles Chinula, likewise, worked for seventeen years as teacher, inspector and evangelist, before becoming a minister in 1925, and Yona Lengwe, one of the pioneer evangelists at Chitambo, was not ordained until 1927.[133] Yesaya Chibambo, the Ngoni historian, became the first recipient of the Honours Diploma for Schoolmasters in 1920, nine years before his ordination and George Nyasaru, though admitted to the theology class as early as 1913 and having worked with great success in Tanganyika, was still an evangelist in 1932, when he was dismissed from his post for sending Christians in need of advice to the miracle worker, Mzimu.[134] When the pioneer missionaries retired, they were replaced by young men in their mid or late twenties: Martin, Faulds, Robertson, Youngson, Galbraith. But for African pastors, age and experience had become essential qualifications. Rather than choosing from the best of the new generation the church was coming to rely increasingly on veterans educated at the Institution in the golden, prewar years.

It is difficult to determine how far active Christian membership can be equated with economic innovation. As I have tried to show, Livingstonia's influence was more keenly felt in the transformation of the Northern Province into a reservoir of skilled labour than it was in the development of commercial agriculture. Indeed, it is possible to argue that in some respects the mission positively hindered agricultural advance. By banning beer-drinking, the CCAP prevented Christians from utilising hoeing-for-beer parties in order to prepare their fields for planting. Yet according to Gregson, these groups of males were a more effective form of labour group than any other operated in the north.[135] All the same, so many Nyasa entrepreneurs were also active Presbyterians that it would be idle to deny that a connection existed. The first two-storied house in the West Nyasa district was built by a former cook and teacher employed by the Livingstonia Mission.[136] In the Henga valley, Yakobi Harawa, an elder

[132] Overtoun Institution Roll Book; Liv. Presb. minutes entry for 19 October 1928

[133] Personal communication from Rev. Charles Chinula; Moffat to Laws, 25 September 1917; November 1923; 15 February 1927, Liv. Corr. Box 7

[134] Liv. Presb. minutes, entries for 21 August 1913; 11 July 1929; 26 July, 22 October 1932; Liv. Mis. Council minutes, entry for 14 July 1920

[135] Gregson, 'Work, Exchange and Leadership', 86 and 112

[136] Diary of A. G. Macalpine for 24 June 1904

of the church, 'proved himself the most progressive in seeking to experiment and make advances in agriculture'. In 1923 he had 500 tea bushes under his care and was producing tea 'of a very fair quality'.[137] Philemon Chirwa, the senior schoolteacher at Bandawe in the 1920s, owned a dhow which he used to make himself 'one of the leading traders on the Lake', and consequently, 'quite a wealthy man'. And other teachers also traded, a practice which the missionaries excused on the grounds that it was 'only a variation of the old Scottish practice of raising money for fees by work in the holidays'.[138] It is true that some successful entrepreneurs in Malawi, the most outstanding perhaps being Peter Mwakasungulu, the Kyungu of Ngonde, made greater use of political and economic influences gained in the precolonial years than they did of their missionary contacts in order to establish new wealth in the 1920s.[139] Others, notably Chewa tobacco farmers, lacked any contact with Christianity, so Chanock has argued.[140] Others were educated by missionaries like those from the UMCA, who positively disapproved of commercial involvement.

But though the correlation between Presbyterianism and innovation was far from complete, some links can be detected. Skills taught at the Institution, though of primary value in the European sector of the economy, could sometimes be employed in the African sector as well. The ideological emphasis on thrift, sobriety and hard work, though not resulting in the widespread acceptance of a Protestant ethic, did possibly contribute to the emergence of entrepreneurial habits. Success in European employment, while by no means inevitably resulting in success in other economic fields, could provide sources of capital to be used in the employment of labour and the purchase of modern implements. By the 1960s active membership of the Presbyterian Church in the Henga valley was largely the preserve of an 'emerging rural elite'. In Chimwemwe village, which Gregson has studied in detail, both mill-owning cotton farmers

137 Alex Caseby, 'Report on the Agricultural Department', 1923 (?), NLS 7887

138 J. R. Martin to Ashcroft, 24 January 1922, NLS 7885

139 Wilson, *Constitution of Ngonde*, 78–9

140 M. L. Chanock, 'The Political Economy of independent agriculture in Colonial Malawi: The Great War to the Great Depression', *Journal of Social Science*, 1, 1972, 125n, Chanock's assumption that African production of cash crops was carried out by those least affected by Christianity should only be provisionally accepted until such time as the relationship of the Dutch Reformed Church and leading African farmers is explored more thoroughly. The DRC's economic ideology was almost certainly more appropriate for budding rural entrepreneuers then Livingstonia's industrially-oriented approach.

were retired government servants, who had been trained at Livingstonia and remained active members of the CCAP.[141]

Although they are often associated, there is no automatic connection between economic innovation and the desire for political and social change. Christian leaders, trained at the Overtoun Institution, combined a tradition of critical questioning with one of respect for mission authority. In consequence, their concern for change was sometimes tempered by a desire for social continuity. In theory, African and Scottish agents were at one in seeking to break the control of polygamous husbands over their wives, thus transforming the position of women in society. In practice, however, as Chanock suggests, the impact of the church was much more limited.[142] Girls filled some thirty to forty per cent of student places at Livingstonia's village schools, but many of them married early or were refused additional school fees by their families. At the Institution, fifty-two girls were examined, out of 232 pupils in 1898, but only twenty-seven out of 193 in 1900, five out of 110 in 1935 and none at all in the next four years.[143] And the skills taught were frequently of use only in a subordinate and domestic role. Following a brief interlude, when co-educational classes were conducted at the Institution, the Senatus decided in 1903 to reduce the academic standard of the Girls' School and to concentrate instead on such subjects as cooking, sewing, nursing, house-maid work and laundry work.[144] Sweeping, dusting, scrubbing, washing and ironing were all regarded as the ordinary duties of the girls' department in 1910; sewing lessons were carried on and 'a good deal of pounding of maize took place'.[145] In 1917, girls were once more admitted to the same classes as men, but the results achieved were unimpressive. In contrast to the significant proportion of Scottish women teachers employed by the mission, Nyasa women teachers were rarely recruited. In 1927, only thirteen women were so employed, as opposed to 1403 men, while in 1939 the figure had dropped to twelve women out of a total of 1334 teachers. In Ngoniland, as a result of Fraser's efforts, the Balakazi or female elders, played an active role as congregational advisers, settling disputes and supervising morals among women. But as late as 1935, so Agnes Fraser pointed out, they had not been admitted to full membership of the Sessions and had never been invited to participate at Presbytery.[146]

141 Gregson, 37 and 39–40

142 Chanock, 'Development and Change' in *Early History of Malawi*, 438

143 Annual returns for the Overtoun Institution, MNA

144 Senatus minutes, entry for 1 July 1903

145 Institution Educational Diary, reports for 1910 and 1911

146 Liv. Presb. minutes, entry for 5 July 1935

Rather than encouraging the genuine emancipation of women, then, Livingstonia opened up new areas where men were supreme. And though African church leaders commented in 1936 on the absence of training facilities for women, there is little evidence to suggest that they were seriously interested in extending opportunities significantly.[147]

A further consequence of the conflicting traditions associated with Livingstonia was the ambivalent political attitude which many of its leaders displayed. As the products of a highly-disciplined, fact-orientated educational system, the early pastors tended to combine an autocratic aloofness from the members of their congregations with a deference to the Scottish missionaries who had in many cases been their teachers. Patrick Mwamulima, the first pastor to be ordained at Karonga and Peter Thole, were only two of the ministers accused by Y. Z. Mwasi in 1933 of assuming that because the missionaries were of the same nationality as the colonial authorities their opinions had inevitably to be supported. Thole, according to Mwasi, argued that the pastors would be unable to 'remain alone by themselves', without Scottish support; he and his fellows refused to continue discussions in Presbytery in the absence of the European members.[148]

The fact that these charges were made by an African pastor indicates that such deference was by no means a universal characteristic among them. But while Mwasi could never be accused of subservience, he was no less high-handed in his approach to church members than the majority of his ministerial colleagues. Drawing upon the paternalist tradition established by Laws, he maintained strict control over the Sanga and Lumphasa congregations, to whom he ministered. Evangelists whose work was not up to standard were promptly denounced in Presbytery, and Kirk Sessions were treated with scant respect. When disagreements arose with elders from the Rumphasa district in 1932 Mwasi forbade them to preach and refused to celebrate the Lord's Supper in their district until they publicly proclaimed the error of their ways.[149]

Such actions were as important in the creation of new political attitudes as the experiences of anti-colonial and anti-missionary protest that historians have more frequently described. It is true that Livingstonia

147 'Resolutions of the Native Session in attendance at the 5th General Conference of the Federated Missions of Nyasaland', 1926, Liv. Corr. Box 1, MNA

148 Y. Z. Mwasi, 'My essential and Paramount Reasons for Working independently', 12 July 1933. I would like to acknowledge Professor B. Pachai's generosity in lending me a copy of this document.

149 Liv. Presb. minutes, entries for 22 August 1931, 27 and 28 July 1932

offered to a limited elite educational and bureaucratic opportunities of a type closed to those in government service, at least up to the 1950s. Through the network of church courts, pastors and elders gained first-hand experience in the practicalities of local self-government, keeping minutes and running committees. Through the Institution, a probing approach was developed which, with all its limitations, provided church leaders with the assurance that final authority could be arrived at only on the basis of personal judgement. But if the tradition was questioning, it was also in some senses inegalitarian and concerned with the extension of personal privilege. 'The age of improvement and differentiation', which John Iliffe has described for Tanzania, has a direct counterpart in Malawi.[150]

[150] John Iliffe, 'The age of improvement and differentiation (1907–45)' in I. N. Kimambo and A. J. Temu, *A History of Tanzania*, Nairobi, 1969

10

The politics of privilege

In the years following the downfall of Charles Domingo political activities in northern Malawi were largely concentrated in the hands of a small group of teachers, pastors and clerks, many of them educated at the Livingstonia Mission. In some respects, these men differed from the disaffected pastors of the prewar period. The latter had allied themselves with underprivileged groups in the north, who were envious of the success of Livingstonia's converts; the former tended to represent the more privileged sections of the community, though not all remained members of the Presbyterian Church. Yet if the new politicians were less radical in their social aspirations than the pioneer independent churchmen, it would be rash to assume that they were less important. It is through their activities that we can best appreciate the often-quoted remark that Livingstonia was the seed-bed of the Nyasaland African Congress.[1] Their political attitudes, it has been argued, reflected the distinctive traditions of the mission.[2] The grievances they articulated arose out of an economic and educational environment which Livingstonia had helped to create. As a comparatively ineffective elite, they were unable to challenge the colonial system with the force displayed by an embittered peasantry in the late 1950s. But through their efforts to reform the local administration, to promote economic change in certain directions, and to improve educational facilities, they did maintain a certain independence of initiative, crabbed and constrained by imperialist pressures, which played a part in the shaping of colonial Malawi.

The most effective improvers were also the architects of class formation.[3] Compared with their European or even West African counterparts, petty bourgeois clerks and teachers like Levi Mumba, E. A. Muwamba and Charles Chinula lived in conditions of austerity only marginally different

1 Shepperson and Price, *Independent African*, 414

2 Cook, 'The Influence of Livingstonia Mission upon the Formation of Welfare Associations in Zambia' in Ranger and Weller, *Christian History*

3 Kimambo and Temu, *A History of Tanzania*, 124–5

from those experienced by their peasant neighbours. But, while it can be argued that the most significant feature of social change in Malawi in the inter-war years was the absence of major differentiation, the effects of differential access to education should also be noted. In one sense, the northern improvers identified with Malawians as a whole in their efforts to better conditions. In another, they represented mainly themselves in their bid to maintain and extend privileges gained before the First World War.

Native associations

The emergence of a group of political activists in northern Malawi in the 1920s was intimately connected with the impact of Livingstonia during the previous 30 years. Up to the First World War over 800 students had passed through the educational classes at the Institution, many of whom subsequently worked for the mission. At Khondowe, as I have argued, they were subjected to a variety of influences, among which the tradition of critical discussion was uppermost. Those who served as teachers had taken part, from as early as 1894, in strikes, usually short and ineffective; those who became church elders practised in Kirk Sessions and Presbytery procedures of discussion and debate, of the keeping of minutes and the passing of resolutions, which they were to employ successfully in the political associations they later founded.

Furthermore, the missionaries both encouraged the foundation and influenced the character of the early associations. Laws believed that to deny Africans the instruments of political expression was to encourage a radicalism that the Scots would be unable to control. As early as 1907, he suggested in an unsigned article, published in the mission journal *Aurora*, that:

> Some constitutional means should be provided whereby the natives who form the majority of the population should have by a native council or otherwise the means of expressing an opinion on legitimate changes which concern themselves. Were this done, and done early, we believe the gradually increasing educated native community would be enlisted on the side of constitutional government and peace and so be prevented from becoming in the future the prey of any noisy demagogue.[4]

In 1912 the issue became more pressing. Laws, according to one witness, was stimulated by his imminent co-option to the Legislative Council to seek the establishment of a body of moderate African opinion whose

[4] *Aurora*, December 1907

suggestions he could take up with the government at Zomba.[5] At the same time, it seems likely that he saw in the foundation of an association a counterweight to the disturbing views propagated by Kamwana's successors. In the North Nyasa district, the incursion of Watch Tower evangelists in 1911 had been followed at Kasisi by a ground swell of opposition to mission teaching and a revival of beer drinking and dancing.[6] At Karonga, the central town in the district, former Livingstonia pupils, some of them now separated from the mission, were working in the government office and hospital and in the stores belonging to the ALC and the Tanganyika Concessions Company. Fearful that such men would be attracted by separatist claims, the missionaries in March 1912 opened a reading room in the town 'into which we put weekly such papers as are likely to be useful to them, along with books which they can read with profit'.[7] But, by itself, the provision of literature was recognised to be an inadequate safeguard. The missionaries were anxious to channel, rather than suppress, the aspirations of the new intelligentsia. When Laws, prior to the opening of the reading room, was approached by a group of predominantly Tumbuka clerks and teachers, who were anxious to form their own pressure group, he therefore welcomed the scheme. Permission was given for the reading room to be used as a meeting place of the North Nyasa Native Association, as the new body was entitled, but Laws insisted that 'members should be educated up to the highest standard going in the local schools', with most having attended the Institution; 'that good character should be an essential qualification'; and 'that they should be loyal to the government'.[8] Personal improvement was made the central theme of the meetings, at which infant mortality and sanitation were discussed, along with marriage payments and village reconstruction. The local missionary, Mackenzie, became a regular attender and a government medical officer, Doctor Conran, lectured on public health.[9] For a short period during the war, the association took over the mission's educational responsibilities and functioned as a school board, collecting fees and appointing teachers.[10]

Many of the interests brought together in the North Nyasa Native

[5] S. A. Bwingo, 'The North Nyasa Native Association', History Seminar Paper, Chancellor College

[6] Livingstonia Mission Report, 1911, 39; *Livingstonia News*, October 1912, 66

[7] *FCSMR*, August 1912, 350

[8] Laws to Acting Chief Secretary, Zomba, 12 January 1920, MNA S1/2065/9

[9] *Livingstonia News*, October 1912, 66; Livingstonia Mission Report, 1912, 42

[10] Notes on the Fifth General Conference of the Federated Missions of Nyasaland, 1926, Liv. Corr. Box 1.

Association can be identified in the four leading office holders. The first president, Peter Mwakasungulu, the brother of the Ngonde ruler and subsequently Kyungu himself, represented both the dominant chiefly family in the area and also a new breed of Ngonde entrepreneur, who benefited from the cattle trade to the south and from the involvement of the Ngonde in the growing of cotton. In 1912 he was employed, as he had been for a decade, by the ALC, but a year later he went into partnership with the company and used his local political contacts to such effect that, in 1919, he was able to strike out on his own as a successful free-lance trader. The profits he made from trading and planting he ploughed back into the Ngonde chieftaincy, with the result, so Godfrey Wilson has argued, that the prestige of the office remained high, though its pre-colonial economic assets had been lost.[11] His active participation in the Association's affairs is indicative at once of the alliance established by the Association with at least some of the traditional authorities and also of the complex interrelationship between economic wealth and political influence that existed in the North Nyasa district.

Simon Mhango, the Association's vice-president, personified a different tradition. A Tumbuka migrant, subsequently a government interpreter, he returned from South Africa only in 1912, and is credited with being the architect of the new Association.[12] Despite suggestions to the contrary, there appears to be no concrete evidence to link his action with the foundation of the South African Native National Congress in January, some two months before the inaugural meeting at Karonga.[13] But it is possible to speculate that, as a migrant, he had developed a sense of Nyasa identity transcending, though not obliterating, tribal differences and that in his travels he had acquired ideas and techniques that could be utilised in the political context of his homeland. Martin Chanock has usefully reminded us that 'South African mines and Rhodesian farms have historically shown little evidence of being radical hatching grounds'; that because of the absence of social and economic security in the south, many migrants concerned themselves obsessively with land claims and succession disputes in the districts from which they came.[14] But to discount the argument

[11] Wilson, *Constitution of Ngonde*, 78–9; Evidence of P. H. Chungu, 15 May 1929 before North Nyasa Commission of Inquiry, MNA J8/5/3. It should be noted that this evidence has recently been questioned; Kalinga, 'Ngonde of Northern Malawi', 151.

[12] See documents relating to a quarrel within the NNNA 1919, MNA S1/1481/19

[13] See Pachai, *Malawi: the History of the Nation*, 226

[14] M. L. Chanock, 'Development and Change in the history of Malawi' in Pachai, *Early History of Malawi*, 438–9. Also J. van Velsen, 'Migrant Labour

that migrancy fostered 'the emergence of a new, dynamic form of leadership'[15] is not to deny that it had some influence. Isolated groups of Tonga domestic servants or Chewa agricultural labourers on Rhodesian farms are unlikely to have experienced much that could have contributed to the creation 'of a sense of common homeland'. But for urban workers – Nyasa interpreters at Livingstone, hospital assistants like Kamwana, clerks in Rhodesian mines, perhaps oppressed by a 'cruel' compound manager as Kadalie had been – the situation was much less clear cut. Just as Eliot Kamwana was converted to Watch Tower in the south, so Clements Kadalie and Robert Sambo obtained their first contact with socialist and Garveyite ideas while travelling outside their homeland.[16] To a large extent, political patterns in Malawi emerged from the logic of the local situation. But just as ideas, whether concerning witchcraft eradication or political organisation, could spread from Malawi to other areas so Malawi itself, through returning migrants, imported ideas from the south.

If Mhango symbolises the labour migrant element in the North Nyasa Association, Uriah Chirwa and Levi Mumba, vice-president and secretary respectively, represent the important Livingstonia connection. Uriah Chirwa was the very model of the moderate, responsible voice which Laws had wished to encourage. A schoolmaster, later senior assistant at the Overtoun Institution, he led the numerous teachers who joined the association in loyal support of mission policies. Christian education, he was to tell the 1915 Commission of Enquiry, had utterly transformed his Tonga compatriots: 'In Tongaland houses were dark and small, but now they have nice houses and they do all the work which civilised people do here.' He praised the colonial government without reservation: 'We... are thankful that we are under such a Government which greatly cares for her people, and that she has helped to bring into the peace which we now enjoy.'[17]

Compared with Chirwa, Levi Mumba, secretary and for twelve years the driving force of the association, can be almost classed as a radical. At the Institution, from 1897 to 1903, he played the part of a model pupil, never coming lower than third in his form. His reward was a job in Laws's office followed in 1904 by a place in the new commercial course that T. C. Young was starting. In July 1905 he was sent to gain experi-

as a Positive Factor in Tonga Tribal Society' in Aidan Southall (ed.), *Social Change in Modern Africa*, London, 1961

15 Gray, *Two Nations*, 170

16 Kadalie, *My Life and the ICU*, 35; Ranger, *African Voice*, 151

17 Written statement by Yuria Chatonda Chirwa, Overtoun Institution, 3 July 1915, CO 525/66

ence at the Chinsali *Boma* in Northern Rhodesia and by September 1906 he was back, working in the Institution and proving to be 'of immense value' in 'all the business work'.[18]

Mumba's subsequent disenchantment with the mission can be traced only with difficulty. According to Tangri, whose account is based on oral information, he left the Institution in 1911, having contracted a polygamous marriage and found employment in the government hospital at Karonga, where the European medical officer, Meredith Sanderson, became his mentor and friend.[19] By 1912 he had thus joined the ranks of those in exile from Livingstonia and critical of its policies. However, the minutes of the Institution senate present a different picture. Mumba, they indicate, may have worked temporarily at Karonga in 1912, but by September 1913 he was back at Khondowe as a clerk in the Institution post office. Next year he was given responsibility for signing official letters, bills and weigh bills and for typing examination papers for students on probation. Not until 1915 did he leave the mission and then it was the low rate of pay he received, £3 a month, that precipitated his decision.[20] But the uncomfortable independence of mind that was to characterise his utterances on religious affairs in the 1920s may well have alarmed the missionaries even earlier. In 1908 he was refused permission to enrol in the theological class, ostensibly on the grounds that he was required full time in the office.[21] Four years previously he had discussed with Donald Siwale why 'Africans were being called boys by Europeans although they were grown men'.[22]

In the two years prior to the outbreak of war, the example set at Karonga by a small group of Livingstonia graduates was followed throughout the mission sphere with varying degrees of success. 'Invitations to form local associations in the adjoining districts of Mombera and West Nyasa were not at first entertained,' Levi Mumba later wrote, 'as the educated natives in those districts did not feel inclined to start them owing

[18] Overtoun Institution Roll Book entry 156; T. Cullen Young (ed.), 'The Religion of My Fathers' *International Review of Missions*, June 19, 1930, 362; Institution Senatus minutes entry for 19 March 1905

[19] Roger K. Tangri, 'Levi Z. Mumba, "A Political Biography of a Pioneer Malawi Nationalist"' (unpublished paper)

[20] Institution Senatus minutes, entries for 9 September 1913, 13 February 1914, 12 January and 9 February 1915. Mumba's salary of £36 a year should be compared with the starting salary of £75 a year offered by the Northern Rhodesian Government at Livingstone in 1913 to clerks trained at Livingstonia

[21] Institution Senatus minutes, entry for 8 December 1908

[22] Quoted in Cook, 'The Influence of Livingstonia Mission', 107

to other pressing duties.'[23] However, a branch of the Karonga association was formed at Khondowe, while at Mwenzo, an informal discussion group of teachers, sometimes attended by Dr Chisholm, was transformed before 1914 into the first welfare association in Northern Rhodesia. Its initial impetus came from Levi Mumba, who sent a copy of the constitution of the North Nyasa Association to his college friend Donald Siwale. The evacuation of the station following the German invasion scattered the teachers and brought the Mwenzo association's meetings to a close. But in 1923, following the reconstitution of the Malawi associations, this body was revived once more.[24]

The change of character within the associations that took place during the 1920s may be ascribed at once to the economic crisis of that period and to the inadequacy of Livingstonia's response. In the prewar years, so Levi Mumba claimed in an article published in 1924, the aim of the members was largely 'to better local conditions' and to represent 'public opinion' to the local Residents more effectively than the annual meetings of chiefs and headmen had been able to do.[25] How frequently they communicated their views to the central government is unclear – the Governor received a copy of the minutes of at least one meeting – but by and large they appear to have confined their activities to discussion of general issues at a district level and to have accepted a measure of European control.[26]

The 1920s, however, was a period of trouble in which the compromises of the past were gradually abandoned. During the war, at least 37 members of the North Nyasa Association served with the army, 23 as interpreters,[27] and when they resumed their meetings in June 1919, they exuded a new assurance. Proud of the contribution they had made in 'helping to win freedom for mankind' they looked to the government to reward their efforts and to listen to their requests with sympathy. All members of the association who had served in the army should receive medals, they argued in a memorandum directed, significantly, to the Superintendent of Native Affairs; widows bereaved by the war should not be molested by askaris on the tax raids they periodically made.[28]

[23] Levi Z. Mumba, 'Native Associations in Nyasaland', *The South African Outlook*, 2 June 1924. I owe this reference to Dr Roger Tangri

[24] Cook, 106–10

[25] Mumba, 'Native Associations'

[26] Livingstonia Mission Report, 1912

[27] Minutes of a meeting of the NNNA June 1919, MNA S1/1481/19. Four of the remaining ex-servicemen were clerks, four were carpenters, one was a hospital assistant, one a linesman, one a storekeeper, one a scout and one a 'captain in Military Transport'

[28] ibid.

But in the wake of the post-war influenza epidemic, which carried off thousands of victims, hopes were dashed and disillusionment spread. Prices for cloth and other commodity goods spiralled upwards but wages remained stationary and local employment opportunities shrank. Cash-crop farmers, like the Manganja of the lower Shire valley, benefited from the boom in cotton, but where no cash crops were grown standards of living declined.[29] 'It is unquestionable to everybody,' the comment was made in Ngoniland in 1921, 'that natives, since the hideous war broke out, find great difficulty in supporting themselves and find that goods in stores are beyond their means.' 'Prices,' it was claimed, 'are still high in stores as in wartime' but wages of plantation labourers at Blantyre had fallen from seven or six shillings a month to five. Products grown by the European community were sold at a fixed price, it was erroneously believed, while the price of African-grown foodstuffs fluctuated in accordance with market conditions. People in the Northern Province suffered particularly badly, the argument went, because they 'have no chance at all, or very little, of selling their products in the country because there are no market places at all'.[30] 'Since the war the cost of living has been very high now,' the West Nyasa Association later complained, 'but the wages of the labouring classes are stationary in Nyasaland only.'[31]

Adding to these grievances, the policies pursued at Livingstonia appeared to worsen, not ameliorate the crisis. Faced by the pressing need to economise, the missionaries cut back the number of teachers employed from the six major Nyasaland stations by some 8 per cent compared with 1913 (913 compared with 996) and froze wages at prewar and pre-inflation levels.[32] Demands for higher pay, made by evangelists at Loudon and teachers at Bandawe, were rejected without discussion by the mission council. When, in 1927, a deputation of teachers carried their complaint to the Director of Education, Laws deducted from their pay the amount covering the time spent going to and returning from their interview.[33] The list of criticisms made by Yesaiah Chibambo to the mission council in 1921 represented, as the council admitted, 'the opinion of many other workers in the mission'.[34] Chibambo contrasted the regular terms of

29 Chanock, 'Political Economy', 122

30 Minutes of MNA 26, 27 September 1921, MNA S1/210/20

31 Quoted in Chanock 'Political Economy', 123

32 Livingstonia Mission Reports 1915 and 1921. If the whole mission-field including Northern Rhodesia, is considered the cut back in the number of teachers employed was approximately thirteen per cent. However, by 1925 employment had risen to the prewar level.

33 A. J. Macalpine to Laws, 22 January and 19 February 1927, Liv. Corr. Box 9

34 Livingstonia Mission Council minutes entry for 15 July 1921

service offered to government employees with the poor conditions of work that prevailed for servants of the mission. Certificated teachers, he pointed out, had no security of tenure and lacked adequate materials for their work. No travelling expenses were paid to African employees; pensions and gratuities were denied to the old; 'the families of the natives who have died in the mission service are not cared for by our mission'. The African, he suggested, had no 'voice in the mission work', was 'not regarded as a co-worker with the missionary', was 'commonly called Boy by his missionary without any distinction'. No African was allowed to report directly to the Council on his work, 'and sometimes the missionary who writes the same report perhaps does not understand really about the work done by the native'.[35]

Further annoyance was felt at the inability of the mission to maintain the dominance over post-primary education upon which the prosperity of a minority in the north depended. As Fraser's agriculturally-based educational policies took effect from the late 1920s, a chorus of complaint arose from local educational boards and councils of chiefs concerning the limited opportunities which Livingstonia now provided.[36]

The introduction of a new English–African reader in the upper primary levels, about 1930, in the place of the Chambers Graduated Readers hitherto used, marked only one of several steps on the road to a specifically African education which northern Malawians often deeply resented.[37] How total was the fall in standards at the Institution following Laws's defeat and the setbacks of the First World War it is difficult from external evidence alone to determine. But that the decline was major became the opinion not only of W. P. Young, the new principal, but also of most graduates of the mission prior to 1914.[38] 'The early men who came from Khondowe were far more highly educated than those who came out of Khondowe in the twenties and thirties' Dr Banda declared some years ago, in words that echo the conviction of his contemporaries:

> Men like Chinula or the father of Chiwambo and others, my uncle Reverend Phiri, were far more, far better educated those days than those who came after them. When I left this country I had not even started Standard III or IV but my uncle used to talk to me about

[35] Y. M. Chibambo to the Mission Council, n.d., enclosed in Liv. Mis. Council minutes, 15 July 1921

[36] See pp. 236–43 and 286–7

[37] Minutes of a meeting of the North Nyasa District School Committee, 2 June 1936, MNA NNI/10/3

[38] This opinion was forcibly expressed in separate interviews I held with three prewar graduates from the Institution, Rev. Charles Chinula, Mr Alexander Muwamba and Mr Hanoc Ngoma.

political economy as the British call it and which the Americans call economics. Dr Laws was teaching the rudiments of economics at Khondowe – Latin, Greek, because he was planning that place to be a University of Central Africa.[39]

A similar view was expressed by the Atonga tribal council in a petition of October 1943:

> It is generally said that the Nyasaland Protectorate was second to South Africa in receiving education . . . It is clear that the Protectorate is now far behind comparing the education which neighbouring territories are obtaining . . . If Nyasaland was given a sound general education which is or would be a stepping stone to high educational qualifications there would have been similar chances as those of South African natives today.[40]

It was against these conditions of economic depression and educational decline that the Livingstonia-educated elite reacted in the 1920s and 1930s. Surprise has been expressed that political initiatives at this period should have arisen in the north when the abuses suffered by southerners were so much more dramatic.[41] But given the grievances that we have seen created, it was almost inevitable that attempts to deal with them should have come from the area containing the highest proportion of the educated and politically adept, particularly when education provided for their compatriots, in the absence of significant local opportunities outside the mission, the main means through which they could aspire to privileged positions in the work markets of south and central Africa.

The result was that pastors, teachers and clerks were drawn into a variety of organisations, all concerned with the social consequences of the emergence of colonial economy, though some aimed to bring particular issues to the notice of the government, while others attempted to supply the facilities which the Europeans had failed to provide. The native associations, independent churches and local tribal councils, which they dominated and encouraged, differed from each other in a number of ways, and friction sometimes occurred between one organisation and another. However, the overlap of membership in the inter-war years was so extensive that an identity of purpose was usually maintained. Most leaders in the wake of the Chilembwe Rising accepted the realities of the

39 Official Report of the Proceedings in the Parliament of Malawi, 1st session, 3rd meeting, 27 October 1964, 154

40 Petition by Tribal Council of Atonga Chiefs to the Governor, 6 October 1943, MNA NNC5/1/1

41 J. van Velsen, 'Some Early Pressure Groups in Malawi' in Stokes and Brown, *Zambesian Past*, 378

colonial system and shrank from challenging it directly; most resented the loss of African initiative and looked to re-establish personal dignity as a means of recapturing the dignity of Africans as a whole. Above all, they were concerned with 'improvement', and though improvement meant utilising European techniques, it also meant adapting them to a particular African context. For this reason the native associations which, before the war, were essentially outcrops of the mission, came in the 1920s to take on a character and a force of their own.

The emergence of native associations as a significant political force in Malawi can be dated from the revival of the North Nyasa Association in June 1919. Proposals to form similar bodies were discussed at Khondowe in July, and after the plan for a single society, drawing its membership equally from Ngoniland and the lake shore, had been discarded, the Mombera Native Association was inaugurated in January 1920 and the West Nyasa Native Association at Bandawe some two weeks later.[42] In the same year, members of the North Nyasa Association were unsuccessful in their attempt to encourage the formation of similar organisations in the south. In 1923, however, the Southern Province Native Association was begun, and in 1924 a Representative Committee of the Northern Provinces Associations was set up at Zomba by Levi Mumba, who had been transferred from Karonga that year. Subsequently at least four more associations were started, all of them operating in the Southern and Central Provinces.

Opposition to the new bodies was expressed by the Resident at Chinteche, A. J. Brackenbury, who warned of the WNNA that it would 'probably amount to a Native Mission Union which under the guidance of some kinds of European Missionaries might very likely be continually pressing the Government for better conditions for the blacks'.[43] But Dr Laws's more sophisticated beliefs were those which carried the day. As he told the acting Chief Secretary in 1920, Laws was convinced that: 'the vast multitude of the natives . . . cannot be expected to remain dumb with regard to their own affairs, and safety valves for the expression of their opinions are needed in the interests of peace and safety'. The associations would admirably fill the part, he believed, for their middle-class members would tend to support a government which protected their possessions.

> We have to take notice of the fact that no suppression can prevent the natives from discussing political and other subjects . . . Very often . . . there is lacking in these discussions the guidance of a better-educated person than his companions who can give the other side a

[42] Laws to acting CS Zomba, 12 January 1920, MNA S1/2065/19

[43] Resident Chinteche to CS Zomba, 6 November 1919, MNA S1/2065/19

> wider view of things. This counteractive the associations can supply . . .
>
> Of course in all such movements there is a certain amount of risk that some hot-headed demagogue might abuse the liberty given just as is the case at home, but if there is a conservative party of native opinion behind this which knows that it can make itself heard in what for want of a better phrase, I might call, a 'constitutional way', I think such a danger is accordingly minimised.
>
> The increase of comparative wealth among the natives steadily brings the native to the side of law and order securing him the peaceful possession of his earnings and protection in his efforts to improve his position and his surroundings. This leads him to be a supporter of the Government as the cause of bringing about such favourable conditions.[44]

The accuracy of Laws's analysis was demonstrated in considerable measure by the actions of the associations. All three northern bodies retained the prewar requirement that 'members . . . are to be persons of good knowledge and character' and at least one, the West Nyasa Association, specifically ruled that: 'No member [is] eligible unless educated' and that 'Proposed members must have a certificate of education'.[45] The high annual levy of 2 shillings appears to have discouraged all but the most affluent of applicants and, in consequence, the number of those enrolled was small. Meetings of the Mombera Association were attended by a maximum of 37 and a minimum of 15 members between 1920 and 1927, while up to 1929, the attendance at meetings of the West Nyasa body rarely rose above 25. Teachers and clergymen in the service of the mission remained the most effective participants along with a scattering of government clerks like Hezekaiah Mwanza, chief clerk at Chinteche *Boma*. Apart from Levi Mumba, secretary at Karonga until 1925, active office holders were largely drawn from those in employment with Livingstonia: some, like Mumba's successor, Patrick Mwamulima and Philemon Chirwa, the schoolmaster secretary at Bandawe, representing the moderate, accommodationist wing; others like Charles Chinula in Ngoniland and Y. Z. Mwasi, secretary at Bandawe after Chirwa, representing a more radical, independent tradition. As for those chiefs and headmen who attended meetings, the majority were educated and in some cases affluent men, who identified with the 'progressive' ethos which the associations sought to propagate. Few were as well off as Peter Mwakasungulu, Chief

[44] Laws to acting CS Zomba 12 January 1920, MNA S1/2065/19

[45] Constitution of the West Nyasa Native Association, 15 January 1920, MNA S1/2065/19

Kyungu who, in the early 1920s, claimed to be cultivating up to 900 acres of cotton.[46] But most had attended Livingstonia schools and several had served in mission employment. Amon Jere, Chief Mtwalo, the president of Mombera's association from 1921 to 1926, was one of the pioneer Christians in his region and a former mission teacher.

The topics raised with the government by the associations frequently reflected social attitudes not dissimilar to those held by Laws. Whatever their affection for the past, most members would have agreed with Yesaiah Chibambo that 'the country is now in a new era with new life, new knowledge, new resolutions, new laws and new sanctions'. They accepted that 'it would be foolish and ridiculous if people of this country dislike the civilisation' and regarded as one of their aims 'making people understand the necessity and value of order and . . . of industrious labour – and in short the value of civilisation as against ignorance, laziness, disloyalty and anarchy'.[47] Taxes should be promptly paid, the Mombera Association argued; wailing at funerals should be discouraged.[48] Popular attempts to adjust to the colonial situation they regarded with disfavour as tending to undermine the authority of the existing network of local elites. The Mombera Association joined with local chiefs in calling for the suppression of immigrant witchfinders, who were active in Ngoniland in 1920. 'Marini' bands, introduced into Tongaland by ex-soldiers from Tanganyika, were condemned by the West Nyasa Association in 1921 on the grounds that they contributed to laziness and disobedience.[49]

Yet to regard the associations simply as the upholders of established order would be to ignore much that was most central to their aims. During the 1920s, they forwarded a flood of complaints to central government, some of them concerned with trivial issues, but some with questions of major importance. The actions of government agents, and the indignities suffered by Africans under the colonial power were continual sources of grievance. Thus demands were made that women should not be seized as hostages when their husbands were in default of tax and that forced labour should not be exacted from men seeking passes to leave the country. Africans, it was argued, should not be discouraged by settlers and govern-

[46] Evidence of P. H. 'Chungu', 15 May 1928, before North Nyasa Native Reserves Commission, MNA J8/5/3

[47] Constitution of WNNA 15 January 1920, ibid., minutes of MoNA 1–2 September 1920, MNA S1/210/20

[48] Minutes of MoNA, 28–31 July 1922, MNA S1/210/20; Minutes of MoNA 24 July 1925, MNA S1/2859/23

[49] Minutes of MoNA, 1–2 September 1920; Minutes of WNNA 11 May 1921, MNA S1/2065/19. See also T. O. Ranger, *Dance and Society in Eastern Africa*, London 1975, 38–47, 71–6

ment officials from wearing hats, jackets and long trousers, as was the practice in the early 1920s; European sexual offenders against Africans should be treated under the same laws as Africans against Europeans.[50]

Demands were also made for government economic action, to improve conditions for wage labourers and to create opportunities for peasant production. The Mombera Association complained on a number of occasions of the ill treatment meted out by European settlers to their African employees and the West Nyasa Association expressed a similar view in 1929 in a comprehensive indictment of conditions on the Vizaro and Chombi estates near Nkata Bay, owned by the African Lakes Company. Wages rates were desperately low, the Association's secretary alleged; *posho* – the food supply given to workers – consisted only of ten pounds of maize in the rainy season and nothing thereafter. Working hours fluctuated between nine and ten hours a day in the dry season and eleven hours during the rains. Some of the workers were 'tender women with babes on their backs while others are children of only twelve or thirteen years of age'. The huts erected for workers were 'foully untidy', lacked doors and were plagued by 'venomous insects'. To Y. Z. Mwasi, the author of the Association's minute, the poverty that resulted was fundamentally un-Christian: 'The man who is underpaid, underfed and badly housed, the man who is sweated and overdriven, the child who is wronged in body and mind are not easily accessible to the message of God's grace.'[51]

What was required, associationists believed, was government assistance for African enterprise. Members pleaded for reforms that would widen the scope for local initiative rather than condemning the colonial economic system outright. They made requests for government aid in growing cotton at Karonga and Mzimba and for the restriction of Indian retail trading activities, so that African traders (some of whom possessed up to £300 of capital in 1929, according to the WNNA) would not be undercut. The Mombera Association, responsive to anxiety concerning the prices paid for Ngoni cattle, asked for dipping tanks and for the assistance of a veterinary surgeon. The North Nyasa Association, anxious to exploit the agricultural potential of the district, sought government loans for 'progressive' independent farmers.[52] Implicit in their requests was the

[50] Minutes of MoNA, 26–7 September 1921, MNA S1/210/20; 12 June 1924; 26 May 1926, MNA S1/1365/24

[51] Minutes of WNNA 1–2 May 1929; Y. Z. Mwasi to DC Chinteche, 29 October 1927, S1/2065/19

[52] Minutes of WNNA, 1–2 May 1929, ibid.; Minutes of MoNA 23–31 July 1922, MNA S1/210/20; Minutes of NNNA forwarded to Government, 19 March 1924, MNA S1/1481/19

belief that, once abuses had been demonstrated, they would be speedily rectified and that the road to prosperity lay in the expansion of the export market. The government, it was assumed, should play a dynamic, interventionalist role in stimulating economic advance, but the key agents of change would be small capitalist traders and farmers rather than state owned public concerns.

For the majority of members, the key to economic improvement lay in the type of education available. Most leading Livingstonia missionaries – Fraser, as well as Laws – were sympathetic towards the associations, which they regarded as 'schools of training in national self-responsibility', preparing the ground for the grant of substantial rights of franchise to Africans in the not too distant future.[53] In their turn members reciprocated the sympathy by defending Protestant missions against the criticisms of the Commission of Enquiry into the Chilembwe Rising in 1919 and subsequently by sending messages of goodwill to missionaries on their retirement.[54] Nevertheless, the inadequacies of Livingstonia's educational system were increasingly plainly spelt out. In the early 1920s, the main demand was for government financial support in extending the mission's educational network. But by 1929, criticism of mission policies was being openly and vigorously expressed. Writing on behalf of the substantial schoolmaster body, Mwasi accused the mission, of which he was still a prominent member, of failing to provide the material conditions which teachers had come to expect. Ever since the 1870s, he claimed, the village schools had been organised '*on the mendicant system, begging mats, food, lodging and what else from the villagers*'. Villagers were now discontented at being forced to provide food supplies for the teachers; the latter were demoralised by the failure of the mission to provide them with 'model houses', which would set an example to the rest of the village. Earlier in the 1920s, J. R. Martin, the missionary at Bandawe, had argued that teachers should not expect to receive better food and better housing than other villagers. To Mwasi, however, this attitude 'degrades ethical worth of his native teachers and consequently stirs no ideals in the hearts of scholars or villagers to regard them as teachers of good things'. Schools, he claimed, had been closed at the whim of an individual missionary; in

[53] Fraser, *New Africa*, 162. Laws's attitude is summarised in his letter to the acting chief secretary, Zomba, 12 January 1920: 'Full electoral native franchise and native members of the Legislative Assembly are a long way off yet, but this has to come in the future, and the sooner the ABC of such responsibilities are learnt the safer for the country.'

[54] Minutes of NNNA, June 1919, MNA s1/1481/19; Chinula to Ashcroft 6 August 1925, NLS 7888; Y. M. Chibambo to Dr and Mrs Elmslie, 13 June 1924, MNA s1/1365/24

1929, Dr Burnett had closed Kakwewa school 'because the villagers failed to entertain him hospitably'. Children of suspended church members had been refused higher training: the son of Hezekaiah Mwanza, the head *capitao* at Chinteche, had been denied entrance to the Institution for this reason.[55] 'School,' the Association recognised, 'is necessary for any human being', but 'ecclesiastics stand in the way of people's real progress'.[56]

The quality of mission education was also the target of criticism. Most associationists would have agreed with the member from Blantyre, who claimed in 1930 that what was wanted was 'an education which will give us initiative and rouse our inertia to stand and venture on our own as carpenters, builders, traders etc.'.[57] By concentrating on primary education up to Standard IV, the mission had failed to meet the aspirations of the new intelligentsia. 'In the Northern Province the people are restless in their demand for better education', Levi Mumba and I. M. Jere, chairman and secretary of the Representative Committee of the Northern Province Native Association claimed in a memorandum written in January 1932. They reiterated an earlier complaint from the West Nyasa Association (made in January 1930) that 'almost all . . . village schools are run by mere youths, incapable of religious knowledge and school-management', and protested that despite the institution of the government Education Department, the mission had been 'tied down to Std IV without substituting something else for those classes that had been cut off'. Their conclusion was that the government should open 'a properly equipped and efficient High School', independent of the mission and open to all, to take pupils from Standards V to VIII. As a makeshift, they recommended that the Overtoun Institution should be taken over by the government for this purpose, 'the at one time open door of the mission school' having now been closed.[58]

What is the significance of the native associations? In a pioneer article, van Velsen has pointed to the continuing pressure which they exerted on the central government and to the extent to which they transcended tribal particularisms.[59] Though each association was based within a separate communal area, they shared identical constitutions drawn up by

[55] Y. Z. Mwasi to DC Chinteche, 29 October 1929, MNA S1/2065/19

[56] Minutes of WNNA, 1–2 May 1929, ibid.

[57] Paper read before the Blantyre Native Association, 18 January 1930, MNA S1/3263/23

[58] Memorandum on Native Education from the Representative Committee for Northern Province Native Associations, 25 January 1932, Liv. Corr. Box 2

[59] van Velsen, 'Pressure Groups'

Levi Mumba and represented substantially similar economic interests. All northern associations made considerable efforts to keep the others informed of their actions, and as early as 1924, Levi Mumba expressed the hope 'that before long these associations may assume national importance by amalgamation under a central body'.[60] Both in their central focus and in their supra-tribalism they looked forward to the advent of the nationalist party.

What they lacked was the kind of machinery that could turn anguished pleading into concrete action. Despite the radical tone adopted by the West Nyasa Association in the late 1920s, when Y. Z. Mwasi was secretary, the associations shrank from direct confrontation with the government and never queried the legality of colonial rule. Up to the early 1930s, their requests were carefully scrutinised by the Governor and the Chief Secretary; but whereas abuses, such as the practice of forcing men to cut grass outside the Provincial Commissioner's office, while awaiting the issue of passes, were occasionally rectified, major demands went largely unheeded. Government officials, faced by requests for the improvement of African education, took refuge in platitudes concerning the need for patience, and the time required to accomplish reforms. Apart from the provision of strychnine for the destruction of wild beasts and of a dipping tank in Ngoniland, no action was taken to widen economic opportunity. The Overtoun Institution remained in mission hands; loans were not given to capitalist farmers; Indian merchants continued to trade in Ngoniland.

In his analysis of the emergence of modern African nations, John Lonsdale has urged historians to be wary of identifying associations as the precursors of the political parties of the 1950s. Such bodies, composed of 'Africans already represented on the official missionary hierarchies' were essentially transitory phenomena, he argues, doomed in the rural areas to be swept away at a time of more popular political involvement.[61] Though the warning is justified, it can be modified for Malawi in two different ways. In the first place, while it is true that tactics were transformed in the 1950s, aspirations towards improvement continued to be influential. Many of the educational and economic policies pursued by the independent Malawi government of the 1960s can be shown to have had antecedents in the demands of associationists some 30 years earlier.[62]

[60] Levi Mumba, 'Native Associations in Nyasaland'

[61] John Lonsdale, 'The Emergence of African Nations: A Historiographical Analysis', *African Affairs*, vol. 67, 1968

[62] See M. L. Chanock, 'Ambiguities in the Malawian political tradition', *African Affairs*, 74, 1975

Secondly, the contemporary influence of the associationists was more deeply rooted than might be expected. Their leaders were equally active in two other forms of organisation, each more broadly based than the associations, and each essentially complementing the other. Independent churches and native authority courts were both vehicles for the politics of privilege.

Independent churches

The emergence from the late 1920s of a new group of independent churches in northern Malawi marks one of the first attempts by Africans between the wars to take the process of improvement into their own hands. Some churches founded in the north during this period reflected their members' rejection of Livingstonia's Eurocentric code of morality. The Last Church of God and His Christ, founded by the Tonga evangelist, Jordon Msumwa in 1925, appealed to suspended members of the Scottish church through its forceful defence of polygamy and of other long established customs.[63]

Other churches drew support, as Watch Tower had done, from members of the community who felt themselves to be excluded from the benefits gained by their neighbours in contact with the mission. The Seventh-day Adventists in the Karonga district received temporary encouragement in 1934 from the Kyungu and his sub-chiefs. These Ngonde leaders resented the control by Henga teachers, using the Henga language, of Livingstonia's schools in that region and disliked the claims made by the missionary, Cullen Young on their behalf, in his *History of the Tumbuka–Kamanga*, which had been published only two years previously.[64]

Most new churches, however, reflected these tendencies to only a minor extent. Between 1928 and 1934, four major secessions took place from Livingstonia, three of them led by long-established church leaders. In 1928 the African National Church was founded at Deep Bay and Florence Bay by five middle-grade Institution graduates, three of them school teachers, one, Simon Mkandawire, a printer, and the fifth, Paddy Nyasulu, a mission storekeeper, subsequently a government clerk. The church drew its members initially, according to a government report, from 'the intelligentsia of the Livingstonia Mission who had been excommunicated for polygamy'. In 1930 the schoolteacher, Isaac Mkhondowe, extended its activities from the north into the West Nyasa district, and in the same year Nyasulu established an outpost in Nyakyusa country in Tanganyika.

[63] Resident Chinteche to PC Northern Province, 28 April 1925, MNA NN1/20/3

[64] Annual Report by DC Karonga, 1931, 1932, 1934 MNA NNK2/12

Branches were also opened in the Mzimba district by Simon Mkandawire and at Lilongwe by Robert Sambo, formerly a member of the Industrial and Commercial Workers Union of South Africa, who had been deported from Southern Rhodesia in 1927 on account of his union activities. By 1940, the church boasted over 3000 members in Malawi, almost all of them living within Livingstonia's sphere.[65]

The establishment of the ANC was followed by the secession of three of Livingstonia's most experienced pastors. Yaphet Mkandawire, after fourteen years' blameless service as pastor in the Karonga area, was accused in July 1932 of taking *phemba* medicine as a safeguard against poisoning. The committee appointed to investigate the affair upheld the allegation and, on 24 October, Mkandawire was deposed from office and suspended from church membership, despite the plea from a minority in Presbytery that he should be reprimanded and forgiven. Less than a month later he established the African Reformed Presbyterian Church in the Deep Bay area and applied to the DC at Karonga for official recognition.[66]

Ten months later, in September 1933, Y. Z. Mwasi, the first African Moderator of Presbytery, also turned his back on the mission. In July 1932, elders from the Sanga and Lumphasa congregations complained to the Presbytery that their pastor had over-reached his powers by refusing to celebrate the Lord's Supper in one district and by forbidding certain elders to preach in another. Mwasi replied that the complaints were invalid as they had not been accompanied by the minutes of the respective Kirk Sessions, but nevertheless the Presbytery decided to look into the affair, and subsequently reprimanded the minister. Mwasi then protested against what he regarded as the unlawful proceedings of the Presbytery and announced his intention of resigning if satisfactory answers were not given to five questions he had framed concerning the relations between Kirk Sessions and Presbytery and between elders and their minister. The clerk of Presbytery played for time by conveniently 'losing' the questions, but Mwasi remained insistent, and on 26 September publicly withdrew from the CCAP, having previously read a paper to the Presbytery explaining his reasons for doing so.[67] Several hundred members of his flock went

65 'Historical Survey of Native Controlled Missions . . . ', MNA 1A/1341; C. T. Mwalwanda, 'The African National Church', University of Malawi research paper. For further information on the ANC see T. O. Ranger, *The African Churches of Tanzania*, Historical Association of Tanzania, Paper No. 5, and R. J. Macdonald 'Religious Independency as a means of social advance in Northern Nyasaland in the 1930s', *Journal of Religion in Africa*, Vol. III, 1970

66 Livingstonia Presbytery minutes, entries for 28 July and 24 October 1932

67 Livingstonia Presbytery minutes, entries for 27–8 July 1932, 26 September

out with him to form the nucleus of the Black Man's Church of God which is in Tongaland, based at Ching'oma, some ten miles north of Chinteche. The Black Man's Church claimed possession of ten churches belonging to the CCAP, but built through the self-help of its members and also of the manse in which Mwasi had previously lived. But, after a protracted legal battle, they were deemed to be Livingstonia's property and were handed back to the mission.[68]

Meanwhile, in July 1934, the fourth secession took place. Charles Chinula joined the teaching staff of the mission in 1908 and in 1923 was singled out as 'the best teacher' in the Loudon area.[69] He was ordained pastor in 1925, but was convicted of adultery in November 1930 and was suspended from membership of the church. During the next four years he worked devotedly to demonstrate his sincere repentance, but his attempts to gain readmittance to the pastorate met with repeated failure. Grieved at what he believed to be a lack of Christian charity within the Presbytery, he founded his own church the Eklesia Lanangwa (Church of Freedom) in 1934, at the village of Jenda (or Bethlehem) on the Kasungu–Mzimba road. It was upon the transforming power of repentance and Christ's infinite forgiveness that the main theological tenets of the Eklesia Lanangwa were subsequently based.[70]

A year later, in May 1935, the three pastors joined forces in what they called the *Mpingo wa Afipa wa Africa* (the Black Man's Church in Africa), a body containing 50 elders in 1935 and over 2000 members. In the next decade, the Black Man's Church remained divided into three clearly defined sections, each with its virtually autonomous local leader. By 1940, it had acquired some 3500 adherents.[71]

These new churches differed in a number of important respects from those founded in the first wave of independency in Malawi from 1909 and their descendants, the various branches of Watch Tower, the Messenger of the Covenant Church, and the Last Church of God. Several of the latter had Livingstonia-trained leaders who included in their pro-

1933; Y. Z. Mwasi, 'My Essential and Paramount Reasons for Working Independently', 12 July 1933

68 DC Chinteche to PC Northern Province, 8 and 23 March 1935, MNA NNI/22/1; 'Historical Survey of Native Controlled Missions' MNA IA/1341

69 C. Stuart to Laws, 22 May 1923, Liv. Corr. Box 7

70 Livingstonia Presbytery minutes entry for 20 August 1931, 'Historical Survey' personal communication from Rev. Charles Chinula, Loudon, 25 July 1964.

71 'Historical Survey'; C. C. Chinula to DC Mzimba, 22 May, 1935, MNA NNI/20/4

grammes demands for free universal education. But in the rural areas they tended towards millenarianism and a consequent rejection of worldly authority that brought them into conflict with members of the chiefly hierarchy and precluded their participation in directly political concerns. Watch Tower adherents were conspicuous by their absence from meetings of native associations, whose members, according to Laws, were largely 'opposed to the attitude of the society'.[72]

By contrast, the new church leaders were intimately involved in the association's work. Mwasi, founder of the Black Man's Church was for several years the secretary and, according to the local District Commissioner in 1931, the dominant influence in the West Nyasa Association.[73] There can be little doubt that he was responsible for the critical tone of the association minutes in the late 1920s, as exemplified by his eloquent complaint that: 'whatever pays which does not answer, better food, better clothing, better home, better education, more leisure, more ease, and more pleasure in life to the workers, are not just pays at all'.[74] S. K. Mkandawire played an active part in the affairs of the North Nyasa Association; Charles Chinula for several years was Secretary and leading spirit of the body at Mombera's, and Levi Mumba, the leading coordinator of the associations, gave valuable advice on the constitution of the African National Church, though his work in Zomba prevented him from being an active participant.

The circumstances which led these men to break from a church to which they had given the greater part of their lives are too complex and varied to be susceptible to a single explanation. Friction over questions of the transfer of authority undoubtedly occurred in the 1920s and early 1930s. But, while it is noteworthy that Mwasi gave as one reason for his secession the overpowering influence of the European missionaries, this factor alone can hardly explain the timing.[75] Mwasi was involved in fierce controversies with individual missionaries from as early as 1915, when the Resident at Chinteche warned that 'a man of his temperament might be a source of unrest or possible danger if he should hereafter sever his connection with the Mission and begin independent preaching among the local natives'.[76] During the 1920s, however, Laws's hope that 'a gradual devolution of work, responsibility and authority [should] take place from the European

[72] Laws to acting CS Zomba, 12 January 1920, MNA S1/2065/19

[73] 'As I have stated on other occasions this is a *one man* Association – Revd. Yesiah Mwase' Annual Report for the West Nyasa District 1931, MNA NNC3/1/4

[74] Y. Z. Mwasi to DC Chinteche, 29 October 1929, MNA S1/2065/19

[75] 'My . . . Reasons for Working Independently'

[76] H. N. Duff to Laws, 26 March 1915, Liv. Corr.

to the native', was slowly being put into effect.[77] Laws himself clashed with Mwasi at a Presbytery meeting in 1927 on the question of whether it was wise to appoint an African as General Treasurer to supervise the financial arrangements of the church. But it is significant that Mwasi's motion carried the day and that an African treasurer was subsequently appointed.[78] Friction in relations was not thereby resolved – Mwasi blamed Macalpine for the reprimand he received in 1932 – but increasing weight, it is clear, was beginning to be given to the opinion of African pastors.

Similarly, while differences over the approach to religious institutions and beliefs were still an endemic source of tension, they too should not be over-emphasised in explaining why the break took place. It is true that the African National Church permitted polygamy and specifically referred in its constitution to the 'need [in Africa] of a Church that would correspond to her God-given customs and manners',[79] but the others all followed Presbyterian codes of worship. Chinula, from 1908 at least, had disapproved of the prohibition on dancing. Mwasi was a fervent evangelical preacher whose effect upon a congregation could be cataclysmic.[80] Yet neither, in practice, found great difficulty in adhering to their beliefs within the framework provided by Livingstonia until the crises of the 1930s provoked them into independent action.

Three new factors, I suggest, throw light on the character and timing of the break. Firstly there is evidence to suggest that the historical traditions and theological foundations of Livingstonia predisposed her members to independent action. Barrett has demonstrated that unrestricted access to the Bible, particularly when it has been translated and published in the local vernacular, can be of great importance in providing Africans with an independent source of authority with which to challenge and contradict missionary teaching.[81] It is therefore highly significant that Laws made study of the scriptures the central activity in all mission schools and that translations in Tumbuka at least of substantial portions of the Bible were widely available from 1911. Furthermore, whereas the concept of the single indivisible church as the only true source of salvation

[77] Laws to Lyell Grant, 2 July 1915, Hetherwick Papers

[78] Livingstonia Presbytery minutes, entry for 18 July 1927

[79] Copy in DC Karonga to CS Zomba, 21 March 1929, MNA NN1/20/3

[80] Personal communications from Rev. Charles Chinula and from Mr E. A. Muwamba. According to Mr Muwamba, Mwase based his highly emotional style of preaching on that of Dr Charles Inwood whose evangelical tour of northern Malawi in 1910 made a great impression on Europeans and Africans alike.

[81] David B. Barrett, *Schism and Renewal in Africa*, Nairobi, 1968, 127–34

was an essential feature of Roman Catholic and High Anglican teaching, the primacy of individual conscience was repeatedly emphasised by the Free Church missionaries. Men like Mwasi, Chinula and Mkandawire had been brought up on stories of Scottish covenantors and on sermons dealing with such topics as 'Jeroboam's Established Church . . . and the Disruption of Priests and Levites who went out of their livings in Israel rather than officiate in Jeroboam's Church'.[82] Mwasi, in explaining his reasons for working independently, utilised his theological training to good purpose in order to enlist John Knox's Scots Confession of 1560 in his support, and to enrol Christ, Moses, Luther, Zwingli and Calvin as fellow 'agitators' whose 'just cause' had triumphed, despite the 'various and painful measures' taken against them by 'the Jews, Egyptians and Popish church'.[83] Charles Chinula went one stage further by paying formal tribute to the 'Livingstonia Mission which trained me', in asserting his right to seek God 'according to the liberty of my own conscience by sticking myself to the Holy Bible, which I strongly believe to be the supreme rule in all spiritual matters'.[84]

Developments within the CCAP also facilitated the emergence of independent churches. As long as they remained assistant ministers, subject to the directions of a European missionary, African pastors had little opportunity of building up a personal following. From 1916, however, an increasing number were called to take charge of specific congregations, and in some cases they were able to attract a core of followers, whose loyalty was to their minister as an individual rather than to the Presbytery. Despite his dispute with certain elders, Mwasi was thus able to carry the greater part of the Sanga and Lumphasa congregations with him, when he left the CCAP in 1933, and Chinula likewise was followed by personal supporters.[85]

At the same time, the declining financial involvement of the overseas mission in the running of the church resulted in the increasing self-sufficiency of individual congregations. Most congregations in Ngoniland and the Bandawe district were frequently in arrears with their contri-

[82] James Henderson to Margaret Davidson, 25 April 1897 in Ballantyne and Shepherd, *Forerunners of Modern Malawi*, 234. Henderson was clothing the Old Testament story in the imagery of the famous 1843 Disruption in the Church of Scotland which resulted in the creation of the Free Church

[83] 'My . . . Reasons for Working Independently'

[84] Chinula to DC Mzimba, 5 July 1934, MNA NN1/20/4

[85] The number of communicants attached to the Sanga and Lumphasa congregations of the CCAP appears to have dropped from 1147 in 1927 (the last year for which Mwase supplied statistics) to 397 at the end of 1933 after the founding of the Blackman's Church

butions to the central fund. Nevertheless, during the 1920s, they succeeded in paying the stipends of their ministers and evangelists, in building churches with free labour, and in supplying their pastors with gowns and Communion vessels.[86] It is not surprising, therefore, that Mwasi should have felt himself able to reject the 'foreign denomination' in favour of 'the church of the locality'.[87] He and his supporters regarded his manse and the thatched school–churches in the neighbourhood as their own, for the good reason that they had been responsible for building them. By the same token, Chinula took possession of the school–church at Jenda and was only persuaded to leave it in October 1934 through Dr Turner's personal intervention and 'very wise' diplomacy.[88]

A second factor, which may have contributed to the re-emergence of independency in this period, was a growing disillusionment with some aspects of the Christian message, as propagated by European missionaries. Christianity, so Ranger has argued, was widely welcomed in the late nineteenth century, at least partly in the belief that, following the adoption of a new religion, witchcraft would disappear, divisions within and between African societies would be vanquished and evil would be driven out.[89] In practice, however, as he notes, orthodox missions like Livingstonia, for all their influence were remarkably unsuccessful in dealing with the central moral problems that confronted them. Faced by beliefs concerning the causes of misfortune, which they frequently failed to comprehend, Scots missionaries took refuge in general denunciations of belief in the existence of witchcraft, which were of little consolation to those who were convinced they were caught in its grasp. Individual assaults on witchfinders occasionally took place. In 1902, Fraser responded to the challenge of the Kayayi cult in Ngoniland, whose agents sold a medicine said to 'make man proof against curses and death' by setting a Christian headman onto them and having them severely thrashed.[90] Eighteen years later, in May 1920, he led a campaign against sorcery at Loudon, in which he called upon witchdoctors to give up their instruments and elicited a dramatic response.[91] But such campaigns were not

[86] Macalpine to Laws, 19 February 1927, Liv. Corr. Box 9; Livingstonia Presbytery minutes entry for 25 July 1932

[87] 'My . . . Reasons for Working Independently'

[88] Chinula to DC Mzimba, 2 October 1934; Turner to DC Mzimba, n.d. MNA NNM1/12/2

[89] Ranger, *African Churches*, 6–11

[90] *FCSMR*, October 1902, 450

[91] Donald Fraser, 'Exit the Witch Doctors', ibid., October 1930, 180–1; A. R. Fraser, *Donald Fraser*, 193–5. The point has been made elsewhere that the 152 'witch-doctors' who gave up their implements were probably not

repeated and thus had little lasting impact. Few Free Church converts appear to have accepted in practice the code of Christian conduct, relating to the use of protective charms, laid down by a Commission of Presbytery in August 1915.[92] Many may have experienced a widening of the gulf between belief and practice in the early 1930s, as economic tensions, stemming from the world depression, exacerbated social tensions inherent in village life.[93] Kirk session reports to the Livingstonia Presbytery provide illuminating glimpses of the state of affairs. Many Christians in the Karonga district had consulted a witch-finder at Wenya, it was reported in 1926. The use of protective amulets and charms was widely practised, even by elders, at Loudon and Elangeni. In 1932 the pastor Y. M. Mkandawire followed the example of many of the humbler members of his flock by taking *Phemba* medicine in the hope that it would protect him from being poisoned. In the same year a prophet, 'Mzimu', who forbade contributions being made to the Church so impressed the evangelist George Nyasuru that he recommended the prophet to his fellow Christians as being sent by God to work his miracles.

The extent of the crisis was vividly demonstrated in 1933 by the success of the witchcraft-eradication movement, *Mchape*, which swept through Malawi from its point of origins in the Mlanje area before being carried north into Zambia and Tanganyika. From the available evidence, it seems likely that *Mchape* vendors made less impact in the Livingstonia sphere than they did in the area worked by the UMCA, perhaps because Kamwana's Watch Tower disciples had previously functioned in the north as witchcraft eradicators.[94] Nevertheless, it is clear that many Presbyterians did drink the medicine, in the hope that *Mchape* would succeed where Christianity had failed, in freeing them from the scourge of evil. In the Bandawe district, the first *Mchape* vendor arrived from Chiradzulu on 8 June 1933 and was received with such enthusiasm that, by late July, at least 365 church members and catechumens had been suspended for agreeing to drink the medicine.[95] Chimtunga, the Ngoni paramount,

diviners but ordinary people seeking to exchange one form of protection for another. Andrew Roberts, *The Lumpa Church of Alice Lenshina*, Lusaka, 1972, 19

92 Livingstonia Presbytery minutes entry for 26 August 1915

93 This argument is examined briefly in T. O. Ranger, 'Mchape and the Study of Witchcraft Eradication', Conference on the History of Central Africa Religious Systems, Lusaka, 1972

94 An excellent study that implicitly makes the contrast is: Richard G. Stuart, 'Mchape and the UMCA, 1933', ibid.

95 DC Chinteche to DC Mzimba, 8 June 1933, MNA NNM1/17/2; Livingstonia Presbytery minutes, entry for 20 July 1933

invited the vendors to the Mzimba district, where they were said by the local missionary in August to be 'causing terrible trouble' and intimidating other chiefs.[96] African Christians, so one Institution graduate noted, were singled out by the vendors as hypocrites, on the grounds that 'they are the people who are hiding in this religion and are great wizards more than anyone else'.[97] Edward Shaba, who witnessed a *Mchape* ceremony at Chief Samuel Jere's village, estimated that some 2000 people attended, many of them Free Church members. The leading official informed his audience that 'What we are here for is to purge the country and save the people, by casting away all evils which have been in force for many years.' Everyone present was examined, and those who were declared to be witches were given medicine to cleanse them from their sin. A sense of communal purity was thus created, though inevitably it failed to last for long.[98]

How far the new churches provided alternative answers to the continuing problems of insecurity and division is a difficult question to answer. In some senses, the Black Man's Church and the ANC were as fundamentally opposed to *Mchape* as they were to the Watch Tower movement, which experienced something of a resurgence in Malawi in the 1920s, following the relaxation of government controls. No attempt was made in these churches to detect witches, or to provide new types of protection against sorcery. No mass-cleansing ceremonies were performed.

At the same time, it is possible to detect within these churches an impatience with the effect of mission Christianity, which may reflect the same sense of disillusionment upon which *Mchape* fed. It can hardly be a coincidence that Y. Z. Mwasi reached the conclusion that 'Mission shall never be corporated into the lifeblood of the native church . . . shall never uproot evil customs of the native lands and in short shall never conquer for Christ', in July 1933, when *Mchape* vendors were still working in his district.[99] The ANC, in legalising polygamy and beer drinking, likewise argued that 'The commission of the Christian church to Africa was to import Christ and education in such a way as to fit in with the manners and customs of the people and not that it should impose on the Africans,

96 Duncan Campbell to DC Mzimba, 29 August 1933, MNA NNM1/17/2

97 Edward Shaba 'A Brief History of the Proposed Visit of the "Mchape" People', Sumbawanga, Ufipa, 3 March 1934. Dar es Salaam 77/18/15NA. I owe this reference to Professor T. O. Ranger

98 Shaba, 'A Brief History'

99 Mwasi 'My Reasons . . . for Working independently'

the unnecessary and impracticable methods of European countries.'[100]

In its constitution, probably composed by Levi Mumba, the ANC criticised the divisive consequences of mission Christianity and proclaimed an alternative approach, based on a fundamental respect for African traditional beliefs, which would have the effect of removing divisions by Christianising the community as a whole:

> The aim of this Church is the uplifting of the African en masse taking in its rise the old people which are at present being left out by the religions of the north and its civilization as well as winning those who are considered bad because of polygamy and drink and are refused any latent qualities for doing good any more.[101]

In the general confession he composed for the church, Robert Sambo admitted the existence of a sickness within African society: 'We have done wrong in our village, Father. Witchcraft, adultery, and hatred, all these are in our village . . . Our chiefs do not love one another in their hearts.' His cure was to adapt the liberating message of Christ to a code of conduct sanctioned in the precolonial past. 'A new commandment you have given unto us all to love one another as in Heaven, where there is no quarrelling . . . We have forgotten all the laws you gave to our forefathers . . . Turn us to a life of new marriages, according to the ways of our forefathers.'[102]

A respect for African institutions, however, did not involve a rejection of modern techniques. Leaders of the ANC and of other churches were concerned with re-establishing social unity, but they were also enthusiastic improvers, who followed 'European methods' in organising their churches, sent their own children to school at Livingstonia and at Lovedale, and successfully participated in capitalist farming.[103] During the

[100] Copy of constitution of the ANC enclosed in Simon Mkandawire and others to DC Karonga, 11 January 1929, MNA NNI/20/3

[101] ibid. For Levi Mumba's connections with the ANC see DC Karonga to CS Zomba, 21 March 1929, NNI/20/3 and C. T. Mwalwanda, 'The African National Church'

[102] The General Confession is quoted in full in Wilson, *Communal Rituals*, 194–5. My analysis of the significance of the ANC closely follows Ranger, *African Churches*, though I believe that an ambiguity existed within the ANC that Ranger ignores. Its leaders were themselves representatives of the elite, the creation of which the Church by implication deplored. Their solution to contemporary problems was a self-conscious and intellectual one of greater attraction to other graduate Malawians than to the majority of Malawi villagers

[103] Constitution of ANC, MNA NNI/2013; DC Karonga to Commissioner of Police, Zomba, 28 January 1937, MNA NNI/20/4; Wilson, *Communal Rituals*, 195

1920s, they had witnessed what they believed to be a reduction in the educational and economic facilities made available in the Northern Province and, by the early 1930s, they had become sufficiently disillusioned to seek to organise their own schools, in an attempt to create the opportunities which Livingstonia now failed to provide. The mission had taught him the science of 'working independently', Mwasi complained in 1933, for so few resources were reaching his parish that he was compelled to tend his congregation 'without a help of a newspaper, medicine, or teacher from the mission'. 'Children around me grow wild yearly, my own children go to Bandawi area in search of central school.'[104]

The answer, Y. M. Mkandawire argued in January 1934, was the establishment of African-controlled 'normal' schools, open to all, irrespective of religious beliefs. Such schools, he hoped, would provide the facilities to make each pupil 'independent in his own living', by teaching children 'duties which they can do to support themselves and others without leaving their own country such as ... carpentry ... fishing ... and building'.[105]

Even more important was formal academic instruction. In August 1934, Y. Z. Mwasi unveiled his plans for a Nyasaland Black man's Educational Society, an African response to Laws's earlier initiative. The society was to collect funds from migrants in Northern and Southern Rhodesia as well as from workers in Malawi. Its expressed aim, perhaps influenced by Marcus Garvey's *Negro World*, to which Mwasi subscribed,[106] was 'to improve and develop the impoverished condition of the black man, religiously, morally, economically, physically and intellectually by starting a *Purely Native Controlled high school or college*'. The society, Mwasi wrote, was 'neither denominational or particular to a single tribe in Nyasaland, but is national and coextensive with the Black man as a race within and outside Nyasaland'. It would collect funds not only for the college, but for the training of teachers and the building of hospitals. Despite its pan-African pretensions, it would be securely based in Tongaland, with Chief Marenga as general chairman, and Mwasi himself as director.[107]

104 Mwasi 'My Reasons ... for Working independently'

105 Y. M. Mkandawire to DC Karonga, 13 January 1934, MNA NNK1/2/7

106 Ass. Supt. i.c. CID to Resident Kota Kota, 4 September 1926, MNA NN1/20/3

107 Y. Z. Mwasi, 'Submission of an Application to Government for adoption and sanction of the Scheme entitled: "The Nyasaland Blackman's Educational Society"', 18 August 1934 enclosed in DC Chinteche to PC Northern Province, 7 November 1934, MNA NN1/20/4

The failure of these schemes, set against the hopes of their creators, does much to explain the limited impact of independent churches in Malawi. Independent schools could flourish in areas like eastern Nigeria, or even the highlands of Kenya, where cash-crop farmers provided financial assistance, but in the absence of such an economy funds were in short supply. With the exception of Watch Tower none of the northern sects enjoyed financial support from any international body.[108] Apart from certain village schools, run by the African Reformed Presbyterian Church, and the ANC in the North Nyasa district, none of the schools they founded was deemed to be of sufficient quality to be eligible for a government grant in aid. Y. Z. Mwasi attempted to enlist the support of Tonga migrants in Northern Rhodesia at meetings held at Livingstone, Ndola and Broken Hill in May and June 1934,[109] but, though Tonga workers in Katanga had successfully organised a similar scheme of self-help on more modest lines from 1931, the obstacles placed in Mwasi's path proved insuperable.[110] John Moffat in Northern Rhodesia, warned his African friends against becoming involved with Mwasi's society; the Tonga Tribal Council of Chiefs reacted with hostility; the Director of Education in Nyasaland expressed disapproval.[111] In May 1935, Chinula optimistically described the Blackman's Society as the educational extension of the *Mpingo wa Afipa*, a body whose function was 'to collect money for a college or two for the Nyasalanders'.[112] But the harsh truth was that, in face of government opposition, little money was collected and the colleges remained stillborn. Mwasi was forced to recruit his teachers from among pupils at the Livingstonia school at Sanga, thus arousing the opposition of Chief Mankhambira, who accused him in March 1935 of having 'destroyed my plans in education' and Chinula

[108] An exception to this generalisation was the branch of the African Methodist Episcopal Church founded by Rev. Hanoc Phiri near Kasungu in 1924. Phiri, the uncle of Dr Banda, was a graduate from the Overtoun Institution who left Nyasaland for the Transvaal in 1916 and returned as an ordained minister in the AMEC in 1924. Responding to the hunger for English which the Dutch Reformed Church mission was reluctant to teach, he built up a comparatively successful network of schools with some financial assistance from his South African headquarters 'Historical Survey of Native Controlled Missions...' MNA IA/1341

[109] Act. Officer i.c. CID Livingstone to CS, Livingstone, 21 February 1935 (copy) MNA NN1/20/4

[110] Church of Scotland Foreign Missions Report for 1931, 85

[111] DC Chinteche to PC Northern Province, 7 November 1934; CS Zomba to PC Northern Province, 29 January 1935, MNA NN1/20/4; personal communication from Mr E. A. Muwamba

[112] Chinula to DC Mzimba, 22 May 1935, MNA NN1/20/4

likewise was unable to attract competent colleagues.[113] In 1937 the Superintendent of Education for the Northern Province described Mwasi as 'an old man of boundles ambition . . . still determined to carry out his elaborate scheme for the education and betterment of the native peoples of Nyasaland'. He controlled several vernacular schools in the vicinity of the station, but had no certificated teachers, and the Superintendent believed, 'that there is little likelihood of any of his high flown schemes coming to fruition at this stage of his career'.[114]

Elected chairman of the newly-formed Council of the Blackman's Church in December 1939, he made a final plea for government assistance, only to be rebuffed once more. Unmoved by Mwasi's claim that the schools were 'an effort of the native community in representation', the Superintendent recommended on 24 June 1940 that no further support should be given to any branch of the Church.[115] If changes were to be made in the educational system, they would have to come through political action rather than through the efforts of independent schoolmasters.

Local politics

A third type of political organisation was used by the northern-based mission-educated elite at this period. From 1933, increased government attention was given to the various local administrative councils, in an attempt to apply more vigorously the principles of indirect rule. As organs of the chiefs and their councillors, these courts were sometimes regarded as conservative and reactionary. Yet, though their establishment was unrelated to Livingstonia's influence – unlike the native associations and the independent churches – the role of Livingstonia graduates within them was one of considerable importance. Their rise coincided with, and in part caused, the decline of native associations, many of whose members came to transfer their activities from the one type of organisation to the other.

The early political alliance of traditional leaders and new intellectuals has been noted for South Africa by Mary Benson and for Matabeleland and Barotseland by Terence Ranger.[116] In northern Malawi such an alliance arose in part from the high proportion of official leaders who themselves had access to education. As a result of policies pursued at

113 Hearing by Atonga Tribal Council of dispute between Mwasi and Mankhambira, 30 March 1935, MNA NN1/22/1; Atonga Tribal Council minutes, entry for 16 March 1935, MNA NNC5/1/1

114 'Historical Survey . . .' MNA 1A/1341

115 ibid.

116 Mary Benson, *The African Patriots*, London, 1963; T. O. Ranger, 'Nationality and Nationalism: the case of Barotseland', *Journal of the Historical Society of Nigeria*, IV (1968).

Livingstonia, all five principal headmen appointed in Tongaland in 1917 had been educated by the Scottish missionaries, and three had taught in their schools; six out of seven principal headmen in Ngoniland in the 1930s had a similar background and one was still an active teacher.[117] In part too, it developed from the desire of chiefs, educated or not, to involve mission teachers prominently within their councils. The District Commissioner at Karonga believed that 'almost every highly educated native of the Livingstonia mission is politically minded and race conscious.'[118] But despite his disapproval, he was unable to prevent the Tumbuka Native Authority, Chikulamayembe, from turning more frequently for advice to the Reverend Edward Bote Manda than he did to his tribal elders. Manda, it was claimed in the 1930s, often acted as spokesman for Chikulamayembe and liaised between him and the District Commissioner.[119] Similarly the Tonga Tribal Council of Chiefs, set up by the government in 1932 partly as a means of reducing the influence of mission teachers, co-opted educated representatives to their meetings in 1938 drawn from a list of 14 men all educated at Livingstonia and including eleven employed by the Presbyterian church.[120] And the same trend was noted in Ngoniland, where the composition of the Jere (or Mbelwa's) council was so similar to that of the Mombera Native Association, that the District Commissioner was forced to ask at a meeting in 1936, which body was in session. Chinula combined the task of secretary to the association with that of secretary to the council. 'The educated element in the mission teachers and preachers were concentrated in one place' the report of one meeting with the District Commissioner runs 'and it was obvious that their reaction to any proposal was closely watched by Chinula and Mbelwa who conducted the meeting'.[121]

The consequence was that the councils pursued policies on certain matters that were just as vigorously improving as those followed by the native associations. Between 1934 and 1940 they passed measures in favour of compulsory primary education in their districts, petitioned for the establishment of government secondary schools and criticised the low standard of teaching materials that the Livingstonia Mission provided. In

117 West Nyasa District Note-Book; 'Memorandum compiled as an introduction to the subject of the application of Indirect Rule to the Mombera District' DC Mzimba, 21 January 1937, MNA NNM1/13/6

118 DC Karonga to PC Northern Province, 27 January 1931, MNA S1/148/17

119 Annual Report of the PC for the Northern Province, MNA NN2/1/1; Annual Report of the DC for North Nyasa District, 1932, MNA NNK2/12

120 Atonga Tribal Council minutes, entry for 15 January 1938, MNA NNC5/1/1

121 Notes on Proceedings at a meeting of the District Commissioner with the Jere Council, 19–20 March 1936, MNA 1/15/2

1935, the Tonga Tribal Council deplored the failure of the Nyasaland government to open industrial schools, of the same type to those of Domboshawa and of Tjoloto in Southern Rhodesia.[122] A chiefs' meeting at Deep Bay in 1937 complained that only schoolteachers were now admitted to the higher classes of the Overtoun Institution and asked that the government should open a secular school for all children whose parents could afford the fees.[123] The Mbelwa council in 1938 passed a by-law fining parents living within reach of school who kept their children away; though on instructions from the District Commissioner, the rule was not enforced.[124] Only in five villages controlled by Chief Chikulamayembe was a system of compulsory education permitted. And that system, introduced in 1935, proved so expensive and time consuming that neither Livingstonia nor the government were prepared to recommend its extension.[125]

Local administrative courts also provided convenient vehicles for the one serious attempt between the wars to change the structure of government in any fundamental way – the attempt to reduce government interference by seeking to increase African powers at the local level. By the late 1920s mission graduates held considerably greater responsibilities in the sphere of church government than they did in secular affairs. Encouraged by their experience and partial independence in Kirk Sessions and Presbytery, they were quick to seize what opportunities they could within the governmental system. Their problem was that in seeking changes at a local or tribal level, they accentuated differences among themselves which had gone undetected as long as their concern had been with central government reforms. Thus while in some areas demands for administrative change were aimed at recapturing or extending African rights vis-à-vis the colonial regime, in other areas they were concerned principally with safeguarding the interests of certain groups against their immediate neighbours.

One example, notable for the exceptional unity within the society which it evoked, was the successful campaign for the restoration of the northern Ngoni paramountcy. In consequence of the treaty negotiated with Sharpe in September 1904, Ngoni chiefs enjoyed up to the First World War, a measure of self-government unparalleled elsewhere in Malawi. But, after

[122] Atonga Tribal Council minutes, entry for 30 September 1935, MNA NNC5/1/1

[123] Memo. from the Chiefs' Meeting, Deep Bay, 29 April 1937, MNA NNK1/2/3

[124] Minutes of Mbelwa Native Administrative Council, entry for 18 August 1938; DC Mzimba to N.A. M'mbelwa Jere, 3 September 1938, MNA NNM1/15/2

[125] Report of the Education Department for the Nyasaland Protectorate, 1935,

Sharpe's retirement, government officials became increasingly critical of a policy which had the effect of putting the Ngoni rulers 'in a position altogether different from and superior to that of ordinary native headmen'. In 1915, they seized the opportunity presented by the refusal of chiefs to deliver requisitions for labour and foodstuffs to the military authorities to deport the paramount chief, Chimtunga, from his homeland and to declare that henceforth only one paramount power would be recognised in Mombera district 'namely the power of the government represented by the resident'. The other chiefs were reduced to the status of principal headmen and all special privileges guaranteed by Sharpe were withdrawn.[126] In subsequent years, Chimtunga's cause was championed not only by representatives of the royal Jere family, seeking the restoration of the monarchy, but also by Tumbuka councillors, like Charles Chinula, who may have been at least as interested in limiting colonial power. The Mombera Native Association took up the case enthusiastically and, partly through its efforts, Chimtunga was allowed to return to the district in 1920, though only with the authority of a village headman. In 1924, a widespread movement began, aimed at having him reinstated as paramount. When he died in that year, elders and teachers combined to press the claims of his son, Lazaro Jere, a young man who had spent four years as a clerk in the Labour Bureau at Fort Jameson, following his education at the Livingstonia Mission. In 1926 there was an attempt, foiled by the local Resident, to call a meeting of all Ngoni at which he would be publicly proclaimed as paramount, and petitions were sent to the government both by the Jere Council and the Native Association, asking that his position should be recognised. When these were ignored, the Ngoni took matters into their own hands, and from 1930 began to give him the royal salute, 'Bayete', and treat him as de facto paramount; though it was not until the introduction of indirect rule in August 1933 that the government accepted the situation and officially appointed him Native Authority over two thirds of the Mzimba district.[127]

While some Livingstonia graduates worked to restore the power of the Ngoni authority, others used the techniques of education for different and contradictory ends. The emergence of the Chikulamayembe as an inde-

18–21; 1937, 20. For further details see Macdonald, 'African Education', 398–407

126 G. Smith, Gov. of Nyasaland, to S. of S. for Colonies, 17 January 1916; H. L. Duff, CS to Governor Nyasaland, 26 November 1915; message from H. E. the Governor to the Angoni chiefs enclosed in Duff to Resident Mzimba, 6 January 1916, PRO CO 525/66

127 'Memo compiled as introduction . . . of Indirect Rule'. DC Mzimba, 21

pendent Native Authority, recognised as Paramount Chief of the Tumbuka, was to some degree the result of the influence of Livingstonia graduates. At the time of the Ngoni arrival, so Vail has argued, the economic base of the Chikulamayembe had been eroded, and his state had virtually disintegrated.[128] In 1907, however, the British administration officially re-established the state, and during the 1920s and 1930s, Tumbuka graduates, unwittingly assisted by T. Cullen Young, drew inspiration from this action to promulgate a persuasive interpretation of Tumbuka history that glorified the Chikulamayembe chieftainship. Aided by informants like Saulos Nyirenda, a schoolmaster turned telegraphist, whom Young dubbed 'father of History so far as the Northern Province of Nyasaland is concerned', the missionary produced a number of articles and books which emphasised the unity of the Tumbuka and the strength of the Chikulamayembe dynasty.[129] His view received active support from the Livingstonia pastor, Edward Bote Manda, in some respects the most ideologically radical member of the Institution's staff. Manda employed his knowledge of history in an attempt to create 'a united Utumbuka without the stigma of subserviency to Angoni rule'. His aims ran counter to those of the DC at Mzimba, who as late as January 1935, hoped to establish 'the Angoni as the natural tribal chiefs in Utumbuka working in the interests of the heterogeneous people under them'. But, though Manda's powers of persuasion were insufficient to achieve 'the immediate elimination of the Angoni', they did ensure that no radical diminution of Chikulamayembe authority took place with the introduction of indirect rule.[130]

Further south in Tongaland, three groups of Livingstonia graduates made use of different historical traditions to enhance their personal status. A group of teachers headed by the senior schoolmaster, Philemon Chirwa, were the first to achieve results. During the 1920s, these men, most of them members of the underprivileged Phiri clan, had come to resent the dominance in the area between the Dwambazi and Luweya rivers of two powerful principal headmen from the Banda clan, Marenga and Guru. Using his influence as an intermediary with the government, and, it is claimed, his knowledge of Scottish clan history, Philemon Chirwa

January 1937, MNA NNM1/18/6; Minutes of Jere Council entries for 5 and 8 August 1933; W. Y. Turner to DC Mzimba, 19 August 1933, MNA NNM1/15/2

128 Vail, 'Tumbuka History' in Pachai, *Early History of Malawi*, 162.

129 Vail, ibid., 149; Saulos Nyirenda 'History of the Tumbuka–Henga People' trans. and ed. by T. C. Young, *Bantu Studies*, v, 1930; Cullen Young, *Notes on the History of the Tumbuka–Kamanga Peoples*

130 DC Mzimba to W. P. Young, 4 January 1935, Liv. Corr. Box 1

persuaded the Resident in 1932 that, as no chief was senior to another in this area, the principal headmen should be deprived of office, and instead should take part in a council with other, often Phiri chiefs.[131] However, Chirwa's success in influencing the establishment of the Tonga Tribal Council, brought him into conflict with two other groups of Livingstonia graduates, and ultimately led to the destruction of the council. Y. Z. Mwasi, as a representative of the Kapanda Banda, dismissed Chirwa's claim as 'the working of . . . Bolshevism', and turned instead to an alternative historical tradition. He used his extensive knowledge of missionary history and especially of the early contacts of Laws and Livingstone with Tonga chiefs, to advance the claim of Chief Marenga whom he wished to see proclaimed as Paramount Chief in Tongaland.[132] Mwasi in turn met with ferocious criticism, for Isaac Clements, and Ernest Alexander Muwamba of the chiefly family at Chifira advocated the rival claims of their relation, Chief Chiweyu, with a skill that bore witness to their long experience as senior clerks and chairmen of welfare associations, at Lusaka and Ndola. The two Muwambas united with Mwasi in condemning the schoolteachers' argument as a fraudulent one that derived from their membership of 'inferior clans in this district'. But whereas Mwasi related chiefly authority to early missionary connections, they argued that Livingstonia had 'deliberately meddled' with Chiweyu's chieftainship by inflating the importance of Marenga, one of the mission's African staff'.[133]

In a letter written in April 1923 to his cousin, Alexander Muwamba, Clements Kadalie put into perspective the passionate concern with local politics which gripped so many of the northern intellectuals in the years between the wars. As a proud member of Chifira's 'noble family', Kadalie supported the campaign 'to reclaim the throne now temporarily with Marenga'. But as a shrewd political organiser, busy transforming the ICU in South Africa into a mass organisation, he was well aware of the limitations involved in such an approach.

> I frankly confess that that family and its throne ought to be maintained but what will that be when speaking after modern civilization? It is the white man that is ruling Nyasaland and not Marenga or any black chief. The white man is determined to turn the country his own and it behoves us now to be up and doing to culture

131 DC Chinteche to PC Northern Province, 3 March 1933, MNA 1/21/3. Annual Report for the West Nyasa district 1932, NNC3/1/4. For an excellent survey of administrative change in Tongaland see J. van Velsen, 'Administration'

132 Y. Z. Mwasi to DC Chinteche, 4 April 1935, MNA NN1/22/1; to DC Chinteche, 5 April 1947, MNA 27A/108

133 IC. K. Muwamba to PC Northern Province, 27 April 1947, MNA 27A/108

> ourself in the white man's modern Government. To do this, our beloved Chifira must produce most cultured and educated men who will participate to agitate for the modern Government alongside the white man. What we require is that we shall send men to sit as legislators at Zomba where laws are made to govern Nyasaland.[134]

But Kadalie's argument that power should be seized at the heart of the colonial system was not shared by the majority of his compatriots in the 1920s and 1930s. Men like Y. Z. Mwasi and Edward Bote Manda were in the van of those pressing reforms on the government, but as Tangri has noted, they never attempted to seek the political kingdom.[135] Livingstonia graduates had political influence but not just the centrally-directed influence of those men linked by common educational ties forged at the Overtoun Institution. Groups of graduates also possessed locally-directed influence and competed with each other on a variety of issues. Rather than taking the form of a struggle between 'conservatives' and 'progressives', local politics in the Livingstonia sphere involved the clash of competing modernisers. Not until the 1950s was mass support to be associated with a centrally-focussed political movement and even then local politics are likely to have been of greater importance than conventional accounts of Malawi nationalism suggest.

This is not the place to make an analysis of mass nationalism in Malawi, except to note that its rise was accompanied by the decline in political influence of the mission elite. With the founding of the Nyasaland African Congress in 1944, political initiatives began to slip to the Southern and later to the Central Province, and new men – civil servants, traders and farmers – took the place that pastors and teachers had formerly held. Livingstonia-educated politicians did not disappear from the Malawi scene – both the first President of Malawi and the first President of Congress received their primary education in Livingstonia schools – but no longer were they to be tied to employments connected with the mission. Though the role of the CCAP in the campaign against the federation of Rhodesia and Nyasaland in the 1950s had been extensively publicised, it may well be that detailed research will show that its significance has been somewhat exaggerated. Certainly in 1953, the year when Federation was imposed, the Reverend W. H. Watson, minister at Livingstonia, took a deliberately detached view of the issue. Though one pastor, the veteran Patrick Mwamulima, registered his protest by refusing to conduct a service celebrating the coronation of the British Queen, most CCAP

134 C. Kadalie to E. A. Muwamba, 29 April 1923, MNA s2/71/23. See also Kadalie, *My Life and the ICU*, 31

135 Tangri, 'Inter-war "Native Associations"', 89

ministers complied with the request to hold services, if sufficient people had gathered to worship.[136] It was only later in the 1950s that the CCAP emerged into the political prominence that the Devlin Report describes.[137]

Conclusion

At the time of Malawi's independence in July 1964 British newspapers made much of the extensive influence of Scottish Protestant missionaries in the country, and suggested, somewhat fancifully, that Malawi was an African Scotland writ large. A central conclusion of this book must be that such a view is seriously misleading. Already by 1940, Roman Catholic converts probably outnumbered members of the Scottish branches of the CCAP, and Blantyre and Livingstonia between them possessed only 29 per cent of all government-assisted schools in the country. In the West Nyasa district where 7300 CCAP communicants were recorded in 1938, there may have been as many as 6000 members of independent churches. At a village level, Christianity coexisted with older religious institutions and beliefs. Most Christians remained unconvinced by the church's explanation of misfortune; many turned to alternative explanations when the opportunity presented itself. Hundreds of CCAP communicants between 1959 and 1964 turned to the witchcraft eradicator, Chikanga, himself a member of the Presbyterian Church; the anti-sorcery movement, Kamcape, aroused considerable interest among Livingstonia congregations in 1963. In the Northern Province of Zambia, the Presbyterian congregation at Lubwa, built up initially by David Kaunda, was catastrophically depleted in 1955 when over 80 per cent of its members joined Alice Lenshina's Lumpa Church, a Christian anti-sorcery cult.[138] Social behaviour in Ngoniland in the late 1930s, Margaret Read has demonstrated, involved a complex intermingling of Christian and non-Christian elements. At marriages and funerals, church rites were combined with Ngoni rites, and Ngoni proverbs were used by ministers in their sermons to illustrate their ethical teaching.[139] For most villagers, Linden has commented, 'changes in daily life were largely the product of labour migration rather than mission interference'.[140] And though Livingstonia, to a far greater

136 W. H. Watson to A. W. Kayira, 30 May 1953; Kayira to Watson, 3 June 1953, Liv. Corr. Box 6

137 *Report of the Nyasaland Commission of Inquiry* 1959, Cmd. 814, 23

138 R. G. Willis, 'Kamcape: an anti-sorcery movement in south-west Tanzania', *Africa* XXXVIII, 1968; Principal's Report for the Overtoun Institution, 1959, Liv. Corr. Box 1; Roberts, '*The Lumpa Church*'

139 Margaret Read, 'The Ngoni and Western Education' in Victor Turner (ed.), *Colonialism in Africa 1870–1900*, vol. III, Cambridge 1971, 360–2.

extent than the Roman Catholic missions which Linden has studied, contributed to the character of the new Malawi economy, the importance of her impact must be put into perspective. The initial impetus towards the southern-orientated labour migrant system came from the Protestant missions, but it was reinforced by tax and labour policies followed by H. H. Johnson and his successors, by the demand for Malawi labour from southern Africa and by the willingness of imperial and colonial authorities to accede deliberately or tacitly to those demands. In 1925 the Phelps-Stokes Commission singled out the Dutch Reformed Church station at Mkhoma as a model of the rurally-based institution which it wished to see created. But there is little evidence to suggest that the Dutch Reformed Church converts were conspicuously more successful in resisting the demands of migrant labour than were their compatriots trained at the Overtoun Institution further north.[141]

Yet to emphasise the limits of Livingstonia's influence is not to deny the importance of her impact. Secular historians lack the means to measure the extent and totality of Christian conversion, but it is surely significant that religious protest in the north, even when it involved a break with the CCAP, so frequently took a Christian or quasi-Christian form. *Mchape* vendors, at the village of Chief Samuel Jere in 1933, criticised the hypocrisy of African Christians, but they added: 'We follow the Commandment of God who says "Thou Shalt Not Kill".'[142] Christianity had become the dominant ideology of the region, in the sense that those who

[140] Linden, *Catholics, Peasants and Chewa Resistance*, 207

[141] The following table, printed in the Report of the Education Department of the Nyasaland Protectorate for 1943, shows the occupation in that year of all boys who had been enrolled in the upper and middle sections of the DRC school at Mkhoma from 1933 to 1939. Though the proportion 'living in villages' is slightly higher than one would expect from graduates of the Overtoun Institution, the general pattern is remarkably similar.

Serving in the mission as teachers	69
Living in villages	58
Working in S. Africa or S. Rhodesia	36
Enlisted in the KAR	20
Clerks	18
Still at school	12
In medical work	10
Employed as overseers	7
,, carpenters	6
,, storekeepers	5
,, tailors	3
Died	1
In prison	1
Total	239

wished to propagate new messages had to do so in Christian terms. Social anthropologists and historians working since the 1950s among the Chewa, south of Livingstonia's sphere, have found abundant evidence of the vitality of pre-Christian religious institutions. Yet J. van Velsen, following his researches among the lakeside Tonga between 1952 and 1955, concluded that, at least in the Nkata Bay area, such institutions were moribund.[143]

The educational impact of Livingstonia has also had important repercussions. In a country where few Africans could accumulate much wealth as farmers, access to Western education provided the main means through which social differentiation took place during the colonial period. The educational patterns established as a consequence of the initial reaction of various societies to the mission in the 1880s and 1890s thus remained of considerable importance, at least until the 1950s. Just as the Yao of the Lake Malawi region still remained substantially isolated from educational contacts before independence, so the northern peoples, particularly the Tonga, still included a higher proportion of the educationally qualified than did those of other regions, and still were forced to put their education to use outside their own home province. Though Livingstonia may have affected the extent of labour migration only marginally, she undoubtedly influenced the type of job that her graduates obtained. A survey conducted by Margaret Read in 1939 demonstrated that 25 per cent of all those in employment from northern Ngoniland could be placed in a special category of 'skilled worker' – a higher proportion than in any other of the regions she had studied.[144] The Northern Province provided a disproportionately high number of the African clerks employed on the Copperbelt and in government offices at Lusaka in the 1930s and 1940s, with the result that many Zambians came to resent the influence gained by their more privileged neighbours.[145] Opposition in Northern Rhodesia in 1938 to amalgamation with Nyasaland came largely from members of local elite groups who complained that 'these educated [Nyasa] natives will have all the work before our children are educated, because none of our children are educated'.[146] Livingstonia contributed to the enlargement of social scale and the creation of a community of believers, but she also influenced the establishment of divisions of a new and threatening type.

142 Shaba, 'Brief History'

143 van Velsen, 'Missionary Factor', 22

144 Read, 'The Ngoni and Western Education', 371

145 See Evidence of Major G. St J. Orde-Browne, 19 May 1938, Record of the Oral Evidence presented to the Bledisloe Commission, 1938, FCOL

146 Evidence of Native Authorities, Shirwa Nganda, 5 August 1938, ibid.

Bibliography

ARCHIVAL SOURCES

Listed abbreviations as they appear in footnote references

NATIONAL LIBRARY OF SCOTLAND (NLS)

Letterbooks of the secretaries of the Foreign Missions Committee of the Free Church of Scotland, 1873–1923

Letterbook of the secretary of the Livingstonia Committee, 1901–34

Letters from missionaries at Livingstonia to the secretaries, 1874–1926

Letters from missionaries and others to Dr Laws, 1875–1900

Mission journals covering the pioneer journey to Lake Malawi, the years at Cape Maclear, 1875–80, the establishment of pioneer settlements at Bandawe and Kaningina, 1878–9, and the first years at Bandawe, 1881–7

Minute book of the sub-committee of the Livingstonia Mission, 1871–90 and 1894–1895

Letterbooks of the convenors and secretaries of the Foreign Missions Committee of the Church of Scotland, 1872–1907

EDINBURGH UNIVERSITY LIBRARY (EUL)

Laws's Papers

Macalpine Papers

Morrison Papers

DEPARTMENT OF RELIGIOUS STUDIES, ABERDEEN UNIVERSITY (ABERDEEN)

Laws Papers

PROFESSOR GEORGE SHEPPERSON, EDINBURGH UNIVERSITY (SHEPPERSON COLLECTION)

Livingstonia Papers

Moir Papers

MALAWI NATIONAL ARCHIVES (MNA)

(*i*) *Government Records*

District and Provincial reports for the Northern Province from 1901

District books of the West Nyasa and Mzimba districts

Secretariat files relating to native associations, independent churches and education; evidence presented to the North Nyasa Commission 1929; Minute book of the Atonga Tribal Chiefs

(*ii*) *Church records*

Minutes of the Livingstonia Presbytery, 1899–1933

Minutes of the Mission Council, 1909–38

Minutes of the Overtoun Institution Senatus, 1901–31
Education Diary, Livingstonia, 1895–1915
Roll-Book of the Overtoun Institution
Miscellaneous Livingstonia Correspondence
Hetherwick Papers (now incorporated into Blantyre Presbytery Papers)
(*iii*) *Private Papers*
Wordsworth Poole Papers

NATIONAL ARCHIVES, SALISBURY, RHODESIA (SALISBURY)
(*i*) *Government records*
The papers of the British South Africa Company
Files relating to the Watch Tower movement
(*ii*) *Private papers*
James Stewart Papers
H. H. Johnston Papers

PUBLIC RECORD OFFICE, LONDON (PRO)
FO 84 (Slave Trade)
FO 2 (African Consular)
CO 525

EDINBURGH HOUSE, LONDON
Files relating to education in Nyasaland

FOREIGN AND COMMONWEALTH OFFICE LIBRARY, LONDON (FCOL)
Record of the Oral Evidence heard by the Rhodesia–Nyasaland Royal Commission, 1938

RHODES HOUSE, OXFORD
Waller Papers
Lugard Papers

UNIVERSITY LIBRARY, CHANCELLOR COLLEGE, MALAWI
Domingo Letters (photocopies)

NATIONAL ARCHIVES OF ZAMBIA, LUSAKA (LUSAKA)
Files on Missions: United Free Church of Scotland, Livingstonia

NATIONAL ARCHIVES OF TANZANIA, DAR ES SALAAM
Files on the African National Church
Edward Shaba, 'A Brief History of the Proposed Visit of the "Mchape" People' (copy made by Professor T. O. Ranger)

PERIODICAL PUBLICATIONS MISSIONARY SOCIETIES

The Livingstonia Mission, 1875–1900, a collection of pamphlets bound together in the possession of Professor George Shepperson
Livingstonia Mission Reports to 1914
United Free Church Foreign Mission Reports, 1914–28
Church of Scotland Foreign Mission Reports, 1929–36
General Assembly Papers of the Church of Scotland
Minutes of the Livingstonia Mission Committee
Minutes of the Foreign Missions Committee of the Free Church of Scotland

Proceedings of the Nyasaland United Missionary Conference, Livingstonia, 1901

Proceedings of the Third General Missionary Conference of Nyasaland, Mvera, 1910

Aurora, 1897–1902

The Livingstonia News, 1903–12

Life and Work in British Central Africa (originally *Life and Work Blantyre Mission Supplement*) 1888–1916

The Free Church of Scotland Monthly Record (continued as *The Missionary Record of the United Free Church of Scotland* etc.) 1874–1928

The Church of Scotland Home and Foreign Missionary Record (1870–1900)

Life and Work

Other Lands

Central Africa

The Nyasa News, 1893–4

OFFICIAL PUBLICATIONS

Papers relative to suppression of Slave-raiding in Nyasaland, 1892, Cmd. 6899

Papers relative to the suppression of Slave-Raiding in British Central Africa, 1893–1894, Cmd. 7031

Correspondence respecting Operations against Slave Traders in British Central Africa, 1896, Cmd. 7925, 8013

Report by Commissioner Johnston of the first three years' Administration, 1894, Cmd. 7504

Report by Commissioner . . . Johnston . . . on the Trade and General Condition of the British Central Africa Protectorate, 1895–96, Cmd. 8254

Report by Consul. . . Sharpe on the Trade and General Condition of the British Central African Protectorate, 1896–97, Cmd. 8438

Annual Report on the British Central Africa Protectorate for 1897–98, Cmd. 9048

Report on the Trade and General Conditions of the British Central Africa Protectorate for 1902–03, Cmd. 1772

Report for 1903–04, Cmd. 2242; *for 1904–05*, Cmd. 2684; *for 1905–06*, Cmd. 2684; *for 1906–07*, Cmd. 3729

Nyasaland Protectorate, Report of Commissioner for 1907–08, Cmd. 3729

Nyasaland Protectorate, Report . . . for 1908–09, Cmd. 4448; *for 1909–10*, Cmd. 4964; *for 1910–11*, Cmd. 5467; *for 1911–12*, Cmd. 6007; *for 1912–13*, Cmd. 7050; *for 1913–14*, Cmd. 7822; *for 1914–15*, Cmd. 6172

Correspondence relating to the Recruitment of Labour in the British Central Africa Protectorate for Employment in the Transvaal 1903, Cmd. 1531

Correspondence relating to the Recruitment of Labour in the Nyasaland Protectorate for the Transvaal and Southern Rhodesia Mines, 1908, Cmd. 3993

General Information as to the British Central African Protectorate, HMSO, London 1905

Census of the Nyasaland Protectorate, 1911, 1921, 1931, Zomba

Report of the Commission . . . to Inquire into . . . the Native Rising within the Nyasaland Protectorate, Zomba, 1916

Report of the Native Education Conference... held at Zomba, May 17–20 1927 Zomba, 1927

Eric Smith, Report on the Direct Taxation of Natives in the Nyasaland Protectorate, Zomba, 1937

Report of the Committee to Enquire into Emigrant Labour 1935, Zomba, 1936

Report of the Nyasaland Commission of Inquiry, 1959, Cmd. 814

Reports of the Education Department, Nyasaland Protectorate, 1934–53

The British Central Africa Gazette, 1894–9

The Nyasaland Government Gazette, 1908–14

NEWSPAPERS – NON-MISSIONARY

The Times

The Scotsman

The Edinburgh Courant

The Glasgow Herald

These have been consulted for particular issues such as the General Assembly debate on the Blantyre atrocities, March 1881, the campaign in Scotland for the declaration of a protectorate over the Malawi regions, and for obituary notices of leading mission supporters

INTERVIEWS

Rev. Charles Chinula, interview Loudon, 25 July 1964

Mr A. E. Muwamba, interview Zomba, 9 June 1966

Mr Hanok N'goma, interview Nkata Bay, 22–3 June 1966

Rev. Z. P. Ziba, interview Loudon, 24 July 1964

UNPUBLISHED THESES AND PAPERS

Alpers, E. A., 'The role of the Yao in the development of trade in East-Central Africa, 1698–c.1850', London PhD, 1966

Bwingo, S.W., 'The North Nyasa Native Association', History Seminar Paper, University of Malawi

Cross, Sholto, 'The Watch Tower Witch-Cleansing and Secret Societies in Central Africa'. Conference on the history of Central African religious systems, Lusaka, 1972

Brock, Sheila M., 'James Stewart and Lovedale: a reappraisal of Missionary Attitudes and African Response in the Eastern Cape, South Africa, 1870–1905', Edinburgh PhD, 1974

Gavin, R. J., 'Palmerston's policy towards East and West Africa, 1830–1865', Cambridge PhD 1959–60

Gregson, R. E., 'Work, Exchange and Leadership: the Mobilisation of Agricultural Labor among the Tumbuka of the Henga Valley', Columbia PhD, 1969

Horton, Robin, 'Conversion: Impact versus Innovation', paper presented at a meeting of the African Studies Association of the United Kingdom, Liverpool, 1974

Iliffe, John, 'Ecological Crisis and Economic Change in Sukumaland Tanzania, 1890–1970', Seminar paper, Institute of Commonwealth Studies, London, 1975

Kalinga, O. J., 'The Ngonde of Northern Malawi c.1600–1895', London PhD, 1974

Krishnamurthy, B. S., 'Land and Labour in Nyasaland, 1891–1914', London PhD, 1964

Macdonald, R. J., 'A History of African Education in Nyasaland, 1875–1945', Edinburgh PhD, 1969

Macmillan, H. W., 'The Origins and Development of the African Lakes Company, 1878–1908', Edinburgh PhD, 1970

Mwalwanda, C. T., 'The African National Church', Research Paper, University of Malawi, 1967

Ranger, T. O., 'Mchape and the Study of Witchcraft Eradication', Conference on the history of Central African religious systems, Lusaka, 1972

Rau, W. E., 'The Ngoni Diaspora and Religious Interaction in East and Central Africa', Seminar Paper, UCLA, 1970

Ross, A. C., 'The Origins and Development of the Church of Scotland Mission Blantyre, Nyasaland, 1875–1921', Edinburgh PhD, 1968

Schoffeleers, J. M., 'The Chisumphi and M'bona cults in Malawi: a comparative history', Conference on the history of Central African religious systems, Lusaka, 1972

Stuart, Richard G., 'Mchape and the UMCA, 1933', Conference on the history of Central African religious systems, Lusaka, 1972

Tangri, R. K., 'The Development of Modern African Politics and the emergence of a Nationalist movement in Colonial Malawi, 1871–1958', Edinburgh PhD, 1970

'Levi Z. Mumba: a political biography of a pioneer Malawi Nationalist', Seminar paper, University of Malawi

Thompson, T. J., 'Early Missionary Attitudes towards African Leadership in the Livingstonia Mission, 1875–1900', History Seminar Paper, University of Malawi

Vail, H. Leroy, 'Religion, Language and the Tribal Myth: the Tumbaka and Cewa of Malawi', Conference on the History of Central African religious systems, Lusaka, 1972

BOOKS AND ARTICLES

Abdallah, Yohanna B., *The Yaos*, trans. and ed. by Meredith Sanderson, Zomba, 1919

Addison, W. Innes, *A Roll of the Graduates of the University of Glasgow, 1727–1897*, Glasgow, 1898

Agnew, Swanzie, 'Environment and history: the Malawian setting', in Bridglal Pachai (ed.), *The Early History of Malawi*, London, 1972

Ajayi, J. F. A., *Christian Missions in Nigeria, 1841–1891: The Making of a New Elite*, London, 1965

Alpers, Edward A., *The East African Slave Trade*, Historical Association of Tanzania Paper No. 3, Nairobi, 1967

Alpers, Edward A., 'Trade, State and Society among the Yao in the nineteenth century', *Journal of African History*, x, 1967
'The Yao in Malawi: the importance of local research' in Bridglal Pachai (ed.), *The Early History of Malawi*, London, 1972
'Towards a History of the Expansion of Islam in East Africa' in T. O. Ranger and I. Kimambo (ed.), *The Historical Study of African Religion*

Anderson-Morshead, A. E. M., *The History of the Universities' Mission to Central Africa, 1859–1909*, London, 6th edition 1955

Appeal to the Students of the Free Church of Scotland Missionary Union, Glasgow University, Glasgow, 1896

Austen, Ralph A., 'Patterns of Development in Nineteenth-Century East Africa', *African Historical Studies*, IV, 1971

Ayandele, E. A., *The Missionary Impact on Modern Nigeria, 1843–1914: A Political and Social Analysis*, London, 1966

Baker, C. A., 'Nyasaland, the History of its Export Trade', *Nyasaland Journal*, xv, 1962

Ballantyne, M. M. S. and Shepherd, R. H. W., *Forerunners of Modern Malawi: The Early Missionary Adventures of Dr. James Henderson, 1895–1898*, Lovedale, 1968

Barnes, Bertram H., *Johnson of Nyasaland*, London, 1933

Barnes, J. A., *Politics in a Changing Society: A Political History of the Fort Jamieson Ngoni*, London, 1954

Barrett, David B., *Schism and Renewal in Africa*, Nairobi, 1968

Bennett, N. R. and Ylvisaker, M., (ed.), *The Central African Journal of Lovell J. Procter, 1860–1864*, Boston, 1971

Bismark, Joseph, 'A Brief History of Joseph Bismark', *Occasional Papers of the Department of Antiquities*, no. 7, Zomba, 1969

Blaikie, W. G., *The Personal Life of David Livingstone*, London, 1880

Blake, George, *B.I. Centenary, 1856–1956*, London, 1956

Boeder, Robert B., 'The Effects of Labor Emigration on Rural Life in Malawi', *Rural Africana*, no. 20, 1973

Bolink, Peter, *Towards Church in Zambia*, The Netherlands, n.d.

Brock, Sheila, 'James Stewart and David Livingstone', in B. Pachai (ed.), *Livingstone: Man of Africa*, London, 1973

Brown, Richard, 'Aspects of the Scramble for Matabeleland', in Eric Stokes and Richard Brown (ed.), *The Zambesian Past: Studies in Central African History*, Manchester, 1966

Buchanan, John, *East African Letters*, Edinburgh, 1880
The Shire Highlands, Edinburgh, 1885

Buell, Raymond Leslie, *The Native Problem in Africa*, vol. 1, New York, 1928

Cairns, H. Alan C., *Prelude to Imperialism: British Reactions to Central African Society, 1840–1890*, London, 1965

Cardew, C. A., 'Nyasaland in 1894–5', *Nyasaland Journal*, 1, 1948

Carswell, Donald, *Brother Scots*, London, 1927
Chadwick, Owen, *Mackenzie's Grave*, London, 1959
Chanock, M. L., 'Development and Change in the history of Malawi', in B. Pachai (ed.), *The Early History of Malawi*, London, 1972
'The Political Economy of Independent Agriculture in Colonial Malawi: the Great War to the Great Depression', *Journal of Social Science*, University of Malawi, I, 1972
'Ambiguities in the Malawian political tradition', *African Affairs*, 74, 1975
Charsley, S. R., *The Princes of Nyakyusa*, Nairobi, 1969
Chibambo, Y. M., *My Ngoni of Nyasaland*, translated by Rev. Charles Stuart, London, 1942
Chirnside, Andrew, *The Blantyre Missionaries: Discreditable Disclosures*, London, 1880
Cook, David J., 'The Influence of Livingstonia Mission upon the Formation of Welfare Associations in Zambia, 1912–31', in T. O. Ranger and John Weller (ed.), *Themes in the Christian History of Central Africa*, London, 1975
Cornford, L. Cope, *The Sea Carriers, 1825–1925*, Aberdeen, 1925
Coupland, Reginald, *Kirk on the Zambesi*, Oxford, 1928
The Exploitation of East Africa, 1856–1890, London, 1939
Cross, D. Kerr, 'Geographical Notes of the Country between Lakes Nyassa, Rukwa and Tanganyika', *Scottish Geographical Magazine*, VI, 1890
'Crater Lakes North of Lake Nyasa', *Geographical Journal*, V, 1895
Drummond, Henry, *Tropical Africa*, London, 1888
Duff, Alexander, *The Proposed Mission to Lake Nyassa*, Edinburgh, 1875
Duff, H. L., *Nyasaland under the Foreign Office*, London, 1903
African Small Chop, London, 1932
du Plessis, J., *A History of Christian Missions in South Africa*, London, 1911
Thrice through the Dark Continent, London, 1917
The Evangelisation of Pagan Africa, Cape Town, 1930
Elmslie, W. A., *Among the Wild Ngoni*, Edinburgh, 1899
Elton, J. F., *Travels and Researches among the Lakes and Mountains of Eastern and Central Africa*, edited by H. B. Cotterill, London, 1879
Ewing, Rev. William, *Annals of the Free Church of Scotland, 1843–1900*, Edinburgh, 1914
Eyre-Todd, George, *Who's Who in Glasgow in 1909*, Glasgow, 1909
Ferguson, H., 'Social Problems in the Nineteenth Century', *Scottish History Review*, XL, 1962
Fleming, J. R., *A History of the Church in Scotland*, two volumes *1843–1874*, Edinburgh, 1927; *1875–1929*, Edinburgh, 1933
Foskett, Reginald (ed.), *The Zambesi Journal and Letters of Dr. John Kirk*, 2 vols., Edinburgh, 1965
Fotheringham, L. Menteith, *Adventures in Nyasaland*, London, 1891
Fraser, Agnes R., *Donald Fraser of Livingstonia*, London, 1934

Fraser, Donald, *The Future of Africa*, Edinburgh, 1911

Winning a Primitive People, London, 1914

Livingstonia, Edinburgh, 1915

African Idylls, London, 1923

The Autobiography of an African, London, 1925

The New Africa, London, 1927

'The Growth of the Church in the Mission Field: VI The Livingstonia Mission', *International Review of Missions*, II, 1913

'The Church and Games in Africa', ibid., x, 1921

'The Evangelistic Approach to the African', ibid., xv, 1926

Galbraith, John S., *Mackinnon and East Africa 1878–1895: a study in the 'New Imperialism'*, Cambridge, 1972

Gamitto, A. C. P., *King Kazembe and the Marave, Cheva, Bisa, Bemba, Lunda and other Peoples of Southern Africa*, translated by Ian Cunnison, Lisbon, 1960

Gann, L. H., *A History of Northern Rhodesia*, London, 1934

The Birth of a Plural Society, Manchester, 1958

A History of Southern Rhodesia, early days to 1934, London, 1965

'The End of the Slave Trade in British Central Africa, 1889–1912, *Human Problems in British Central Africa*, XVI, 1954

Gelfand, Michael (ed.), *Doctor on Lake Nyasa. Being the Journal and Letters of Dr. Wordsworth Poole*, Salisbury, 1961

Gelfand, Michael, *Lakeside Pioneers*, Oxford, 1964

Gouldsbury, Cullen and Sheane, Hubert, *The Great Plateau of Northern Rhodesia*, London, 1911

Gray, Richard, *The Two Nations*, London, 1960

Gray, Richard and Birmingham, David, *Pre-Colonial African Trade*, London, 1970

Green, Steven, 'Blantyre Mission', *Nyasaland Journal*, x, 1957

Groves, C. P., *The Planting of Christianity in Africa*. Volumes Two and Three, London, 1954 and 1955

Gulliver, P. H., 'A History of the Songea Ngoni', *Tanganyika Notes and Records* 40, 1955

Hailey, Lord, *An African Survey*, London, 1938

Native Administration in the British Territories, Part II, London, 1950

Hall, Richard, *Zambia*, London, 1965

Hamilton, Henry, *The Industrial Revolution in Scotland*, Oxford, 1932

Hamilton, J. Taylor, *Twenty Years of Pioneer Missions in Nyasaland*, Bethlehem, Pennsylvania, 1912

Hanna, A. J., *The Beginnings of Nyasaland and North-Eastern Rhodesia, 1859–1895*, Oxford, 1950

Henderson, James, 'Northern Nyasaland', *Scottish Geographical Magazine*, XVI, 1900

Hetherwick, Alexander, *The Romance of Blantyre*, London, 1932

Hewat, E. G. K., *Vision and Achievement, 1796–1956*, London, 1960

Hine, J. E., *Days Gone By*, London, 1924

Hole, H. Marshall, 'The Rhodesian Railways' in Leo Weinthall (ed.), *The Story of the Cape to Cairo Railway and River Route*, London, n.d., Vol. II

Holmberg, Ake, *African Tribes and European Agencies*, Göteborg, 1966

Hooker, J. R., 'Witness and Watchtower in the Rhodesians and Nyasaland', *Journal of African History*, VI, 1965

Hopkins, A. G., *An Economic History of West Africa*, London, 1973

Horton, Robin, 'African Conversion', *Africa*, XLI, 1971

Illiffe, John, *Tanganyika under German Rule*, Cambridge, 1969

Agricultural Change in Modern Tanganyika, Historical Association of Tanzania Paper No. 10, Nairobi, 1971

'The Age of Improvement and Differentiation (1907–45)', in Kimambo, I. N. & Temu, A. J., *A History of Tanzania*, Nairobi, 1969

Inglis, K. S., *Churches and the Working Classes in Victorian England*, London, 1963

Inwood, Charles, *An African Pentecost: the record of a missionary tour in Central Africa*, London, 1911

Issacman, Allan, 'The Origin, Formation and Early History of the Chikunda of South Central Africa', *Journal of African History*, XIII, 1972

Jack, J. W., *Daybreak in Livingstonia*, Edinburgh, 1901

Jeal, Tim, *Livingstone*, London, 1973

Johnson, W. P., *Nyasa, The Great Water*, London, 1922

My African Reminiscences, London, 1924

Johnston, Alex, *The Life and Letters of Sir Harry Johnston*, London, 1929

Johnston, Sir H. H., *British Central Africa*, London, 1897

The Story of my Life, London, 1923

'England and Germany in Africa', *The Fortnightly Review*, July, 1890

Johnston, James, *Reality versus Romance in South Central Africa*, London, 1893

Dr. Laws of Livingstonia, London, n.d.

Johnston, Col. William, *Roll of the Graduates of the University of Aberdeen. 1860–1900*, Aberdeen, 1906

Jones, Thomas Jesse, *Education in East Africa*, report prepared for the Phelps-Stokes Fund, New York, 1925

Kadalie, Clements, *My Life and the ICU*, London, 1970

Kaunda, Kenneth, *Zambia Shall Be Free*, London, 1962

Keltie, J. Scott, *The Partition of Africa*, London, 2nd edition, 1895

Kimambo, I. N. & Temu, A. J., *A History of Tanzania*, Nairobi, 1969

King, Kenneth, *Pan-Africanism and Education*, Oxford, 1971

Klein, Martin A., 'Slavery, the slave trade and legitimate commerce in late nineteenth century Africa', *Etudes d'Histoire Africaine*, II, 1971

Krishnamurthy, B. S., 'Economic Policy, Land and Labour in Nyasaland, 1890–1914', in Pachai, B., *The Early History of Malawi*, London, 1972

Kuczynski, R. R., *Demographic Survey of the British Colonial Empire, Volume* II, London, 1949

Lamb, John A., (ed.), *The Fasti of the United Free Church of Scotland, 1900–1929*, Edinburgh, 1956

Lamb, J. A., (ed.), *Fasti Ecclesiae Scoticanae*, IX, 1929–54, Edinburgh, 1961
Langworthy, Emily Booth, *This Africa was Mine*, Stirling, 1952
Langworthy, H. W.,'Swahili influence on the area between Lake Malawi and the Luangwa River', *African Historical Studies*, IV, 1971
'Chewa or Malawi Political Organization in the Pre-colonial Era' in Pachai, B., *Early History of Malawi*, London, 1972
Latourette, K. S., *A History of the Expansion of Christianity, Volume V*, London, 1943
Laws, Robert, *Women's Work at Livingstonia*, Paisley, 1886
Reminiscences of Livingstonia, London, 1934
'Native Education in Nyasaland', *Journal of the African Society*, XXVIII, 1929
Linden, Ian, *Catholics, Peasants and Chewa Resistance in Nyasaland, 1889–1939*, London, 1974
Linden, Ian, and Linden, Jane, 'John Chilembwe and the "New Jerusalem"', *Journal of African History*, XII, 1971
'The Maseko Ngoni at Domwe, 1870–1900', in Pachai, B., *The Early History of Malawi*, London, 1972
Livingstone, David, *Missionary Travels and Researches in South Africa*, London, 1857
Narrative of an Expedition to the Zambesi and its Tributaries, London, 1865
The Last Journals of David Livingstone, edited by Horace Waller, London, 1874
Family Letters, 1841–1856, edited by I. Schapira, London, 1959
Livingstone, W. P., *Laws of Livingstonia*, London, 1921
A Prince of Missionaries: Alexander Hetherwick, London, 1931
Lohrentz, Kenneth, 'Joseph Booth Charles Domingo and the Seventh Day Baptists in Northern Nyasaland, 1910–12', *Journal of African History*, XII, 1971
Long, Norman, 'Bandawe Mission Station and Local Politics, 1878–86', *Human Problems in British Central Africa*, XXXII, 1962
Lonsdale, 'The Emergence of African Nations: A Historiographical Analysis', *African Affairs*, vol. 67, 1968
Lucas, C. P., (ed.), *The Empire at War. Volumes I and IV*, London, 1921
Lugard, F. D., *The Rise of Our East African Empire*, Edinburgh, 1893
Macalpine, A. G., 'Tonga Religious Beliefs and Customs', *Journal of the African Society*, V, 1905–6; VI, 1906–7
McCracken, K. J., 'Livingstonia as an Industrial Mission, 1875–1900', *Religion in Africa*, Edinburgh, 1964, mimeo
'African Politics in twentieth-century Malawi', in Ranger T. O. (ed.), *Aspects of Central African History*, London, 1968
'Religion and politics in Northern Ngoniland, 1881–1904', in Pachai, B., *The Early History of Malawi*, London, 1972
'Livingstone and the Aftermath: the Origins and Development of Livingstonia Mission' in Pachai, B., *Livingstone: Man of Africa*, London, 1973
MacDonald, Duff, *Africana: Or the Heart of Heathen Africa*, London, 1882

Macdonald, R. J., 'Religious Independency as a means of social advance in Northern Nyasaland in the 1930s', *Journal of Religion in Africa*, III, 1970

'Reverend Hanock Msokera Phiri and the Establishment in Nyasaland of the African Methodist Episcopal Church', *African Historical Studies*, III, 1970

Mackenzie, D. R., *The Spirit-Ridden Konde*, London, 1925

Macmillan, H. W., 'Notes on the origins of the Arab War', in Pachai, B., *The Early History of Malawi*, London, 1972

Macpherson, Kenneth, *Kenneth Kaunda of Zambia*, Lusaka, 1974

Maples, Ellen, *The Life of Bishop Maples*, London, 1897

(ed.), *Journals and Papers of Chauncey Maples*, London, 1899

Marwick, M. G., 'Another Modern Anti-Witchcraft Movement in East Central Africa', *Africa*, xx, 1950

'History and Tradition in East Central Africa through the eyes of the Northern Rhodesian Cewa', *Journal of African History*, IV, 1963

Marwick, W. H., *Economic Developments in Victorian Scotland*, London, 1936

Maugham, R. C. F., *Africa as I have known it*, London, 1929

Nyasaland in the Nineties, London, 1935

Mechie, Stewart, *The Church and Scottish Social Development, 1780–1870*, London, 1960

Meebelo, Henry S., *Reaction to Colonialism: a prelude to the politics of independence in northern Zambia, 1893–1939*, Manchester, 1971

Mitchell, J. C., *The Yao Village*, Manchester, 1956

'The Political Organization of the Yao of Southern Nyasaland', *African Studies*, VIII, 1949

'An Outline of the Social Structure of Malemia Area', *Nyasaland Journal*, IV, 1951

Mitchell, Sir Philip, *African Afterthoughts*, London, 1954

Moir, Fred L. M., *After Livingstone*, London, 1923

'The Story of the African Lakes Corporation', in Leo Weinthal (ed.), *The Story of the Cape to Cairo Railway and River Route*, London n.d., Volume I

Morrison, J. H., *Streams in the Desert: A Picture of Life in Livingstonia*, London, 1919.

Mumba, Levi Z., 'Native Associations in Nyasaland', *The South African Outlook*, June, 1924.

Murray, A. Victor, *The School in the Bush*, London, 1929

Murray, S. S., *A Handbook of Nyasaland*, London, 1922

Mushindo, Paul Bwembya, 'The Life of a Zambia Evangelist', University of Zambia Institute for African Studies, Communication No. 9, 1973

Newitt, M. D., *Portuguese Settlement on the Zambesi*, London, 1973

Norman, L. S., *Nyasaland Without Prejudice*, London, 1939

Northcott, Cecil, *Robert Moffat: Pioneer in Africa 1817–1870*, London, 1961

Nyirenda, Saulos, 'History of the Tumbuka–Henga People', trans. ed. by T. C. Young, *Bantu Studies*, v, 1930

Oliver, Roland, *The Missionary Factor in East Africa*, London, 1952

Sir Harry Johnston and the Scramble for Africa, London, 1957

Oliver, Roland, and Gervase Matthew (ed.), *History of East Africa Volume 1*, Oxford, 1963
Omer-Cooper, J. R., *The Zulu Aftermath*, London, 1966
Pachai, Bridglal (ed.)., *The Early History of Malawi*, London, 1972
(ed.)., *Livingstone: Man of Africa, Memorial Essays 1873–1973*, London, 1973
Malawi: the History of a Nation, London, 1973
'The State and the Churches in Malawi during early Protectorate rule', *Journal of Social Science*, University of Malawi, I, 1972
Perham, Margery, *Lugard: The Years of Adventure, 1858–1898*, London, 1946
Pike, J. G. and Rimmington, G. T., *Malawi: A Geographical Study*, London, 1965
'A Pre-colonial History of Malawi', *Nyasaland Journal*, XVIII, 1965
Pollock, J. C., *The Keswick Story*, London, 1964
Pollock, Norman H., *Nyasaland and Northern Rhodesia: Corridor to the North*, Pittsburgh, 1971
Poole, E. H. Lane, *The Native Tribes of the Eastern Province of Northern Rhodesia*, Lusaka, 1938, 2nd edition
Pretorius, J. L., 'The Story of the Dutch Reformed Church Mission in Nyasaland', *Nyasaland Journal*, x, 1957
Price, Thomas, 'Malawi Rain-cults', *Religion in Africa*, Edinburgh, 1964, mimeo
Rangeley, W. H. J., 'Mtwalo', *Nyasaland Journal* v, 1952
'The Makalolo of Dr. Livingstone', *Nyasaland Journal*, XII, 1959
'The Amacinga Ayao', *Nyasaland Journal*, xv, 1962
'The Ayao', *Nyasaland Journal*, XVI, 1963
Ranger, Terence (ed.), *Aspects of Central African History*, London, 1968
The African Voice in Southern Rhodesia, London, 1970
'The "Ethiopian" Episode in Barotseland, 1900–1905', *Human Problems in British Central Africa*, XXXVII, 1965
'African Attempts to control Education in East and Central Africa 1900–1939', *Past and Present*, XXXII, 1965
'The Early History of Independency in Southern Rhodesia', *Religion in Africa*, Edinburgh, 1964, mimeo
The African Churches of Tanzania, Historical Association of Tanzania Paper No. 5, Nairobi
Ranger, Terence, and Kimambo, Isaria (ed.), *The Historical Study of African Religion*, London, 1972
Ranger, Terence, and Weller, John (ed.), *Themes in the Christian History of Central Africa*, London, 1975
Rankin, D. J., *The Zambesi Basin and Nyasaland*, Edinburgh, 1893
Rankine, W. H., *A Hero of the Dark Continent*, Edinburgh, 1896
Read, Margaret, *The Ngoni of Nyasaland*, Oxford, 1956
'The Ngoni and Western Education', in Turner, Victor (ed.)., *Colonialism in Africa 1870–1960*, III, *Profiles of Change: African Society and Colonial Rule*, Cambridge, 1972

Rennie, J. K., 'The Ngoni States and European Intrusion', in Eric Stokes and Richard Brown (ed.)., *The Zambesian Past: Studies in Central African History*, Manchester, 1966

Retief, Dr M. W., *William Murray of Nyasaland* translated from the Afrikaans and abridged by Mary H. Roux and M. M. Cherholster-Le Roux, Lovedale South Africa, 1958

Richards, Audrey I., 'A Modern Movement of Witch-Finders', *Africa*, VIII, 1935

Riddel, Alexander, *A Reply to 'The Blantyre Missionaries: Discreditable Disclosures', by Andrew Chirnside*, FRGS, Edinburgh, 1880

Ritter, E. A., *Shaka Zulu*, London, 7th impression 1962

Roberts, Andrew, 'The nineteenth century in Zambia', in Ranger, T. O. (ed.), *Aspects of Central African History*, London, 1968

'Pre-colonial Trade in Zambia', *African Social Research*, x, 1970

The Lumpa Church of Alice Lenshina, Lusaka, 1972

A History of the Bemba, London, 1973

Robertson, William, *The Martyrs of Blantyre*, London, 1892

Robinson, R. E. and Gallagher, J., 'The Partition of Africa' in F. H. Hinsley (ed.), *The New Cambridge Modern History, Volume XI*, Cambridge, 1962

Robinson, R. E. and Gallagher, J., with Alice Denny, *Africa and the Victorians*, London, 1961

Roome, W. J. W., *A Great Emancipation: A Missionary Survey of Nyasaland Central Africa*, London, 1926

Ross, Andrew C., 'The Foundations of the Blantyre Mission, Nyasaland', *Religion in Africa*, Edinburgh, 1964, mimeo

'The African – A Child or a Man', in Eric Stokes and Richard Brown (ed.), *The Zambesian Past: Studies in Central African History*, Manchester, 1966

'Scottish missionary concern 1874–1914: a golden era?', *Scottish Historical Review*, LI, 151, 1971

Rotberg, Robert I., *Christian Missionaries and the Creation of Northern Rhodesia, 1880–1924*, Princeton, 1965

The Rise of Nationalism in Central Africa: The Making of Malawi and Zambia 1873–1964, Harvard, 1966

Rowley, Henry, *The Story of the Universities' Mission to Central Africa*, London, 1866

St John, Christopher, 'Kazembe and the Tanganyika–Nyasa Corridor, 1880–1890', in Gray, Richard and Birmingham, David (eds.), *Pre-Colonial African Trade*, London, 1970

Sanderson, F. ,.E 'The Development of Labour Migration from Nyasaland, 1891–1914', *Journal of African History*, II, 1961

Saunders, Laurence J., *Scottish Democracy, 1815–1840: The Social and Intellectual Background*, Edinburgh, 1950

Schoffeleers, J. M., 'Livingstone and the Mang'anja Chiefs', in Pachai, B., (ed.), *Livingstone: Man of Africa*, London, 1973

'The Interaction of the M'bona Cult and Christianity, 1859–1963', in Ranger T. O.

and Weller, J., *Themes in the Christian History of Central Africa*, London, 1975
Schoffeleers, J. M., and Linden, I., 'The Resistance of the Nyau Societies to the Roman Catholic Missions in Colonial Malawi', in Ranger, T. O. and Kimambo, I. (ed.), *The Historical Study of African Religion*, London, 1972
Scott, David Clement, *A Cyclopaedic Dictionary of the Mang'ania Language*, Edinburgh, 1892
'Living Stones'. *Sermon upon the Church of Scotland Blantyre Mission in British Central Africa*, Edinburgh, 1901
Seaver, George, *David Livingstone: His Life and Letters*, London, 1957
Sharpe, Sir Alfred, *The Backbone of Africa*, London, 1921
Shepherd, R. M. W., *Lovedale South Africa: The Story of a Century, 1841–1941*, Lovedale, South Africa, 1941
Shepperson, George (ed.), *David Livingstone and the Rovuma*, Edinburgh, 1965
'Nyasaland and the Millenium' in Sylvia L. Thrupp (ed.)., *Millenial Dreams in Action*, The Hague, 1962
'The Jumbe of Kota Kota and some aspects of the history of Islam in British Central Africa', in I. M. Lewis (ed.), *Islam in Tropical Africa*, London, 1966
'The Politics of African Church Separatist Movements in British Central Africa, 1892–1916', *Africa*, XXIV, 1954
'External Factors in the Development of African Nationalism with particular reference to British Central Africa', *Phylon*, XIXII, 1961
Shepperson, George (ed.), and Thomas Price, *Independent African*, Edinburgh, 1958
Sim, A. F., *The Life and Letters of Arthur Fraser Sim*, London, 1896
Smith, George, *The Life of Alexander Duff*, London, 1879
The Lake Regions of Central Africa, Edinburgh, 1891
Smith, L. A., *George Adam Smith: A Personal Memoir and Family Chronicle*, London, 1943
Stevenson, James, *The Civilization of South Eastern Africa*, Glasgow, 1877
Notes on the Country between Kilwa and Tanganika, Glasgow, 1877
The Arab in Central Africa, Glasgow, 1888
Stewart, James, *Lovedale Past and Present*, Lovedale, South Africa, 1887
Livingstonia: Its Origin, Edinburgh, 1894
Dawn in the Dark Continent, London, 1903
'The Second Circumnavigation of Lake Nyassa', *Proceedings of the Royal Geographical Society*, 1879
Stokes, Eric, 'Malawi Political Systems and the Introduction of Colonial Rule, 1891–1896', in Eric Stokes and Richard Brown (ed.), *The Zambesian Past: Studies in Central African History*, Manchester, 1966
Stone, W. V., 'The Livingstonia Mission and the Bemba', *Bulletin for the Society of African Church History*, II, 1968
Sundkler, B. G. M., *Bantu Prophets in South Africa*, London, 1948
The Christian Ministry in Africa, London, 1960
Swann, Alfred J., *Fighting the Slave Hunters in Central Africa*, London, 1910

Tangri, Roger, 'Inter-war "Native Associations" and the formation of the Nyasaland African Congress', *Transafrican Journal of History*, I, 1971

Taylor, John V., *The Growth of the Church in Buganda*, London, 1958

Taylor, John V., and Dorothea Lehmann, *Christians of the Copperbelt: The Growth of the Church in Northern Rhodesia*, London, 1961

Temple, Merfyn M., 'Profile of Kaunda', in *Black Government? A Discussion between Colin Morris and Kenneth Kaunda*, Lusaka, 1960

Terry, P. T., 'The Rise of the African Cotton Industry in Nyasaland, 1902–1918', *Nyasaland Journal*, xv, 1962

Tew, Mary, *Peoples of the Lake Nyasa Region*, London, 1950

Thomson, Joseph, *To the Central Lakes and Back*, London, 1881

Thrupp, Sylvia L. (ed.), *Millenial Dreams in Action, Comparative Studies in Society and History*, Supplement II, The Hague, 1962

Trimingham, J. Spencer, *Islam in East Africa*, Oxford, 1964

Vail, H. L., 'Suggestions towards a reinterpreted Tumbuka history', in Pachai, B. (ed.), *The Early History of Malawi*, London, 1972

'The Making of an Imperial Slum: Nyasaland and its Railways, 1895–1935', *JAH*, XVI, 1975

van Velsen, J. *The Politics of Kinship: A Study in Social Manipulation among the Lakeside Tonga of Nyasaland*, Manchester, 1964

'Labour Migration as a Positive Factor in the Continuity of Tonga Tribal Society', in Southall, A. W. (ed.), *Social change in Modern Africa*, Oxford, 1961

'The Missionary Factor among the Lakeside Tonga of Nyasaland', *Human Problems in British Central Africa*, XXVI, 1959

'Notes on the History of the Lakeside Tonga of Nyasaland', *African Studies*, XVIII, 1959

'The Establishment of the Administration in Tongaland', *Historians in Tropical Africa*, Salisbury, 1962, mimeo

'Some Early Pressure Groups in Malawi' in Eric Stokes and Richard Brown (ed.), *The Zambesian Past: Studies in Central African History*, Manchester, 1966

Waller, Horace, *The Title-Deeds to Nyasa-Land*, London, 1887

Wallis, J. P. R., (ed.), *The Zambesi Expedition of David Livingstone, 1858–1863*, London, 1956

The Zambesi Journal of James Stewart, 1862–1863, London, 1962

Ward, Gertrude, *The Life of Charles Allan Smythies*, London, 1896

Webster, James Bertin, *The African Churches among the Yoruba, 1888–1922*, Oxford, 1964

Weinthal, Leo, *The Story of the Cape to Cairo Railway and Route from 1887 to 1922*, London, n.d.

Wells, James, *Stewart of Lovedale*, London, 1908

Werner, A., *The Natives of British Central Africa*, London, 1906

Willis, R. G., '"Kamcape": an anti-sorcery movement in South-west Tanzania', *Africa*, XXXVIII, 1968

Wilson, G. H., *A History of the Universities' Mission to Central Africa*, London, 1936

Wilson, Godfrey, *The Constitution of the Ngonde*, Rhodes–Livingstone Papers No. 3, 1939

Wilson, Monica, *Good Company: a Study of Nyakyusa Age-Villages*, London, 1951

The Peoples of the Nyasa–Tanganyika Corridor, Cape Town, 1959, mimeo

Winspear, Frank, 'Some Reminiscences of Nyasaland', *Nyasaland Journal*, XIII 1960

Wishlade, R. L., *Sectarianism in Southern Nyasaland*, London, 1965

Wright, Marcia, *German Missions in Tanganyika, 1891–1941*, Oxford, 1971

Wright, Marcia, and Lary, Peter, 'Swahili settlements in Northern Zambia and Malawi, *African Historical Studies*, IV, 1971

Wrigley, C. C., 'The Christian Revolution in Buganda', *Comparative Studies in Society and History*, II, 1959

Young, E. D., *The Search after Livingstone*, London, 1868

Nyassa: A Journal of Adventures, London, 2nd edition, 1877

Young, T. Cullen, *Notes on the History of the Tumbuka–Kamanga Peoples in the Northern Province of Nyasaland*, London, 932

Young, T. Cullen, and Banda, Hastings Kamuzu (ed.), *Our African Way of Life*, London, 1946

Young, T. Cullen (ed.), 'The Religion of my Fathers', *International Review of Missions*, XIX, 1930

'How far can African Ceremonial be incorporated in the Christian system?', *Africa*, VIII, 1935

'The "Native" Newspaper', *Africa*, XI, 1938

'The "Henga" People in Northern Nyasaland', *Nyasaland Journal*, V, 1952

Index

Abdallah, Y. B., 6
Aberdeen, 29, 52, 158, 181, 234
Abeokuta, 36
Aborigines Protection Society, 66
Aden, 26
African Lakes Company: origins, 43–4; early operations, 44–6, 54; employees, 48, 62, 75, 170–1, 259; and Livingstonia, 44, 72, 77, 82, 138, 159–61, 170–1; treaties, 77, 94, 110, 159–60, 171; and labour migration 82–3, 113, 115, 258; and 'Arab War', 103–6; and Indian traders, 117; rubber estate, 114, 186, 269
African Methodist Episcopal Church, 201
African National Church, 273–4, 277, 281–2, 284
African Presbyterian Church, 71n
African Reformed Presbyterian Church, 274, 284
African Sabbath Recorder, 215
African Transcontinental Telegraph Company, 138, 140
Aitken, George, 105
Ajayi, Professor, 195
Alliance High School, Kenya, 242
Amanda, Sam, 226
America, 201, 203, 209, 213, 233
Amon Jere, Chief Mtwalo II, see Muhawi
Amuhoni, Andrew, 211
Anjos, Paul Marianno Vas dos, 11
Ansumba, Jordan, 212
apprentices from Overtoun Institution, 127, 138–42, 237–8
'Arab War', 103–4, 110; and Scottish missionaries, 157–8, 168, 171–3
Arabs, 4–5, 12–13, 23, 35–6, 39, 41–2, 45–6, 60–1, 63, 78, 82–3, 85, 88, 94, 103–6, 110–11, 157–8, 162, 168, 172
Argyllshire, 249
Arthington, Robert, 29
Ashcroft, Frank, 230, 232–3, 236
Atonga Tribal Council *see* Tonga Tribal Council
Aurora, 257
Austen, Ralph, 11

Bain, Rev. J. H., 72–3, 75, 102–5, 108, 171, 178
Balakazi (female elders), 253
Balfour of Burleigh, Lord, 160
Balowoka, 3, 5
Banda clan, 289–90
Banda, Dr H. K., vii, 155, 264
Banda, John Afwenge, 129–30, 197, 222
Banda, Lamek Mankwalwa, 147
Bandawe: observation post, 57–8, use of force at, 52, 62–4, 75–6; new policy introduced, 69–70; relations with Tonga at, 77–85, 119–22, 186–9; and Ngoni, 90, 93–5; contrast with Karonga, 106; and colonial authorities, 111, 168, 174; evangelisation from, 127, 129–30; students at Institution from, 144, 149–51; and elephant hunters, 170; and Watch Tower, 184, 202–5, 209; and Inwood, 219; and the War, 223, 225; and soil erosion, 240; and schools, 240–1, 249, 283; and teachers, 252, 263; and WNNA, 266–7, 270, and *Mchape*, 280
Barbour, George, 29
Barnes, J. A., 88
Barotseland, 34, 36, 191, 285
Barrett, D. B., 277

Batoka Plateau, 18
Bechuanaland, 155
Bedford, Cape Province, 191
Bell, Miss, 100
Bemba, 7, 12, 13, 86–7, 107, 125–6, 127–30, 134
Benson, Mary, 285
Berlin Mission Society, 131, 223, 226, 229–30
Bible, the: as source of power, 88–90, 92; as text-book, 146, 181; and baptism, 187–8; taught, 191; as source of authority, 130, 152–3, 215, 250, 277–8
Binnie, Thomas, 133, 136, 227
Bisa, 2, 4, 12, 53, 86, 127–8
Bismark, Joseph, 47–8
Black, Dr William, 178–9
Black Man's Church of God which is in Tongaland, 275–6, 281
Blantyre Mission: founded, 29, 41; early dependants at, 47, 49; and Livingstonia, 52, 58; and atrocities, 65–8; under D. C. Scott, 69–70; and Maseko Ngoni, 100–1; and education, 132, 141, 235, 238; and colonial occupation, 157–69; social attitudes, 163–4, 173–4; end of monopoly, 175; financial resources, 176–7; forms of worship, 195; conference, 196; Church members, 199, 250, 292; and German missions, 223–4; and CCAP, 247–8
Blantyre Mission Sub-Committee, 66–8; 100
Blantyre Presbytery, 247–8
Blantyre (town and district), 48, 102, 139, 148, 158, 162, 165, 173, 175–6, 200, 223, 263, 271
Blyden, Edward, 215
Blythswood, 27
Boers, 18
Bombay, 26–7
Booth, Joseph: founds Malawi missions, 175–6, 189; and Kamwana, 189, 201; and Seventh Day Baptists, 209–10, 214; and Domingo, 212–13, 215, 218
Boquito, Thomas, 47–8
Bowie, Dr John, 162–3
Bowring, Sir Charles, 234–6
Boxer, Dr E. A., 129, 186
Brackenbury, A. J., 266
Brink, Pastor, 209
British Central Africa Gazette, 166
British Government, and imperial policy, 24–5, 114, 239; and colonial occupation, 110–13, 157–62, 168
British India Steam Navigation Company, 26, 29
British South Africa Company, 125, 135, 141, 155, 157, 160–1, 166, 168–70, 174
British West African territories, 114
Broken Hill, 200, 209, 284
Brooke, Rajah, 161
Bruce, A. L., 161
Buchanan Institute, Glasgow, 178
Buchanan, John, 65, 157
Buganda, 35–6, 75, 84, 90, 97
Bulawayo, 200
Burnett, Dr, 271
Burton, Richard, 21, 24
Bwana Mkubwa mine, 150

Cabora Bassa rapids, 18
Cairns, H. A. C., 157
Calabar, 232
Cape Maclear: Free Church settlement at, vii, 35, 37–40, 42, 46–54, 70, 73, 77, 80–2; and Bandawe, 57–8, 62–3, 84; and Lovedale evangelists, 71, 190–1, 193, 228
Cape Town, 47, 85, 135, 155, 169, 189–90, 206, 208–9, 214
Carnegie Trust, 238
Cetshwayo, 90
Chabisa, 13, 111
Chalmers, Thomas, 179
Chamaranda, Edward, 200
Chambers Graduated Readers, 264
Chambezi river, 129
Chancellor College, 242
Chanock, Martin, 252–3, 259
Chewa, 3, 7, 12–15, 19, 73, 84, 86, 92, 96, 100–1, 114, 125, 127, 130–1, 148, 225, 252, 260
Chibambo, Yesaya, 96, 246, 251, 263–4, 268
Chibeza village, 128
Chibisa, 11, 49, 171
Chicago, 28, 155
Chidionga, 100
Chifira village, 202–3, 212, 290–1
Chifisi, 13, 100–2
Chigowo, Jacob, 211

Chihayi, Gilbert, 209, 211
Chikanga, 292
Chikang'ombe shrine, 15
Chikhumba, 166
Chikulamayembe: empire, 3, 5, 7, 11; and Livingstonia graduates, 286–9
Chikundu, 2, 15
Chikuru, 58, 61, 77, 79–80, 85, 202n
Chikusi, 13, 40, 73, 100–2, 191
Chikwa village, 127
Chilembwe, John, 207–8, 210, 217–218
Chilembwe Rising, 207–8, 218–19, 224, 226, 245, 265
Chimbono, 58, 62, 64, 77–9, 85, 202
Chimlolo, 49, 51, 53–4
Chimtunga (Mbelwa II), 110–11, 124, 149, 226, 280–1, 286, 288
Chimwemwe village, 252–3
China, 24, 118
Chinde, 141
Chinese, 233
Chindio, 114
Ching'oma, 275
Chingoni, 119, 191
Chinsali, 129–30, 226, 250
Chinsali *boma*, 261
Chinteche, 58–60, 75–8, 80, 86–7, 95–6, 115, 202–3, 275. *See also* Mankhambira
Chinteche *boma*, 205, 266–7, 271
Chinula, Charles: at Overtoun Institution, 149; at Loudon, 196, 264, 277; ordained, 251; class, 256; and MoNA, 267, 276; and Eklesia Lanangwa 275–9, 284; and local politics, 286, 288
Chinyama, Filipo, 215
Chinyanja (Chichewa), 2, 100, 120–1, 148, 182, 241
Chinyera, 97, 191
Chipata village, 211, 213–14
Chipatula, 34
Chiputula *see* Nhlane, Mayayi Chiputula
Chiradzulu, 166, 280
Chirenje *see* Mweniwanda's
Chirnside, Andrew, 66–7
Chiromo, 157, 200
Chirwa, Jonathan, 199, 222, 226
Chirwa, Philemon, 252, 267, 289–90
Chirwa, Timon, 212
Chirwa, Uriah, 199, 260
Chisholm, Dr James, 129–30, 170, 222, 250
Chisumphi cult, 15
Chitezi, 98, 192
Chiuta, 84
Chitambo, 130, 250
Chitonga, and Livingstonia missionaries, 84, 121
Chitumbuka, 148, 241, 277
Chiwere Ndhlovu, 7–9
Chiweyu, 290
Chombi estate, 269
Christian Native Marriage Ordinance, 196
Chualo, 51
Church Missionary Society, 31, 35, 90
Church of Central Africa Presbyterian, viii, 247–51, 253, 274, 278, 291–4. *See also* Livingstonia Presbytery
Church of Scotland, 21–2, 29–30, 65, 68, 136, 161, 163. *See also* Blantyre Mission
Church of Scotland Foreign Missions Committee: and Blantyre atrocities, 66–8; and colonial occupation, 158, 160–1
Church of Scotland Home and Foreign Missionary Record, 31
Coillard, François, 171
Clarendon, Lord, 25
Clegg, Thomas, 36
Cochrane, Rev. M., 200–1
Commission of Inquiry into Nyasaland Rising, 206, 211, 217, 270
Congo, Belgian (Zaïre), 126
Conran, Dr, 258
conversion to Christianity: and religious crisis of late nineteenth century, 13–16, 279; in East and West Africa, 35–6; Yao rejection, 39–42, 44–6, 50–6; at Cape Maclear, 48–9, 54; in Tongaland, 73–85; and northern Ngoni, 85–99; and Ngonde, 106–9; popular demand for, 120–3, 186–9, 219–20, 229; through African evangelists, 121, 125–30; nature of, 130–1, 292–4; and evil 279–82
Copperbelt, the, 294
Cotterill, H. B., 42

cotton, 4, 10, 17–21, 23, 61, 81, 113, 139, 240, 263
Cowan, Sir John, 30
Cowgate (Edinburgh), 179
Crooks, Thomas, 51–2
Cross, Dr David Kerr, 73, 104–5, 107, 119, 134, 168, 172–3, 179
Cross, Sholto, 204
Crowther, Bishop, 194, 244

Daly, J. F., 128, 183, 227
Dar es Salaam, 155
Dedza, 8, 111
Dedza highlands, 11, 73
Deep Bay, 273–4
Delagoa Bay, 7–8
Devlin Report, 292
Dewar Alexander: at Karonga, 118; at Mwenzo, 125, 129; critical of Overtoun Institution, 134; critical of colonial administration, 172, 174; and Livingstonia Presbytery, 243
Disruption in Church of Scotland, 21, 30
district (Nyasaland)
  Blantyre, 212
  Mzimba, 239, 274, 281, 288
  Mombera, 214, 261, 288
  North Nyasa, 258–9, 284
  Lower Shire, 113, 212
  Upper Shire, 113, 212
  West Nyasa, 155, 184, 189, 207–9, 225–6, 239–40, 251–2, 261–2, 273, 292
  West Shire, 212
Domasi, 69, 165–6, 241
Domboshawa, 287
Domingo, Charles: brought to Malawi, 47; at Overtoun Institution, 144, 150, 156; on African dances, 196; quits Livingstonia, 198–9; joins Seventh Day Baptists, 210–15; as political philosopher, 175, 215–17; later career, 218; and Livingstonia agents, 227; downfall, 256
Domingo, Sarah, 213
Domira Bay, 8
Domwe mountain, 7–8
Drummond, Henry, 121, 181
Duff, Dr Alexander, 26–7, 31
Duff, Hector, 179, 224
Dundee, 29
Dupont, Bishop, 129
Durban, 26
Dutch Reformed Church mission, 126, 131, 148, 175, 177–8, 180, 221, 229–30, 238, 241, 246–47, 293
Dwambazi: village and district, 80, 202, 212–13; river 289
Dwanga river, 114

Edinburgh, 21–2, 29–30, 143, 158, 163, 179, 181
Edinburgh Daily Review, 32
Edinburgh House, 230
education
  African-controlled, 211–14, 217, 282–5; government, 56, 241–2; demands for, 271, 286–7; Islamic, 35, 55
Education mission: in East and West Africa, 35–6; at Cape Maclear, 38, 48–9, 53–4; in Tongaland, 80–3; in Ngoniland, 93, 97–9, 124; at north end of lake, 106, 118; growing demand for, 118–20; at Overtoun Institution, 132–3, 143–55, 232–8, 240; European attitudes towards, 116–17, 176–86; and church membership, 187–8; and the underprivileged, 203–4, 211–12; and the War, 222–3, 228, 230–1; and women, 253; and the government, 231–2, 241–2; in the 1930s, 238, 240–3; African criticisms of, 264–5, 270–1, 283, 286–7; and politics, 151–6, 253–5, 257, 264–6
Edwardes, Major C. A., 180
Eklesia Lanangwa, 275
Ekwendeni, 96–9, 115–16, 119, 122–4, 127, 130, 144, 151, 187, 219, 223, 225, 249
Elangeni, 197, 280
Eldorado mine, 212
Elisabethville, 155
Elmslie, Dr W. A.: and Ngoni, 72, 86–9, 91–5, 97–9, 124; and Livlezi, 101; and colonial occupation, 111, 171; on educational expansion, 119; on revivalism, 121; on Institution, 134, 137, 139; on Blantyre mission, 164; on Rhodes, 170; and admission to church membership, 187–9; and Lovedale assistants, 191–3; and African culture, 194–7; and Watch

Tower, 199, 203–4; and Seventh Day Baptists, 214; on teacher shortage, 231; and Livingstonia Presbytery, 243, 245; and African pastors, 244
Elton, Captain, 37, 47, 55
Emcisweni, 251
English language: taught at Institution, 146, 148, 153; Livingstonia graduates expert in, 153; DRC reluctant to teach, 178; and women, 180; congregations seek expertise in, 201; passion for learning deplored, 237

Faulds, M. H., 251
Federation of Rhodesia and Nyasaland, viii
Fife, 125, 222–3
firearms, 5–6, 12, 18, 39–41, 83, 86–7, 94, 96
First World War, 129, 156, 199, 208, 264; effects on Livingstonia's stations, 221–3; on African agents, 225–7, 245; on native associations, 262; and Scottish missions in Tanganyika, 223–5; and financial crisis, 228–9
Florence Bay, 273
Forbes, Major P. C., 135, 138, 169–70
Fort Jameson (Chipata), 115, 141, 288
Fotheringham, Dr David, 75–6
Fotheringham, Monteith, 75, 103–4
Fraser, Mrs A. R., 253
Fraser, Donald, 38, 96; as intermediary, 112, 171; at Loudon, 119, 238; and revivalism, 121–3, 186; and Luangwa valley, 127; on need for European control, 128, 244–5; on Laws, 174, 179; upbringing, 178; social attitudes, 179–80; and African culture, 194–7; and Domingo, 197–8, 210; on labour migration, 200; on the War, 228; as fund-raiser, 227, 229; and education, 232–3, 235–6, 264; and Balakazi, 253; and native associations, 270; and witchcraft, 279
Free Church of Scotland: and origins of Livingstonia, 21–2, 26–30; and Church of Scotland, 68; and 'Wee Frees', 128n; beliefs, 152, 177, 195, 278; organisation, 182; and CCAP, 247
Free Church of Scotland Foreign Missions Committee, 21, 26, 28–9, 31–2, 36, 162, 227–30, 234–6
Frere, Sir Bartle, 26–7
Fuka, 61, 77, 80

Galbraith, W. C., 242, 251
Galla, 27
Gamitto, A. C. P., 2, 19
Garanganze Mission, 148
Garvey, Marcus, 260, 283
Gaunt, R. F., 233
Gemuseus, Oscar, 223, 225
German East Africa, 104–5, 222–3; missions and Livingstonia, 123, 223–5, 229–30
Germany, 105
Glasgow, 22, 28–9, 32, 43, 151, 158, 178–9, 181, 209, 234; industrialists and Livingstonia, 28–32, 43–4; University, 122, 147
Globe and Phoenix mine, 212
Golinga, 50
Gomani, 100, 102
Gondwe, Nathan, 201
Goodrich, Consul, 60, 77–8, 88
Gordon, Sir Arthur, 66, 68
Gossip, Robert, 104–5
Granville, Lord, 158
Gregson, R. E., 251–2
Gulungula, 64
Gunn, John, 48
Guru's village, 226, 289

Halliday, A. C., 245
Hand, Rev. G. B., 177
Harawa, Yakobi, 251–2
Hardie, Keir, 30
Harding, Major, 111
Harrow (school), 42
Harry's Catechism, 120
Hawes, Consul, 54, 160
Henderson, Henry, 41, 47, 52
Henderson, James, 38, 143–7, 153, 182, 198, 228–9, 236
Henderson, John Riddell, 130, 206
Henderson, William, 29
Henga, 76, 86–7, 96, 104, 106, 116, 135, 143–4, 148, 273
Henga valley, 7, 107, 115, 143, 238, 251–2

Henry, Dr George, 101
Henry Henderson Institute, 132, 177
Hetherwick, Alexander: quoted 115, 117–18; background, 163; and colonial occupation, 160, 165–6, 168n, 169; paternalist attitudes, 173–4; and migrants, 200; and Domingo, 210; and CCAP, 247–8
High God, 13, 14, 15, 84, 120
Hoho village, 71, 91
Hora, Mount, 76
Horton, Robin, 14–15, 120

Ikawa *boma*, 174
Ilala, the, 34–5, 42, 44, 45, 53, 77–8, 82, 137
Ilala, 25
Iliffe, John, 225
Illustrated London News, 47
India, 21, 24, 26, 118, 158
Indian Civil Service, 62
Indian Ocean, 36
Indians, 5, 26, 117, 233, 269, 272
Industrial and Commercial Workers Union of South Africa (ICU), 150, 274, 290
Innes, Dr Frank, 174, 178
Inverness, 151
Inwood, Dr Charles, 123, 219
Inyati, James, 148–9
Iosko, 230
Irvine, Miss, 231
Islam, 6, 15, 35, 54–6, 117, 120
Itete, 230

Japan, 211
Jeal, Tim, 25
Jeanes School, 182, 238; Training Centre, 241
Jenda, 275, 279
Jere clan, 87–8, 95, 99, 124, 288; Council, 286–8
Jere, I. M., 271
Jere, Lazaro, 288
Jere, Chief Samuel, 281, 293
Johannesburg, 155, 189, 200
Johnston, George, 52, 67
Johnston, H. H., 102, 110–12, 135, 151, 158, 162, 165–70, 172–3, 293
Johnston, Lorenzo, 47
Johnston, William, 209–10
Jones, T. Jesse, 232–3, 238
Jumbe of Nkota Kota, 12–13, 42, 46, 55, 86

Kachindamoto, 102
Kadalie, Clements, 141, 150, 155, 203, 260, 290–1
Kafue Training Institute, 132
Kakwewa school, 271
Kalinga, Owen, 3
Kambombo village, 127
Kambwiri, Harry, 101
Kamcape, 292
Kampata, 49
Kamwana, Eliot Kenan: and the evangelical tradition, 123; proselytises, 184; and tax, 186; career, 189; attracts suspended Presbyterians, 197, 199; in mining compound, 201; at Chifira, 203; appeals to underprivileged, 204–5; political significance, 205–8; rejects Sabbatarianism, 209; and Domingo, 211; and Watch Tower after 1909, 212–13, 258; and Inwood, 219; and migration, 260
Kaningina, 57–9, 61–2, 71
Kangoma, 58, 63, 77, 79
Kapangasina, 49, 51
Kapayenze, 131
Kapeni, 41, 164
Karamuka, 104–5
Karemteta, 238
Kariba Gorge, 127
Karonga: plain, 4; focus for trade between Arabs and the ALC, 45–6, 94; and 'Arab War', 103–4, 82, 110; mission station, 105–6, 118, 125, 222–3, 226–7, 241, 249, 254; and colonial occupation, 172, 174; pupils at Institution from, 148, 151, 155; and Watch Tower, 212, 258; and the War, 222–3, 225; and cotton, 240, 269; and the NNNA, 258–9; and independent churches, 273–4; and witchcraft, 280
Karonga (Phiri ruler), 2
Kasanga, 53
Kasisi, 258
Kasungu, 110; mission station, 125–6, 129, 229; transferred to DRC, 229–30, 246–7; and Watch Tower, 212
Katanga, 12, 140, 284

Kateta, Andreya, 155
Katonga, 79
Kaunda, David: at Chinsali, 129–30, 197, 292; political influence, 131; ordination delayed, 250
Kaunda, Kenneth, 131
Kaunda, Stefano Mujuzi, 121
Kawinga, 167
Kayayi cult, 204, 279
Kazembe (Lundu kingdom), 10
Keltie, J. Scott, 104
Kenya, 36, 118, 136, 231, 234, 242, 284
Keswick (conference), 123, 195
Khondowe, 115, 123, 133, 138–9, 143, 197, 199, 233, 238, 241, 257, 261–2. *See also* Overtoun Institution
Khondowe plateau, 125
Kibwezi, 136
Kilwa, 1, 9
King's African Rifles, 209
King's College, Aberdeen, 181, 234
King Williams Town, 201
Kircaldy, 62
Kirk, John, 18, 25
Kirkwood, Peter, 147
Kiungani, 148
Kololo *see* Makololo
Konde, Charles, 53, 84
Kongone mouth of the Zambezi, 34, 47
Kopa Kopa, 103
Koyi, William: at Cape Maclear, 47–8, 190; and northern Ngoni, 71–2, 90, 191; dies, 93; Scottish attitudes towards, 191–3
Krumen, 83
Kunda, 127
Kundu, prophetess, 186
Kurukuru, John, 84
Kuwira, 80
Kydd, 105
Kyimbila, 226
Kyungu, 4, 103, 105, 108, 252, 259, 268, 273

Labour migration: and belief in High God, 14, 120; and Tonga, 82–3, 186; and northern Ngoni, 98, 186; and Maseko Ngoni, 102; after establishment of colonial rule, 114–18; and Overtoun Institution students, 140–1, 155–6; and tax, 143, 186; and Christian independency, 199–202; Malawi's role in, 239; and political influence, 259–60; and Livingstonia, 292–4
Lacey, A. L., 242
Lady Nyassa, 45
Lagos, 35
Lambya, 102
Lancashire, 21
Last Church of God and His Christ, 273, 275
Laws, Mrs Margaret, 141, 143
Laws, Robert, 68, 75, 117, 119, 260, 290; record-keeping, ix; pioneer missionary, 33–4, 36–7; qualities, 38; on conversion, 15–16; on Kololo, 36–7; and Mponda, 40; at Blantyre, 52; evacuates Cape Maclear, 53; on Tonga, 59; on mission's use of civil powers, 50, 64–5, 69–70; and northern Ngoni, 71–2, 90, 93–5; and Maseko Ngoni, 100–1; at Bandawe, 58, 78, 85; economic strategy, 81–3; occupies Karonga, 105; speaks Chinyanja, 121; advocates European control, 128; at Overtoun Institution, 132–53, 156; and colonial occupation, 159–64, 167–8, 172–4; and BSAC, 169; and DRC, 175; influence of upbringing, 178–9; as head of mission, 182–3; on church admission, 188; on African culture, 194; and Lovedale assistants, 190–3; distaste for emotional preaching, 121, 123; response to labour migration, 200; and Watch Tower, 219; as provision merchant, 223; and German missions, 223–4; educational aims, 232–3; plans for Institution, 234–6; resigns, 236; on position of Africans in church, 245–46, 276–7; and CCAP, 247–8; influence on African pastors, 254, 283; and native associations, 257–8, 266–8, 270
Laws, Robert, senior, 179
Lengwe, Yona, 251
Lenshina, Alice, 292
Lettow-Vorbeck, von, General, 222
Lindsay, Professor, 159, 169
Life and Work Blantyre Mission Supplement, 161

Lilongwe, 274
Linden, Ian and Jane, 208, 292
Linthouse, 29
Lisbon, 162
Liverpool, 22, 122
Livingstone, David, viii, 4, 6, 11, 17–21, 23–8, 34, 36, 42, 45, 47, 60–1, 66, 70, 130, 133, 290
Livingstone, Mrs, 23
Livingstone (town), 200, 260, 284
Livingstone expedition *see* Zambesi expedition
Livingstone mountains, 58, 224
Livingstone search expedition, 33
Livingstonia: Kirk Sessions, 183, 197, 230, 243, 246–7, 250, 254, 257, 274, 280
Livingstonia mission: African agents: at Cape Maclear, 47–9, 52–3, at Bandawe, 57, 82, 84–5, 121; in Ngoniland, 98–9; at north end, 104, 106; growing influence of, 124–31; at Overtoun Institution, 132, 144–56; frustration suffered by, 190–9; pastors, 197–9, 250–1, 254–6; teachers, 221, 240–1; in Rhodesia, 200–1; in Tanganyika, 224–5; and Christian independency, 204–5, 209, 211; and the War, 221–3, 225–7, 262; in Presbytery, 243–9, 276–7; and entrepreneurship, 251–3; and women, 253–4; in politics, 124–45, 131–2, 151–6, 254–5, 256–92 *passim*. *See also* Lovedale evangelists
Livingstonia mission: economic influence: and underdevelopment, viii; antecedents, 17–22, 27–33; 'Commerce and Christianity', 38–46; at Bandawe, 81–4; in Ngoniland, 98; in the Northern Province, 114–18, 180, 238–40, 293–4; at Khondowe, 133–43, 151–2, 155–6, 232–3, 237–8; and entrepreneurship, 251–3; and women, 180, 253–4; and African responses, 263–5, 269–71, 282–3, 286–7
Livingstonia mission: financial and administrative structure: initial sources of support, 29–31; Scottish administration to 1914, 31–2; and Blantyre, 176–7; administration in Malawi, 182–3; new structures, 227–9
Livingstonia mission: Scottish agents: composition of expeditionary party, 32–3; artisans, 33, 44, 51–2, 62–5, 67–8; political attitudes, 164, 167–75; social background, 178–9; social attitudes, 179–82. *See also under individual missionaries*
Livingstonia Mission Council: abolishes Arts Course, 147; and Laws, 172, 182–3, and Presbytery, 197–8, 243–7; transfers stations to DRC, 230; suggests that Laws should resign, 235–6; scraps building programme, 236
Livingstonia Mission Estates Committee, 136
Livingstonia Mission sub-committee: foundation, 31; membership, 32; response to Blantyre atrocities, 67–70; and mission expansion, 72–3, 105, 129, 133–4; and Institution estate, 136; and ALC, 159–60; and Laws, 183; and Lovedale evangelists, 191–3; amalgamates with FMC, 227–8
Livingstonia Presbytery (Presbytery of North Livingstonia): autocratic tradition behind, 182–3; and marriage laws, 195–6; established, 197, 243; influence of Africans within, 197–8, 243–7; and Tanganyika mission, 224–5; union with Blantyre, 247–8; prejudice within, 249; and ordination, 250–1; and women, 253; political influence, 254–5, 257, 287; and Y. Z. Mwasi, 199, 274, 277, 280, 287
Livlezi, 54, 73, 101–2, 168, 172
London, 33, 141
London Missionary Society, 72, 126, 131, 148, 157, 191, 248
Lonsdale, John, 272
Loram, C. T., 238
Loudon, 119, 127, 131, 196, 198, 210, 219, 223, 229, 232, 238, 240–1, 249, 263, 275, 279–80
Lovedale evangelists, 37, 47–8, 71, 88, 93–4, 190–4 *passim*, 197, 199
Lovedale Institution, 27–8, 33, 37, 146, 191, 193, 210, 282
Lozi, 81

Luangwa river, 7; valley, 10, 12, 96, 112, 116, 126–31, 209, 224, 230
Lubwa, 130, 249, 292
Lugard, Captain Frederick, 83, 104
Luhanga, 3
Lumpa Church, 292
Lumphasa, 254, 274, 278
Lundu, 2–3
Lusaka, 290, 294
Lutherans, 180, 230
Luweya river, 59, 289

McCallum, Peter, 96, 129
Macalpine, A. G., 84, 121–2, 149, 174, 184, 187–9, 194, 205, 214, 243, 277
McCurrie, J. B., 52
Macdonald, Rev. Duff, 46, 52, 65–6, 164
McDonald, H. C., 125
McFadyen, John, 52
Mackenzie, D. R., 106, 147, 222–3, 225–6, 230–1, 258
Mackenzie, Bishop, 47
Mackinnon, Peter, 29
Mackinnon, William, 26, 29–30, 42–3, 160
Maclagen, J., 32
Macmillan, Hugh, 45
McMinn, R. D., 130, 205–6, 249–50
McMurtrie, John, 161–2
Macrae, Dr, 66, 69
Macvicar, Dr Neil, 163
Magomero, 20, 49
Main Reef mine, 189
Makandanji, 49
Makani, 198
Makanjira, 6, 10, 13, 39, 46, 55, 81
Makololo (Kololo), 11–12, 34–5, 48–9, 159
Makua, 5
Makwanga, Mark, 227
Malamia, 166
Malanda, 64
Malawi, Lake, 1, 7, 10, 12, 17–19, 27, 28, 30, 33, 35–6 71–2, 83, 90, 101–3, 113–14, 133, 137–8, 142, 158, 190, 204, 234, 247, 252
Malawi–Tanganyika corridor, 126, 159
Malilima, 34
Malinda, Amon, 211
Malmesbury, Lord, 19
Malombe, Lake, 35
Malungu, 166,
Mambwe, 107
Manchester, 19, 22, 141
Manda, Edward Bote, 149, 153–5, 246, 286, 289, 291
Mandala (ALC depot), 82, 159
Mandala (nickname of John Moir and by extension African name of ALC), 77
Manganja, 3–6, 9, 11, 13, 19, 23, 34, 38, 41, 46, 103, 113, 263; mission dependants, 47–50, 84
Mankhambira (headmen and village), 57–61, 64, 71, 78–80, 84–6, 89, 284. *See also* Chinteche
Mankhokwe, 2
Marambo, the *see* Luangwa valley
Marau, 124
Maravi, 1–3, 5, 11
Marenga (headmen and village), 58–9, 62–4, 76, 78–80, 83, 85, 202–3, 283, 289–90
Marini bands, 268
Martin, George, 29
Martin, J. R., 251, 270
Masea, 34, 49
Maseko Ngoni *see* Ngoni, Maseko
Mashonaland, 7, 118
Matabele, 85, 171
Matabeleland, 157, 170, 285
Matete valley, 76, 80
Maviti *see* Ngoni
Mazero, 47
Mazoe, 200–1
Mbande, 105, 108
Mbelwa, 7–8, 12, 71, 78, 88–95, 97, 107, 110, 124, 171, 191
Mbelwa II *see* Chimtunga
Mbelwa council *see* Jere council
Mbelwa's Ngoni *see* Ngoni, northern
M'bona cult, 15
Mbozi district, 226
Mchape, 280–1, 293
Mchimi, 84
Messenger of the Covenant Church, 275
Mgayi, 7
Mhango, Simon, 259–60
Miller, A. C., 62–3, 71, 89–90
mines, southern African, 114, 120, 141, 155, 189, 200–1, 212, 259–60
Mitchell, Clyde, 6–7
Mitioche, 166

Mkandawire, Simon, 273–4, 276
Mkandawire, Y. M., 246, 274, 278, 280, 283
Mkhoma, 238, 247, 293
Mkhondowe, Isaac, 273
Mkochi, Andrew, 226
Mlanje, 69, 165–6, 207, 280
Mlima, 97
Mlozi, 12, 103
Moffat, J. S., 171
Moffat, John, 284
Moffat, Malcolm, 130, 138, 142
Moffat, Robert, 85, 95
Moir, Dr, 159
Moir, Fred, 44–5, 149, 159
Moir, John, 44–5, 149, 159–61
Moloko, 48
Montfort Marist Fathers, 176
Moody and Sankey, 121
Moore, N. O. and Wilcox, Wayland, 214
Moravians, 131, 223–6, 230, 248, 250
Moray House Training College, 243
Morrison, Frederick, 60, 77, 107–8
Mozambique, 2, 5, 87, 155, 239
Mpama, 164
Mpasa, 49, 51, 54
Mperembe, 7, 89, 95–6, 124
Mpezeni, 7–8, 13, 111–12
Mphande, Yoram, 224–26
Mpingo wa Afipa wa Africa, 275, 284–5
Mponda (village and headmen), 6, 10–11, 13–14, 35, 39–41, 45–6, 48–9, 51, 54–5, 63, 101–2
Mpongo, 70
Mputa, 8
Msumwa, Jordan, 273
Mtusu, Daniel, 199
Mtwalo, 7, 89, 93, 95–6, 99, 124, 171
Muhanga, Simon, 155
Muhawi (Amon, Mtwalo II), 99, 124, 268
Mumba, Levi: at Institution, 149, 156; on African religion, 197; higher education memorandum, 242, 271; as associationist, 256, 260–2, 267, 271–2; and ANC, 276, 282
Murchison cataracts, 34, 43
Murray, A. C. 175
Murray Mitchell, J., 26–7, 32
Mushinda, P. B., 249
Mutesa, 90
Muwamba, E. A., 149–50, 256, 290
Muwamba, I. C. K., 150, 290
Muwamba, William, 149
Muwamba, Y. M., 121, 144, 149, 210
Mvera, 148, 175, 178
Mvula, John Brown, 49, 84
Mwakasungulu, Peter, 252, 259, 267–8
Mwamba, 129
Mwamulima, Patrick, 227, 254, 267, 291
Mwanza, Hezekaiah, 267, 271
Mwase Kasungu, 11–12, 86, 111, 125
Mwasi, Yesaya Zerenje: and Chitambo, 130; at Institution, 149, 156; delays in ordination, 199; and Dr Turner, 199, 244; pastor at Sanga, 226, 245, 254; in Presbytery, 244–6; on other pastors, 254; secretary of WNNA, 267, 269–70, 272, 276; leaves CCAP, 274; and Black Man's Church, 275, 277–9, 282; and plans for college, 283–5; and local politics, 290–1
Mwavi, 13–14, 54
Mwaya, 224
Mweniwanda's, 72–3, 102–4, 107, 131
Mwenzo, 125–6, 128–30, 134, 148–9, 151, 170, 174, 222–3, 228, 262
Mweru, Lake, 131, 148
Mzikuwola (Yohane), 99, 124
Mzilikozi, 95
Mzimba *boma*, 218
Mzimba, Rev. Pambani, 71
Mzimu, 251, 280

Namalambe, Albert, 49, 53–5, 73, 100, 121, 147, 193
Namwanga, 107, 125, 129, 148
Natal, 7
Native Associations: in Northern Rhodesia, 131, 262; and Institution, 132; antecedents, 257–8; North Nyasa, 258–62, 266, 269; Mwenzo, 262; West Nyasa, 263, 266–72; Mombera, 266, 286, 288; Southern Province, 266; Representative Committee of the Northern Provinces, 266; significance, 271–3; and local councils, 285–90
Ncheu, 101, 215
Ndirande, 166

Ndola, 150, 284, 290
Negro World, 283
New College, 21
New Langenburg, 223–4
Ngerenge, 105–6
Ng'oma, Noa Chiporuporu, 121
Ngonde, 3–4, 12, 86, 96, 102–10, 114, 118, 123, 125, 148, 172, 252, 273
Ngoni, 1, 7–15, 107
Ngoni, Maseko, 7–8, 11, 40, 73, 100–2, 111
Ngoni, Mpezeni, 11, 85, 111
Ngoni, northern, 12, 36, 57–62, 71–2, 76–8, 80, 85–101, 107, 110–26, 132, 135, 145, 148, 165, 171–2, 191–2, 195, 226, 287–8
Ngoniland, northern, 61, 76, 84–7, 91, 97, 100–1, 116, 123, 170–1, 191–2, 195, 197, 199, 211, 213–14, 263, 279–81, 286, 292, 294
Ngoniland, southern 73, 100–1, 168, 172
Ng'onomo, 8, 87, 95–7, 111
Ngunana, Shadrach, 48, 190–1
Nhlane, Mayayi Chiputula, 12, 59, 71, 89
Niger Expedition, 24
Nigeria, 180, 190, 194, 232, 284
Nile, 28
Njobvu, Andrew Mwana, 53, 84
Njuyu, 71–2, 90–3, 97–9, 197, 251
Nkata Bay, 18, 61, 112, 115, 186, 269, 294
Nkota Kota, 5, 10, 12–13, 42, 50, 57, 61, 86, 111, 114, 125, 184
North-Eastern Rhodesia, 126, 131, 170
Northern Rhodesia *see* Zambia
Northey, General, 222
Nsenga, 87, 98
Nsenga country, 7
Ntinili, Mapas, 190–1, 193
Nyakyusa, 4, 102, 104, 106–8, 123, 273
Nyamwezi, 4
Nyasaland African Congress, vii, 291
Nyasaland Blackman's Educational Society, 283–4
Nyasaland Legislative Council, 174, 257
Nyasaland Missionary Conference, 182, 187, 198
Nyasulu, Paddy, 273
Nyasuru, George, 226–7, 251, 280
Nyau cult, 84
Nyiha, 102
Nyika plateau 116, 133
Nyirenda, Saulos, 289

Old Calabar, 35
Oldham, J. H., 230
O'Neill, Consul, 69
Overtoun Institution (Khondowe, Livingstonia), vii, 98, 124–8, 132–56, 164, 177, 189, 190, 196, 199, 210, 219, 221, 223, 225, 227–8, 231–8, 240–4, 249, 251, 253, 255, 260–2, 264–5, 271–2, 282, 291, 293
Overtoun Institution Senatus, 139, 223, 253, 261
Overtoun, Lord *see* White, John Campbell

Palmerston, Lord, 24–5
Panthumbi, 101
Pemba, 5, 104
Petrie, Miss, 231
Phelps-Stokes Commission, 139–40, 178, 231–2, 293
phemba medicine, 274, 280
Phiri clan 289–90
Phiri, Rev. Hanoc, 264, 284n
Phoka, 116, 148
Plainfield Industrial Mission, 189, 209
Plainfield, New Jersey, 209, 214
Plymouth Brethren, 131
Pollockshields, 179
Poole, Dr Wordsworth, 83
Port Herald, 114
Portugal, 162
Portuguese, 2, 7, 12, 18–19, 23, 43, 157–9
Prentice, Dr George, 127, 129, 179, 230
Presbyterian Church of South Africa, 200–1
Pretoria, 201
Pretorius, J. L., 178
Pringle, Alexander, 66–8
Procter, Lovell, 47
Province (Nyasaland) Central, 291
  Northern, 48, 57, 139, 143, 156, 213, 218, 239, 242, 263, 283, 294
  Southern, 82, 176, 291
Punjab, 62, 65

Que Que, 212

Queen's Hall, Glasgow, 28
Quelimane, 1, 24, 41, 47

railway, 18, 114, 127, 239
Ramakukan, 34, 48–9
Rand, the, 155, 206
Ranger, T. O., 208, 279, 285
Rankine, Dr, 66, 68
Read, Margaret, 292, 294
Report on Emigrant Labour (1935), 239
Rhodes, Cecil, 127, 135, 160–1, 166, 169–70
Riddel, Alexander, 52, 62, 67–8, 70–1, 89–90
Rigby, Consul, 9
rinderpest, 114–16
Robertson, D. M., 251
Robertson, W. Govan, 168, 172–3
Roman Catholic Church, 105, 126, 175, 220, 241, 278, 292–3
Ross, Andrew, 164, 247
Royal College of Physicians and Surgeons, 181
Ruarwe, 9, 189
Rukuru river, 112; plain, 116
Rungwe, 104, 131
Ruo river, 158
Russell, Lord, 20, 24–5
Russell, Pastor Charles Taze, 189, 205, 207–10
Rutenganio, 224, 230
Rutherglen, 29–30
Ruvuma river, 19, 36

St Lawrence river, 18
Salim bin Abdallah, 5
Salim bin Najim, 103
Salisbury, 115–16, 141, 149, 155, 200, 212
Sambani, Samuel, 47–8
Sambo, Robert, 260, 274, 282
Sanderson, Meredith, 261
Sanga, 212, 245, 254, 274, 278, 284
Sarawak, 161
Schoffeleers, Dr, 15
Scotland, 29–30, 32–3, 62, 64, 67, 121, 134, 143, 147, 159–60, 163, 180, 182, 195, 198, 203, 209, 229, 232, 235–6, 238, 243–4, 246–7, 292
Scotsman, The, 68
Scott, David Clement, 69–70, 101, 160–9, 173, 195, 248
Scott, Henry, 163
Scott, Dr William (Blantyre missionary), 163, 167
Scott, Dr William (Livingstonia missionary), 77
Scottish influence on: discipline, 48, 62–3; hymn tunes, 84; forms of worship, 121; school syllabus, 151; social reform, 179, 182; educational policy, 181; church government, 183, 243; theological training, 278
Seapoint, 189
Senga, 9, 87, 96, 126–7
Seremani, Walter, 200
Seventh-day Adventists, 189, 273
Seventh Day Baptists, 209–22, 227
Seychelles, 213
Seyid Burgash (Sultan of Zanzibar), 12
Shaba, Edward, 281
Shaka, 88, 92
Shamva, 212
Sharpe, Alfred, 82, 112–13, 117, 125, 166, 171–2, 287–8
Shepperson, George, 207; and Price, Thomas, 184
Shire highlands, 9–11, 13, 18, 19, 22–3, 40, 100, 102, 113, 115, 132, 140, 157–8, 165
Shire river, 8, 17–18, 34, 72, 114, 131, 158, 165
Shire valley, 15, 19, 50, 62, 263
Shire–Zambesi waterway, 1, 19, 23, 30, 43–5, 72
Shona, 149
Sibanda, Yakobi, 148
Siberrad, A., 225n
Sierra Leoneans, 190
Simpson, Alan, 52, 58, 62–4
Sinoia, 212
Sirhind canal, 62
Siwale, Donald, 148–9, 261–2
Smith, Dr George, 32, 68, 160–2, 168, 182–3, 193
Smith, J. A., 159, 166
Smythies, Bishop, 177
social differentiation, viii, 147–51, 256–7, 294. *See also* Education
Sogoli, 51
Somali, 26; -land, 27–8
Songwe river, 102, 104–5
South Africa, 27, 71, 85, 104, 115, 151,

155, 169, 178, 199–201, 206–7, 212, 233, 259, 265
South African General Mission, 131
South African Native National Congress, 259
Southern Rhodesia, 112, 118, 127, 149, 155, 199–200, 208, 231, 259, 266, 274, 283, 287
Speke, J. H., 21, 24
Stanley, H. M., 25
Stanley, Sir Herbert, 234, 236
Steele, George, 99, 179
Stephen, Alexander, 29
Stephen, John, 28, 31, 44, 159
Stevenson, James, 29, 31–2, 42–3, 46, 57, 72–3, 132, 134, 159, 227
Stevenson Road, 102
Stewart, James (civil engineer), 52, 62–3, 65, 68, 70–2, 105, 157
Stewart, Dr James, 20–8, 31–3, 36–7, 42–3, 47–8, 52–3, 65, 67–8, 71, 136, 146, 157–8, 190, 193
Stone, Vernon, 250
Stuart, Charles, 171, 188
Student Volunteer Missionary Movement, 122
Suez Canal, 26
Sundkler, Bishop, 184
Sutherland, James, 72, 90–1
Swahili, 4–5, 10, 12–13, 36, 48, 55, 86, 103–6, 120, 127. *See also* Arabs

Tamanda, 130, 229–30
Tandu, Hanson, 209–11
Tanganyika, 36, 104, 107, 116, 126–7, 140, 234, 240, 255, 268, 273, 280; Scottish missions active in, 223–6, 229–30, 251
Tanganyika Concessions Company, 258
Tanganyika, Lake, 7, 28, 44, 72, 83, 125, 148, 161
Tangri, Roger, 261, 291
tax, 113–16, 143, 166, 168, 174, 186, 205–7, 209, 239
Tembo, Makera, 98, 124, 197
Tembo, Mawelero, 98–9, 124, 197
Tembwe, 127
Territorial cults, 14–15
Thelwall, W. B., 47
Thole, Peter, 250–1, 254
Thonga, 87, 92
Thyolo, 189
Tjoloto, 287
Tonga: origins, 3; resist Ngoni, 9, 11–12; and *mwavi*, 14; attractions of Livingstonia to, 57–61; mission as political factor among, 62–4, 70–1, 75–9; and education, 79–81, 97, 118–19, 186–90, 294; and Christianity, 15, 84–5, 120–3, 186–90, 294; and Ngoni, 86–7, 90, 94, 96; and labour migration, 82–3, 114–15, 117, 186, 200, 239; teachers, 124–5; as missionaries, 129–31, 224; at Institution, 148, 150, 155; treaties made with, 159, 171–2; and colonial occupation, 165, 174; and Watch Tower, 184, 202–4, 208–9, 212; and the War, 225–6; and native associations, 260; and independent schools, 284
Tonga Tribal Council, 265, 284, 286–7, 290
Tongaland, 12, 71, 96, 114, 118, 122, 125, 132, 194, 202, 204, 226, 283, 286, 289
Transvaal mines, 114
tsetse fly, 18, 116, 142
Tukuyu, 104
Tumbuka, 3, 5, 7, 9, 14–15, 76, 86–7, 91–2, 98, 107, 113–15, 118, 120, 132, 135, 195–6, 258–9, 286, 289; farmers, 142, 148, 150
Tumbuka–Henga, 236
Tumbuka-Ngoni, 90n
Turner, Dr W., 199, 225, 244, 279
Tuskagee, 214, 233
Tweedie, Dr, 21
Tweya, Hezekiah, 199, 226, 244

Ufipa, 7
Uganda, 231
Ukukwe, 104–5
Undi, 2–3
Union Minière Company, 155
United Free Church of Scotland, 128. *See also* Free Church of Scotland
United Presbyterian Church of Scotland, 33, 35
Universities Mission to Central Africa (UMCA), 11, 20, 23–5, 49, 125, 148, 160, 166, 170, 175, 177, 223, 252, 280
'University of Livingstonia', 234
Unyamwezi, 7
Usisya, 184, 189, 202, 212

Uwandali, 105

Vail, Leroy, 13, 14n, 239, 289
van Velsen, Jaap, 58, 79, 271, 294
Venn, Henry, 176
Victoria, Lake, 72
Vincente, 210
Vipya plateau, 114
Vizaro (rubber estate), 114, 186, 269

Waller, Horace, 25, 159
Wandya, 102, 104, 107
Wankie (coalmine), 127
Washington, Booker, 233
Watch Tower, vii, 123, 184–209, 211–13, 218–20, 226, 258, 273, 275–6, 280–1, 284
Watch Tower, The, 197, 219
Watch Tower Bible and Tract Society, 184, 209
Watson, W. H., 240, 291
Wauchope, Isaac Williams, 190
Wellington, 122
Wenya, 280
Werner, Miss Alice, 100
West Africa, 21, 35–6, 194, 256
White Fathers, 105, 125–6, 129, 176, 221
White, James, of Overtoun, 29, 32, 43
White, John Campbell (Lord Overtoun) 29–32, 132, 134–6, 193, 227
Wiese, Carl, 85
Williams, George, 88, 93–5, 191–3, 199
Wilson, Godfrey, 3, 259
Wilson, Dr John, 26–7
Wilson, Monica, 124
witchcraft, 13–14, 92, 229–30; eradication movements, 122, 204–5, 280–1, 292
Witwatersrand Native Labour Association, 115
Wright, Marcia, 224, 230
Wrigley, C. C., 75

Yao, 2–7, 10–13, 19, 38, 41–2, 44–7, 49–56, 58, 60, 83–5, 100, 102, 112–13, 117, 120, 159, 165–7, 172–3, 184, 294
Yao, Machinga, 39–40
Yao, Mangoche, 23, 40–1
Yao, Masaninga, 39
Young, E. D., 26, 33, 35, 37, 40–1, 47–8, 54, 157, 190
Young, James, 29, 32, 42, 44
Young, T. Cullen, 141, 211, 260, 273, 289
Young, W. P., 139–40, 235–41, 264
Youngson, James, 251

Zamatgona, Harry, 53
Zambesi, 7, 18–20, 23, 34, 47, 87, 114–15, 157, 159, 160–1, 169, 210
Zambesi expedition, 18, 23–5, 33, 36
Zambesi Industrial Mission, 175
Zambia (Northern Rhodesia), vii, 2, 7, 116, 131–2, 140–1, 150, 155, 197, 207–8, 227, 230, 234, 248–9, 261, 280, 283–4, 292, 294
Zanzibar, 5, 9, 13, 24, 26, 41, 45, 148
Zarakuti, Frederick, 47–8, 85, 121
Ziehl, W. R. 112, 125
Zinyoka, David, 125
Zoani, 61, 63
Zomba, 140, 149, 184, 248, 258, 266, 276, 291
Zulu, 7–8, 90, 92
Zulu Gama, 7
Zumbo, 7
Zwangendaba, 1, 7, 12, 92, 106